Tycoons and Entrepreneurs

MACMILLAN
PROFILES

Tycoons and Entrepreneurs

MACMILLAN LIBRARY REFERENCE USA
New York

Produced and designed by Miller Williams Design Associates,
Lake Villa, IL

Macmillan Library Reference USA
1633 Broadway
New York, New York 10019

Manufactured in the United States of America

Printing number
1 2 3 4 5 6 7 8 9 10

Library of Congress Cataloging-in-Publication Data

Tycoons and entrepreneurs / [editor Judy Culligan].
        p.   cm. — (Macmillan profiles ; 2)
    Includes index.
    Summary: Alphabetical articles profile the life and work of notable
business leaders and entrepreneurs from antiquity to the present, beginning with Ah Quin and concluding with Linus Yale.
    ISBN 0-02-864982-6 (alk. paper)
    1. Rich people—Biography—Juvenile literature. 2. Millionaires—
Biography—Juvenile literature. 3. Capitalists and financiers—
Biography—Juvenile literature. 4. Industrialists—Biography—Juvenile literature. 5. Businesspeople—Biography—Juvenile literature.
[1. Businesspeople—Encyclopedias] I. Culligan, Judy. II. Series.
HC79.W4T93 1998
332′.092′2—dc21
[B]   98–39089
                                                                        CIP

Front cover clockwise from top: Bill Gates (© Peter Turnley/Corbis),
J. Pierpont Morgan (© Oscar White/Corbis), Henry Ford (© Corbis-
Bettmann), Cornelius Vanderbilt (© Oscar White/Corbis)
Cover design by Berrigan Design

This paper meets the requirements of ANSI/NISO A39.48-1992
(Permanence of Paper).

Contents

Preface ix

Ah Quin 1
Antuñano, Estevan de 2
Arkwright, Sir Richard 3
Armour, Philip Danforth 5
   GRACELAND CEMETERY 6
Astor, John Jacob 7

Belmont, August 9
Boeing, William E. 10
Boyd, Henry Allen 12
Brannan, Samuel 13
Briones, Juana 15
Buffett, Warren Edward 17
Butterfield, John 19

Carnegie, Andrew 21
   CARNEGIE'S LIBRARIES 22
Casey, James E. 23
Church, Robert Reed, Sr. 26
Colgate, William 27
Colt, Samuel 29
Culver, Henry 30

De Passe, Suzanne 33
Deere, John 35
Dow, Herbert Henry 36
Du Pont Family 39

Eastman, George 41

Field, Marshall 43
   MARSHALL FIELD'S CHICAGO STORE 44
Fisk, James 45
Forbes, Malcolm Stevenson 46
   THE "FORBES FOUR HUNDRED" 47
Ford, Henry 49
Frick, Henry Clay 52
   THE FRICK COLLECTION 53

Fugger, Jakob 53
Fuller, S. B. 55

Gates, William H. (Bill) 59
    THE CODEX LEICESTER 60
Geffen, David 62
Getty, J. Paul 66
Gibbs, Mifflin Wister 68
Goldwater, Barry (and Family) 69
Gordy, Berry, Jr. 71
    MOTOWN HISTORICAL MUSEUM 72
Gould, Jay 74
Graves, Earl Gilbert, Jr. 76
Guggenheim, Daniel 78

Haggar, Joseph Marion 81
Hall, Joyce Clyde 84
Hammer, Armand 87
Harriman, Edward Henry 93
Harvey, Ford Ferguson 95
Hassenfeld, Stephen David 96
Hauser, Samuel Thomas 99
Hearst, George 100
Hearst, William Randolph 101
    HEARST CASTLE 102
Heinz, Henry John II (Jack) 104
Hershey, Milton S. 109
    HERSHEY, PENNSYLVANIA 111
Hill, James J. 113
Hollerinth, Herman 114
Hughes, Howard 117
Hunt, Haroldson Lafayette, Jr. 119
Huntington, Collis Potter 124
Huntington, Henry Edwards 125
    THE HUNTINGTON LIBRARY, ART COLLECTIONS,
    AND BOTANICAL GARDENS 127

Ilfeld, Charles 129

Jobs, Steven Paul 133
Johnson, John Harold 134
Kaiser, Henry J. 137
Kellogg, Will Keith 140
Knott, Walter 145
    THE RISE OF THEME PARKS 147

Kroc, Raymond Albert 148
    FAST FOOD IN AMERICA 156
Lathrop, Austin E. 157
Lay, Herman W. 158
Lisa, Manuel 161
Llewellyn, James Bruce 163

Malone, Annie Turnbo 165
Marinho, Roberto 166
Marriott, J(ohn) Willard (Bill) 167
Mason, Biddy 171
Mauá, Visconde de 172
Maytag, Frederick Louis 174
McCormick, Cyrus Hall 177
Mellon, Andrew W. 178
    ANDREW W. MELLON FOUNDATION 180
Morgan, John Pierpont 181
    PIERPONT MORGAN LIBRARY 182
Murdock, Rupert 183

Overton, Anthony 187

Pace, Harry Herbert 189
Patiño, Simón Iturri 191
Patterson, Charles R. 192
Peabody, George 193
Penney, James Cash 194
    RICHARD W. SEARS 197
Pcrot, H(enry) Ross 198
Pillsbury, Philip Winston 201
    THE PILLSBURY BAKEOFF 203
Pullman, George Mortimer 204
    THE PULLMAN STRIKE 206

Rhodes, Cecil John 207
Ripley, Edward Payson 210
Rockefeller, John Davison 211
Rothschild Family 213
Ryan, John Dennis 216

Simmons, Jake, Jr. 219
Spalding, Albert Goodwill 221
Spaulding, Charles Clinton 223
Spielberg, Stephen 225
Spreckels, Claus 228

Stanford, Leland 229
Stein, Julian Caesar (Jules) 230
Steinway, Henry Englehard 235
Stetson, John Batterson 237
   COWBOY HATS 237
Strauss, Levi 238
   THE HISTORY OF BLUE JEANS 239
Studebaker, John Mohler 240
Sutton, Percy Ellis 242

Trump, Donald 245
Tupper, Earl Silas 248
Turner, Robert Edward (Ted) 251
   TED TURNER'S DONATION TO THE UNITED NATIONS . . . 253

Vanderbilt, Cornelius 255
   GEORGE VANDERBILT'S BILTMORE ESTATE 258

Walker, Madam C. J. 261
   ELIZABETH ARDEN AND HELENA RUBINSTEIN 262
Walton, Sam 264
Ward, Aaron Montgomery 267
   MAIL ORDER CATALOGUES 268
Waterhouse, Frank 270
Weinberg, Harry G. 271
Whitney, John Hay 274
Winchester, Oliver Fisher 278
Winfrey, Oprah Gail 280
   THE OPRAH BOOK CLUB 281
Woodruff, Robert Winship 282
Woolworth, Frank Winfield 287
Wozniak, Stephen G. 289
Wright, William 292
Wrigley, William, Jr. 293

Yale, Linus 297

Sources/PhotoCredits 299
Suggested Reading 303
Glossary 323
Index 333

Preface

Macmillan Profiles: *Tycoons and Entrepreneurs* is a unique reference featuring over 100 profiles of notable tycoons and entrepreneurs from the eighteenth century to the present. Macmillan Library Reference recognizes the need for reliable, accurate, and accessible biographies of notable figures in world and American history. The Macmillan Profile series helps meet that need by providing new collections of biographies that were carefully selected from distinguished Macmillan sources. Macmillan Library Reference has published a wide array of award-winning reference materials for libraries across the world. It is likely that several of the encyclopedias on the shelves in this library were published by Macmillan Reference or Charles Scribner's Sons. All biographies in Macmillan Profiles have been recast and tailored for a younger audience by a team of experienced writers and editors. In some cases, new biographies were commissioned to supplement entries from original sources.

Our goal is to present an exciting introduction to the life and times of important figures in the world of business, industry, and finance. Articles describe transportation tycoons, media moguls, restaurant and real estate magnates, mail order merchants, computer developers, investors, and financial wizards, as well as the manufacturers of everything from candy, hats, and clothing to airplanes and electric appliances. The article list was based on the following criteria: relevance to the curriculum, importance to history, name recognition for students, and representation of as broad a cultural range as possible. The article list was refined and expanded in response to advice from a lively and generous team of high school teachers and librarians. The result is a balanced, curriculum-related work that brings these important people to life.

FEATURES

To add visual appeal and enhance the usefulness of this volume, the page format was designed to include the following helpful features:

■ **Time Lines:** Found throughout the text in the margins, time lines provide a quick reference source for dates and important accomplishments in the life and times of these tycoons and entrepreneurs.

■ **Notable Quotations:** Found throughout the text in the margins, these thought-provoking quotations are drawn from interviews, speeches, and writings of the businessperson covered in the article. Such quotations give readers a special insight into the distinctive personalities of these great men and women.

■ **Pull Quotes:** Found throughout the text in the margin, pull quotes highlight essential facts.

■ **Definitions and Glossary:** Brief definitions of important terms in the main text can be found in the margin. A glossary at the end of the book provides students with an even broader list of definitions.

■ **Sidebars:** Appearing in shaded boxes throughout the volume, these provocative asides relate to and amplify topics.

■ **Suggested Reading:** An extensive list of books and articles about the tycoons and entrepreneurs covered in the volume will help students who want to do further research.

■ **Index:** A thorough index provides thousands of additional points of entry into the work.

ACKNOWLEDGMENTS

We thank our colleagues who publish the *Merriam Webster's Collegiate® Dictionary*. Definitions used in the margins and many of the glossary terms come from the distinguished *Webster's Collegiate® Dictionary*, Tenth Edition, 1996.

The biographies herein were written by leading authorities at work the fields of American, European, and world history. *Tycoons and Entrepreneurs* contains over 70 photographs. Acknowledgments of sources for the illustrations can be found on page 301.

This work would not have been possible without the hard work and creativity of our staff. We offer our sincere thanks to all who helped create this marvelous work.

Macmillan Library Reference

Ah Quin

1848–1914 ● BUSINESSMAN & LABOR CONTRACTOR

Ah Quin received his education in his native Canton from missionaries, who taught him English, the concepts of Christianity, and other subjects. As a young man, he immigrated to the American West Coast and labored for several years as a house servant and cook in San Francisco, Santa Barbara, and Alaska. Employment was not hard to find, as he had a network of relatives in America, could speak English, and had adopted Western manners and dress.

In 1878, Ah Quin visited San Diego and met local businessman George Marston. The two maintained a correspondence, and when the California Southern Railroad began planning a line from San Diego, Marston urged Ah Quin to become a labor contractor for the railroad. He hired hundreds of Chinese laborers, housed them in makeshift camps, and

> Ah Quin became recognized as the unofficial mayor of San Diego's Chinatown.

Ah Quin and other Chinese immigrants to the United States formed Chinatowns in many major cities, including San Diego, Chicago, New York, and San Francisco (pictured here, ca. 1892).

sold them provisions from a store he had opened in San Diego's Chinatown. Construction of the railroad, which extended from National City through desert and solid rock to San Bernardino, was completed in three years, although stretches of the line had to be rebuilt when heavy winter rains in 1884 washed away some thirty miles of lumber and steel.

Ah Quin continued as a labor contractor while he developed interests in ranching, mining, produce farming, and real estate. He became recognized as a spokesman for the Chinese community in San Diego and as the unofficial mayor of the city's Chinatown. When he died after being struck by a motorcycle, he passed on to his twelve children a substantial commercial empire. ◆

Antuñano, Estevan de

1792–1847 ● TEXTILE MANUFACTURER

Antuñano had a vision of national development for Mexico.

One of Mexico's first modern industrialists, Estevan de Antuñano was born in Veracruz into a Spanish immigrant family. He was educated in Spain and in England, where he became familiar with industrial production. In the 1830s he led the modernization of the textile industry in Puebla, setting up Mexico's first mechanized spinning factory, La Constancia Mexicana, which produced cotton yarn on Arkwright spindles powered by the waters of the Río Atoyac. By the early 1840s, he owned four such factories in Puebla.

An enlightened entrepreneur, Antuñano recognized that the mechanization of spinning deprived women and children of employment and tried to alleviate the problem by turning La Constancia into a model experiment in the employment of family labor. He provided both housing and health care for his workers. Unfortunately, wages were low and people worked eleven to sixteen hours daily.

A vigorous **propagandist**, who authored over sixty pamphlets, Antuñano had a vision of national development. He

propagandist: a person who actively spreads a belief or view.

wanted to see the traditional manufacturing center of Puebla wrest control of northern Mexican markets, then dependent on **contraband**. Trade with the north would revitalize Mexico's central cities and agricultural districts. Silver exports would bring in foreign exchange. His vision floundered on the realities of the scarcity of raw cotton and currency, the persistence of contraband, and national disintegration. Antuñano died of natural causes during the U.S. Army's occupation of the city of Puebla. A French merchant, to whom he owed money, acquired most of his properties. ◆

contraband: smuggled goods.

Arkwright, Sir Richard

1732–1792 ● SPINNING MACHINE INVENTOR & MANUFACTURER

Richard Arkwright was a British inventor whose innovations in spinning machinery fostered the Industrial Revolution. Richard Arkwright was born to a humble family in the town of Preston, Lancashire, the youngest of thirteen children. As a child he was expected to learn a trade and therefore received little formal education. He was apprenticed at 18 to Edward Pollit, a wigmaker in Bolton.

While working there he developed a new method for dyeing hair, enabling him to have his own business.

Upon his father's death Arkwright inherited a small shop. He continued in the wigmaking profession but took an interest in cotton spinning. By 1767 Arkwright had made considerable improvements on a spinning machine invented several years earlier by Louis Paul. His own model—the famous spinning frame—was exhibited at the Preston fair of 1768, where it attracted much attention. In June of that year Arkwright opened a horsepowered spinning mill in Nottingham incorporating his own improvements. Despite the cost involved, he had found partners who foresaw great promise in his in novations. Arkwright obtained a patent on his first spinning machine in 1769.

Although the new machinery had mechanized some of the spinning process, much of the work continued to be done by hand. Arkwright spent the next years developing machinery for carding, drawing, and roving. In 1771 he bought property in Cromford, Derbyshire, on which he constructed a water-driven mill, and by the following year was producing a superior quality of yarn. Earlier machinery had produced threads that were suitable only for use as **woof** in weaving; Arkwright's threads were strong enough to be used as **warp**.

Despite the protests of competing spinners, who expected his improvements to cost them business, in 1775 Arkwright received additional patents on his machinery. At the same time, these competitors began to imitate Arkwright's machinery; he sued them for patent infringements in 1781, but lost his case because his patents were said to be lacking in specifications. A second suit in 1785 was also lost. Despite his legal failures Arkwright was earning a fortune from his own mills and from the sale of his machinery. By 1789 he owned five mills in Derbyshire and three in other counties. Several other mills had adopted his machinery. However, because he had initiated the large-scale production of yarn he was also the object of agitation on the grounds that his inventions cut the demand for labor; in 1779 his mill in Chorley was destroyed by a mob.

Although he was not an original inventor, preferring to improve on previous inventions, his innovations won him the esteem of his community. Arkwright was knighted in 1786 after delivering his county's congratulatory address to King

1768 Arkwright exhibits his new spinning frame at the Preston Fair.

1769 Arkwright patents his spinning machine.

1771 Arkwright constructs a water-driven spinning mill.

1779 A mob destroys Arkwright's mill in Chorley.

1786 Arkwright is knighted.

woof: threads running side-to-side across a loom.

warp: threads running lengthwise in woven fabric.

George III following an assassination attempt. The next year he was appointed high sheriff for his county. Arkwright earned over £200,000 in his career and spent the last years of his life completing the formal education he had missed as a child and in the construction of Willersly Castle, dying before its completion. ◆

Armour, Philip Danforth

1836–1901 ● MEATPACKING TYCOON

"The fundamental principles which govern the handling of postage stamps and of millions of dollars are exactly the same. They are the common law of business, and the whole practice of commerce is founded on them."

Philip D. Armour

Born in Stockbridge, New York, Philip Danforth Armour was the meatpacker principally responsible for developing the Chicago stockyards. Armour's first vocation was as a miner, from which he moved into farming and then the wholesale-grocery business. By the late 1860s, a primitive form of refrigerated railroad car became available, and Armour, seeing an opportunity, went into the meatpacking business in 1870. Since Chicago had already developed into the rail hub at which Eastern lines met Western and Southwestern routes, it was the logical place for a meatpacking industry. Armour pioneered the shipping of hogs to Chicago, where they were slaughtered, canned, and shipped

Graceland Cemetery

Philip Armour, Marshall Field, Cyrus McCormick, and George Pullman are all buried in the same place—Chicago's historic Graceland Cemetery. Armour came to Chicago in the late 1800s to take over his ailing brother's meatpacking company. A large tombstone bearing the word "Armour" identifies his spacious family plot. A large bronze statue called "Memory" overlooks the Marshall Field plot. The seated figure with its melancholy gaze is the work of sculptor Daniel Chester French. It resembles the statue of Abraham Lincoln that French later sculpted for the Lincoln Memorial in Washington, D.C. Only a small headstone marks the grave of Cyrus McCormick. But the McCormick family's grassy plot is the largest in Graceland. Land is the monument for the man whose invention revolutionized farming. Over George Pullman's grave stands a tall Corinthian column flanked by stone benches. Pullman died a few years after the bitter 1894 strike at the Pullman Palace Car Company. His family, afraid that angry ex-employees might try to steal the body, took extraordinary measures. Beneath the monument, Pullman's coffin is encased in a room-sized block of concrete.

both nationally and internationally. He also purchased his own fleet of refrigerator cars to ship fresh meat to the East Coast.

Armour made a fortune and greatly expanded the market for Western beef producers, but he also be came the target of censure—in the East as well as the West—for his strong-arm antilabor tactics and **monopolistic** practices. Like other captains of industry of his day, he did have a **philanthropic** side; he established the Armour Institute, which subsequently became the prestigious Illinois Institute of Technology.

monopolistic: characterized by complete control of an industry.

philanthropic: showing love and care for humankind.

Late in his life, Armour was among those in the packing industry charged with purveying what the Muckraking press called "embalmed beef"—inferior canned meat, treated with toxic chemicals—to the armed forces during the Spanish-American War of 1898. The tainted meat was responsible for numerous cases of food poisoning, including fatalities, among soldiers. The scandal helped spark a reform movement that culminated in such Progressive legislation as the Pure Food and Drug Act of June 30, 1906.

antitrust: concerning laws that protect business from unfair practices.

Despite **antitrust** actions and the "embalmed-beef" scandal, Philip D. Armour's son, J. Ogden Armour, continued to build Armour and Company and made it the world's largest meatpacking firm. ◆

Astor, John Jacob

1762–1848 ● FUR TRADER

"The man who has a million dollars is as well off as if he were rich."

John Jacob Astor III, attributed

The wealth of John Jacob Astor, the richest man of his time in the United States, was based on a fur trading business. He arrived in the United States in 1783, with about twenty-five dollars in cash and a number of flutes to sell and start a business. He went into the fur trade at once, and built his twenty-five dollars into an immense fortune. He arranged to buy furs from the Indians, first in Ohio and Michigan, then in Canada. He extended his business into the Louisiana Territory after 1803, and soon was conducting the largest fur trade in the United States. His trading post at Astoria, Oregon, played a part in the contest between the United States and Great Britain for control of the Oregon territory.

The War of 1812 practically destroyed Astor's post at Astoria. After the war he tried to rebuild it as a base for controlling the fur trade of the Northwest. He also tried to control the fur trade of the Rocky Mountains, but was not successful in this. Astor put a great deal of his money into New York City real estate. He bought open land just north of the city limits, and as New York developed north through Manhattan Island, his land became enormously valuable. Astor died in 1848, the richest man in the United States. He left money in his will to the Astor Library, which is

1783 Astor arrives in the United States.

1803 Astor extends his business into the Louisiana Territory.

1848 Astor dies the richest man in America.

today an important part of the reference services of the New York Public Library. The Waldorf-Astoria hotel in New York City is named in his memory. ◆

Belmont, August

1816–1890 ● BANKER

August Belmont started his career in finance at the age of 14, when he began work in Germany for the famous international banking house of Rothschild. He soon won a reputation as a brilliant young banker. For several years he worked in Italy for the Rothschilds and was sent to handle that firm's affairs in Havana in 1837. Deciding to try his fortune on his own in New York, at the age of 21 he gave up his position with the Rothschilds and established himself as a banker in New York City. He made a great deal of money and became one of the city's leading social figures. Belmont supported the Democratic party in New York and in national politics, but when the Civil War broke out he offered his help to the Union government. He outfitted a regiment of German troops for the Union Army, and he traveled twice to Europe to persuade European governments and banks not to help the Confederacy. ◆

Belmont made a great deal of money and became one of New York's leading social figures.

Boeing, William E.

1881–1956 ● AIRCRAFT MANUFACTURER

1920	Boeing builds a flying boat.
1927	Boeing wins a contract for airmail service in the West.
1933	Boeing cuts coast-to-coast passenger flights to 19.75 hours.
1934	Boeing wins a Guggenheim Medal.

A pioneer in aircraft manufacture and transport, William E. Boeing (1881–1956) was born to a wealthy family engaged in the lumber business in Detroit. He attended Yale University for two years and learned to fly from Glenn L. Martin. He competed with Martin during World War I in supplying military aircraft to the government, and after the war, he founded the Pacific Aero Products Company. Aided by Phil Johnson and Claire Egtvedt, young engineering professors from the University of Washington, Boeing built a flying boat for the first private airmail service (in July 1920), flying between Seattle, Washington, and Vancouver, British Columbia. In March 1927, his Seattle-based Boeing Air Transport won the first contract for private airmail west of Chicago. The contract led to a merger with Pratt and Whitney and later with National Air lines. Then named United Aircraft and Transport, Boeing's company offered coast-to-coast passenger flights in 28 hours. Three years later, in 1933, the flight time was cut to 19.75 hours, thanks to the Boeing 247 Monomail, the first all-metal, stress-skinned monoplane structure. Other firsts for Boeing included night flights for passengers over long distances and two-way radio communications. He won the cov-

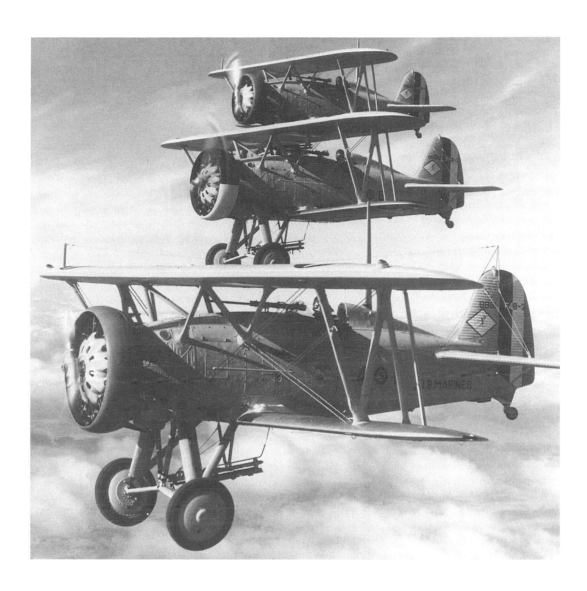

eted Guggenheim Medal in May 1934 for "successful pioneering and achievement."

Boeing retired as president of United Aircraft in mid-1933, but he remained chairman of the board. During that time, the company split into United Airlines, United Aircraft, and Boeing Airplane Company. Boeing remained in constant touch from his farm while his company constructed flying boats for international transport, bombers for World War II, jet transports of the 707 series, and Bomarc and Minuteman missiles. He died at the age of 74 on his yacht in Puget Sound. ◆

Three Boeing F4B-3 U.S. Marine Corps fighters fly in echelon formation in 1933 over the San Diego coast.

Boyd, Henry Allen

1876–1959 ● BUSINESSMAN & PUBLISHER

Henry Allen Boyd was born in Grimes County, Texas. Accounts of his education differ, though it is likely that Boyd studied theology at the Hearn Academy in Texas and at Guadalupe College in Seguia, Texas. After graduating, he worked in San Antonio, Texas, as a headwaiter and then as a postal clerk; but, due to eye problems, Boyd left the post office just before 1900 and moved with his family to Nashville, Tennessee, where he lived for the rest of his life. The son and business heir of Richard Henry Boyd, Henry Allen Boyd followed his father into the higher echelons of the National Baptist Convention and, particularly, the National Baptist Publishing Board. With the aid of his father, Boyd ran the *Nashville Globe and Independent*, a weekly African-American newspaper established in 1905.

When the National Baptist Convention divided in 1915—in part over the Boyds' domination of the successful publishing firm and the desire by some other members of the convention to incorporate—the Boyds became sole owners of the publishing facilities and leading members of the National Baptist Convention, Unincorporated. Upon the death of his father in 1922, Henry Boyd became publisher and president of the *Globe and Independent*, and took control over the publishing firm as well as his father's bank, the One Cent Savings Bank and Trust Company, now the Citizens Savings Bank and Trust Company of Nashville.

Boyd proved an able businessman. When many African-American banks collapsed during the Great Depression, Boyd guided the One Cent to success. With his capital, as well as his influential position as editor of the *Globe and Independent*, Boyd became the principal advocate for numerous local and statewide black concerns and campaigns, including the founding in Nashville of the Tennessee Agricultural and Normal School (now Tennessee State University).

Boyd had an abiding concern with the success of blacks in the United States, and as a banker, businessman, and publisher, did his utmost to help other African Americans and their business projects. At the time of his death, Boyd was a

1905 The *Nashville Globe and Independent* is established.

1915 Boyd helps lead the National Baptist Convention.

1922 Boyd publishes the *Globe and Independent*.

director of the Supreme Liberty Life Insurance Company, an executive of the Negro YMCA of Nashville, secretary of the National Sunday School Congress of the National Baptist Convention of America, and was on the board of trustees at Fisk University, Meharry Medical College, the National Negro Business League, the NAACP, and the National Council of Churches. ◆

Brannan, Samuel

1819–1889 ● BUSINESSMAN

An "empire builder" in early San Francisco, Mormon leader, and initiator of the California Gold Rush, Samuel Brannan was born in Maine to parents of Irish descent. He left home in 1833, fleeing a drunken and abusive father, and moved to Ohio to live with his sister and her husband. There, the young man became an apprentice printer.

In 1843, Brannan converted to the new religion, the Church of Jesus Christ of Latter Day Saints. In part to escape an unhappy marriage, he plunged into the work of the church, remarried, and moved to New York to publish a **sectarian** journal entitled *The Prophet*.

Although he was closer to Prophet Joseph Smith Jr. than to Smith's successor, Brigham Young, the latter chose him to lead a colony of 238 Saints to Mexican California at about the same time as the 1846 Mormon trek overland to the Great Salt Lake. From the deck of his chartered *Brooklyn*, Brannan saw the American flag flying over Yerba Buena (later San Francisco), just captured in the United States-Mexican War. Because of the persecution of Mormons in the United States, Brannan was said to have exclaimed either "there's that damned *flag*, again!" or "there's that damned *rag*, again!"

The dynamic young Mormon quickly made his peace with the citizens of San Francisco. He was the first since Francis Drake's Chaplain Fletcher (1579) and the Orthodox priests at

"Gold! Gold from the American River!"
Samuel Brannan, 1848

sectarian: relating to a certain religious group.

Fort Ross (1812 to 1841) to preach a non-Catholic sermon in California. He built the second or third flour mill on the West Coast. He also set up a job printing press and published one of the state's first two newspapers, the *California Star*.

Brannan then made the arduous and dangerous crossing of the Sierra Nevada and the Utah desert to try to persuade Brigham Young to shift his Zion to the San Francisco area from Salt Lake City. Back in San Francisco, his religious ardor began to cool, and his business opportunism turned into a new faith: materialism and even hedonism. Accusations of misuse of Mormon tithes eventually led to his excommunication, but he was already drifting into **apostasy**.

apostasy: desertion of one's religion.

While running a prosperous general store at Sutter's Fort (later Sacramento), Brannan ignited the explosive California gold rush. Parading through the streets of San Francisco in May 1848, he flaunted a vial of "dust" and shouted, "Gold! Gold from the American River!" But Brannan, himself, made his money as a storekeeper and real-estate speculator, not in the drudgery of placer mining.

Brannan diversified his business interests. He owned office buildings, a bank, a lumber mill, a bookstore, a biscuit factory, a cattle ranch, and even a vineyard, distillery, and posh resort, Hot Springs, in Napa Valley's Calistoga. He made the latter into the Saratoga of the Pacific. It was said that, at one time, he owned a fifth of San Francisco. He was probably the state's first millionaire in 1856.

Brannan was also a civic leader. He founded the prestigious Society of California Pioneers and organized an informal vigilante movement in 1849 to rid the city of a predatory gang of criminals. He was named president of the First Vigilance Committee (1851) to repeat the process. As a vigilante, Brannan revealed flaws in his character, such as a penchant for reckless meddling and violence. He was always the first to haul away a criminal suspect on a hangman's rope. In 1851, he dabbled in a filibustering fiasco in Hawaii. From 1864 to 1865, he sent arms and mercenaries to Mexico to help Benito Juárez fight Maximilian. In 1868, he was badly wounded at Calistoga when his hot temper got him into a shooting incident.

After a costly divorce in 1870, the spendthrift and overextended Brannan lost his Midas touch. As he acquired notoriety as a hard drinker and a womanizer, the remnants of his fortune slipped through his fingers. He faded into obscurity.

1833 Brannan flees his drunken father; moves to Ohio.

1846 Brannan leads 238 Mormons to Mexican California.

1848 Brannan parades a vial of "gold-dust" through the streets of San Francisco.

1849 Brannan organizes vigilantes to rid San Francisco of criminals.

1856 Brannan becomes one of California's first millionaires.

1864 Brannan begins funneling arms to Benito Juárez in Mexico.

During his last years, he was virtually forgotten. After he died in Escondido, California, his body lay in an undertaker's vault for sixteen months until a nephew paid the embalming bill and arranged for burial in San Diego. ◆

Briones, Juana

1802–1889 ● RANCHER

Juana Briones was a first-generation Californian who amassed a personal fortune by ranching in the San Francisco area. Her parents, Marcos Briones and Isidora Tapia, were born in Mexico. Her mother arrived in California as a child with the Juan Bautista de Anza colonizing expedition of 1775 to 1776. Her father, a soldier at Monterey, accompanied the expedition to San Francisco. During the late eighteenth century, Spain discouraged commerce to avoid foreign influence in California. Without markets, settlers grew and produced little more than they themselves required. Mexico lifted these trade restrictions after achieving independence from Spain in 1821. A **seigniorial** style of living evolved as the government provided settlers with lands from the vast mission holdings and in an atmosphere that encouraged trade, many rancheros, including Briones's family, prospered.

seigniorial: like a wealthy, noble person.

Juana Briones married and took on the duties of a young wife and mother during this period of transition. Briones was an industrious and hospitable woman, who cared for orphaned children and the sick. Exceptionally skilled in healing, she educated her nephew, Pablo Briones, who was for fifty years the respected doctor of Bolinas, a community north of San Francisco.

Juana Briones's most remarkable achievement was the prosperity that she maintained throughout her life despite overwhelming disadvantage. Through persistence, careful management, and good judgment, she reached and sustained a position of honor and affluence. The American occupation

marginal: barely
making enough to live.

in 1846 and the acquisition of statehood in 1850 greatly diminished the status of the Hispanic people and drove many of them to destitution or to **marginal** employment. Furthermore, even under the relatively equitable property and business laws of Spanish and Mexican California, the status of women was far from equal. Women received only 13 percent of the land grants, and property was usually registered under the name of husbands. After the death of her own husband in 1847, Briones pursued her claim to the property at the foot of Lyon Street hill along the present-day boundary of the San Francisco Presidio. It took her fifteen years to validate the title and her claim to it for herself and her children.

She moved in 1835 to land at the foot of Alta Loma, now Telegraph Hill, to increase her farmland holdings and to live closer to the ships that were her market for fresh food. She was one of the first inhabitants of the newly founded pueblo of Yerba Buena (later San Francisco). She built a brush fence to provide a corral, garden, and orchard—a rectangular plot that today is Washington Square Park. Her ranch buildings angled across the land that is now the corner of Filbert and Powell streets. One early map identifies the nearby cove as Juana Briones Beach.

In 1844, Briones took three steps to strengthen her position as the sole supporter of her eight children. She applied to religious authorities for a separation from her second husband; she petitioned the local authorities for the third time for title to the property she had farmed since 1835 in Yerba Buena; and she purchased from Indians a forty-four-hundred-acre ranch thirty-five miles to the south, where Los Altos Hills and Palo Alto now draw their political boundaries.

Part of the house she constructed on the Purisima ranch still stands in present-day Palo Alto and is occasionally opened to the public as a historic site. Chester Lyman, a visitor in 1847, wrote that he had arranged for his comfortable stay at Briones's home, meaning probably that he paid for his accommodations. He noted that Briones was caring for two sick people and that there was considerable coming and going of guests and members of the bustling household.

Available evidence suggests that Juana Briones never left the San Francisco Bay area, yet her name and accomplishments remain a California legacy. ◆

1821 Mexico achieves independence from Spain.

1835 Briones moves to the foot of Alta Lorna, now Telegraph Hill.

1844 Briones takes steps to strengthen her role as sole supporter of her children.

1847 Briones' husband dies.

1850 California becomes an American state, diminishing the status of Hispanic people there.

Buffett, Warren Edward

1930–PRESENT ● INVESTOR

> *"It is better to be approximately right than precisely wrong."*
> — Warren Buffet, 1994

Warren Edward Buffett is an American business executive. He is the chairman of Berkshire Hathaway Inc., a major long-term investment company with holdings in insurance companies and manufacturing, retail, and communications businesses. In the late 1900s, he became one of the wealthiest men in the United States and one of the world's most celebrated investors.

Buffett was born in Omaha, Nebraska on August 30, 1930, to Lila (Stahl) Buffett and Howard Homan Buffett. His father, a known fiscal conservative, worked as a stockbroker and a Republican congressman for the U.S. House of Representatives.

Buffett grew up in Omaha and in Washington, D.C., where he lived during his father's terms in Congress. As a boy, he displayed an early interest in business, holding several paper delivery routes, a lost-golf ball retrieval and sales service, a small pinball machine business, and other odd jobs. Buffett started playing the stock market on a small scale when he was 11. By the time he graduated from high school, he had earned enough from his various businesses to purchase forty acres of farmland in Nebraska.

In 1947, Buffett began his undergraduate studies at the University of Pennsylvania. He transferred to the University of Nebraska in 1950 and graduated with a bachelor's degree in

Buffett invested in companies whose stocks were cheap and undervalued by the market.

business that same year. As an undergraduate, Buffett became interested in Benjamin Graham, a professor at the graduate school of business at Columbia University in New York City, who pioneered the "value approach" to purchasing stocks. In this approach, investments are made in companies whose stocks are cheap and undervalued by the market. Graham believed that the price of stocks for such firms would rise with time, resulting in a profit for the investor. Buffett did his graduate work with Graham and received a master's degree in business administration from Columbia University in 1951.

After graduation, Buffett worked as an investment salesman in his father's brokerage firm in Omaha. He moved to New York City in 1954 to become a security analyst under his mentor Graham at the Graham-Newman Corporation. In 1956, he returned to Omaha and borrowed money from friends and relatives to form an investment firm called the Buffett Partnership. One of his most successful purchases for the partnership was made in 1963, when he invested in the American Express Company. At that time, the credit card company was in the throes of a scandal involving fake inventories of salad oil. The scandal caused the price of AmEx stocks to tumble, leading many investors to believe that the company was near collapse. Buffett relied on what he observed—the continued use of American Express cards by consumers around Omaha—rather than what he heard from other investors, and he bought 5 percent of the company's stock. The company soon revived and rose from about $35 a share to $189 a share over the following five years.

In 1969, Buffett dissolved the partnership, and the investors received 30 times their original investment. He then devoted his attention to Berkshire Hathaway, a textile firm in New Bedford, Massachusetts, that he had personally bought control of in 1965. He installed new management at the firm and slowly began to build it into a profitable holding company. The textile end of the business failed, and Buffett closed it in 1985, but profits in other areas of Berkshire Hathaway grew, including holdings in insurance companies, steel service industries, retail businesses, and communications businesses.

Through the years, Buffett followed Graham's staunch advocacy of buying stocks in companies that make more money than all their stocks are worth. But he also sought companies with strong brand recognition, such as Gillette

1950 Buffett graduates with BA in business from the University of Nebraska.

1954 Buffett becomes a security analyst at Graham-Newman Corporation in New York.

1956 Buffett returns to Nebraska and establishes the Buffett Partnership.

1958 Buffett buys a $31,500 house in Omaha.

1963 Buffett invests in the American Express Co.

1965 Buffett buys control of Berkshire Hathaway.

Co., manufacturer of razors and razor blades. Of his investment in Gillette, Buffett has expressed pleasure in going to bed at night knowing that there are billions of males who have to shave in the morning. Buffett also invested heavily in Coca-Cola Co., which trades at many times its earnings but is recognized all over the world for its product. Other notable investments over the years have included the packaged foods manufacturer General Foods Corporation; the fast-food giant McDonald's Corporation; Federal Home Loan Mortgage Corporation (known as Freddie Mac), a private corporation chartered by the United States government to increase funds for housing; the *Washington Post* Company, which owns the *Washington Post*, one of the most influential newspapers in the United States; See's Candy Shops, a San Francisco-based shop where Buffett has bought fudge for years; and Capital Cities/ABC Inc., which was purchased in 1995 by the Walt Disney Company.

Buffett is known as a congenial man with a self-deprecating humor, a folksy manner, and a fondness for Cherry Coke. He lives frugally, residing in the Omaha house he bought for $31,500 in 1958. He is a voracious reader of newspapers and business reports and is an avid bridge player. Buffett married Susan Thompson in 1952 and had three children. He separated from his wife and has subsequently lived with his companion Astrid Menks. ◆

> Buffett has expressed pleasure in going to bed at night knowing there are billions of males who have to shave in the morning.

Butterfield, John

1801–1869 ● TRANSPORTATION & COMMUNICATIONS MOGUL

Expressman, businessman, and financier John Butterfield was born on a farm at Berne, near Albany, New York. More interested in horses and transportation than in farming, at the age of 19 he obtained his first job as a stagecoach driver in Albany and later in Utica. He soon bought a small stable and went into the **livery** business,

livery: the renting of horses and carriages.

which he expanded to include a boarding house after his marriage to Melinda Harriet Baker in 1822. As his business interests prospered, Butterfield obtained a controlling interest in most of the stage lines carrying mail and passengers in northern and western New York. He invested in packet boats on the Erie Canal, steamers on Lake Ontario, and post roads. In 1849, he formed the express company of Butterfield, Wasson and Company and, the following year, merged his interests with Wells and Company and Livingston, Fargo and Company to form the American Express Company. At the same time, he was interested in telegraphic communication, and with Henry Wells and Crawford Livingston, he established the New York, Albany and Buffalo Telegraph Company. He took great pride in his home town of Utica and invested his growing fortune in real estate there. In 1856, he was elected mayor of Utica as a Republican.

The greatest achievement of Butterfield's career was his role in founding and organizing the Overland Mail Company to undertake a federal-government contract in 1857 to deliver the mails on a transcontinental route twenty-eight hundred miles long from St. Louis through Texas and the Southwest to San Francisco. A highly competitive man of great energy and determination, he planned to establish a daily, rather than a semiweekly, mail service and proposed to establish a pony express service to compete with that on the central route. His partners were unwilling to expand further and Butterfield was relieved from the presidency of the Overland Mail Company in 1860.

Already past the customary age of retirement, Butterfield remained in seclusion for more than two years. He then engaged in business activities in New York City until October 1867 when he suffered a stroke. He died at his home in Utica two years later. ◆

1822 Butterfield marries Melinda Harriet Baker.

1850 The American Express Co. is formed.

1856 Butterfield becomes mayor of Utica, New York.

1857 Butterfield founds the Overland Mail Co.

1867 Butterfield suffers a stroke.

Carnegie, Andrew

1835–1919 ● INDUSTRIALIST

"Surplus wealth is a sacred trust which its possessor is bound to administer in his lifetime for the good of the community."

Andrew Carnegie, 1889

A ndrew Carnegie, who became one of the wealthiest men in American history, was born in Dunfermline, Scotland, on November 25, 1835. He arrived in the United States as a penniless Scottish immigrant. He was 13 when his parents brought him to America. He began work almost at once, in a textile factory. His second job, as messenger boy for a Pittsburgh telegraph company, led to a rapid rise. Carnegie was a quick learner, and became an expert telegraph operator. As a result, he came to the attention of Thomas Scott, then superintendent of the Pennsylvania Railroad, who made the bright young Carnegie his secretary and his personal telegrapher.

At the start of the Civil War, Carnegie helped work out a signal system for use in handling military shipments. He soon discovered that the wartime needs of the country offered great business opportunities. He left the railroad, and began a career of organizing and reorganizing iron and steel companies, beginning with a bridge company that he reorganized in

> Carnegie discovered that America's wartime needs offered great business opportunities.

21

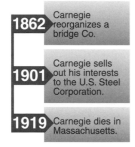

1862. Recognizing the great need for steel in the United States, he turned all his talent for work and organization to the business of making steel. His mills became the most important and best managed in the United States, at the time when the nation was moving ahead to lead the world in steel production.

Carnegie was a hard-driving manager and an expert at selecting aides and assistants. He never organized his companies as corporations, but kept them as partnerships which he controlled himself. His chief associates were rewarded with shares of the ownership of companies, and were placed in positions where their talents were able to produce very successfully. Carnegie was also a clever judge of business trends and used this skill to help improve his companies. During times of depression or slow business, he often bought the newest equipment available at relatively low prices. When business improved, his factories were able to produce better steel, faster and cheaper, than his competitors. Carnegie's policies were very strongly anti-labor unions. His steel mills were involved in several long, bitter strikes, and the Carnegie Company was never successfully unionized.

Carnegie's Libraries

Andrew Carnegie lacked a formal education, but he had a strong respect for books and education. He also believed that wealthy people had a duty to use their money to make life better for others. When Carnegie sold his steel company in 1901, he retired with a fortune estimated at $500 million. Before he died, Carnegie donated more than $350 million to educational, cultural, scientific, and peace institutions. Carnegie made one of his greatest gifts when he began paying for the construction of libraries in the United States and other English-speaking countries. In 1911, he founded the Carnegie Corporation of New York to "promote the advancement and diffusion of knowledge and understanding." One of the foundation's original purposes was the establishment of free public libraries. Carnegie believed people should improve themselves through hard work and education. Thus he opposed straight charity, but he supported projects that helped people to help themselves. For each library he built, the agreement was the same. Carnegie provided the funds for the building itself, but the local government had to provide the land, purchase the books, and agree to future maintenance of the library. Altogether, Carnegie endowed more than 2,500 public libraries; nearly 1,700 of them were in the United States.

In 1901, Carnegie decided that he had made enough money and had spent enough of his time in business. He sold out all his interests to the new United States Steel Corporation, acquiring a quarter of a billion dollars. Carnegie planned to use his money as a means of improving the lives of others. He began with the men who had worked for him and set up a five-million-dollar pension fund for the employees of the Carnegie Company. During the rest of his life, he spent a great deal of his time and effort supervising ways to put his enormous wealth to work for general public good. Among his special gifts were funds to build "Carnegie Libraries" to be operated as public libraries in many parts of the United States and the world. His gifts were largely responsible for starting public libraries in many American cities. He also created funds to improve schoolteaching, to support scientific research, and to advance international peace. Many of his funds were used for organizations in Great Britain as well as for United States groups. Carnegie provided funds for building the "Peace Palace" at The Hague.

He died in Lenox, Massachusetts, in August, 1919. ◆

> *"Gentlemen, I would almost as soon leave a curse as I would leave excessive wealth to a child."*
> Andrew Carnegie

Casey, James E.

1888–1983 ●FOUNDER OF UNITED PARCEL SERVICE

James E. Casey was born on March 29, 1888, in Candelaria, Nevada. He was the eldest of four children of Annie E. and Henry J. Casey; his father was an innkeeper whose establishment served silver miners in Candelaria. When gold was discovered in Alaska, Casey's father moved the family to Seattle and set off for the Klondike, hoping to strike it rich. He had no success and returned penniless and ill. Casey left school at age 11 to help support the family. His first job was a department store delivery boy, which brought in $2.50 weekly. For a time in his teens Casey returned to Nevada and tried gold prospecting himself.

"Each employee should be treated as a special asset that needs to be appreciated and developed—when someone leaves our company, that's a failure."

James E. Casey

1907 Casey and a partner start the American Messenger Co.

1919 The Co. is renamed United Parcel Service.

1929 Casey experiments with using trucks to feed shipments to airplanes.

1930 Casey brings his service to New York City.

1957 UPS begins gaining interstate operating rights.

1975 UPS secures interstate shipping rights for the lower 48 states.

In 1907 Casey and a partner started a courier service, the American Messenger Company, in Seattle, employing six carriers and two bicycles and operating out of a basement under a saloon in what is now known as the city's underground. A free lunch counter served as both work space by day and as a bed at night. The company was soon serving local department stores as well as small businesses; its initial success was based on keeping clients accurately informed of the pickup times. The messenger service also picked up odd jobs, occasionally including a little detective work. In 1913 the company, after merging with a local delivery service, bought its first motor vehicle—a Model T Ford.

Casey's partner, Claude Ryan, sold out in 1917, but by then Casey and his new partners had delivery agreements with every department store in Seattle. In 1919 the company expanded to Oakland and was renamed the United Parcel Service. At the suggestion of his partner Charles Soderstrom, Casey painted his trucks brown in emulation of Pullman coaches, hoping that this would, in his words "make us equally famous on the streets of America." Soon UPS trucks were rolling in all the big cities along the West Coast. In 1929 Casey experimented with using his trucks to feed shipments to airplanes, but the disruption of the airline industry by the stock market crash put an end to this innovation. Casey's focus on using air service remained a stumbling point with company directors until the time of his death.

In 1930 Casey brought his service to New York City, immediately picking up the prestigious Lord & Taylor department store as a principal customer. Soon Casey obtained contracts with nearly all of New York's great retail emporiums. Shortly thereafter, *Business Week* reported that the stores had scrapped their individual fleets of delivery equipment in favor of Casey's service because they could achieve savings as much as 50 percent of previous costs. (UPS generally bought the stores' fleets and hired some of the workers.) By 1940 the company was serving thirty-seven New York stores with 320 vehicles, including large trucks for furniture transport and several models of cars for special bulk items and package delivery. This use of specialized equipment was perhaps unique in the early trucking industry and led transportation planners to think in terms of the highly specialized equipment that would be required for highway conveyance of all commodities. Casey soon moved UPS corporate headquarters to Greenwich, Connecticut, and bought a modest two-bedroom home in the area. Later, he moved to an apartment in the Waldorf Towers in Manhattan.

Casey is considered a founder of modern management. He once cut out the side of a truck in order to observe how shipping clerks sorted and handled parcels. Casey eliminated 30 percent of worker movements this way. He would then establish work quotas based on his observations. A stickler for detail, Casey authored 138 employee rules. An employee in need of a haircut paid a fifty-cent fine; one who used profanity paid a dollar (one must remember that UPS deliverymen usually arrived at private homes, not a business establishment).

Casey also had advice for his managers. "Each employee should be treated as a special asset that needs to be appreciated and developed–when someone leaves our company that's a failure," he wrote. He also insisted on promoting from the ranks, opening up management positions to employees. Casey established one of the first profit-sharing systems in the nation. By the time of his death United Parcel Service was one of the largest employee-owned companies in the world. Lower-level executives frequently attended conferences with Casey. "Ideals of our company cannot be carried out from the top alone," he wrote. Casey would sometimes anonymously stop a UPS truck and ask the driver how he liked his job.

After World War II, UPS expanded into a new markets. Frequently, it did so not in his own name, but rather through a local affiliate. For example, in Philadelphia Casey's company called itself Common Carrier. The company started gaining interstate operating rights in 1957, and the system of regional carriers continued until the early 1970s, when the carrier applied to the Interstate Commerce Commission for permission to operate as a single entity. Beginning in 1975, the firm finally had interstate rights for the contiguous forty-eight states and functioned as a single operating entity.

Casey never married, he had no children, and he was reportedly somewhat of recluse. He did, however, maintain strong community ties through his philanthropic activities, notably with the Annie E. Casey Foundation, named in honor of his mother, and the Casey Family Program; the latter organization specialized in finding permanent homes for

A UPS employee in need of a haircut paid a fifty-cent fine; one who used profanity paid a dollar.

foster children. Casey also contributed $100,000 to the restoration of a park, Pioneer Square Triangle, in Seattle.

In the early 1960s Casey's dispute with UPS executives over air freight transportation led to his dismissal as chief executive officer. A series of bitter labor disputes with the **Teamsters** union had also weakened Casey's position with the firm. In the early 1980s the aging Casey was frequently hospitalized, and in 1983 Casey retired from the board of directors of United Parcel Service, becoming honorary director. Shortly thereafter, he died of undisclosed causes at a Seattle hospital at age ninety-five. He is interred at Holyrood Mausoleum in Seattle. At the time of his death, United Parcel Service was delivering 6 million packages daily nationwide and had more that 115,000 employees. ◆

teamster: a worker who hauls things with a truck.

Church, Robert Reed, Sr.

1839–1912 ● INVESTOR

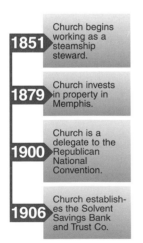

1851	Church begins working as a steamship steward.
1879	Church invests in property in Memphis.
1900	Church is a delegate to the Republican National Convention.
1906	Church establishes the Solvent Savings Bank and Trust Co.

Born a slave in Mississippi, Robert "Bob" Church was the son of a white riverboat owner and captain, and an African-American slave mother. When Church's mother died in 1851, his father took him aboard the steamboat as a steward. After the end of the Civil War, Church settled in the growing community of Memphis, Tennessee. He invested his savings in a saloon and pool hall. Spending as little as possible, he invested in saloons and other businesses in the black waterfront area of Beale Street, personally visiting and monitoring each one. He made a name for himself as the "Boss of Beale Street." In 1879, following a yellow fever epidemic that ravaged the city and drove real estate prices down, Church invested in property throughout the city. Through shrewd investments his personal fortune skyrocketed, and it is likely that Church was the first African American to become a millionaire.

Conscious of his lack of education and unsavory business activities, as well as the need to keep harmonious business relationships with whites, Church generally avoided political and civil rights issues, although he served as a delegate to the Republican National Convention of 1900. He did encourage his children, who included activists Mary Church Terrell and Robert R. Church Jr. to fight for education and respect for blacks. Church participated in civic affairs on a nonpartisan basis. Concerned about leisure facilities for black Memphians, who were excluded from city parks, he provided land for a public park, which was named in his honor. He also sponsored the construction of a large auditorium and concert hall. Church's most significant community enterprise was the Solvent Savings Bank and Trust Company (1906), which he started in part to encourage saving, and which enjoyed enormous success before folding during the Great Depression. Church died suddenly in Memphis in 1912, following a brief illness. ◆

> **Church was probably the first African American to become a millionaire.**

Colgate, William

1783–1857 ● SOAP MANUFACTURER

William Colgate, American manufacturer, was born in the Hollingbourn, Kent County, England, on January 25, 1783. His father, Robert Colgate, was so strongly in sympathy with the democracy of France and America that the British government was about to deal with him as a traitor when William Pitt, his personal friend, warned him of his peril, and he fled to this county with his family. He settled on a farm in Hartford county, Maryland, in 1795, but subsequently moved to Delaware County, New York.

In 1804, the son, William Colgate, found employment in the store of Slidel & Co., **tallow-chandlers**; at 50 Broadway, New York, and two years later, when the firm was dissolved, he started in business on his own account. He lived in the same building in which he worked, namely Nos. 4 and 6 Dutch Street, which was still standing and occupied by the

tallow-chandler: candle maker.

business of his descendants after 100 years. Intelligence, energy, thrift, and honorable dealing met their natural rewards, and before many years he was rated as one of the most prosperous in his line of business throughout the city. At first the business was limited to the manufacture of laundry soap, but a toilet soap department was added in 1847 and perfumery department in 1870. The manufacturing plant was moved from New York to Jersey City in 1847, although the office and salesroom remained in New York. The original name of the enterprise in 1806 was William Colgate & Co., which was changed upon the admission of the son Samuel in 1838, to Colgate & Co.

Colgate was one of the most prominent members of the Baptist Church for many years. In 1850 he was one of the thirteen founders of the American Bible Union. From the time that the Hamilton Literary and Theological Seminary was established at Hamilton, New York, he contributed largely to its support, and by the time it became Madison University, in 1846, five-eighths of the entire property had been contributed by Colgate and his sons. In his honor the name was changed to Colgate University in 1890. Since that time the institution has been greatly helped and supported by Samuel, Robert, and James Boorman Colgate.

Samuel carried on the business founded by his father; Robert became the head of the Atlantic White Lend works of Brooklyn; and James Boorman organized the banking firm of J. B. Colgate & Co., in Wall Street, New York City. These were all the sons of William Colgate by his wife, Mary Gilbert, to whom he was married in New York in 1811. William Colgate died in New York, March 25, 1857. ◆

1804 William Colgate begins working for Slidel & Co., tallow-chandlers.

1806 Colgate establishes William Colgate & Co.

1847 Colgate & Co. adds a toilet soap department.

1850 Colgate helps found the American Bible Union.

1870 Colgate & Co. adds a perfumery department.

1890 In honor of Colgate's contributions, Madison University changes its name to Colgate University.

Colt, Samuel

1814–1862 ● FIREARMS MANUFACTURER

> *"God made men, Samuel Colt made them equal."*
>
> Proverb from the Old West

ounder of an industrial empire based on revolving cylinder, repeating firearms that played an instrumental role in Western settlement, Samuel Colt was born near Hartford, Connecticut. During a sea voyage from 1830 to 1831, the mechanically minded young man carved a wooden pistol with a multichambered, revolving cylinder that rotated to fire successive charges. Back in the United States, he hired gunsmith John Pearson to perfect working models and raised money for the endeavor by conducting demonstrations of nitrous oxide (laughing gas) as the "Celebrated Dr. Coulte of New York, London, and Calcutta."

Colt received a patent for his invention in February 1836, and the Patent Arms Manufacturing Company of Paterson, New Jersey, was incorporated with Pliny Lawton as superintendent. Colt moved from inventor to salesman-promoter and persuaded the government of the Republic of Texas to buy his arms. In the hands of the Texas Rangers, his No. 5 Belt Revolver clearly demonstrated its superior firepower in mounted combat with Comanche Indians during the 1840s.

Although Colt's Paterson enterprise failed, his early revolvers won the devotion of frontiersmen. During the United States-Mexican War, former Texas Ranger Samuel H.

Colt revolvers became icons of America's frontier myth.

Walker collaborated with Colt in creating the Colt-Walker revolver, an improved design adopted by the military. The new revolver helped ensure Colt's success with a new firm, Colt's Patent Fire Arms Manufacturing Company of Hartford.

During the California gold rush and the subsequent period of increased westward immigration, the innovative arms maker introduced a series of improved weapons—notably the .36 caliber, Model 1851 Navy Revolver—to an appreciative market. With foreman Elisha Root, he opened the largest, most advanced private armory in the world in Hartford in 1855, a facility using the machinery and mass-production principles of the "American System of Manufacturing." Although Colt died in 1862, his enterprise was secure, in part, because of a growing Western market.

Colt's inventive and entrepreneurial genius helped advance and protect the Western frontier for several decades. Historian Walter Prescott Webb has cited the Colt revolver (in company with barbed wire and windmills) as a decisive technological factor in the settlement of the Great Plains. Colt firearms—in particular the famed Single Action Army Revolver, or "Peacemaker"—were so popular and ubiquitous that they ultimately became icons of America's frontier myth. ◆

1830 Colt carves a pistol that fires successive charges.

1836 Colt receives a patent for his pistol.

1855 Colt and Elisha Root open the world's largest private armory.

Culver, Henry

1880–1946 ●REAL ESTATE DEVELOPER

Culver pitched a new life, not just a new home.

Southern California real-estate developer in the years of Los Angeles's phenomenal growth, Henry Culver provided thousands of middle-class families with their first homes. Born in Nebraska, Culver spent his early career in a series of dissatisfying civil service and sales positions. Heading to the Los Angeles area in 1910 at the age of 30, he spent three years learning the real-estate business before founding his own Culver Investment Company through which he developed Culver City, a community of homes located between the cities of Los Angeles and Venice.

Culver mastered every step of land development. With only five thousand dollars of his own money, he secured capital for his city from Los Angeles land owners, bankers, and corporations. With a staff of 150 salesmen, he pitched home ownership to the legions of families pouring into the Los Angeles area in the 1920s. Ever sensitive that most of his customers were new to the area and first-time buyers, he pitched a new life, not just a new home. And he offered them easy terms: five hundred dollars down, eighty dollars a month at 7 percent interest, furnishings included.

Culver's success, however, lay in his promotions. His baby contests, raffles, road races, and booster parades attracted customers. Culver's sales soared when he convinced film producer Thomas H. Ince to locate his movie studios in Culver City in 1915, which became the Metro-Goldwyn Mayer (MGM) studios of the 1920s.

Culver's fortunes grew along with his city throughout the 1920s; he sat on the boards of corporations and cultural organizations, maintained a private plane and pilot, spent his summers in Europe, enjoyed memberships in Los Angeles's best country clubs, and built a magnificent home for himself in 1928 on a four-acre lot near the California Country Club.

Culver City continued to prosper as well. RKO movie studios followed MGM to the community; the television studios of Desilu Productions moved there in the 1950s; and petroleum, aircraft, and electronics industries fueled the economy throughout the twentieth century. ◆

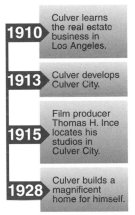

1910 Culver learns the real estate business in Los Angeles.

1913 Culver develops Culver City.

1915 Film producer Thomas H. Ince locates his studios in Culver City.

1928 Culver builds a magnificent home for himself.

De Passe, Suzanne

1946?–PRESENT ● ENTERTAINMENT
EXECUTIVE

Suzanne de Passe grew up in Harlem. She guards her private life carefully, and as a result little is known about her early life and career. De Passe apparently was working as a booking agent at the Cheetah Disco in New York when she met Berry Gordy, then the head of Motown Records. Her strong criticisms of Motown's business operations, delivered directly to Gordy, earned her a position as his creative assistant. Until 1972 she served as road manager, costume designer, and choreographer for the Jackson Five, then Motown's newest sensation. She was also responsible for signing the Commodores, who went on to become one of Motown's biggest sellers during the 1970s.

In the 1970s de Passe became increasingly involved with Motown's theater, television, and film productions. In 1971 she helped write *Diana*, the first production by Motown's television and theatrical division. That project was so successful that the next year Gordy named de Passe corporate director of Motown's Creative Production division, and vice president of Motown's parent corporation, positions that allowed her to work almost exclusively in television and film. De Passe was nominated for an Academy Award for cowriting the Motown-produced film *Lady Sings the Blues* (1972)

In the late 1970s Gordy began to entrust de Passe with the fastest-growing, most profitable divisions of Motown. In 1977 she was promoted to vice president of Motown Industries, another television and film subsidiary, and in 1981 she was named president of Motown Productions. Under de Passe, the

1971 De Passe helps write Motown's *Diana*.

1972 De Passe is nominated for an Academy Award.

1977 De Passe becomes vice president of Motown Industries.

1981 De Passe becomes president of Motown Productions.

1985 De Passe pays $50,000 for the rights to *Lonesome Dove*.

1990 De Passe is inducted into the Black Filmmaker's Hall of Fame.

budget for the company grew from $12 million in 1980 to $65 million in 1989. She won Emmy awards for *Motown 25: Yesterday, Today, Forever* (1982–1983) and *Motown Returns to the Apollo* (1984–1985).

By the early 1980s de Passe was considered one of the rising black female Hollywood executives. In 1985 her reputation soared further after she paid $50,000 for the rights to *Lonesome Dove*, the Larry McMurtry novel about a nineteenth-century western cattle drive that had been rejected by every major Hollywood studio. De Passe sold telecast rights to CBS for $16 million, and by 1989 she had produced an eight-hour program that won seven Emmy awards and drew one of the largest audiences ever for a miniseries. In 1990 de Passe produced *Motown 30: What's Goin' On*.

In the early 1990s de Passe started a new company, de Passe Entertainment, and produced the five-hour miniseries *The Jacksons: An American Dream* (1992). In that year she also was co-executive producer of the film *Class Act*. Considered one of the most powerful female black executives in Hollywood, de Passe won a 1989 Essence award, and the next year was inducted into the Black Filmmaker's Hall of Fame. In 1990 de Passe received a Micheaux award for her contribution to the entertainment industry. ◆

Deere, John

1804–1886 ● FARM EQUIP-
MENT MANUFACTURER

*"I will never put my name on a
plow that does not have in it
the best that is in me."*

John Deere

John Deere developed the steel plow which made it easier to cultivate the tough soil of the American prairies. He began experimenting with steel plows in the late 1830's. By 1846, he was turning out about a thousand steel plows a year for farmers in Illinois, where he had his headquarters.

Deere was born in Vermont and was trained as a blacksmith there. He moved to Illinois in 1837 and set up shop as a blacksmith. His work brought him in touch with farmers who needed a tougher and more reliable plow than the ones they were using, which were generally wooden with some metal tips. Deere and a partner devised the steel plow to satisfy this need. In 1846, he moved his shop to Moline, Illinois. The business grew to become a major producer of farm equipment in the United States. ◆

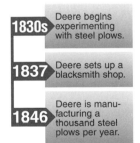

1830s Deere begins experimenting with steel plows.

1837 Deere sets up a blacksmith shop.

1846 Deere is manufacturing a thousand steel plows per year.

Dow, Herbert Henry

1866–1930 ● CHEMICAL MANUFACTURER

Herbert Henry Dow, chemist, was born at Belleville, Ontario, Canada, February 26, 1866, son of Joseph Henry and Sarah Jane (Bunnell) Dow. His first American ancestors, Henry and Joane (Nudd) Dow, came from, Ormsby, Norfolk, England, to Watertown, Massachusetts, in 1637. From them the descent is through their son Henry Dow, who was senior justice of the New Hampshire court of common pleas, 1699–1707, and his wife Hannah Page; Samuel and Abigail Hobbs; Samuel and Mary Page; Joseph and Dorothy Blake; Josiah and Hanna Moulton; Joseph and Abigail French; and Joseph Henry Dow, the father of the chemist. Six of the above ancestors in succession from the first Henry to Josiah held the office of town clerk at Hampton, New Hampshire.

Herbert Dow's father, who was master mechanic at the Chisholm Steel Shovel Works, Cleveland, invented the first steam turbine produced in the United States. Herbert Dow was graduated as a chemical engineer at the Case School of Applied Science in 1888 and for the ensuing years was professor of chemistry and toxicology at the Huron Street Hospital College in Cleveland. In 1889, he developed a process for the manufacture of bromine from brine (patent No. 11,232, April 12, 1892). In the following year he established a laboratory at Midland, Michigan, where there was one of the most valuable brine fields in the United States, and began the production of bromine and its derivatives under the name of the Dow Process Company.

The Midland Chemical Company was organized in 1892 with Dow as director and the manufacture of bromine and bromides continued to occupy his attention until 1895. In that year he began the manufacture of chlorine and its derivatives in partnership with several friends and business associates, using brine obtained from the Midland Chemical Company after the bromine had been extracted. In 1897 the Dow Chemical Company was organized to manufacture chlorine and caustic soda, with Albert E. Convers as chairman of the board and Dow as president and general manager. The new company acquired the property of the Dow Process Company and gradually added to its line of products magnesium sulfate (Epsom salts), magnesium chloride and magnesium carbonate. In 1900 it absorbed the Midland Chemical Company. Two years later a new Midland Chemical Company was organized to manufacture **chloroform** by a new process, which he perfected. As by-products in the manufacture of chloroform the company produced carbon bisulfide and carbon tetrachloride, which eventually became equally as important as chloroform.

chloroform: a colorless liquid with many industrial uses.

The Midland Chemical Company continued as a separate organization until 1914 when it was purchased by the Dow Chemical Company and Dow became president of the latter. A succession of new products for pharmaceutical and industrial uses served rapidly to enlarged the range and volume of the company's business. These included phenol (carbolic acid), salicylic acid, methyl salieylate (oil of wintergreen), acetyl salicylic acid (aspirin), aniline oil, calcium chloride (marketed as Dowflake for laying dust on roads), Ferric chloride, Paradow (a moth repellent and insecticide for peach tree borers), and magnesium metal and alloys of magnesium (for airplane and automotive parts).

During World War I, when Dow served on the advisory committee of the Council of National Defense, the Dow Chemical Company produced large quantities of mustard gas and other war chemicals. It was the first American company to produce synthetic indigo. At the time of its founder's death it had become one of the leading manufacturers of heavy, industrial, pharmaceutical and aromatic chemicals, solvents, insecticides, dyes and magnesium metal. Its products, numbering more than 200, were sold throughout the United States and Canada and in some foreign countries. It was the largest producer of carbon tetrachloride, magnesium chloride, magnesium metals and bromide in this country and operated the largest phenol plant in the world. Its plant at Midland, Michigan, covering nearly 250 acres, comprised 325 buildings and employed 3,000 hands. The company also had plants at Mt. Pleasant, Michigan, Long Beach, California, and Wilmington, North Carolina. The Dow Chemical Company owned 620 patents, of which 100 were issued to Herbert H. Dow personally or jointly with other inventors.

In recognition of his scientific achievements, Dow was awarded the honorary degree of Doctor of Engineering by the

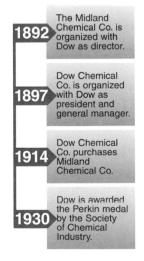

1892 The Midland Chemical Co. is organized with Dow as director.

1897 Dow Chemical Co. is organized with Dow as president and general manager.

1914 Dow Chemical Co. purchases Midland Chemical Co.

1930 Dow is awarded the Perkin medal by the Society of Chemical Industry.

Case School of Applied Science in 1924, by the University of Michigan in 1929. Dow was also awarded the Perkin medal by the Society of Chemical Industry in 1930 for "his development of improvements in the production of chlorine, magnesium and numerous other chemical materials."

For many years Dow served as a consultant to the Westinghouse Electric & Manufacturing Company. He was a trustee of the Case school of Applied Science, and a member of the Chemical Alliance, Inc., American Association for the Advancement of Science, American Chemical Society, American Electrochemical Society, American Institute of Chemical Engineers, Franklin Institute, National Museum of Engineering and Industry, Society of Chemical Industry (Great Britain), the Sigma Xi and Phi Kappa Psi societies, and the advisory board of the department of engineering research, University of Michigan. He was also a 32nd degree Mason. In religion, he was a Presbyterian.

Besides Dow's industrial activities, he was prominent in public affairs at Midland, Michigan, serving on the council and the boards of public works and education and as superintendent of parks. He gave liberally of his time and wealth to promote and develop civic enterprises, such as Midland's community center, welfare association, airport and court house, and a major promotion of a $100,000 clubhouse for the Midland Country Club. Gardening was his chief recreation. Dow was married in 1892 to Grace Anna, daughter of George Willard Ball, of Midland, and had seven children. He died in Rochester, Minnesota, on October 15, 1930. ◆

Du Pont Family

INDUSTRIALISTS

The Du Pont family of Delaware is one of the most influential family groups in the history of American industry; it has included individuals who distinguished themselves in politics, and in military and cultural affairs as well. The family was founded in Delaware by Eleuthère Irénée du Pont de Nemours (1771–1834). He also founded E. I. du Pont de Nemours & Co., established about 1802 as a gunpowder-making firm, which, under his able successors, became the largest chemical manufacturing company in the United States. Other members of the family have won major reputations.

Samuel Francis du Pont (1803–1865) served as a naval officer before and during the Civil War. Du Pont commanded blockading squadrons operating off the coast of the Confederate states. Forces under his command were ordered

> *"The thing about Du Ponts is that some are very, very rich and the others are just plain old rich."*
> Pierre Samuel Du Pont II, 1992

Eleuthère Irénée du Pont de Nemours

1802 ► E.I. du Pont de Nemours & Co. is founded.

1861 ► Henry Algernon du Pont graduates first in his West Point class.

1906 ► Henry becomes U.S. senator from Delaware.

to capture Charleston, South Carolina, in 1863, but were repulsed by the Confederate defenses. A controversy over this attack overshadowed du Pont's effective work as a blockading officer. Du Pont Circle, in Washington, D.C., is named in his honor.

Henry Algernon du Pont (1838–1926) was a West Point graduate, standing first in the class of 1861, which graduated directly into Civil War service. He served throughout the war in a number of commands as an artillery officer and was frequently decorated for bravery and resourcefulness in battle; he held the nation's highest decoration for bravery, the Congressional Medal of Honor. Henry A. du Pont was responsible for changing the family business from a partnership into a corporation, but he refused to become president of the firm. He served as U.S. senator from Delaware, 1906–1917. ◆

Eastman, George

1854–1932 ● PHOTOGRAPHY
EQUIPMENT MANUFACTURER

"Thus far in our industrial development the workers have not evidenced any particular desire for a vacation."

George Eastman, 1919

George Eastman, the most successful figure in the photographic business during his lifetime, devised and marketed a system of picture-taking that revolutionized photography. Instead of relying on large, expensive, and bulky photographic plates of glass, Eastman developed a system of film that could be rolled and inserted into a small, portable camera—the "Kodak." This system gave great impetus to amateur photography in the United States. Eastman was very talented in business management and in the use of sales techniques. His cameras and films were offered nationally with great success, beginning in the 1880s and 1890s. The Eastman Kodak Company developed into a leading manufacturing company, not only in the photography field but in production of related chemicals and in precision engineering.

George Eastman's camera and film products made him one of America's wealthiest men. Like several other wealthy

"To my friends: My work is done. Why wait?"

George Eastman, in a suicide note, 1932

Americans, he devoted a great deal of his wealth to educational projects. He donated well over $75 million to various colleges and universities. The Eastman School of Music became part of the University of Rochester, which received large sums from George Eastman. Other schools that he helped included Hampton Institute, Massachusetts Institute of Technology, and Tuskegee Institute. ◆

Field, Marshall

1834–1906 ● MERCHANT

"Good will is the one and only asset that competition cannot undersell or destroy."
Marshall Field, 1887

Marshall Field, one of the leaders in establishing department stores in the United States, was born in 1834 in Conway Township, Massachusetts. He began his career as a teenaged clerk in a store in Pittsfield, Massachusetts. He decided that prospects were better in the growing West and moved to Chicago in 1856. He clerked in a Chicago store and did some traveling as a salesman in the country sections of Illinois. After a short time as an employee, he was admitted as a partner in the store for which he worked. This was the start of a career that led to the development of one of the world's largest stores, Marshall Field & Company.

The Field system of running a store included uncompromising courtesy toward customers and fixed prices on all goods offered for sale. Many competing firms charged whatever they could get for merchandise. Field expanded his operations, eventually buying the total output of factories to supply his store. He was represented by buyers in many parts of the world, and he developed a habit of buying supplies of goods at

> The Field system of running a store included uncompromising courtesy toward customers.

43

Marshall Field's Chicago Store

The flagship Marshall Field store occupies an entire block fronting on State Street in downtown Chicago. Marshall Field and his partner at the time, Levi Leiter, had moved their business to the site in 1868. The State Street store has been designated a national historic landmark. A number of the store's notable features date back to 1907. These include Corinthian columns throughout the main floor, an atrium called the north light well that soars through the entire building, and a 6,000-square-foot Tiffany mosaic dome. It took 50 workers about 18 months to put in place the 1.6 million pieces of colored glass that make up the dome. The store's bronze clock on State Street was immortalized in 1945 when a painting by artist Norman Rockwell appeared on a cover of the magazine *Saturday Evening Post*. A writer in the mid-1900s joked about enjoying a visit to Chicago, "a suburb of Marshall Field's." A renovation completed in 1992 added an atrium in the center of the store that reinforces the city-within-a-city image. The atrium, with its cast-iron fountain, resembles a town square.

low prices for future delivery and sale through his Chicago store. Marshall Field did not engage in political activity or in public appearances. He endowed the Field Museum of Natural History in Chicago, one of the foremost institutions of its kind in the country; he made important gifts to other public institutions, including the University of Chicago. ◆

Fisk, James

1834–1872 ● SPECULATOR

James Fisk was one of the most sensational speculators in American business history. He began his career buying and selling dry goods. During the Civil War he became interested in war supply contracts, and after the war, he became a leading figure in New York City's financial circles. He was a very successful manipulator of stocks. He worked his way into an important railroad company, the Erie; once in control, he and his accomplices took many of the company's assets as their own. They then forced the price of Erie stock up in such a way that they could make money without any relation to the true value of the stock. Fisk, with one of his associates, Jay Gould, tried to "corner" the U.S. supply of gold in 1869, believing that they had enough influence with President Grant to keep the government from stepping into the market situation. They failed in this, but went on to other flashy business operations.

Fisk used his money to influence New York politics, and to sponsor plays, operas, and musical performances. He had control of several steamship lines working between New York and New England; he named the largest ferry on the Hudson River the *James Fisk*; and he had himself made colonel of a New York militia regiment. Fisk became involved in a quarrel with Edward Stokes over the affections of an actress and

> In 1869, Fisk and Jay Gould tried to corner the U.S. supply of gold.

Stokes shot Fisk in one of the most publicized murders of the nineteenth century. ◆

Forbes, Malcolm Stevenson

1919–1990 ● PUBLISHING TYCOON

> *"Often when on university campuses to address graduating classes, I am asked how one becomes successful, and I explain that my own success was attributable to sheer ability—spelled i-n-h-e-r-i-t-a-n-c-e."*
> Malcolm Forbes

Malcolm Forbes was the chairman and editor-in-chief of *Forbes* magazine, a biweekly journal for business and finance. He was a cosmopolitan multimillionaire known for his extravagant parties, his conspicuous consumption, and his passionate interests in ballooning, motorcycling, and yachting. At the time of his death in 1990, his personal fortune was estimated at between $400 million and $1 billion.

Malcolm Stevenson Forbes was born on August 19, 1919, in Brooklyn, New York, to Adelaide (Stevenson) and Bertie Charles Forbes, a Scottish emigrant. In 1917 his father founded *Forbes* magazine. For many years, *Forbes* was the only business journal published in the United States.

Malcolm was raised in Englewood, New Jersey. In 1941, he graduated from Princeton University, where he majored in political science. After graduation, Forbes became the owner and publisher of two weekly newspapers in Lancaster, Ohio. In 1942, he joined the United States Army as a private. He became a machine gun sergeant and served in Europe during World War II (1939–1945). Forbes was wounded in the thigh during combat in 1944 and was subsequently awarded the Bronze Star and the Purple Heart. He received an honorable discharge in August 1945 after recuperating in a military hospital.

After the war, Forbes joined the staff at his father's magazine as assistant to the publisher and he quickly rose through the ranks. In 1949 he explored his interest in politics and ran successfully for the Borough Council of Bernardsville, New Jersey. In 1951 he was elected to the New Jersey legislature for a six-year term. In 1957 he pitted himself as Republican candidate against the Democratic incumbent governor Robert B. Meyner of New Jersey, but he lost by a landslide vote.

Throughout his political career, Forbes maintained ties with the family business. In 1954, after his father's death, Forbes became publisher and editor of the magazine, while his older brother Bruce took over the presidency and the business side of the parent company, Forbes Inc. Forbes became editor-

> *"I'd say capitalism's worst excess is in the large number of crooks and tinhorns who get too much of the action."*
> Malcolm Forbes, 1979

The "Forbes Four Hundred"

In 1982 *Forbes* magazine compiled its first list of the 400 richest Americans, called the "Forbes Four Hundred." The requirements for inclusion on the list, which is released every October, are simple. A person merely has to be a United States citizen, and to have a net worth that ranks him or her among the top 400 people in the country. The original list contained many people who had inherited their wealth, and there were no software executives; Bill Gates did not appear until 1986, with a paltry $315 million net worth. But by the late 1990s, the composition of the list had changed drastically. The 1997 list contained 170 billionaires, quite a jump from the 13 named in 1982. To make the list in 1997, a person's net worth had to be at least $475 million. And most of the people with "old wealth" (including many women) had slipped off the list. In fact, only 106 people from the original list still remained there 15 years later. During the mid-1990s, Bill Gates and investor Warren Buffett fought over the top position on the list. By October 1997 Gates (whose net worth had doubled in a year, to almost $40 billion) had pulled far ahead of Buffett, who was worth only $21 billion. However, Buffett still held the distinction of having been on every list since 1982.

in-chief and publisher of the magazine in 1957. After his brother died of cancer in 1964, Forbes became president of Forbes Inc. and inherited a healthy, debt-free business. He soon bought out Bruce's widow and his brothers Wallace and Gordon and became the sole owner of the firm.

The magazine flourished under Malcolm. He was an active editor, and he contributed regularly to an opinion column called "Fact and Comment." In the tradition of his father, Forbes continued to focus his magazine stories on the people running companies rather than just the facts and figures of a business. To broaden his customer base, he also expanded the magazine's coverage to include reports on personalities outside the business world. Under Malcolm the magazine also developed the "*Forbes* 400," a descriptive list of the nation's richest men and women that became society's measure of capitalist success. Forbes dubbed his magazine "The Capitalist Tool," a phrase he had printed on the side of his yacht and private jet to help market his publication.

Over the years, Forbes diversified the company's holdings to include real estate and a motorcycle dealership. Forbes was also a serious art collector who owned about 2,000 paintings and a distinguished collection of jeweled Fabergé eggs that had been created for the czars of Russia.

Forbes was renowned his opulent lifestyle and for courting business associates with lavish parties on his yacht. In later years he was often seen in the company of actress Elizabeth Taylor, who added to his aura of fame and success. Forbes was also a ballooning enthusiast and in 1973 he became the first person to cross the United States in a hot-air balloon.

In one of his final shows of extravagance, Forbes spent $2 million on a party celebrating his 70th birthday. He flew hundreds of friends, business associates, and journalists to join him at his Moroccan palace overlooking the Strait of Gibraltar, where his guests were showered with rose petals and treated to exotic entertainment that included acrobats, belly dancers, and Berber horsemen.

Forbes died in 1990 at age 70 of a heart attack. He had five children with Roberta Remsen Laidlaw, his wife of 39 years, from whom he was divorced in 1985. The oldest son, Malcolm "Steve" Forbes Jr., became chairman and editor-in-chief of the magazine empire upon his father's death. Steve brought the notoriety of the Forbes family and fortune back

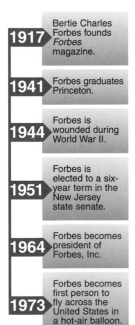

1917 ▶ Bertie Charles Forbes founds *Forbes* magazine.

1941 ▶ Forbes graduates Princeton.

1944 ▶ Forbes is wounded during World War II.

1951 ▶ Forbes is elected to a six-year term in the New Jersey state senate.

1964 ▶ Forbes becomes president of Forbes, Inc.

1973 ▶ Forbes becomes first person to fly across the United States in a hot-air balloon.

into the public eye in the mid-1990s, when he became a candidate for the Republican presidential nomination in 1996, vowing to spend $10 million of his personal fortune on the campaign. He was defeated by Robert Joseph Dole, Republican senator from Kansas. ◆

Ford, Henry

1863–1947 ●AUTOMOBILE MANUFACTURER

"Let a man start out in life to build something better and sell it cheaper than it has been built or sold before, let him have that determination and the money will roll in."

Henry Ford

Henry Ford was the first automobile manufacturer to use assembly line labor-saving devices to produce automobiles more economically and efficiently. Ford was born to Irish immigrants in Springwells Township, Michigan. As a youngster he displayed mechanical skills and a knack for innovation and invention, and in 1879 Ford dropped out of school and went to Detroit, where he took a job as a machinist's assistant. When he returned to his father's farm he set up a small machine shop and sawmill, later working for different companies and honing his skills by working on clocks and watches. As an employee of Westinghouse, Ford set up and repaired their steam engines.

> *"The cure for 'materialism' is to have enough for everybody and to spare. When people are sure of having what they need they cease to think about it."*
>
> Henry Ford, 1931

Ford moved to Detroit in 1891 and two years later he was made chief engineer of the Edison Illuminating Company. That same year he built his first one-cylinder gasoline motor. Soon after he began to build his first car, a two-cylinder light carriage that he completed in 1896. He did this while working for Edison during the daytime and working on his inventions well into the night.

Ford took his wife and 2-year-old son for their first automobile ride the day after he and a friend road tested the car. During the next week he drove all over Detroit, with a friend bicycling ahead as his flagman. In 1899, Ford quit the Edison Company and started the Detroit Automobile Company. This venture lasted about two years, ending with the company's bankruptcy. Ford's father approved of his son's interest in mechanics but thought Ford was wasting his time working on automobiles, telling Henry, "You'll never make a go of it." Ford then decided to try his hand at making racing cars, more for the purpose of gaining a name than because he supported this use of automobiles. In 1901 he entered his car in a race at the Detroit Fairgrounds, at which the first prize was $1,000 and a crystal punch bowl. It was a twenty-five-mile race, with Ford's major competitor being Alexander Winton, who had an auto-manufacturing company. For more than half the race Ford was behind the Winton car but he ended up the winner. When he got out of his car, covered with dirt and visibly shaken, Ford said, "Boy, I'll never do that again! I was scared to death."

In 1903, with the help of a group of backers, Ford organized the Ford Motor Company, of which he owned 25 percent of the stock, and the company began to produce cars that sold well. In 1906 he had a disagreement with Alexander V. Malcolmson, a major stockholder, and bought him out, purchasing 255 shares for $175,000, which made him the majority stockholder. Ford's plans to build an affordable car took off after that. He told one of his employees, "This is a great day. We're going to expand this company, and you will see it grow by leaps and bounds." He began with the low-priced Model N and went on to produce the Model T, which first came out in 1908. The Model T caught the nation's imagination and newspapers praised its virtues. In 1913 Ford introduced the conveyor-belt assembly line and the following year 250,000 Model Ts were sold. Altogether fifteen million Model Ts, also known as Tin Lizzies or Flivvers, were marketed. By manufacturing a large number of the same model, Ford was able to take advantage of mass production, utilizing standardized parts. Although he understood and promoted the benefits of assembly line production, he said, "The idea of repetitive labor—the doing of one thing over and over again and always in the same way—is nothing less than terrifying."

Ford was innovative in rewarding his employees and established an excellent relationship with his workers. Will Rogers said of Ford, "It will take a hundred years to tell whether he helped us or hurt us, but he certainly didn't leave us where he found us."

By 1919 the Ford family had gained complete control of the Ford Motor Company; Ford had become such a powerful force in the company that even key people who disagreed with him were not retained. In 1919 Ford's son Edsel was made president of the company, and he showed a talent for the position. There were differences of opinion between father and son, primarily because Henry Ford failed to see changing trends in automobile styling, color, and manufacture. Although the Model T continued to sell well in the 1920s, General Motors and Chrysler were beginning to make inroads in Ford's sales. In 1927 Ford stopped producing the Model T and it was replaced by the Model A.

Ford dabbled in politics and ran unsuccessfully as a Democratic candidate for the Senate. In World War I he chartered a "Peace Ship," which he sailed "to get the boys out of the trenches by Christmas," but at the same time he was making a fortune in military materiel. In 1918 he bought the weekly *Dearborn Independent* to publicize his political views and published a ninety-issue series of anti-Semitic articles blaming the Jews for the ills of the world, including a reprint of the notorious forgery *The Protocols of the Elders of Zion*. After being sued for libel by a Chicago Jewish lawyer, Ford issued an apology in 1927 and retracted his attacks on Jews; that same year he closed the *Dearborn Independent*.

Over the years, Henry Ford and his son Edsel had many disputes and the senior Ford again assumed presidency of the company after his son's death in 1943. In 1945 Edsel's son, Henry Ford II, became president of the Ford Motor Company.

In 1936 the Ford Foundation was set up primarily to fund international scientific, educational, and charitable projects. ◆

"Do you want to know the cause of war? It is capitalism, greed, the dirty hunger for dollars."

Henry Ford

1891 Ford moves to Detroit.

1893 Ford becomes chief engineer of the Edison Illuminating Co.

1896 Ford builds his first car.

1899 Ford organizes the Detroit Automobile Co.

1903 Ford organizes the Ford Motor Co.

1908 Ford introduces the Model T.

1913 Ford introduces assembly line production.

Frick, Henry Clay

1849–1919 ●INDUSTRIALIST

Henry Clay Frick was first employed as a bookkeeper. He invested in coke ovens, which were a vital part of the steelmaking process in the Pittsburgh area of Pennsylvania during the early 1870s. The investment was so profitable that he gave up his regular job to give full time to the coke company. Frick was a millionaire before he reached the age of 30.

Frick's business ability brought him in contact with Andrew Carnegie, the leading steelmaker of the time. They worked together on several ventures, and Frick became chairman and manager of Carnegie's company in 1889. Frick assembled a net work of companies, including mining firms, railroad and shipping companies, and steel mills, under one management. He was effective as a manager, and selected his subordinates carefully; however, he was notoriously anti-labor. In 1892 he was responsible for bringing armed guards into the Homestead (Pennsylvania) mills, which resulted in a tragic gun battle with striking steelworkers.

Frick was one of the key figures in organizing the United States Steel Company in 1901. He was also active in railroad and insurance company activities. Frick built a mansion in New York City in which he collected notable art masterpieces. On his death, he left the building and the art collection to the public, plus an endowment to support them. ◆

1889 Frick becomes chairman of Andrew Carnegie's steel company.

1892 Frick brings armed guards into the Homestead mills.

1901 Frick helps organize the United States Steel Co.

The Frick Collection

The Frick Collection is a museum exhibiting European art from the 14th through 19th centuries. The artworks were collected over several decades by Henry Clay Frick and displayed in his home on Fifth Avenue in New York City. Architect Thomas Hasting designed the building, which was constructed in 1913–14. Before Frick died, he bequeathed the house and the art collection to the public, along with a fund for maintenance and further acquisitions. The museum was opened to visitors in 1935, after the death of Frick's wife in 1931. The Frick Collection includes many well-known paintings by such artists as Rembrandt, Bellini, Vermeer, and Titian. Among the Frick's most famous paintings are Jean-Honoré Fragonard's four-canvas *Progress of Love*, painted in 1773. The museum also boasts a superb collection of 18th-century furniture, including a chest of drawers that once belonged to Marie Antoinette, as well as French and Chinese porcelains, French Limoges enamels, English silver, and oriental rugs. The art is displayed in a manner that preserves the ambiance of Frick's private residence, and therefore few ropes or glass cases are used to guard fragile and priceless artworks, as in most art museums.

Fugger, Jakob (Jakob the Rich)

1459–1525 ● FINANCIER & BUSINESSMAN

Jakob Fugger was the grandson of Johannes Fugger, who founded one of the most influential families in the history of finance. Johannes Fugger, a master linen weaver, settled in Augsburg, Bavaria, in 1367, one year before **guilds** obtained a share in the management of the city. He capitalized on this newfound political power and developed a successful international business in spices, silk, and woolen materials, with a family branch in Venice. His son, Jakob I, married a daughter of the master of the Augsburg mint. After settling his father-in-law's debts, he moved to Tyrol as a mint master and extended the family business into mining. Jakob II had been destined to work for the church; however, at the age

guild: a union of craftsmen or merchants.

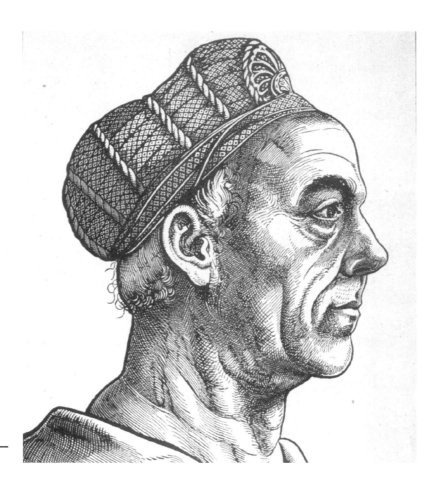

Jacob Fugger

of 14, his older brother, Peter, died and he was called upon to join the family business.

Jakob II displayed great genius for business. The Holy Roman emperor Maximilian I extensively utilized his financial services; as a result, the Fuggers secured interests in silver mines in the Tyrol, copper mines in Hungary, and large tracts of real estate, and controlled the copper market in Venice. Jakob II profitably employed bills of exchange to move large amounts of money for use by the Habsburgs. Without great risk, he skillfully made large profits from the price differential of bills of exchange. The procedure was called *cambiro arbitrio* and is now known as arbitrage.

Historians agree that without the Fuggers' help, Charles V of Spain probably would not have become Holy Roman emperor in 1519. Jakob II influenced the German princes to support Charles V in return for cash and lines of credit;

Charles, in turn, ennobled the family and permitted them to coin their own money.

As a result of Jakob II's business acumen and the financing arrangements made with the extended Habsburg family, the Fuggers became the richest family in Europe. From 1511 to 1527 the Fugger balance sheet showed an increase in equity from 196,796 florins to 2,021,207 florins, an increase of 927 percent or an average annual growth of over 54 percent. Jakob II died childless, leaving his financial interests to his nephews. They and their descendants continued the business until 1607, when bankruptcy occurred. The family made the mistake of extending loans to the Habsburg Philip II of Spain, who lost his Armada in 1588 in a war with England, and later defaulted on his debts to the Fuggers.

Jakob II was described as being a handsome man of merry disposition and pleasant to all. He gave gala skating and dance parties for society. For the less fortunate he built low-rent housing and established a program to provide bread at subsidized prices. He built many churches and enriched the Church of St. Ann at Augsburg with splendid statues and a family tomb. When the church fell into the hands of the Lutherans he requested that his nephews have him buried elsewhere as he was opposed to the Reformation. His motto was "I want to gain while I can." ◆

"I want to gain while I can."
Jakob Fugger

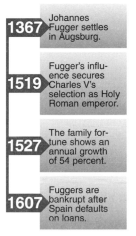

1367 Johannes Fugger settles in Augsburg.

1519 Fugger's influence secures Charles V's selection as Holy Roman emperor.

1527 The family fortune shows an annual growth of 54 percent.

1607 Fuggers are bankrupt after Spain defaults on loans.

Fuller, S. B.

1905–1988 ● SOAP MANUFACTURER

S. B. Fuller, no relation to Alfred C. Fuller, founder of the Fuller Brush Company, was born in 1905, in ◆ Parish Monroe, Louisiana. He was a self-made entrepreneur who became one of the wealthiest African Americans in the United States during the 1950s and 1960s. At the height of its success in the early 1960s, the Fuller Products Company, with eighty-five branches in thirty-eight states, had annual gross sales of $10 million and employed 5,000 workers. By the late 1960s, however, a series of reverses had toppled Fuller's empire and forced him into bankruptcy in 1971. Although he was able to revive his cosmetics business in the 1970s, Fuller could never rejuvenate all the enterprises he had controlled during his company's glory days.

Born into in Louisiana and raised in Memphis, Tennessee, Fuller had only a sixth-grade education. As a schoolboy in Memphis he started selling soap to neighbors, convinced by his mother, who died when he was 17, that door-to-door sales was the best way out of poverty. In 1928 Fuller, already married and a father, hitchhiked to Chicago and found work in a coal yard. Eventually, he became an agent for and then manager of an insurance company, but he always knew that sales held the key to his future.

In 1935, in the middle of the Great Depression, he borrowed twenty-five dollars on his car and used the money to purchase a load of soap from Boyer National Laboratories. He began selling door-to-door and had, by 1939, a dozen sales representatives peddling thirty items from a little-known cosmetics line he produced in his small factory on Chicago's South Side.

As Fuller's business grew he acquired several other companies including, in 1947, Boyer International Laboratories, which made and sold Jean Nadal Cosmetics. The company's clientele was predominately white and located in the South. Other acquisitions included the Courier Newspaper Group, which owned the *New York Age*, the country's oldest black newspaper, and the *Pittsburgh Courier*, the black newspaper with the largest circulation in the United States. Fuller's other businesses included the South Center Department Store and the Regal Theatre in Chicago, and financial interests in farming and beef cattle production. By the early 1960s, Fuller Products had sales of more than $10 million and Fuller was widely regarded as one of the wealthiest African Americans in the country.

In the midst of his prosperity, Fuller in the late 1950s had a $250,000, twelve-room ranch house built for himself and his wife, Lestine. Located in Robbins, Illinois, forty-five minutes from Chicago, it had 4,000 feet of floor space and included a patio and greenhouse.

Fuller's troubles began as he found himself under attack from both blacks and whites. In the late 1950s the White

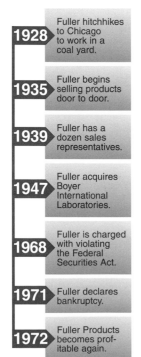

1928 Fuller hitchhikes to Chicago to work in a coal yard.

1935 Fuller begins selling products door to door.

1939 Fuller has a dozen sales representatives.

1947 Fuller acquires Boyer International Laboratories.

1968 Fuller is charged with violating the Federal Securities Act.

1971 Fuller declares bankruptcy.

1972 Fuller Products becomes profitable again.

Citizens Councils, a white racist Southern group, learned that an African American owned Jean Nadal Cosmetics. The Council organized a successful boycott of Nadal merchandise at a time when Boyer products accounted for 60 percent of Fuller Company business.

A few short years later Fuller had to endure a boycott from his black customers. In 1963, at his induction into the National Association of Manufacturers, Fuller said in his acceptance speech that "a lack of understanding of the capitalist system and not racial barriers was keeping blacks from making progress." He expressed similar sentiments in a 1963 interview in U.S. News and World Report in which he said

> Negroes are not discriminated against because of the color of their skin. They are discriminated against because they have not anything to offer that people want to buy. The minute that they can develop themselves so they excel in whatever they do—then they are going to find that they don't have any real problems.

This apparent Uncle Tom attitude angered black nationalists, who boycotted Fuller Products and its owner's gospel of black entrepreneurship.

The combined effects of the two boycotts plus some poorly timed business decisions put financial pressure on the continued viability of Fuller Products. In 1968, in an effort to bail out his company, Fuller sold promissory notes in interstate commerce without registering them. For this action he was charged in 1968 with violating the Federal Securities Act. He pleaded guilty, was placed on five-years' probation, and was ordered to repay $1.6 million to creditors. Faced with a severe cash crunch, Fuller Products entered bankruptcy in 1971. After reorganization the company reported profits of $300,000 in 1972, and, Fuller successfully ran the cosmetics portion of the old company for several years, though never at the firm's previous levels of size or profitability.

On the occasion of his seventieth birthday, Fuller, a Baptist, was the guest of honor at a special tribute organized by John H. Johnson, publisher of Ebony and Jet, and other prominent black entrepreneurs of Chicago whom Fuller had mentored. Besides the compliments and cake, Fuller was given the net proceeds of the dinner, some $70,000, plus

Fuller's apparent Uncle Tom attitude angered black nationalists.

$50,000 worth of stock certificates. Nearly 2,000 guests attended the event, including Illinois governor Dan Walker and the Reverend Jesse Jackson, head of Operation Push.

On 15 June 1985 more than 2,000 people, including Chicago mayor Harold Washington, Jesse Jackson, and Illinois governor James Thompson, gathered at a Chicago hotel to honor Fuller on his eightieth birthday. This would be the last major public event of his life. Just over three years later, the "Godfather of Black Business" died of kidney failure at the age of 83. ◆

Gates, William H. (Bill)

1955–PRESENT ● COMPUTER DEVELOPER

> *"When communication gets inexpensive enough and is combined with other advances in technology, the influence of interactive information will be as real and as far-reaching as the effects of electricity."*
> Bill Gates, *The Road Ahead*

William H. Gates was born in Seattle, Washington, on October 28, 1955. His father is a prominent lawyer and his mother has served on numerous corporate, charitable, and civil boards. He taught himself programming at age 13, having taken up computer studies in 1967 as a seventh grader at the private Lakeside School in Seattle. Gates and a ninth grader named Paul Allen were enthralled about using the school's time-shared computer. Gates and Allen's enthusiasm has not waned since. In the late 1960s, Gates and some other Seattle teenagers would ride their bicycles each afternoon to the Computer Center Corporation office, where they searched for errors in the programs being run on the Center's computer. They eventually went on the firm's payroll. Throughout their high school years, Gates and Allen worked as programming consultants.

TRW, a large software firm in Vancouver, Washington, offered Gates and Allen $20,000 a year, each, to work in a software development group. Gates took a yearlong leave from high school during his senior year to go to work for TRW. When work diminished, he entered Harvard University. He was planning to stay away from computers. Allen went to work as a systems programmer for Honeywell, near Boston.

Gates entered Harvard in the fall of 1973. Allen happened to be strolling through Harvard Square one day when he noticed the January issue of *Popular Electronics* on a news stand. Allen bought a copy and went on to visit Gates. The Altair microcomputer, based on the Intel 8080 chip, made by an Albuquerque, New Mexico, firm called MITS, and selling for $350, appeared on the cover. Here was the first truly cheap computer! To anyone who knew computers then, it was instantly clear that the Altair required, more than anything else, a BASIC interpreter, to permit users to write programs in a high level language rather than in machine code. Allen proposed to Gates that the two try to write a BASIC interpreter for the Altair. Gates and Allen phoned Edward Roberts, the MITS founder who had built the Altair, with an offer to write a BASIC interpreter for the Altair. Roberts was interested, and the pair started working. Allen and Gates spent February

The Codex Leicester

When Bill Gates began to design his new home in Seattle in the late 1980s, he imagined having wall-sized screens that could digitally display famous works of art. First, he set up a new company, Corbis, to develop the needed technology; and then he began to build an art collection. One of his most famous purchases was Leonardo da Vinci's *Codex Leicester*, which Gates bought at a Christie's auction in 1994 for $30.8 million. The *Codex Leicester* is an illustrated notebook written by da Vinci between 1506 and 1510, in which he discussed scientific phenomena such as water, light, and celestial bodies. It was written in Italian—but in a mirror image. In 1717 the manuscript was bought by Thomas Coke, Earl of Leicester, and it became known as the *Codex Leicester*. It remained in that family until 1980, when industrialist Armand Hammer bought it and gave it a new name, the *Codex Hammer*. Many art lovers were concerned that the only remaining da Vinci manuscript in private hands would vanish from public view, but Gates surprised them. First, the manuscript (once again named the *Codex Leicester*) went on a tour through Italy. Then it was exhibited at New York's American Museum of Natural History and the Seattle Art Museum; viewers there could use computer stations to read pages in Italian or English (written left to right). Corbis also developed a da Vinci CD-ROM that used material from the *Codex*.

and March of 1975 working in Gates's small dormitory room at Harvard. Allen flew out to Albuquerque to demonstrate the interpreter. Roberts bought it and Gates and Allen had created an industry standard, one that would hold the field for the next six years.

Allen promptly became MITS's software director. Gates dropped out of Harvard at the end of his sophomore year in 1975 and went to work as a freelance software writer. It was then that Gates and Allen formed Microsoft Corporation. Within 18 months, the two had made a few hundred thousand dollars for their new firm. They were writing programs for Apple Computer, Inc., and Commodore. During the first year, Gates and Allen expanded BASIC so that it would run on other microcomputers.

In 1980, IBM asked Gates to design the operating system for their new machine, what would become the incredibly popular IBM PC. In early 1981, Gates delivered the operating system that would control the IBM PC. Microsoft Disk Operating System (MS-DOS) very quickly became the major operating system for personal computers in the United States. Over two million copies of MS-DOS had been sold as of the spring of 1984.

Other companies turned to Gates as well. Apple Computer, Inc., asked him to develop software for the Macintosh computer. He helped design the Radio Shack Model 100. Beginning in the mid-1980s, Microsoft Corporation started developing applications software, including Microsoft Word, for word processing; Microsoft Works, for business applications; and Flight Simulator, which permits someone to sit at a computer and simulate the piloting of a plane.

In 1982, Gates dreamed of a piece of software, called Windows, that he hoped would push his company to the top of the personal computer software industry. The product was developed, and on April 2, 1987, IBM chose Windows as a key piece of software for their new generation of personal computers—IBM PS/2. Windows is built into the operating system—the software that controls a computer's basic functions and runs applications software such as spreadsheets, word processors, and database managers. Windows, which uses graphics similar to those of Apple Computer's Macintosh computer, makes IBM PCs much easier to use by simplifying the commands needed to operate them.

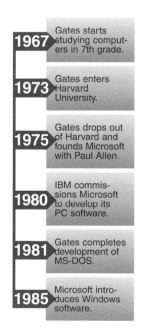

1967 Gates starts studying computers in 7th grade.

1973 Gates enters Harvard University.

1975 Gates drops out of Harvard and founds Microsoft with Paul Allen.

1980 IBM commissions Microsoft to develop its PC software.

1981 Gates completes development of MS-DOS.

1985 Microsoft introduces Windows software.

*"I never antici-
pated Microsoft's
growing so big,
and now, at the
beginning of this
new era, I
unexpectedly find
myself a part of
the establish-
ment"*

Bill Gates, *The
Road Ahead*

Microsoft Corporation has set standards for the software industry in languages, operating systems, and application software. Gates has provided the vision for the company's new product ideas and technologies. Microsoft sold millions of copies of Windows.

During the 1990s, the Microsoft Corporation continued to grow. Gates provided the vision for the company's new product ideas and technologies. By the end of the decade, Bill Gates had an estimated net worth of over $50 billion, making him the richest person in the world. In 1997, Gates contributed $200 million to launch the Gates Library Foundation, which aimed at improving computer services at public libraries in the United States and Canada and providing internet access to low-income communities. Despite Gates's success, the United States Justice Department began investigating Microsoft for unfair business practices. In 1998, the government charged Microsoft with illegally using the market dominance of its Windows operating system to monopolize the internet browser market. ◆

Geffen, David

1943–PRESENT ● ENTERTAINMENT INDUSTRY MOGUL

*"Power is an illu-
sion. No one is
powerful, really,
finally. In my
business, you
often end up a
beggar: 'Please
sign with us.'"*

David Geffen,
Details interview,
1996

David Geffen is a business executive in the entertainment industry. He created and ran two highly profitable record companies and produced some of the most successful musicians of the 1970s and 1980s. He also produced a number of popular motion pictures and hit Broadway plays. Geffen has become one of the entertainment world's wealthiest and most influential businessmen and by the late 1990s he had a personal fortune worth over $2 billion.

Geffen was born on February 21, 1943, in Brooklyn, New York, to Abraham and Betya (Volovskaya) Geffen. Abraham, a Polish emigrant, was as an intellectual who knew a number of languages and who spent much of his time reading books because he had difficulty holding jobs. Betya, who was Russian, supported the family by making and selling undergarments. The Geffen household was poor, and David frequently went to the movie theater for entertainment. As a student, Geffen fared poorly, and he flunked out of both the University of Texas in Austin and Brooklyn College in New York.

After giving up on a college education, Geffen got his first job in show business as an usher for CBS in New York City. Then in 1964, he landed a job in the mailroom at the William Morris Agency, a talent agency. The job required a college degree, so he lied and said he had graduated from the University of California at Los Angeles (UCLA). Convinced that the agency would check up on him, he searched the mailroom daily for a letter from UCLA. When the letter finally arrived, he steamed it open and inserted a forged letter saying he was a UCLA graduate, an act that allowed him to keep his job.

From the mailroom he worked his way up the company ladder. Even before he was an agent, he scouted the New York clubs for talent and worked to sign artists to recording contracts. Eighteen months after starting at William Morris, Geffen became an agent. By that time he had already signed the folksinger Joni Mitchell and the Association, a popular band with a hit called "Windy." In 1966 he began managing singer and songwriter Laura Nyro, who had written some hits for other musicians. In 1969 he and Nyro sold their jointly owned music publishing company to CBS for $4 million, making Geffen his first big profit of $2 million by his mid-twenties.

The following year Geffen and Elliot Roberts started a new record label called Asylum Records and a management company called Geffen-Roberts. Asylum signed such artists as Jackson Browne, Joni Mitchell, the Eagles, and Linda Ronstadt, and the label was a success. In 1972 he sold Asylum to Warner Communications for $7 million, a sale he later regretted because the company was worth several times that much the following year. In 1973 he signed a seven-year contract with Warner and continued as president of Asylum. He merged it with Warner's Elektra label and Elektra/Asylum become one of Warner's most profitable companies.

1964 Geffen lands a job in the mailroom at William Morris Agency.

1969 Geffen earns $2 million from the sale of Laura Nyro's music to CBS.

1972 Geffen sells Asylum to Warner Communications for $7 million.

1973 Geffen begins working for Warner as president of Asylum records.

1979 Geffen starts a new record label called Geffen Records.

1983 Geffen sets up Geffen Film Co.

1990 Geffen sells Geffen Records to MCA.

1994 Geffen starts Dreamworks SKG with Steven Spielberg and Jeffrey Katzenberg.

"When you have as much critical mass, so to speak, as I have, even if you do nothing it makes a gigantic amount of money. I have no interest in it anymore."
David Geffen, *Details* interview, 1996

By his late twenties, Geffen had achieved tremendous professional success, wealth, and fame in the music industry, but he felt unhappy with his life and he began psychiatric therapy at the age of 29. After struggling with his sexuality he decided he was a heterosexual and he had a brief, but much talked about relationship with the popular singer and actress Cher. Geffen continued to seek a solution to his personal problems and became involved in a number of New Age self-help programs.

In 1976, Geffen was diagnosed with bladder cancer. He remained an employee of Warner, but believing he was dying, he quit show business and spent time socializing at clubs and teaching business courses at UCLA and Yale University. In late 1979, he learned that he had been misdiagnosed and that he did not have cancer. With that news he happily returned to work at Warner under a new contract and started a new record label called Geffen Records. By the mid-1990s, Geffen Records had become one of the nation's most successful record companies. Its artists have included John Lennon, Elton John, Peter Gabriel, the grunge band Nirvana, the rock group Aerosmith, and Guns N' Roses, a heavy metal band. Guns N' Roses became one of the company's most commercially successful bands, but it also gained notoriety for the misogynistic lyrics in some of its songs and for its recording of a song by murderer Charles Manson. Concerned that Manson would profit from the song, Geffen helped arrange for song royalties to go to the child of one of Manson's victims.

Geffen turned his attention toward the film and theater industry in the 1980s. In 1983, he set up Geffen Film Company, which was financed and distributed by Warner Communications. His early successes included *Risky Business* (1983), a film that launched the stardom of actor Tom Cruise; *Lost in America* (1985), and *After Hours* (1985). Geffen also co-produced a number of hit stage shows, including *Dreamgirls*, which debuted in 1981, *Little Shop of Horrors* and *Cats*, which came out in 1982, *M. Butterfly*, which began its run in 1988, and *Miss Saigon*, which opened in 1991. The award-winning *Cats* became one of the longest running shows on Broadway.

In March 1990, Geffen sold his label to MCA (Music Corporation of America) Inc. and received 10 million shares of MCA stock in return. In November of that year,

David Geffen, 1983

Matsushita Electrical Industrial Company of Japan bought MCA and Geffen cashed out with $700 million. One of his next biggest endeavors came in 1994, when he started Dreamworks SKG, an entertainment company, with Hollywood producer Steven Spielberg and former Disney executive Jeffrey Katzenberg.

Geffen has been described as intensely loyal, arrogant, and fearless. He has long supported liberal causes and has been a big contributor to the Democratic Party and the political campaign of U.S. president Bill Clinton. In 1992, Geffen publicly announced that he was a homosexual, and he has been a vocal supporter of gay rights ever since. He gives generously to AIDS research and arts organizations through the David Geffen Foundation. Aside from his interests in film, theater, and music, Geffen is an avid collector of paintings and owns works by a number of twentieth-century artists, including Willem De Kooning, David Hockney, Jasper Johns, Roy Lichtenstein, and Andy Warhol. ◆

Geffen Records artists have included John Lennon, Elton John, Peter Gabriel, Nirvana, Aerosmith, and Guns N' Roses.

Getty, Jean Paul

1892–1976 ● OIL TYCOON

"I believe that the able industrial leader who creates wealth and employment is more worthy of historical notice than politicians and soldiers."

J. Paul Getty

John Paul Getty was born in Minneapolis, Minnesota, on December 15, 1892. He was the son of George Franklin and Sarah Catherine McPherson (Risher) Getty, grandson of John and Martha (Wiley) Getty, great-grandson of James and Margaret (Cross) Getty, and great-great grandson of John, who came from Gettystown, Ireland, in 1790, settling in western Maryland, and Nelly Getty. J. P. Getty's father was a lawyer, circuit court commissioner in Michigan, and an oil producer. He received his academic education at public schools and the University of California and was graduated with a diploma in economics from Oxford University, England, in 1913.

Upon his return to America, Getty engaged in oil production in Tulsa, Oklahoma. Two years later he moved to Los Angeles, where he acquired further oil properties. In addition to his own interests he headed his father's company, George F. Getty, Inc., of Los Angeles, during 1929–33. He also served as director of the Petroleum Corporation of America and the Tidewater Associated Oil Company. In addition, Getty became president of the Spartan Aircraft Company in Tulsa, Oklahoma, in 1942. For the next several decades, Getty continued to gain control of large independent oil companies and eventually built an immense financial empire, estimated at more than $1 billion at the time of his death.

In the 1930s Getty began collecting fine art, both as a hobby and as an investment, and he continued to build his art collection throughout his life. Getty's collection included paintings, sculpture, carpets, tapestries, eighteenth-century furniture, eighteenth-century English silverware, and rare and first editions of books. His carpet collection included the Ardabil carpet from the Mosque of Ardabil in Persia, rated by some authorities the finest existent specimen of its kind, and the Coronation carpet, a Persian hunting carpet used at the coronation of King Edward VII of Great Britain. He also owned what is considered the finest collection of Beauvais Boucher tapestries in the world. Getty's collection of paintings included examples of the work of Rembrandt, Gainsborough, Renoir, Titian, David, Manet,

J. Paul Getty, 1957.

van Gogh, Munch, and many other important painters. For many years, Getty displayed his artworks in his own home. In 1954, he established a museum to exhibit the collection. A second museum was opened in 1974 to accommodate Getty's growing collection of ancient Greek and Roman art. This museum, located in Malibu, California, is a full-scale recreation of the ancient Villa of Papyri near Herculaneum in Italy. In the mid 1990s, the remainder of the Getty collection was moved to the new Getty Arts Center. This building, located in Santa Monica, California, was designed by renowned architect Richard Meier.

Getty was the author of numerous books including *History of the Oil Business of George F. and J. Paul Getty* (1941) and *Europe in the 18th Century* (1942). Later in life, he published *My Life and Fortunes* (1963), *How to Be Rich* (1966), and *As I See It* (1976). Getty was married and divorced five times. He owned a large sixteenth-century estate near Surrey, England, and from the mid–1940s on, he spent most of his time there. Getty died on June 6, 1976. ◆

Gibbs, Mifflin Wister

1823–1915 ● ENTREPRENEUR

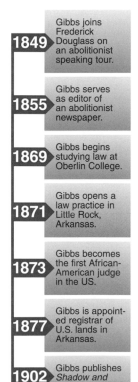

1849 Gibbs joins Frederick Douglass on an abolitionist speaking tour.

1855 Gibbs serves as editor of an abolitionist newspaper.

1869 Gibbs begins studying law at Oberlin College.

1871 Gibbs opens a law practice in Little Rock, Arkansas.

1873 Gibbs becomes the first African-American judge in the US.

1877 Gibbs is appointed registrar of U.S. lands in Arkansas.

1902 Gibbs publishes *Shadow and Light*.

Born free in Philadelphia, Gibbs attended grade school until his father died in 1831. To help his invalid mother support his three siblings, Gibbs drove a doctor's carriage before becoming a carpenter's apprentice at the age of 16 and then a journeyman contractor on his own in 1840. Throughout this period he was a member of the Philomathean Institute, a colored men's literary society, and he was active in the Underground Railroad with William Still and others. In 1849, Gibbs was prominent enough in the Abolition movement to accompany Frederick Douglass on a speaking tour for that cause in western New York.

In 1850, Gibbs relocated to San Francisco, where racial prejudice forced him to abandon carpentry. With savings earned as a shoeshiner, Gibbs opened a successful imported clothing store and quickly rose to prominence. While in California, he became a delegate to the state Negro Convention in 1854, 1855, and 1857, and he served in 1855 as editor of the *Mirror of the Times*, an abolitionist newspaper. Gibbs left California in 1858 for British Columbia, hoping to prosper from recently discovered gold in that area. While there, he acquired a small fortune in real estate and other trades, became a director of the Queen Charlotte Island Coal Company, and was twice elected to the Victoria Common Council (1866 and 1867).

Gibbs returned to the United States briefly in 1859 to marry Maria A. Alexander and again in 1869 to begin studying law at Oberlin College. Two years later, he opened his own practice in Little Rock, Arkansas. Gibbs was appointed county attorney in 1873 and was elected municipal judge of Little Rock later that year, thereby becoming the first African-American judge in the United States. In 1877, President Rutherford B. Hayes appointed Gibbs registrar of United States lands in Arkansas, a position he held until 1889. Gibbs was an active member of the Republican Party, attending as a delegate all but one Republican national convention between 1868 and 1896. Gibbs was also appointed consul at Tamatave, Madagascar, where he served from 1898 until 1901. Upon his return to Little Rock, Gibbs continued his involvement in business, remained active in the civil rights movement, and published his autobiography, *Shadow and Light* (1902), which contained an introduction written by his friend and colleague Booker T. Washington.

Throughout his long and diverse career, Gibbs advocated the creation of a skilled African-American middle class through the acquisition of property and independent control of agriculture and industry. In an attempt to further this cause, Gibbs financed a conference in 1885 aimed at establishing industrial schools for blacks and supported the expansion of African-American business opportunities throughout his career. ◆

> *"The adaptability of the Negro to conditions that are at the time inevitable has been the palladium that has sustained and multiplied him amid the determined prejudice that has ever assailed him."*
> Mifflin Wistar Gibbs, 1902

Goldwater, Barry (and Family)

1821–1998 ● MERCHANTS

> *"Business has become more a system of conglomerates that will make anything, any item and any different variety of items, with the sole idea being to make some money. Nobody has pride in what they're doing: they just want to show a little profit."*
> Barry Goldwater

Senator Barry Goldwater has long been honored as Arizona's most illustrious citizen, but the Goldwater name was well known in the Arizona Territory for nearly a half-century before his birth in 1909.

Polish-born Michel Goldwater (1821) immigrated to California with his younger brother Joseph in 1852. Michel operated a saloon in Sonora, California, and when the business failed, he engaged in other unsuccessful ventures. In 1860, he moved to what would soon become the Arizona Territory, where he sold merchandise from a wagon to gold miners in Gila City, east of Yuma. In 1862, he opened his first general store in La Paz, across the Colorado River from present-day Blythe, California. Goldwater stores were prominent in Arizona history for 120 years thereafter.

Michel and his eldest son, Morris, had moderate success in a general store in Ehrenberg, Arizona, and in 1872, they opened another store in the new town of Phoenix. It failed, but their next venture, in Prescott in 1876, prospered for many decades.

In 1896, after Michel's retirement, Morris sent his youngest brother, Baron, to try the Phoenix market again. Baron proved to be a mercantile genius. His Phoenix department store, catering especially to women, became nationally known and made him a wealthy man.

In 1907, Baron married Josephine Williams, a nurse who had come to Arizona from Nebraska to seek relief from tuberculosis. At her death in 1966 at the age of 91, she was honored as one of the outstanding women of early Arizona.

Upon Baron's death in 1929, his son Barry became president of Goldwater's. When Barry entered politics in 1952, his younger brother, Robert, succeeded him and, over the years, established Goldwater's department stores throughout Arizona and in New Mexico and Nevada.

Several Goldwaters earned prominent places in Arizona history. Michel (known as "Big Mike") was not only a pioneer merchant but also a builder of wagon roads across the wilderness and a founder of several towns. His brother Joseph, severely wounded in an Indian ambush near Prescott in 1872, later established six stores in southeastern Arizona.

Morris, born in 1850, was a giant among territorial pioneers. He was a founder of the Arizona Democratic party, the patriarch of Arizona Freemasonry for a half-century, vice-president of the 1910 Arizona Constitutional Convention, and mayor of Prescott for twenty years. He was the early political mentor of his nephew Barry, whose middle name is Morris.

Barry Goldwater, in his first try for national political office, was elected to the U.S. Senate in 1952. He led the

1852 Michel and Joseph Goldwater immigrate to California from Poland.

1862 Michel opens his first general store in La Paz.

1872 Michel opens a store in Phoenix.

1896 Michel's son Baron opens another store in Phoenix.

1952 Baron's son Barry is elected to the U.S. Senate.

fight to revitalize conservative political philosophy in America and was the Republican presidential candidate in 1964. ◆

Gordy, Berry, Jr.

1929–PRESENT ● MUSIC EXECUTIVE

Born in Detroit, Berry Gordy Jr., the third in his family to carry that name, was attracted to music as a child, winning a talent contest with his song "Berry's Boogie." He also took up boxing, often training with his friend Jackie Wilson. Gordy quit high school to turn professional; however, he soon gave up that career at the urging of his mother. After spending 1951 to 1953 in the Army, Gordy married Thelma Louise Coleman and began to work in the Gordy family printing and construction business.

In 1953 Gordy opened a jazz record store in Detroit. However, since rhythm and blues records were more in demand, the business closed after only two years. Gordy then began working at a Ford Motor Company assembly line, writing and publishing pop songs on the side, including "Money, That's What I Want" (1959). During this time Gordy, who

Motown Historical Museum

In 1959 Berry Gordy Jr. bought a house at 2648 West Grand Boulevard in Detroit and established Motown Records there. Soon Gordy named the house "Hitsville U.S.A." because of the enormous success of the "Motown Sound" that he created. The company moved to other headquarters long ago, but since 1985 the house has been the site of the Motown Historical Museum, created that year to tell the story of Motown Records in its early years. Upstairs is Gordy's old living quarters. The Downstairs Office Area, where young singers waited to audition, has been restored to its 1960–1961 condition. The

Control Room contains the early recording equipment, including a three-track console mixing board that was later upgraded to eight-track capacity by Motown engineers trained by Gordy. Motown's Recording Studio A is preserved in its original form, including its first recording instruments. The Echo Chamber, built to create a reverb effect in the music, has also been preserved. Exhibits include a montage of Motown's history, performance uniforms created for Motown artists to wear in the 1960s, and some of the platinum and gold records that illustrate the success of Motown Records and its sound.

The actual Steinway piano that was used by
Marvin Gaye, Stevie Wonder, and Smokey Robinson.

had separated from his wife, wrote some of Jackie Wilson's biggest hits, including "Lonely Teardrops" (1958), "That Is Why I Love You So" (1959), and "I'll Be Satisfied" (1959). He also sang with his new wife, Raynoma Liles, whom he had married in 1959, on a number of records by the Detroit singer Marv Johnson. In the late 1950s Gordy met and worked with Smokey Robinson and the Matadors, who at Gordy's suggestion became the Miracles. Gordy recorded them on their first record, "Got a Job" (1958).

During this period Gordy became increasingly dissatisfied with leasing his recordings to larger record companies, who often would take over distribution. At the urging of Robinson, Gordy borrowed $800 and founded Tamla Records and Gordy Records, the first companies in what would become the Motown empire. He released "Way Over There" (1959) and "Shop Around" (1961) by the Miracles. Gordy began hiring friends and family members to work for him, and he began to attract young unknown singers, including Diana Ross, Marvin Gaye, Mary Wells, and Stevie Wonder. The songwriting team of Eddie Holland, his brother Brian, and Lamont Dozier began to write songs for Gordy, who had formed a base of operations at 2648 Grand Boulevard in Detroit. From that address Gordy also formed the publishing and management companies that would constitute the larger enterprise known more generally as Motown. Over the next ten years, Motown, with Gordy as chief executive and chief shareholder, and often producer and songwriter as well, produced dozens of pop and rhythm-and-blues hits that dominated the new style known as soul music.

In the mid–1960s Gordy began to distance himself from the company's day-to-day music operations, spending more and more time in Los Angeles, where he was growing interested in the film and television industries. He divorced Raynoma in 1964, and married Margaret Norton, whom he also later divorced. (Gordy again married in 1990, but that marriage, to Grace Eton, ended in divorce three years later.)

In the late 1960s, many Motown performers, writers, and producers complained about Gordy's paternalistic and heavy-handed management of their finances. Some of them—including the Jackson 5, Holland-Dozier-Holland, and the Temptations—left the company, claiming that Gordy had misled and mistreated them. By this time he was also quite wealthy, living in a Los Angeles mansion that contained a portrait of himself dressed as Napoleon Bonaparte. He resigned as president of the Motown Records subsidiary in 1973 in order to assume the chair of Motown Industries, a new parent corporation. The following year he completed what had been a gradual move of Motown to Los Angeles and produced several successful television specials. His film ventures—including the Diana Ross vehicles *Lady Sings the Blues* (1973), *Mahogany* (1975), and *The Wiz* (1978)—were not as successful.

Despite the departure of its core personnel over the years, the company Gordy presided over in the 1980s remained successful, with more than $100 million in annual sales in 1983, making it the largest black owned company in the United States. In 1984 Gordy allowed MCA to begin distributing Motown's records, and the company bought Motown in 1988 for $61 million. Gordy kept control of Gordy Industries,

1953 Gordy opens a jazz record store in Detroit.

1958 Gordy records Smokey Robinson and the Miracles.

1973 Gordy becomes chair of Motown Industries.

1984 MCA begins distributing Motown Records.

1988 Gordy is elected to the Rock and Roll Hall of Fame.

Motown's music publishing, film, and television subsidiaries. His net worth in 1986, as estimated by Forbes, was more than $180 million, making him one of the wealthiest people in the United States. In the late 1980s and '90s Gordy branched out into other fields, including sports management and the ownership and training of racehorses.

Although Gordy, who was inducted into the Rock and Roll Hall of Fame in 1988, began his career as a successful songwriter and producer, his greatest achievement was selling soul music to white pop audiences, thus helping to shape America's youth into a single, huge, multiracial audience. ◆

Gould, Jay

1836–1892 ● RAILROAD MAGNATE

> *"I can hire one-half of the working class to kill the other half."*
>
> Jay Gould, 1886

By the age of 45, railroad magnate Jay (born Jason) Gould had amassed a fortune of more than $100 million, a record for that day. Through a series of astute and sometimes shady financial dealings, Gould, called "the Great Manipulator," left a trail of gigantic fortunes, gutted companies, and ruined entrepreneurs, some of them his former friends.

Born in Roxbury, New York, Gould grew up on his father's farm and learned at an early age that agricultural labor was not for him. He mastered surveying, tried inventing and banking, and turned his leather business into the nation's largest tannery. He amassed his fortune not in these enterprises, however, but in transportation.

After the Civil War, Gould borrowed money from his father-in-law for his first rail investment—the Rutland and Washington—and quickly sold the line at a profit of $130,000. Over the next several years, he refined his technique of buying while the price was low and selling while the price was high and purchased small, vulnerable lines. He also "invested" in legislators, judges, and other influential people who helped him become a director of Daniel Drew's Erie Railroad.

What Gould lacked in scruples, he made up in audacity and acumen. With Drew and speculator James Fisk, he precipitated the Erie "rate war" against rival Cornelius Vanderbilt, at that time the richest man in the country. Gould and Fisk won, partly by printing reams of suspect stock and forcing Drew out of his own line. Vanderbilt dubbed Gould "the smartest man in America." Drew, later driven into poverty, was not so charitable. He said of Gould: "His touch is death."

Gould and Fisk tried to buy enough gold to corner the market and send prices up. When Gould learned the U.S. Treasury Department was about to open its gold reserves, he abandoned Fisk and sold out. Prices plummeted, triggering the gold panic called "Black Friday" on September 24, 1869. Gould then focused on several struggling railroads in the West. He scooped up the troubled Union Pacific, and in turn, the Kansas Pacific, Denver Pacific, Central Pacific, and much of the Texas and Pacific. He said candidly, "I don't build railroads. I buy them."

Gould kept the Missouri and Pacific and added the Texas and Pacific and other lines to form "The Gould System," which controlled more than eight thousand miles of track, more than half of all the lines in the Southwest.

Gould was no more a "robber baron" than other great railroad magnates, but his methods became models for a generation of younger, faster imitators. The financial panic of 1884 cost him $20 million and his health. He had run out of influ-

> *"I don't build railroads. I buy them."*
>
> Jay Gould

1860s Gould starts buying small rail lines.

1867 Gould joins the board of Erie Railroad.

1869 Gould sells his gold, triggering the gold panic known as "Black Friday."

1873 Gould begins buying railroads in the West.

1884 A financial panic costs Gould $20 million and ruins his health.

ential friends, ready investors, and potential victims. He spent his last years dreaming of the coast-to-coast rail network he could not complete before he died of tuberculosis at the age of 57. ◆

Graves, Earl Gilbert, Jr.

1935–Present ● Publisher

> *"No one, black or white, is going to guarantee you career success or financial security. You have to earn that yourself."*
> Earl Gilbert Graves, *How to Succeed in Business Without Being White*, 1997

Born in Brooklyn, New York, Earl G. Graves attended Morgan State College in Baltimore, Maryland, receiving his B.A. in economics in 1958. Graves, who had been enrolled in the Reserve Officers' Training Corps, joined the U.S. Army immediately after graduation, and rose to the rank of captain. After leaving the Army in 1962, he sold houses and then worked for the Justice Department as a narcotics agent. In 1965 he was hired by New York Senator Robert F. Kennedy as a staff assistant, charged with planning and supervising events. Graves occupied that position until Kennedy's death in 1968. That year he started his own business, Earl G. Graves Associates, a management consulting firm specializing in assistance to small businesses.

In 1970, using $150,000 borrowed from the Manhattan

Capital Corporation, Graves became founder, editor, and publisher of *Black Enterprise*, the first African-American business magazine. An immediate success, the journal had sales of $900,000 by the end of its first year. By the beginning of the 1990s, the magazine had 250,000 subscribers and annual earnings of more than $15 million. *Black Enterprise* soon became a black community institution, widely known for its how-to advice on building minority business and its lists of the top 100 black-owned companies. Graves's monthly "publisher's page" served as a forum for examining politics and the black marketplace. The magazine developed two other special features. In 1975 Graves began the *Black Enterprise* Achievement Awards for successful African-American entrepreneurs. In 1982 he organized a board of economists to make periodic reports on the black economy.

While Earl G. Graves Publishing Company, Inc., which published *Black Enterprise*, remained the flagship property of Graves's company, Earl Graves, Ltd., Graves set up five other businesses over the following two decades: EGG Dallas Broadcasting, Inc.; B.C.I. Marketing, Inc.; a development firm; a market research firm; and a distribution firm. In 1990, in a notable deal, a limited partnership led by Graves and basketball star Earvin "Magic" Johnson acquired a $60 million Pepsi-Cola franchise in Washington, D.C. In addition to his business activities, Graves remained involved in social and political activism, and during the 1990s was active in the lobbying group TransAfrica, as national commissioner and member of the national board of the Boy Scouts of America, as a director of Howard University, and as a member on several corporate and foundation boards. ◆

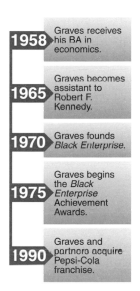

1958 Graves receives his BA in economics.

1965 Graves becomes assistant to Robert F. Kennedy.

1970 Graves founds *Black Enterprise*.

1975 Graves begins the *Black Enterprise* Achievement Awards.

1990 Graves and partners acquire Pepsi-Cola franchise.

Guggenheim, Daniel

1856–1930 ● METAL MOGUL

Daniel Guggenheim was one of several brothers who were active in their father's metal businesses. Meyer Guggenheim, who founded the family business in America after moving from Switzerland in 1948, sent his son Daniel to Switzerland for a period of years to learn European business practices. Daniel Guggenheim returned to the United States, and engaged in the copper business with his father. The Guggenheims won control of the American **Smelting** and Refining Company in 1901 and Daniel Guggenheim served as its president for many years.

The "Guggenheim strategy" in the metals business was credited to Daniel Guggenheim. The plan was to have all operations necessary under one control, rather than to concentrate on any single part of metal processing. The Guggenheims, therefore, engaged in exploration (locating ore-fields) and mapping them, as well as operating mines, smelters, and finishing factories. Gold, tin, rubber, nitrate fertilizers, and diamonds were all areas in which the firm was interested, as well as copper.

Daniel Guggenheim amassed a very large personal fortune, which he used to endow two charitable and educational foundations; in this, as in business activities, he followed his father's example. The Daniel Guggenheim Fund for the Promotion of Aeronautics provided a great deal of money to support experiments and studies in aviation. ◆

Haggar, Joseph Marion

1892–1987 ● Clothing Manufacturer

Joseph Marion Haggar was born on December 20, 1892, in Jazzin, Lebanon. His father, Khalil Hajjar, a tanner, died in Lebanon after falling from a horse when his son Joseph was 2. Joseph Haggar's Lebanese mother died in Dallas, Texas, in 1929. One of five children, Maroun, as Joseph was then called, left the family's impoverished one-room home in a sparse farming community just outside the mountain village of Jazzin at age 13.

In 1906 Haggar boarded a cattle boat bound for Torreón, Mexico, to join an older married sister. He traveled from Beirut to Barcelona to Veracruz, enduring a fierce Atlantic storm on the last leg of the journey. He spent nearly three years with his sister, who taught him to speak Spanish fluently. He contributed to the household income by peddling small goods to the natives.

At age 16, Haggar traveled to the Laredo border, paid the $2 head tax to enter the United States, and crossed the Rio Grande. He joined a gang of Mexican railroad workers and worked his way north to the town of Elgin, Texas. In Elgin he found a job with a cotton farmer, a prosperous German whose wife Haggar remembered as a wonderful cook. At the end of the cotton season, Haggar moved on, hitchhiking to New Orleans. In 1910 he took a job washing dishes in the Grunewald Hotel. Some months later he moved again, this time to St. Louis, where he became a window washer at the Planters Hotel. He worked alongside the Skouras brothers, who later invested in movie theaters in St. Louis. For $200 he

Haggar popularized the word "slacks" and coined the terms "wash-and-wear" and "double knit."

could have joined them, but he did not have the cash. Spyros Skouras later became president of Twentieth Century Fox.

A stocky, handsome, vibrant man, Haggar joined the Lebanese community in St. Louis and attended the Maronite Church, St. Anthony's, where he fell in love with the organist, Rose Mary Wasaff. He rented a room in the Wasaff home and courted Mary. Two years later, when the Wasaffs moved to Bristow, Texas, Haggar quickly followed.

In Bristow he went to work as a cotton weigher for Joe Abraham, a Lebanese businessman he had known in St. Louis, who taught Haggar how to buy cotton in the seed and classify it. Haggar took a second job as a grocery clerk, and paid the rent on a house in Bristow by selling the peaches that grew on the property. In 1914 he applied for his first citizenship papers. In August 1915 Haggar married Rose Mary Wasaff. (She died in 1966 shortly after they celebrated their fiftieth anniversary.) The couple's first child was born a year later.

In 1916 Haggar bought and sold an oil lease, a transaction that earned him enough money to move back to St. Louis. It was the heyday of the wholesale dry goods industry, of which St. Louis was the center. Haggar went to work for Ely & Walker, one of the nation's largest dry goods companies, supplying retailers throughout the United States, Mexico, and Central America. He worked on commission there for five years, dealing in cotton yardage by the belt.

In 1921 Haggar moved to Dallas and began traveling throughout Texas, Louisiana, and New Mexico as a salesman for the King Brand Overall Company based in Jefferson, Missouri. In 1926, when the firm's owner, D. H. Oberman, dropped Haggar's territory, Haggar rented small quarters in the Santa Fe Building in Dallas and went into business for himself, selling Oberman work pants and taking out in trade the commission owed him. Within a year he was buying his own piece goods and contracting with factories in the North and East to make the pants. Not satisfied with the quality of the workmanship, he persuaded the make-and-trim team of Harry Vogel and John Sidor to move from St. Louis to Dallas. In 1928 he bought them out and moved into the eighth floor of the Santa Fe building, with a handful of sewing machines and four full-time employees. By 1929 Haggar had established the Dallas Pant Manufacturing Company, inhabiting 6,000 square feet on two floors and employing 250 workers. During

Haggar sensed what the average man wanted to wear and made the best quality product possible.

the 1930s the Haggars lived on Lakewood Boulevard in Dallas with their three children, Edward, Joseph junior, and Rosemary. By 1941 the Haggar Company moved into a ten-acre site on Lemmon Avenue with nearly 100,000 square feet, completed at a cost of $450,000.

Haggar revolutionized the menswear industry, introducing a "one price policy" and straight-line production. He worked eighteen hours a day, valued his employees, bought the best materials at a competitive price while maintaining good relationships with his suppliers, appreciated his retailers, sensed what the average man wanted to wear, and made the best quality product possible (Haggar has always maintained a state-of-the-art textile laboratory). The Haggar Company popularized the word "slacks," introduced prefinished bottoms for dress trousers, and coined the terms "wash-and-wear" and "double knit." Haggar treated his employees so well that the company was unionized only once, and then for only a short time. His salesmen were typically the best paid in the apparel field.

In the early 1940s Haggar began advertising slacks nationally (through the firm of Tracy-Locke), another first in the apparel industry. He started with *Collier's*, *True*, and *Esquire*, and by the late 1940s and early 1950s had added *Life*, *The Saturday Evening Post*, and *Look*. As slacks became the concept and sports the arena, Haggar moved on to *Sports Illustrated* and to such superstar endorsers as Mickey Mantle, Arnold Palmer, and Roger Staubach. By 1976 the company employed 150 sales representatives and operated out of sixteen facilities with 7,000 employees.

Haggar's sons, both University of Notre Dame Business School graduates, contributed greatly to the success of the company and formed with their father a dynamic triumvirate. They gradually took over the company's operations as their father grew older. Haggar went to his office every day until the time of his death.

In 1972, on Haggar's eightieth birthday, the J. M. and Rose Haggar Foundation, of which Haggar's daughter served as executive director, distributed $3 million dollars among various academic and civic institutions including the University of Dallas, Southern Methodist University, St. Mary's College in South Bend, Indiana, the University of Notre Dame, the city of Dallas, communities in Texas and Oklahoma with Haggar facilities, and St. Jude's Research

1906 Haggar leaves his native Lebanon and heads to Mexico.

1908 Haggar pays a $2 head tax to enter the United States.

1921 Haggar begins working for the King Brand Overall Co.

1926 Haggar starts his own business selling work pants.

1929 Haggar establishes the Dallas Pant Manufacturing Co.

1940 Haggar begins advertising his slacks nationally.

1972 Haggar donates $3 million to academic and civic institutions.

Hospital in Memphis, Tennessee. Haggar was named a Knight of Malta and a Knight of the Grand Cross, was awarded the Golden Torch of Hope Award (1971), an honorary Doctor of Law degree from the University of Notre Dame (1976), and the Horatio Alger Award (1976).

J. M. Haggar died on 15 December 1987 of heart failure in Dallas, Texas, and was buried in Hillcrest Cemetery there. A Lebanese immigrant with no formal education, Haggar had created the largest privately owned apparel manufacturing company in the nation, and a foundation that gave over $1 million a year to charity. His innovations in the menswear industry were widely adopted by clothing manufacturers. Haggar Apparel Company went public in December 1992. ◆

Hall, Joyce Clyde

1891–1982 ● GREETING CARD MANUFACTURER

> *"We weren't poor because my father couldn't make a living—we were poor because he let us be."*
>
> Joyce Clyde Hall

itinerant: traveling from place to place.

Joyce Clyde Hall was one of five children born to George Nelson Hall, an **itinerant** preacher, and Nancy Dudley. The first child died in infancy. With an invalid mother and an absentee father who provided little financial support, the three boys earned money to support the family at very young ages. Hall wrote, "We weren't poor because my father couldn't make a living—we were poor because he let us be. . . . He told my mother that she needn't worry, [that] 'the Lord would provide.' I found out then that it was a good idea to give the Lord a little help." From the age of 8, Hall worked at odd jobs, mostly in sales. In 1902 his brothers, Rollie and William, became partners in a bookstore in Norfolk, Nebraska, a larger town sixty miles north of David City. Joyce joined them after that school year; his mother and sister moved there shortly afterward. Times were hard for the family but Hall's childhood memories were shaped by his belief that his experiences strengthened him. His autobiography, *When You Care Enough* (1979), includes a chapter on his early years called "The Gift of Poverty."

Working in the bookstore before and after school and during lunchtime, Hall learned the basics of retailing. He read and studied the advertisements in the books and magazines. Rollie was a candy salesman and took Joyce, when the latter was 12, on his route through western Nebraska, Wyoming, and South Dakota. The following summer Hall worked part of Rollie's territory for him.

In 1905 he was introduced to picture postcards by a young salesman. Joyce quickly convinced William that they should sell the cards; they invested more than $150 each and committed the absent Rollie to the same amount. They immediately began selling wholesale, getting salesmen who came into the bookstore to sell the postcards to their other customers. The family's finances improved considerably, but Hall left high school in 1910 without graduating. He filled two shoeboxes with postcards and traveled to Kansas City. Within a year Rollie joined him to open a store and form Hall Brothers, Inc. In a few years picture postcard sales began to decline. Beginning in 1913 they added greeting cards, under the name Hallmark, to their wholesale business and soon began designing their own. Hall learned the greeting card business well. "I confess," he once said, "to an overwhelming prejudice in favor of the cards that sell best." What sold were cards with puppies and kittens, not people. Roses were good but a single rose was better, and pansies sold while geraniums did not.

In 1915 a fire destroyed their building and entire stock. The next year the brothers borrowed money, bought an engraving business, and began printing their own cards. Hall

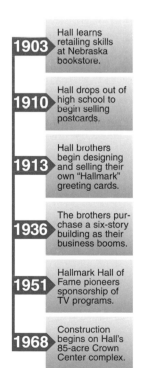

1903 Hall learns retailing skills at Nebraska bookstore.

1910 Hall drops out of high school to begin selling postcards.

1913 Hall brothers begin designing and selling their own "Hallmark" greeting cards.

1936 The brothers purchase a six-story building as their business booms.

1951 Hallmark Hall of Fame pioneers sponsorship of TV programs.

1968 Construction begins on Hall's 85-acre Crown Center complex.

Hall counted Harry Truman, Walt Disney, Dwight Eisenhower, and Winston Churchill among his friends.

took an interest in all aspects of the business, from accounting to design sales. The business grew steadily until the Great Depression, when revenues fell sharply. Hall refused to lay off workers and devised ways of continuing business in the face of new pressures. By 1936 the company had expanded enough so that the brothers purchased a six-story building in Kansas City.

On 25 March 1922 Hall married Elizabeth Ann Dilday, a former schoolmate of his sister. They had three children, the first born in July 1922. Hall wrote that his family wanted to name their one boy Joyce but he refused, saying he was grown before he was no longer ashamed of the name himself. (His mother had named him after a Methodist bishop.) The son, named Donald instead, became president of Hallmark when Hall retired. Hall became friends with public figures and world leaders. In addition to Harry Truman, who often spent time in Kansas City during his presidency, Hall also counted Walt Disney, Dwight Eisenhower, and Winston Churchill among his friends. In 1950 Churchill sold Hall twelve of his paintings to use on greeting cards.

In 1951 Hall took a bold step in deciding to sponsor a new television series, the *Hallmark Hall of Fame*, which brought opera and classic drama to the home screen. He had been advised to choose something more appealing to a mass audience, but the show was a success. Hall held subject approval and vetoed a production of Arthur Miller's *Death of a Salesman* because he did not think it was suitable. Refusing to give in to southern boycott threats in 1957, he sponsored Marc Connelly's all-black *Green Pastures*, repeating it in 1959. The series received a total of forty-four Emmy Awards, including one to Hallmark Cards "for dedication to standards of quality and excellence."

Hall believed strongly that he could help revitalize central Kansas City. In the early 1960s he began planning Crown Center, modeled on Rockefeller Center in New York City. Ground was broken in 1968 for the 85-acre, $400 million development, which would grow to include the Hallmark headquarters, two hotels, a Halls department store and other retail space, and even an outdoor ice-skating rink situated between Kansas City's downtown business district and the Country Club Plaza shopping area, Crown Center dramatically changed the city's landscape.

Although Hall promoted employee ownership of corporate stock, some described him as reluctant to delegate authority. *Fortune* praised him as a man "who single-handedly built a great corporation and then was forced to fight doggedly to prevent . . . [it] from swallowing him up." He resigned as company president in 1966 to devote more time to the Crown Center project, his legacy to Kansas City. He had built the company into a giant in the industry, helping to change the way Americans used greeting cards. When Hall died, Hallmark had 20,000 card shops and annual sales exceeding $1 billion and turned out 8 million greeting cards a day.

While Hall was first and foremost a businessman, he wrote that cards were "a way of giving less articulate people, and those who tend to disguise their feelings, a voice to express their love and affection." He died quietly in his sleep of causes related to old age and was buried in Forest Hill Cemetery, Kansas City, Missouri. He left over $100 million to charity. His estate sold nearly $94 million worth of Hallmark stock to employees, almost doubling the amount owned by employees and bringing the number of shares they held to about one-third of company stock. He was a hardworking, hardheaded businessman who believed that his business could contribute to the good of the community as well as to his own financial interests. ◆

> *"When you care enough to send the very best!"*
> Hallmark slogan

Hammer, Armand

1898–1990 ● INDUSTRIALIST

Born in Manhattan's Lower East Side, Armand Hammer was the son of Julius and Rose Lipschitz Hammer, Russian Jews who had emigrated in the decade before his birth. Julius Hammer was a militant leader of the Socialist Labor Party, and later of the U.S. Communist Party, and he named his son after the party's arm-and-hammer symbol.

Hammer advertised his wealth in the purchase of artwork, an immense yacht, and an award-winning herd of cattle.

Hammer and his siblings—a half brother Harry, born to his mother in 1894 in a previous marriage, and Victor, born in 1902—were raised in the Bronx, where their father practiced medicine and ran a pharmaceutical company. They were nonobservant Jews, and religion never played a large role in Hammer's life.

Hammer attended Columbia University and began medical studies there in 1917. In the same year, his father fell ill and management of the pharmaceutical company fell to Armand. Midway through medical school, Hammer also helped his father by secretly attending to patients. In 1919, either Hammer or his father performed an abortion that resulted in a patient's death. Although Hammer later claimed that he had performed the operation, his father assumed responsibility at the time and was convicted of manslaughter. He was imprisoned until 1923; the truth behind the operation was never established.

Hammer completed his medical degree in 1921 and, although planning to begin a residency that winter, traveled to the Soviet Union at his father's behest, bearing medical supplies to ease a typhus epidemic and planning to establish business connections with Bolshevik friends of his father. Just emerging from the upheavals of revolution, the nation badly lacked basic supplies. Hammer met with Soviet leaders including Lenin and Trotsky, and founded the Allied American Corporation, a trade firm to export furs and minerals in exchange for American wheat, tractors, and machinery. In 1925 Hammer expanded into manufacturing, founding the Soviet Union's first pencil factory, which produced some 45 million pencils a year by 1928. Though Hammer later described his Soviet years as a time of capitalist enterprising, his success owed much to the sponsorship of the Soviet state which, in turn, depended on the use of Hammer's firms as conduits for payments to espionage agents in America. Hammer's father orchestrated these connections. Although these seditious affairs never became public during Hammer's life, beginning in the 1920s, the U.S. Department of State, the Federal Bureau of Investigation, Britain's MI-5, and the Soviet KGB assembled voluminous files documenting his family's ties to international communism.

Hammer met his first wife in the Soviet Union, a singer named Olga Vadina who left her husband to marry him in

March 1927. They had a son, Julian, in May 1929, Hammer's only child born in wedlock. Forced out by Stalin's program of nationalization, Hammer sold his businesses to the government in 1929. Although he maintained a lavish image, historians later determined that Hammer probably stood at least half a million dollars in debt. His next venture, the sale of Russian artwork, aimed to cancel this debt while continuing his furtive connections with the Soviet state. Strapped for currency, the Soviets had approached Hammer in 1925 with plans to sell artwork abroad, and for this purpose he established L'Ermitage Galleries in New York City, but the undertaking failed. Hammer resumed this plan when he returned to New York in 1931. He published *The Quest of the Romanov Treasure* (1932), in which he claimed to have spent vast fortunes in Russia acquiring Romanov artifacts. In fact, he received the artwork from the Soviet state, which had confiscated it during the revolution, and Hammer knew that among his "treasure" was much kitsch and some forgeries. Following a nationwide sales tour, he installed the collection at the Hammer Galleries in New York City. Although Hammer received commissions, he remitted the bulk of the proceeds to the Soviets.

Simultaneous with these art transactions, and perhaps as a means of justifying his ongoing payments, Hammer began importing Soviet barrel staves to the A. Hammer Cooperage Company in Brooklyn. Though Hammer maintained extravagant airs, depressed markets and problems of loan management kept his profits low. Hammer and his first wife separated during the mid-1930s, beginning Hammer's lifelong estrangement from his son. The two divorced in November 1943, and three weeks later, Hammer married Angela Carey Zevely, an opera singer whom he had dated since the late 1930s.

Beginning in the spring of 1940, half a year following the outbreak of World War 11, Hammer devoted himself to building support for American aid to Britain. He donated money to pro-British organizations, took out full-page newspaper advertisements, and, most important, created the idea of exchanging American military equipment for leases on British naval and air bases, a concept that President Franklin D. Roosevelt adopted as the basis for America's lend-lease policy.

Hammer made his first fortune beginning in 1944. Although wartime rationing had ended most production of

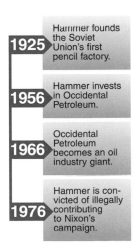

1925 Hammer founds the Soviet Union's first pencil factory.

1956 Hammer invests in Occidental Petroleum.

1966 Occidental Petroleum becomes an oil industry giant.

1976 Hammer is convicted of illegally contributing to Nixon's campaign.

Armand Hammer speaking at a news conference in 1977.

distillery: a company that makes alcoholic beverages.

beverage alcohol, Hammer purchased a defunct New Hampshire **distillery** and, through contacts with New England senators and a handful of presidential officials, gained permission to produce whiskey. Within two years, Hammer built a liquor empire, United Distillers of America, which owned distilleries in nine states and had revenues of $40 million. Hammer advertised his wealth in the purchase of artwork, an immense yacht, an award-winning herd of cattle, and the Roosevelt home at Campobello, an island estate off the Maine coast, which he renovated and donated as a U.S.-Canadian park in 1962. He sold United Distillers in 1953.

In 1953 Hammer began an affair with a Florida waitress named Bettye Murphy, with whom he made vague plans for marriage. After divorcing his second wife in January 1956, however, Hammer married Frances Barrett Tolman, a wealthy California widow. He moved to Los Angeles and relocated Ms. Murphy to Mexico City, where, in May 1956, she gave birth to Hammer's child, a daughter named Victoria. Hammer supported the two but hid their existence to his death. Though he had other affairs, Hammer remained married to his third wife until her death in December 1989.

Hammer's final and largest venture began in 1956 when he invested in Occidental Petroleum, a small California oil firm. Within a year, through strength of finance and personality, he was elected president and chief executive officer. He hired a new head geologist, who struck oil at several domestic sites. In the early 1960s, through a combination of daring expenditures, intensive lobbying, and selective bribery, Hammer succeeded in winning two of the first and largest oil concessions in Libya. From 1966 until the overthrow of Libya's royal family in 1969, the Libyan reserves built Occidental into a titan.

Libyan Colonel Mu'ammar al-Gadhafi's seizure of power threatened to end the nation's oil exports. Unlike the older and larger firms, the so-called Seven Sisters, Occidental would have collapsed without Libyan oil. Thus, while the others maintained solidarity against Gadhafi's ultimatum for greater commissions, Hammer relented in late 1970. His concession forced the Seven Sisters to follow suit, immediately emboldening other petroleum-rich nations to revise their own contracts. None of Hammer's activities was so widely criticized during his lifetime as his Libyan dealings, which many believed responsible for the loss of the Seven Sisters' power over oil pricing, the strengthening of the Organization of Petroleum Exporting Countries (OPEC), and a subsequent rise in global energy prices. Hammer suffered another setback in 1976, when he was convicted of making illegal contributions to President Richard M. Nixon's 1972 campaign; President George Bush pardoned him in 1989.

During the last two decades of Hammer's life, Occidental Petroleum grew to become the United States' eighth largest oil company, controlling diverse mineral reserves throughout the world. Hammer won praise as a capitalist extraordinaire, yet within Occidental, where he maintained an iron grip over leadership, critics charged him with recklessness and egotism: he planned billion-dollar Soviet developments, despite the tenuous cold war climate; he committed the company to a massive speculative coal venture in China; he left a path of bribery through Africa, Asia, and Latin America; he summarily fired executives who voiced dissent; he appropriated and spent millions amassing his collection of artwork and, in the 1980s, constructing the Armand Hammer Museum in Los Angeles. Such practices prompted numerous shareholder lawsuits and Security and Exchange Commission investigations.

> *"People will always work harder if they're getting well paid and if they're afraid of losing a job which they know will be hard to equal. As is well known, if you pay peanuts, you get monkeys."*
> Armand Hammer, *Hammer*, 1987

Hammer increasingly dabbled in public and international affairs. He met with Soviet premiers and hoped that his business there might forge international understanding. He arranged for Occidental to endow the Armand Hammer United World College, establish an annual Armand Hammer Conference on Peace and Human Rights, organize international art exchanges, donate to the cause of cancer research, and finance relief efforts following the 1986 Chernobyl nuclear power plant disaster. In an autobiography, Hammer (1987), he proclaimed two goals for his remaining years: to cure cancer and promote world peace. He lobbied vigorously but unsuccessfully to be awarded a Nobel Peace Prize.

Hammer died of cancer at the age of 92. He was interred in a family mausoleum at the Westwood Village Cemetery in Los Angeles.

At his death, Hammer was praised as an ingenious capitalist. As sources opened within Occidental, the U.S. government, and the former Soviet Union, however, this view unraveled. Hammer's career, it became apparent, included a foundation of espionage, bribery, and bullying. Hidden facts of manipulation and adultery came to light, and with them the image of a man consumed by hubris. Hammer's long-suspected connection to Soviet communism was definitely established by the historian Edward Jay Epstein in 1996, and it is thus possible that Hammer's most novel contribution—the lend-lease concept—was less an effort to protect Britain than one to delay Hitler's aggression against the Soviets. Yet Hammer himself was no communist. Rather, his work for Lenin in the 1920s seems akin to his donations to Roosevelt in the 1930s, to Ronald Reagan in the 1980s, or to his habitual contributions of money and artwork to leaders through his career, all the actions of one fascinated with power and determined to ingratiate himself to those wielding it. Indeed, Hammer's life is a study in the reaches and limits of power. He created a global financial empire and mixed in the destiny of nations, yet, despite assiduous efforts, Armand Hammer could not conceal his own past from posterity. ◆

Harriman, Edward Henry

1848–1909 ● FINANCIER & RAILROAD TYCOON

E dward Henry Harriman, one of the leading railroad organizers and financial wizards of the late nineteenth century, was born in Hempstead, New York, February 20, 1848. He started work as a Wall Street office boy at the age of 14. He learned the operations of stock and bond sales so well that by the time he was 21 years old he had his own seat on the New York Stock Exchange. He grew interested in railroad financial problems during the 1880s after his marriage. His wife's family had been involved in the management of a railroad in upstate New York.

Harriman became an expert in handling the financial end of railroading. Many rail lines had been built and operated during the 1860's and 1870's without careful and thorough money management, so they were in serious trouble, unable to meet their regular expenses, and unable to borrow money or raise money by selling additional stock. Harriman stepped into several such railroad situations, beginning with the Lake Ontario Southern Railroad which he reorganized in 1881-1882. From that success, he moved on to become a director and vice-president of the much larger Illinois Central Railroad, and in 1895 he became the financial manager of a group that took control of the Union Pacific Railroad.

An important objective of the Harriman plan was to get a rail entry into Chicago.

The Union Pacific was the chief link in an extensive rail-road "empire" that Harriman began to develop, including parts of the Southern Pacific and Central Pacific. An important objective of the Harriman plan was to get a rail entry into Chicago, so that his Pacific coast and transcontinental lines would have a gateway into the railroad hub of the country. In order to get this linkage into Chicago, Harriman and his friends engaged in a "stock war" against James J. Hill, another railroad magnate. Both sides were trying to win control of the Chicago, Burlington, and Quincy Railroad, which had the most accessible mainlines into Chicago from the West. Neither Harriman nor Hill won that war. Eventually the two sides joined forces, established the Northern Securities Company, and attempted to settle the railroad control issue by a deal among the chief competitors. This deal gave rise to the Northern Securities Case which was brought eventually to the U.S. Supreme Court. It was decided that the company was illegal, because it was a combination in "restraint of trade" and therefore violated the antitrust laws. Harriman was forced to sell off his stock in Northern Securities, and although he made an enormous profit on the sale, his loss of the law case led to further investigations. The Interstate Commerce Commission looked into his activities and charged that he had used his stock in the Union Pacific, not so much for the good of that railroad, but as a means of borrowing or buying control of other, smaller railroads. The years from 1904 until his death were marked by a series of public investigations of Harriman's business activities, including a study of how he exercised control over the work of the Equitable Life Assurance Society. Harriman was one of the last great individual financiers and managers, although several of his actions appeared to run against the public interests.

He passed away on September 9, 1909. ◆

1881 Harriman reorganizes the Ontario Southern Railroad.

1895 Harriman takes control of the Union Pacific Railroad.

1904 Harriman's business activities are investigated.

Harvey, Ford Ferguson

1866–1928 ● HOTEL & RESTAURANT DEVELOPER

Ford Ferguson Harvey built a major chain of hotels and restaurants throughout the West from 1901 until his death. His empire continued after him, however, until travel by airplane and automobile supplanted tourism by passenger train following World War II.

Born in Leavenworth, Kansas, Harvey attended college briefly before starting work in a restaurant that belonged to his father, Fred Harvey. The elder Harvey had opened a chain of restaurants—the Fred Harvey Houses—along the route of the Atchison, Topeka and Santa Fe Railroad. At the death of his father in 1901, Ford Ferguson Harvey expanded the business to include hotels and dining rooms. In addition, he managed the dining-car service for the railway.

His company, Fred Harvey's, named in honor of his father, was headquartered in Kansas City, Missouri. In addition to the independent chain, he gained the rights to run concessions at the Grand Canyon National Park. His hotels included the Bisonte in Hutchinson, Kansas; the La Fonda in Santa Fe, New Mexico; the Castañeda in Las Vegas, New Mexico; and the El Tovar in the Grand Canyon National Park. With a boom in tourism after the depression of the 1890s and with a growing interest in America's new national parks, Ford Ferguson Harvey's empire was secure.

In 1902, Harvey established the Fred Harvey Indian Department, which bought and sold traditional Native American arts and crafts and gained a reputation for treating the artists and craftspeople fairly. ◆

Harvey gained the right to run concessions at the Grand Canyon National Park.

Hassenfeld, Stephen David

1942–1989 ● TOY MANUFACTURER

"The grass isn't greener elsewhere; it's greenest right here."

Stephen Hassenfeld

Stephen David Hassenfeld, American toy manufactuer, was born on June 25, 1898, in New York City. Hassenfeld was the third-generation owner of the Hasbro toy company. He was a son of Merrill Hassenfeld and Sylvia Kay. His father was the second generation Hasbro toy manufacturer, affording his children the wonders of toy creation. His mother was a housewife. Steven had a brother and a sister, both employed in the family's toy-making enterprise.

As a boy, Stephen lived his entire life encompassed by toys. He told the *New York Times*, "I grew up with everybody's toys." Hassenfeld was showered with factory samples, game prototypes, and salesmen's gifts all due to his father's involvement in the toy industry. Stephen later admitted "it was tough not to be spoiled." With these influences surrounding him, he knew from the time he was very young exactly what he wanted to be, and that was a toy manufacturer. As an adult, he never changed his mind. "Whenever the investment community asks what I'm going to do next," he once said, "I've replied: 'The grass isn't greener elsewhere; it's greenest right here.'"

The Hasbro company (the name stands for Hassenfeld Brothers) had a unique beginning. It was founded in 1923 by three brothers of Polish decent: Stephen's grandfather Henry, and his brothers, Hillel and Herman. They began as distributors of fabric remnants, but soon made profits by wrapping cloth around cigar boxes to produce creative pencil cases. The brothers purchased a pencil manufacturing firm and began marketing school supplies. With the outbreak of World War II, Hasbro was guided into a new direction when plastics became difficult to acquire. The Hassenfeld brothers began to manufacture a new line of toys from paint sets, junior-air-raid-warden sets, wax crayons, and doctor and nurse kits marketed in the same pencil-case boxes. After the war Hasbro continued to make both toys and school items.

Stephen Hassenfeld majored in political science at John Hopkins University in Baltimore from 1959 to 1962. He dropped out in his senior year and went to work for his family's business in 1964, following in the footsteps of his father and grandfather. In 1968 he became executive vice president, in charge of Hasbro corporate hiring. His assignment was to build a new management team inclined to take risks. In the early 1970s Stephen led the company into day-care centers and housewares, both ill-fated ventures that Hasbro eventually lost. After becoming president in 1975 Hassenfeld shackled the company with rigid principles, including a return on investment analysis for each proposed toy. With that standard, not many of the toys reached the production stage. In one instance Stephen authorized an early monster toy called Terron the Terrible. It failed miserably, which helped push the company into the red in 1978.

Subsequently, Hassenfeld threw out many of his earlier, conventional business techniques and developed his own individual management method. As described in a Business Week article, Stephen's philosophy was to "look for three traits in a toy: lasting play value, shareability, and the capacity to stimulate the imagination." While Hassenfeld used common business techniques in most areas, toy selection was still largely intuitive.

When Hassenfeld became chairman of the company in 1980, it was the nation's sixth largest toy manufacturer with annual sales of about $100 million. Stephen methodically transformed Hasbro, once labeled "Hasbeen" by industry humorists, into the company with the broadest production line in the business. During Stephen's tenure, the company was said to have become the world's largest toy manufacturer

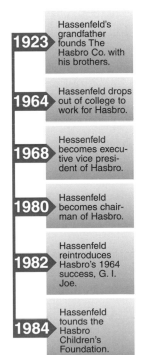

1923 Hassenfeld's grandfather founds The Hasbro Co. with his brothers.

1964 Hassenfeld drops out of college to work for Hasbro.

1968 Hessenfeld becomes executive vice president of Hasbro.

1980 Hassenfeld becomes chairman of Hasbro.

1982 Hassenfeld reintroduces Hasbro's 1964 success, G. I. Joe.

1984 Hassenfeld founds the Hasbro Children's Foundation.

"I grew up with everybody's toys."
Stephen Hassenfeld

Hassenfeld looked for three traits in a toy: lasting play value, shareability, and the capacity to stimulate the imagination.

with sales of more than $1.3 billion. Much of Hasbro's success was attributed to Hassenfeld's enterprising acquisition of other toy producers, such as Milton Bradley, and to the dramatic growth of its G. I. Joe line of soldiers and of its Transformers, vehicles convertible into robot figures. Hassenfeld's first big success was his 1982 reintroduction of G. I. Joe. The doll was originally marketed in 1964 as a World War II-era soldier and in 1970 turned into a organization of quasi-militaristic adventurers. When Hassenfeld reintroduced the doll in 1982, it was marketed as a much smaller, less warlike figure. The new billing for the toy was "a real American hero." The new-fashioned G. I. Joe doll racked up $49 million in the first year of sales. Other basic, perennially favorite toys that contributed to Hasbro's success under Hassenfeld were Raggedy Ann and Andy dolls, Mr. Potato Head, and the Playskool line of products for infants and children.

Hassenfeld, a trim, dark-haired man, was once described as "the curly-haired dynamo, who relies on gestures to help make his points." To him toys and games were not fun, they were part of a battle on the field of business. For both Hassenfeld and G. I. Joe, the toy industry was war. Hassenfeld was an all-work, no-play workaholic who awoke at 5:30 a.m. and rarely quit before midnight. As a bachelor he was devoted to his dream of what Hasbro would become. He found "his challenges and joys in generating profits for Hasbro," and told the *New York Times* in 1985, "I won't say I've been tested as a manager in the last five years. The test for me is in the future."

Hassenfeld received the national humanitarian award of the Rhode Island Council of the National Jewish Hospital and the Humanitarian of the Year award from the Rhode Island Big Brothers Association. He founded the Hasbro Children's Foundation in 1984 to help poor and homeless children. His significant memberships included the Rhode Island Jewish Federation, the National Council of Christians and Jews, the United Way, and the Rhode Island Strategic Development Committee.

Hassenfeld resided in a midtown Manhattan apartment and had homes in Palm Beach, Florida, and Bristol, Rhode Island. His waterfront properties indulged him his hobby of sailing, while his Manhattan home made it easy for him to follow theater and ballet.

Hassenfeld died of pneumonia and cardiac arrest in 1989 at Columbia Presbyterian Hospital in New York City following four weeks of hospitalization. Stephen Hassenfeld was the guiding genius behind Hasbro, Inc. His legacy and lesson were that he proved Hasbro could lose money on promotional toys and still profit overall. His force, imagination, and genius transformed a family-owned toy company into a global, billion-dollar concern. Hassenfeld was a driving force in the playtime business, a mastermind of the toy manufacturers, and a leader in the industry. ◆

Hauser, Samuel Thomas

1833–1914 ● RAILROAD & MINING TYCOON

Among Montana's early entrepreneurs, Samuel Thomas Hauser was remarkable for his diverse investments and for his vision of economic development. Born in Falmouth, Kentucky, he was educated as a civil engineer. In 1854, he moved from Kentucky to Missouri, where he supervised railroad construction. He arrived in Montana in 1862, joined the Bannack gold rush and, in 1863, became a member of James Stuart's Yellowstone Prospecting Expedition

Hauser began building his financial empire in 1865, when he and Nathaniel P. Langford organized a Virginia City bank. At the same time, he founded several mining companies and built the first silver mill in the Montana Territory in Argenta. Ultimately, he controlled banks in Virginia City, Helena, Butte, Fort Benton, and Missoula; financed the construction of numerous short line railroads; owned and operated several smelters; invested in significant real-estate and irrigation projects; and became a partner with A. J. Davis and Granville Stuart in the DHS cattle operation. Hauser backed scores of

1862 Hauser joins the Bannack Gold Rush.

1863 Hauser joins James Stuart's Yellowstone Prospecting Expedition.

1865 Hauser organizes a Virginia City Bank.

1885 Hauser becomes Montana Territory governor.

1908 Hauser's Missouri River hydroelectric dam collapses.

gold-, silver-, copper-, and coal-mining projects across Montana and became the state's preeminent mining promoter.

With Marcus Daly, William Andrews Clark, and Charles Arthus Broadwater, Hauser composed the Democratic party's "Big Four" in Montana. The men wielded great political influence in the territory through the 1880s. In 1885, President Grover Cleveland appointed pointed Hauser the territory's first resident governor.

Hauser's economic fortunes suffered in the panic of 1893, and his hydroelectric dam on the Missouri River collapsed in 1908. Nevertheless, the significant political, social, and financial influence of this competitive capitalist survived beyond his death. ◆

Hearst, George

1800–1895 ● PUBLISHER & MINING PROMOTER

1850　Hearst arrives in California.

1859　Hearst acquires interest in Ophir Mine.

1877　Hearst acquires interest in the Homestake Mine.

1886　Hearst begins serving in Congress.

Enjoying a colorful and spectacular career as a Western mining promoter, publisher, philanthropist, and then United States senator from California, George Hearst amassed one "pile" in the Nevada silver mines only to buy into the most productive property of the Black Hills gold rush—the Homestake lode at Lead near Deadwood—to make another. The son of a Missouri farmer, Hearst had first arrived in California in 1850. Failing to make a fortune as a placer miner, Hearst set up as a storekeeper before returning to mining after he had located two promising quartz claims. Upon hearing about the incredible gold and silver lode named after Henry T. P. Comstock in the Washoe Indians region of the Sierra Nevada, Hearst headed across the mountains in 1859 and, with borrowed money, acquired one-sixth interest in the Ophir Mine for three thousand dollars that returned some ninety thousand dollars in profit. The Comstock Lode was the basis of his ultimately immense fortune. After rich placer deposits were discovered in the Black Hills during the late

1870s, the 57-year-old Hearst arrived in the mining camp of Lead in 1877, where, amid charges of fraud and threats on his life, the California tycoon secured an interest in the Homestake Mine. The industrial colossus he built ultimately took hundreds of millions of dollars out of the Black Hills. Hearst was also one of the principal early investors in the Anaconda Mining Company in Butte, Montana. From 1886 to 1893, Hearst served as California's Republican senator in the U.S. Congress, and he was instrumental in launching the newspaper career of his son, William Randolph Hearst. Having acquired 240,000 acres of old rancho land in San Luis Obispo and Monterey counties and having married socially active and philanthropically minded Phoebe Apperson Hearst, George Hearst died one of the grand figures from California's "frontier" period. ◆

> *"If you want to obtain and retain any person's attention you must say something worthwhile and say it quickly."*
> William Randolph Hearst

Hearst, William Randolph

1863–1951 ● PUBLISHING & MEDIA TYCOON

William Randolph Hearst was born in San Francisco, where his father, a goldmine owner, was elected to the state legislature in 1865 and later to the U.S. Senate. His mother, who always helped the needy, was the founder of the Parents-Teachers Association. In 1882, young Hearst enrolled at Harvard College, where, in his sophomore year, he became the business manager of Harvard's humor magazine, the *Lampoon*, which he put on a sound financial footing. He was expelled from Harvard in 1884 after leading a rally and parade that lasted all night following Grover Cleveland's win in the presidential election. He returned to Harvard in 1885, but was expelled again for a Christmas prank, in which he sent each of his instructors a chamber pot inscribed with their names.

In 1887 Hearst took control of the *San Francisco Examiner*, which his father had bought in 1880 for political reasons. He changed the format, hired the best reporters, and sometimes put a sports or feature story on the front page. He crusaded against corruption and privileges and used sensationalism to enliven his pages. He was well connected to politicians through his father and soon made the newspaper profitable.

Breaking into the New York newspaper market in 1895, Hearst purchased the unsuccessful *New York Journal*, bringing several of his reporters from California with him. He was soon able to lure journalists and editors away from rival newspapers and with a one-cent reduction on the price of his paper, bold headlines, and easy-to-read print, Hearst convinced the newsboys to put the *Journal* on top of the other newspapers. Hearst catered to the common people, and was proud of his "yellow" journalistic style. He told his staffers: "The average man in the street wants everything presented to him briefly as well as brightly. If you want to obtain and retain any person's attention you must say something worthwhile and say it quickly." Hearst's newspapers contained daily articles on sports, music, and drama, as well as literary criticism and practical information. They also included crime stories, which his reporters would often help the police solve.

Hearst Castle

In the Santa Lucia Mountains of California, atop a hill called Cuesta Encantada (the Enchanted Hill) overlooking the coastal city on San Simeon, lies a magnificent estate built over the course of 28 years by publishing magnate William Randolph Hearst. Now called Hearst Castle, the estate comprises a complex of buildings with a total of 165 rooms sprawled over 127 acres of gardens, terraces, pools, fountains, and walking paths. The focal point of the estate is a huge mansion called Casa Grande. Designed in Mediterranean revival style, the mansion is furnished with an opulent collection of priceless European art and antiques, including enormous centuries-old Spanish fireplaces, 16th-century Italian beds, Renaissance paintings, numerous tapestries, ancient Greek vases, and a library with over 5000 books. Other estate buildings include an 18-room guest house called Casa del Sol, a 10-room guest cottage called Casa del Monte, and a theater once used to screen first-run films. After Hearst's death, the Hearst Corporation donated the estate to the State of California; it is now designated a State Historic Monument and is open to the public year round.

A circulation war broke out between Hearst's *Journal* and Joseph Pulitzer's *World*, during which Hearst succeeded in enticing away Pulitzer's best staff. The 1896 presidential campaign between William McKinley and William Jennings Bryan was a battleground not only for the contenders but also for the newspapers. Hearst supported Bryan, and though not agreeing with him on every issue, believed that "the cause he stood for was the people's cause." Hearst's newspaper was the only major one on the east coast to endorse Bryan, who lost the election.

Both the *Journal* and the *World* pursued news stories vigorously and so were influential in shaping the events upon which they were reporting. For a time, Hearst advocated a noninterventionist policy in Cuba, although he supported the insurgents. However, he was soon pushing the U.S. government to recognize Cuba as an independent nation. Hearst was reported to have encouraged his journalists in Cuba to "furnish the pictures" and he would "furnish the war." Hearst denied sending such a telegram but, real or fictional, it displays his philosophy of presenting the news so as to achieve his desired end.

In 1897 and 1898 the *Journal* whipped up public sentiment against Spain and, following the Spanish sinking of the *Maine* in 1898 with the loss of 266 American lives, he demanded a call to war, thus helping precipitate the Spanish-American War. After William McKinley acquiesced to public pressure and Congress declared war on Spain in April, Hearst chartered a steamship to take him to Cuba, where he served as a war correspondent. He also personally participated in the Battle of Santiago and took twenty-nine Spanish prisoners. During the war the *Journal's* daily circulation rate soared to 1.25 million, but when the conflict ended, circulation levels dropped.

Hearst now turned to political pursuits, unsuccessfully seeking the office of governor of New York on several occasions. In 1903 he was elected as a congressman from New York, an office he held for four years. In 1904 he received 263 votes at the Democratic national convention for the presidential nomination. However his political career ended in 1909 after an unsuccessful bid for the mayoralty of New York City. He remained active in politics and in the social reformers' movement but never sought public office again.

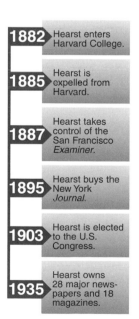

1882 Hearst enters Harvard College.

1885 Hearst is expelled from Harvard.

1887 Hearst takes control of the San Francisco *Examiner.*

1895 Hearst buys the New York *Journal.*

1903 Hearst is elected to the U.S. Congress.

1935 Hearst owns 28 major newspapers and 18 magazines.

Hearst's empire grew as he purchased newspapers in all the major cities; at times he owned up to two or three in one city. He also owned several magazines, including *Cosmopolitan*, *Good Housekeeping*, and *Harper's Bazaar*. Dabbling in the newsreel and motion picture industries, he financed several movies that starred Marion Davies, his mistress of over three decades. His empire now spanned all aspects of the media industry. At the peak of his career in 1935, Hearst owned twenty-eight major newspapers and eighteen magazines, as well as several radio stations, movie companies, and news services.

During the 1920s Hearst had a castle built in San Simeon, California, on a 240,000-acre area with a fifty-mile oceanfront, at a cost estimated between twenty and fifty million dollars; it also housed his private zoo. Decorating it with art works he had collected in Europe, he resided there with Davies. His wife, Millicent Wilson, whom he married in 1903, refused to give him a divorce, and the two remained married but separated.

The Great Depression and his personal extravagances took a heavy toll on Hearst's financial empire. At the pinnacle of his success, Hearst's assets were worth between $200 and $400 million, but his financial straits caused him to sell a number of his less profitable newspapers and parts of his art collection. By 1940, he had lost control of his empire and after World War II, he was forced to leave his castle in San Simeon and move to a smaller house in Beverly Hills.

Hearst left a legacy of expanded news coverage and a journalistic philosophy that the ends justified the means. Orson Welles's famous film *Citizen Kane* was a thinly disguised portrait of Hearst. ◆

Heinz, Henry John II (Jack)

1908–1987 ● PHILANTHROPIST, BUSINESS & CIVIC LEADER

Jack Heinz was the he eldest of the two sons of Howard Heinz, an astute businessman who steered the H. J. Heinz Company through the Depression and guided its growth for twenty-two years, and Elizabeth "Betty" Granger Rust, a housewife. Jack and his brother, Rust, had a rather stern upbringing in an austere and formal Pittsburgh home. Howard traveled constantly and seemed to arouse more respect than affection from his sons. Jack, perhaps in reaction to his father, was considered fun-loving and outgoing by his friends. Educated at Shadyside Academy in Pittsburgh; the Choate School near New Haven, Connecticut; Yale, from which he graduated in 1931; and Trinity College Cambridge, which he attended in 1931 and 1932, Jack was raised with every advantage of wealth and class he and grew into a trim, athletic, handsome young man of great charm.

Part of Heinz's education involved following in his father's footsteps and, during summer vacations, learning the family business from the ground up. It was understood, early on, that Rust, an artist, preferred designing cars to making pickles, and that it would be Jack who would enter and lead the family business.

After college Heinz worked with the British sales force, then returned to the United States, moving up from salesman to branch house manager, to headquarters' sales and advertising manager, and then to Howard's assistant (1937–1941) and to the board of directors. In 1934 his father had enough confidence in his judgment to send him to Australia to locate the company'sfirst manufacturing plant in that country. By then Heinz had married Joan Diehl, an aviator, on 18 June 1935. They lived at Rosemont Farm, outside Pittsburgh. Their son, H. John Heinz III, was born in 1938. (Elected to the U.S. Senate from Pennsylvania in 1976, he died tragically, in an airplane crash, in 1991.)

Heinz shared many family traits, including enormous energy, curiosity, a talent for advertising and promotion, and

Henry Heinz, founder
of H. J. Heinz
Company, and grandfa-
ther of Jack Heinz

**Heinz owned a
fashionable
Manhattan
townhouse on
Fifty-seventh
Street (57
because of the
company's "57
Varieties," its
magic number).**

an unquenchable thirst for travel. He swam the Bosporous as a young man, toured Soviet Russia at the age of 22, married three times and, at one point later in life, owned homes in America, England, the Caribbean, and France, including a fashionable Manhattan townhouse on Fifty-seventh Street (fifty-seven because of the company's "57 Varities," its magic number).

The full burden of leading "the old firm" fell upon Heinz's shoulders in February 1941 upon his father's death. He was only 32—making him one of the youngest men in the United States to head a major company. He was often compared to Henry Ford II, both handsome young scions of immensely successful family-run businesses. His twenty-five years as chief executive spanned enormous changes in America, the food industry, and the H. J. Heinz Company.

When Heinz took over, World War II had begun. In London, where the company had a major facility, the German blitz bombed its Harteen plant and killed two Heinz employees. Heinz traveled to England five times during World War II, three times at the invitation of the British Ministry of

Food, which sought his advice. The company worked overtime to turn out a key wartime protein, baked beans, which remained a much-beloved staple of the English diet. Heinz, a devoted **Anglophile** who socialized with the British royal family, was knighted for his contributions to British-American relations in 1979.

Anglophile: someone who admires England.

Under Heinz's leadership the U.S. company threw itself into the war effort. Its Pittsburgh facilities produced K and C rations, and converted part of a baby-food factory to the production of World War II aircraft parts, accompanied by such slogans as from "beans to bombers," and from "pickles to pursuit planes." Heinz became a highly visible civic and business leader (as had his father during World War I). He chaired the United War Fund; received Pittsburgh's Man of the Year Award in 1942 for his leadership; and delivered speeches promoting food allocation, conservation, and rationing.

After the war Heinz took the company public. The stock offering was snapped up within twenty-four hours. In 1947 Heinz married Jane Ewing. They divorced in 1952. On August 22, 1953 he married Drue Maher, born in England of Irish parents. They loved to entertain and led a jet-set life, mingling with celebrities such as Aristotle Onassis, Winston Churchill, Aly Khan, Truman Capote, and Gianni Agnelli. Known for his impeccable taste in music, literature, architecture, wine, and food, Heinz was described as a man of "**stratospheric** elegance."

stratospheric: very high in style.

Despite the isolationism of postwar America, Heinz devoted himself to European recovery, food programs, and world trade issues, in addition to running the company. He testified in Congress; worked with public-private groups supporting international cooperation; attended International Chamber of Commerce and Bilderberg conferences on Europe, serving as chairman of the U.S. Council of the former organization from 1948 to 1951; assessed an economic assistance program to Pakistan for President Dwight D. Eisenhower in 1954; and continued to contribute to British recovery programs. In Pittsburgh he became a leading member of the Allegheny Conference and Community Chest (later the United Way). In 1947 the company pioneered a national campaign to help feed "the hungry children of Europe."

Between 1945 and 1965 Heinz dramatically expanded the firm in both the United States and abroad. New factories and administration offices were built in Canada, the United

1934 Heinz goes to Australia to open a plant.

1941 Heinz becomes head of the H.J. Heinz Co.

1947 Heinz company organizes a campaign to feed hungry children.

1963 Heinz turns the company over to professional managers.

1971 Heinz Hall opens in Pittsburgh.

1979 Heinz is knighted by the British government.

During World War II, H. J. Heinz Company supplied a key wartime protein, baked beans.

Kingdom, and Pittsburgh. He opened new operations in the Netherlands, Venezuela, Mexico, Portugal, Italy, and Japan. Star-Kist and Ore-Ida were acquired. Worldwide sales boomed but, with the exception of Heinz U.K., profits plummeted. Heinz was more focused on quality, taste, nutrition, advertising, and design than on the bottom line. Generations of loyal employees considered the company "a good place to work," and blessed the Heinz family every day.

Although technically a public company, it was still run paternalistically by an insular board. Heinz relied on a small group of self-made men to steer the ship. Financially, it began to seriously founder. Matters came to a crisis in 1963, when Heinz agreed to become nonexecutive chairman and to turn the company over to professional management. The move freed the company to succeed (and its value to shareholders, including the Heinz family, to rise) under the leadership first of R. Burt Gookin, architect of the modern Heinz, and then Anthony J. F. O'Reilly, who transformed it into a global player. It also freed Jack Heinz to devote himself to his many interests and passions, chief among them the city of Pittsburgh and its renaissance.

The Howard Heinz Endowment, which he headed, funded the Pittsburgh Symphony, the Carnegie Museum of Art, nutrition education programs, and Heinz Hall, in downtown Pittsburgh. Heinz Hall opened in 1971, and was hailed as a stunning contribution to urban restoration and an acoustical gem. Heinz personally supervised the renovation, which transformed an old movie theater into the permanent performing home of the Pittsburgh Symphony Orchestra.

Heinz died of cancer. He was interred in Homewood Cemetery in Pittsburgh.

A Republican and a Presbyterian, Heinz presided over the H. J. Heinz Company's transition from family-run to professionally managed company with dignity and charm, ensuring its survival as an independent company bearing the family name. His civic leadership and generous support of Pittsburgh institutions contributed to the dramatic rebirth of that city, where the Heinz name, family, and company are still regarded with enormous esteem and affection. ◆

Hershey, Milton S.

1857–1945 ● CANDY MANUFACTURER

"Give them quality. That's the best kind of advertising."

Milton Hershey

Milton Snavely Hershey, American industrialist and candy maker, was born in Derry, Pennsyvania, on September 13, 1857. He was the son of Henry II and Fannie (Snavely) Hershey. Following a public school education, Milton Hershey was apprenticed to a confectioner and learned the practical side of the business that was to be his life work. During the Centennial Exposition of 1876 he manufactured and sold candy in Philadelphia. There followed a year in the employ of candy manufacturers in Chicago and other western cities, after which he began the manufacture of caramel candy in New York city.

After moving to Lancaster, Pennsyvania, in 1893, he made his first attempt with chocolate candy, and the venture was so successful that the plant was several times enlarged within the first few years. Two years later he sold his caramel business for $1,000,000 and, continuing the manufacture of chocolate, moved in 1904 to the new plant he built at Derry Church (now Hershey), a small village in Dauphin County, Pennslyvania, where he owned a farm of 500 acres, the site of the family homestead. With ample room for enlargement, he created the first building of the now famous chocolate factory. As operations increased he purchased more land until his holdings totaled 12,000 acres and around the plant grew the present town of Hershey. Its departments consisted of chocolate and cocoa factories, a machine shop, printing plant, and a power station.

The business grow steadily until at the time of Hershey's death it comprised some thirty-four connected buildings of stone and concrete, representing a total floor area of sixty-five acres. At the time of Hershey's death, the Hershey plant was using 400,000 quarts of milk daily in making milk chocolate, a quantity equivalent to the supply from 30,000 cows.

The company imported its supply of cacao beans, which in the process of transformation into the Hershey preparations were roasted at a temperature of between 100 and 135 degrees centigrade, which rendered soluble the starch particles. A crushing and hulling operation separated the husks from the "nibs," the nutritious part, and the nibs were crushed in heated milling machines and reduced to a thick liquor, known as "cocoa mass." Because of it high fatty content, a portion of the fat or cocoa butter was removed by hydraulic pressure and the remaining mass, in the form of hard cakes, was ground to a fine soft powder known as cocoa which was then sifted, automatically weighed, packed, and labeled ready for market. The sweet milk chocolate was made by adding to the cocoa finely ground sugar and concentrated milk thoroughly mixed or blended in melangeur machines, further mixed in granite longitudinal machines, and finally molded into cakes and bars and wrapped for marketing. In addition to the familiar brands of Hershey chocolate confections, the company also originated the now familiar chocolate almond bar, for which the best grade of almond nuts was grown in California and imported from southern Europe and mixed with the milk chocolate mass in the final operation.

This gigantic industry, the world's largest single entity engaged solely in the manufacture of cocoa and chocolate, and founded by the enterprise of one individual, was conducted as the Hershey Chocolate Company from 1893 until it was incorporated in 1908 as the Hershey Chocolate Company, the name being changed in 1927 to the Hershey Chocolate Corp. The company's capital, consisting of 1,000,000 shares, was largely held by Hershey in his own name until 1918. At that time his entire fortune, estimated at $60,000,000 was transferred to the Hershey Industrial School

1876 Hershey sells candy during the Exposition in Philadelphia.

1877 Hershey begins manufacturing caramel in New York City.

1893 Hershey moves to Lancaster and begins making chocolate.

1904 Hershey establishes Hershey Chocolate Co. in Derry, PA.

1909 Hershey founds the Hershey Industrial School for orphan boys.

1936 Hershey forms the M. S. Hershey Foundation.

for orphan boys. The school, founded in 1909 on the Hershey homestead, near the village of Hershey, afforded instruction to orphan boys between the ages of 4 and 18 years who had lost one or both parents. The school was **nonsectarian** but the moral and religious welfare of the students was a vital part of their training. They were instructed in the several branches of a sound education from the kindergarten to the high school grade, including agriculture, **horticulture**, the mechanical-trades, and handicraft. Experienced educators and specialists were in charge, an instructor for every twenty-five boys. Improved methods of instruction and modern systems of housing and care were in practice, the aim being to avoid the distinctively institutional atmosphere, and to prepare all students for self-respecting and successful maturity. In 1934, the students then numbering 450, it became necessary to build an entire group of new buildings, occupying a space 780 by 425 acres on a high ridge of the foothills of the Blue Ridge Mountains.

In 1936, Hershey formed the M. S. Hershey Foundation, with an endowment of 500 shares of Hershey common stock (then worth $400,000) for educational purposes in Derry. Two

nonsectarian: not connected to a religious group.

horticulture: the science of growing plants.

Hershey, Pennsylvania

In 1903 Milton Snavely Hershey established what would become the world's largest chocolate factory in Dauphin County, Pennsylvania. At the same time that he started manufacturing the "Hershey bar," he began developing the town of Hershey as a model community for his workers. Hershey still bears marks of its founder's philanthropic generosity. The Milton Hershey School, established in 1909, provides room, board, and education for over 1,100 disadvantaged children a year. Hershey Park, opened by Hershey in 1907, is one of America's most popular theme parks, including a sports arena, amusement areas with six roller coasters, river rapids for canoeing, and a zoo (originally stocked with Milton Hershey's animals). Also in the park is the Hershey Museum, which traces the story of Milton Hershey and the town and also contains Pennsylvania German and American Indian artifacts. Hershey is sometimes called "the sweetest place on earth," and chocolate is still a central theme of the town. The Hershey chocolate factory offers tours and free samples. Chocolate-related events are common, such as a Chocolate Lovers Weekend sponsored by the Hotel Hershey in 1990. Located thirteen miles east of Harrisburg, the state capital, Hershey has a population of 11,860, according to the 1990 Census.

years later the Hershey Junior College for boys of Hershey grew into a thriving community with a population of 4000, having its own water supply and sewerage system, electric lighting plant, churches, schools, a bank and trust company, a village inn, a resort hotel, four golf courses, swimming pool, sports arena seating 8000, and a ballroom accommodating 4000 dancers. Its up-to-date schools, built and equipped by Hershey and given to the township, constituted the largest consolidated township schools in the United States and comprised a high school, a grade school, a kindergarten, and trade and vocational schools all conducted under one management. Hershey also created and equipped a large community building for public use, containing a library, hospital, gymnasium, moving picture theater, auditorium, swimming pool, ten school rooms, and dormitories.

In 1942, Hershey resigned the presidency of three of his corporations, the Hershey Industrial School, and Hershey Chocolate Corp. Although destined to lasting fame because of his practical contributions to the well-being of humanity, Hershey was modest and retiring. He was devoted to the oversight of the vast business that he founded, and to the improvement of his industrial school, for which childless himself, he expressed a fullness of real fatherly concern. Personally, he was a man of high ideals, born for great works, and nobly accomplishing them; a leader among men, and one endowed with a genius for making and holding friends.

Hershey was married in New York City on May 25, 1898, to Catherine, daughter of Michael Sweeney, of Jamestown, New York. Hershey died at Hershey on October 13, 1945. ◆

Hill, James Jerome

1838–1916 ● RAILROAD TYCOON

James J. Hill is sometimes called an "Empire Builder" and
the story of his rise to power in American railroading and
trade development suggests why. Hill began his career as
a poor young man with visions of going to the Orient. He
only got as far as St. Paul, Minnesota, in 1856, a few days late
for the annual transcontinental caravan. He stayed in St. Paul
and became one of its leading and wealthiest citizens.

He started in the transportation business as agent for a
Mississippi River steamboat company. Recognizing that profits could be made not just by sale of freight and passenger
tickets, but by carrying things to sell as well, he did so and
prospered. Later on, he would apply the same idea by building
business at each end of his railroad lines, thus making his terminals into important shopping centers. In the late 1870s, he
became interested in fuel-wood and coal. He wisely forecast
that coal would be the normal fuel for railroads, and moved
into coal as a business.

His chance for major wealth and influence came in 1878,
when with three partners he bought out a bankrupt railroad
that had been badly mismanaged. Hill turned this small St.
Paul-based railroad into the cornerstone of the Great

1856 Hill moves to St. Paul, Minnesota.

1878 Hill and three partners buy a bankrupt railroad.

1904 The Supreme court splits up the Northern Securities Co.

Northern Railroad. He personally planned and pushed through the construction of this transcontinental line, helping to select the right-of-way and the sites for bridges and "cuts" through the newly developing Dakota Territory, and across Montana, Idaho, and Washington to Puget Sound. Hill managed to keep his railroad operating, and profitable, through many major depressions, when his rivals, especially the Northern Pacific, suffered reverses. He also developed the timberlands along his right-of-way, and labored to make Seattle, his Pacific terminal, a major shipping port for trade with Japan and the Orient.

Hill's methods of personal management and extremely careful financing gave him success. He organized a company, known as the Northern Securities Company, to act as a holding company for the great wealth he had built up over the years. The Supreme Court, in 1904, declared that the Northern Securities Company was an illegal combination, and ordered it split up. Hill's work with the Great Northern was extremely important in opening up the northern sections of the States through which it ran. He sponsored agricultural demonstrations to encourage farming, and he invested heavily in shipping facilities and warehouses at both ends of his lines. He was also a major owner and developer of the **Mesabi Range** iron ore deposits. ◆

Mesabi Range: hills in NE Minnesota.

Hollerith, Herman

1860–1929 ● Computer developer

Herman Hollerith was born in Buffalo, New York, on February 29, 1860, the son of a German immigrant couple. Immediately after graduating from the Columbia University's School of Mines in 1879, he became an assistant to one of his former teachers in the U.S. Census Bureau. During the next few years, he taught briefly at the Massachusetts Institute of Technology in Cambridge, experimented on air brakes, and worked for the patent office in

Washington, D.C. During all of this time, Hollerith was occupied with the problem of automating the tabulation work of the census.

When the tenth **decennial** census was taken in 1880, the country had grown to 50 million people, and 5 years later the Census Bureau was still struggling to compile the results. It was not hard to foresee a situation where a given census would not be published before it was time to take the next one. Hollerith, inspired by watching a conductor punch tickets with a basic description of each passenger, started work on a machine for mechanically tabulating population and other statistics. In 1884, he applied for his first patent on a machine for counting population statistics. He was eventually issued thirty-one patents.

decennial: occurring every ten years.

Hollerith's most important innovations were the sensing of the holes through electrical contacts and the design of electrically operated mechanisms for **incrementing** the proper register in the tabulating machine. He also provided for one step in an electric sort. Each card was coded to fall into the proper pocket in a sorting box. From this point on, sorting had to be done by hand, but it was easier to sort punched cards than handwritten cards because the sorter could sight through the wanted hole or use a sorting needle. The card used in Hollerith's machine was 6⅝ x 3¼ inches and had twenty-four columns, each with twelve punching places. Hollerith worked as an independent inventor, with no commitment from the census authorities to the use of his invention; however, he planned his system keeping in mind the requirements for tabulation of the population census.

incrementing: increasing by a certain amount.

In 1889, a committee was appointed to consider the means of tabulation to be used in the 1890 census. Three systems were tested, one of them Hollerith's. His system took only about two thirds as long as its nearest competitor to transcribe information. The commission estimated that on a basis of 65,000,000 population, the savings with the Hollerith apparatus would reach nearly $600,000. Hollerith's invention was adopted and an arrangement was entered into by the government with its inventor.

Hollerith subcontracted the development and construction of the keyboard punches to the Pratt and Whitney Company of Hartford, Connecticut, and of the tabulator to the Western Electric Company.

In 1890, three major events occurred in Hollerith's life: (1) he married the daughter of Dr. John Billings; (2) he received his doctor of philosophy degree from Columbia's School of Mines; (3) the United States conducted its eleventh census using his system. Dr. Billings was in charge of the work on vital statistics for both the 1880 and 1890 censuses, especially the collection and tabulation of data. While working at the Census Bureau, Billings, who was Hollerith's superior, also suggested to Hollerith that Jacquard-like punched cards might be the answer to the massive tabulation problems of the census.

In 1896, Hollerith formed the Tabulating Machine Company. Word of his success spread rapidly. Insurance companies used his machines for actuarial work, department stores used them for sales analysis, and the New York Central used them to keep track of their railroad cars. The Tabulating Machine Company became world famous.

Hollerith continued to modify and improve his machines, which were used for the 1900 census. In 1910, even though Hollerith had developed a system of hopper-fed machines that eliminated hand feeding of cards, he was unable to reach an agreement with the Census Bureau for their use.

When his Tabulating Machine Company became too large for individual control, Holerith sold it. In 1911, the company became part of the Computing-Tabulating-Recording (C-T-R) Company. The C-T-R Company was a holding company and in 1924 was renamed the International Business Machines (IBM) Corporation.

On November 17, 1929, in Washington, D.C., a heart attack ended his life at the age of 69. What Henry Ford did for manufacturing, Herman Hollerith accomplished for data processing—a means for standardization and a format for the interchangeability of information. ◆

1879 Hollerith works as an assistant at the U.S. Census Bureau.

1880 Census Bureau struggles to tabulate results of nation's tenth census.

1884 Hollerith applies for a patent on a machine for counting population statistics.

1889 The government adopts Hollerith's key-punch invention for the 1890 census.

1896 Hollerith forms Tabulating Machine Co.

1911 Hollerith sells Computing-Tabulating-Recording Co.

1924 CTR is renamed the International Business Machines (IBM) Corporation.

Hughes, Howard

1906–1976 ● AVIATION & FILMMAKING BILLIONAIRE

Considered one of the most innovative yet eccentric billionaires of the twentieth century, Howard Hughes proved his talent as an aviator, filmmaker, record-setter, and entrepreneur.

Howard Robard Hughes Jr. was born on December 24, 1906, in Houston, Texas. His father had built his fortune in the Sharp-Hughes Tool Company, which leased oil-drilling equipment patented by "Big Howard" himself. Howard Jr. was also mechanically inclined, and was fascinated by airplanes. Against his parents' wishes, he took flying lessons from crop dusters as a teenager. His mother, Allene, died in 1923, and his father followed a year later, leaving the 17-year-old with three-quarters of Hughes Tool but little preparation as a businessman or an adult.

In 1925 a family friend sought financing from Hughes for a new film entitled *Swell Hogan*. Hughes agreed on the condition that he be allowed to work on the set and learn everything about the business. The film bombed, and the remain-

Millionaire Howard Hughes and his plane.

ing Hughes family members, who controlled 25 percent of Hughes Tool, chastised Howard for squandering the company's funds in Hollywood. In response, Howard bought their shares at twice the market value, and went on to produce three movies over the next two years, one of which—*Two Arabian Knights*—won an Academy Award in 1927 for best comedy. Hughes then set out to make a film about aviation. *Hell's Angels* cost nearly $4 million to produce and the compulsive Hughes shot over 3 million feet of film (of which only 1 percent was used in production), but the result was a box-office hit that doubled his investment. During these years in Hollywood he developed a reputation as a playboy, dating Jean Harlow, Katharine Hepburn, Ava Gardner, and other stars. Both of his marriages ended in divorce.

Looking for a new challenge after his film success, Hughes returned to aviation. In 1932, he bought a seaplane and traveled cross-country with Glen Odekirk, whom he had hired to customize the plane to his specifications. Obsessed with the idea of producing the fastest plane in the world, Hughes broke the world's record for airspeed at 352.39 miles per hour in an experimental plane that no one had even tested. In the meantime, he founded Hughes Aircraft Company.

By 1939, Hughes had purchased controlling shares of Trans World Airlines, and helped launch the Constellation, one of the first transcontinental passenger planes. When Hughes was ordered by a Federal court to sell his shares for $750,000,000 in the late 1950s, he became America's first billionaire and the richest man in the world at that time.

After a plane crash in 1946 that left him with severe head and back injuries, Hughes became addicted to pain killers. The already eccentric man became irrationally paranoid, and insisted that objects be handed to him covered by tissue paper. By the early 1960s, pursued by the IRS for tax evasion, he hired a former FBI agent named Robert Maheu to shield him from public view. He moved into suites in the upper levels of the Desert Inn in Las Vegas, which he later bought for $14 million, along with other legendary Vegas institutions. Maheu eventually moved Hughes to the Bahamas, and in 1976 the press reported that the magnate had died of heart failure on a plane en route to Texas. He left no valid will, and a string of illustrious court battles over his fortune ensued.

The Hughes legacy lives on in the many companies and organizations he founded, including the Howard Hughes Medical Institute, Baker Hughes Incorporated, Hughes Electronics Corporation, Hughes Space and Communications Company, and Hughes Aircraft. ◆

Hunt, Haroldson Lafayette, Jr.

1889–1974 ● OIL BARON

Haroldson Lafayette Hunt Junior was born in Carson Township, Fayette County, Illinois, on February 17, 1889. He was the son of Haroldson Lafayette and Ella Rose (Myers) Hunt. H. L. Hunt's father was a farmer and sheriff. The younger Hunt received his early education under the tutelage of his mother at home and spent a semester in 1906 at Valparise College. Meanwhile, at the age of 15, he worked his way westward across the country as a cowboy, **mule skinner**, lumberjack, or laborer in Kansas, Colorado, Utah, California, Arizona, Texas, Nevada, Indiana, Washington, Montana, the Dakotas, and Saskatchewan, Canada. In 1911 Hunt went to the area of Lake Village, Arkansas, to begin trading in cotton lands, but floods and the

mule skinner: a person who drives mules.

Hunt drilled numerous "wildcat" wells in high risk, unproved areas.

agricultural depression following the First World War left him virtually bankrupt in 1921.

In that year, Hunt saw his first oil well in El Dorado, Arkansas, and he decided to start a new career of trading in oil leases and in drilling oil wells. Many of the wells he put down were so-called wildcat wells, or wells drilled in high-risk, unproved areas. In 1923 and 1924 he brought in two discovery wells in a new oil field around the Liberty Hill community in the Louann Field north of Smackover, Arkansas, and the Swilley area south of it. He sold a half interest in some forty small wells in Arkansas in 1924 for $600,000, and during the ensuing years he drilled several other discovery wells in Arkansas and in the Tullos-Urania field in Louisiana. After drilling without success in west Texas, he drilled the discovery well in the Rainbow Field east of El Dorado, Arkansas, in 1927. By 1930 he was investigating the possibilities of oil in east Texas in an area that other oil companies had passed over as unlikely to be productive.

In the most important trade of his career, Hunt acquired the Daisy Bradford No. 3 well, which was brought in by another wildcatter, Columbus M. Joiner. Hunt's total financial commitment included $30,000 in cash, $45,000 in notes, and $1.3 million in future production, an example of one of his innovations in oil financing. The Daisy Bradford proved to be the discovery well of the enormous East Texas Field, which was 45 miles long and between 9 and 12 miles wide and at the time of its discovery was the largest oil field in the world. The oil wells owned by Hunt in this field and elsewhere in Texas, Louisiana, and Arkansas continued to produce, and during the Second World War they alone provided more oil and gas than all of the enemy production combined.

By 1944, under the impetus of wartime demand, Hunt began wildcatting in an area where other authorities had decided there could be no significant quantities of oil, and he promptly brought in the Gilbertown Field in southwestern Alabama, which was so productive that he felt called upon to build a special refinery in Tuscaloosa to handle the production of the new field. During the balance of his active career, Hunt continued his wildcatting while broadening his business activities into twenty-four ventures. His oil holdings made him the largest independent operator in the world. Among his enterprises were Hunt Oil Co., the basic entity, which evolved from the original Hunt Production Co. Another Hunt family entity was Placid Oil Co., which evolved from the original H. L. Hunt, Inc. Other Hunt operations included Tenable Oil Co, Penrod Drilling Co., Panola Pipe Line Co., Parade Gasoline Co., HLH Medical Center Drugs, HLH Products, and HLH Aloe Vera Cosmetics. While he built a small refinery, Hunt never attempted to compete with the corporate giants of the oil industry with their vast complexes of refineries, distribution systems, and chains of service stations. His preference was to drill for oil and to sell it to them, chiefly as crude oil.

When the great East Texas Field, beginning with the Daisy Bradford No. 3, came in, the country was at the beginning of the national economic depression of the 1930s, and the demand for oil was low. In order to provide work for as many hands as possible during that difficult time, Hunt initiated a new policy in his operation. The prevailing practice was to hire two 12-hour shifts on drilling rigs that operated twenty-four hours a day. Hunt increased the hourly wage by 10 percent and doubled his work force by running his rigs with four 6-hour shifts. Other oil companies followed his example, with the result that many workers who would otherwise have been idle were able to work. Ultimately, in the later years of the depression, many operators in the construction industry also adopted this means of spreading the available work time among larger numbers of employees.

While he valued his privacy, Hunt began to take an interest in political and social affairs after the Second World War, and his first major project was a one-man campaign to encourage the passage and ratification of the amendment to the United States Constitution that limited the presidency to a maximum of two consecutive terms for any president. Although this amendment, the twenty-second, was passed by both houses of the Congress in 1947, by 1951 twelve additional state ratifications were required to secure its final passage. Acting on the premise that few amendments were adopted if more than three or four years elapsed without ratification, Hunt mounted a personal campaign, speaking in public for the first time in his life and enlisting the aid of friends in various states to secure ratification of the amendment by its acceptance by the twelve additional states required. His efforts were successful. Indiana, Montana,

1911 Hunt goes to Arkansas to begin trading cotton lands.

1921 Hunt sees his first oil well.

1924 Hunt sells half-interest in 40 wells for $600,000.

1944 Hunt discovers a productive oil field in Alabama.

1951 Hunt founds Fact Forum.

1964 Hunt begins writing the column Hunt for Truth.

Idaho, New Mexico, Wyoming, Arkansas, Georgia, Tennessee, Texas, North Carolina, and Utah each ratified; and finally, the twelfth state, Nevada, joined in February, 1951, to make the amendment a part of the Constitution.

It was also in 1951 that Hunt decided that the general public should have available to it a more rounded presentation of divergent political and philosophical views than then seemed to him to be available. With the idea of creating greater involvement in public affairs on the part of the citizenry at large, he founded Fact Forum in that year. At first a sort of town meeting type of **forum**, the movement became a regular radio presentation and in June, 1953, a television program. A wide variety of public figures, reflecting every aspect of political and social opinion, were eager to appear on these programs, including such people as John F. Kennedy, then a congressman from Massachusetts; Estes Kefauver, a senator from Tennessee; other members of the Congress; and Louis Budenz, one-time editor in chief of the *Daily Worker*, the news organ of the Communist party of the United States. Some twelve Democratic governors and a similar number of Republican governors also participated in the program at various times.

forum: a assembly for discussing issues.

While Hunt never involved himself in oil exploration outside North America, he made one attempt to seek oil abroad. It was not successful. He took a trip around South America in the late 1950s, however, and returned with the conviction that in too many cases the populations of Latin American countries had relinquished their freedom of choice in political affairs in favor of the establishment of dictatorships. He expressed his thoughts on this question in a book in the form of a novel entitled *Alpaca*, which he published privately in 1960 as an inexpensive paperback. Its setting was a fictional Latin American country, and in the book Hunt included a constitution, which he maintained was inserted merely for the purpose of encouraging the inhabitants of emerging nations to seek to govern themselves rather than succumb to the easier path of dictatorship. The constitution was widely reprinted and was translated into a number of foreign languages, and it was widely criticized in this country and abroad. Hunt always felt that such criticism of the document, taken out of its total context of the entire book, was unfair and unjustified.

In 1964 he began writing the column "Hunt for Truth," which appeared both daily and weekly in more than eighty newspapers in this country. He continued writing the column until his death. In 1964 Hunt produced another book, *Why Not Speak*, a handbook for public speakers, and in the course of the next few years he wrote and published *Fabians Fight Freedom* (1964), *Hunt for Truth* (1965), *Weekly Strength* (1967), and *Hunt Heritage* (1973). Throughout his writings and speeches Hunt expressed views that were characterized by some of his contemporaries as conservative but which he preferred to call constructive. He considered himself first of all a patriot, and his general philosophy stressed the importance of freedom of the individual. He was a determined defender of individual rights, including property rights, and a determined opponent of communism. He was opposed to some of the findings of the Supreme Court of the United States, particularly during the chief justiceship of Earl Warren; he opposed any tendency toward deficit financing by the federal government or toward the growth of the federal bureaucracy. He was against disarmament, and he distrusted the United Nations.

Hunt increased the hourly wage by ten percent and doubled his work force by running his rigs with four 6-hour shifts.

Hunt's religious affiliation was with First Baptist Church, Dallas, Texas, and in politics he was a registered Democrat, although his political philosophy involved him actively in the affairs of both parties. In 1952, for example, he supported the candidacy of Douglas MacArthur as a Republican nominee for the presidency, but he eventually gave his support to Dwight D. Eisenhower through his two administrations. He supported Lyndon B. Johnson for the Democratic presidential nomination in 1960. Hunt attended the Democratic convention of that year and supported its nominee, John F. Kennedy. In 1964 he attended both the Republican and Democratic conventions, and in 1968 he attended the Republican convention to urge support for Gerald R. Ford, a congressman from Michigan, as a presidential nominee in preference to Richard M. Nixon. Although he was sympathetic toward the policies of George Wallace, then governor of Alabama, he could not support Wallace's presidential aspirations as he did not believe in any third-party movement.

Hunt enjoyed playing checkers, and he was seriously interested in the health-food movement and opposed the use of refined sugar, bleached four, and saturated fats. He also took an interest in the practice of yoga. He was married twice; (1) in Lake Village, Arkansas, November 26, 1914, to Lydia, daughter of Nelson Waldo and Sarah Rebekah Hunnicutt (Kruse) Bunker of that place, and by this marriage had six children: Haroldson Lafayette; William Herbert, who married Galatyn Hill; Caroline, who married Hugo William line Lewis; and Lamar, who married Norma Knobel; his first wife died in 1955; (2) in Dallas, Texas, November 24, 1957, to Ruth, daughter of Walter Lee and Grace Collins (Sims) Ray of Idabel, Oklahoma, and by this marriage had four children: Ray Lee, who married Nancy Ann Hunter; Ruth June; Helen LaKelley, who married Randall Arthur Kreiling; and Swanee Grace, who married Mark Anthony Meeks. H. L. Hunt died in Dallas on November 24, 1974. ◆

Huntington, Collis Potter

1821–1900 ● MERCHANT & RAILROAD BUILDER

A day in the gold fields convinced Huntington that he could make money more easily in business.

Collis P. Huntington began his business career at the age of 15 as a New York peddler. He was a shrewd trader and built up his cash reserve to the point at which he could set up partnership with a brother in the largest store in Oneonta, New York. In 1849, Huntington made the long trip to California with the gold rushers; he traveled by way of Panama. A day in the gold fields convinced him that he could make money more easily and more certainly in business than by prospecting, so he began to trade in Sacramento as a general merchant. This was a prosperous time and Huntington made a great deal of money, but his chance for a vast fortune came in railroading. There was an obvious need for a transcontinental railroad, and, during the early 1860s. Huntington fell in with a group of men who organized and began the Central Pacific Railroad. Huntington became the financing wizard of the group, for he went to New York and arranged to borrow enough money to get the operation started. He continued to finance construction of the line and became one of its principal owners. One of his partners was Leland Stanford, who became governor of California in 1861.

Huntington acted as Central Pacific's lobbyist in Washington, and also as lobbyist for the Southern Pacific, a railroad organization created by his associates and himself which cornered the rail routes from California to Texas and Louisiana. Huntington fought to prevent Federal government aid being given to any competitors, and to block any laws that might limit the kinds of action the railroad interests chose to take. ◆

Huntington, Henry Edwards

1850–1927 ● RAILROAD EXECUTIVE

During the first two decades of the twentieth century, Henry Edwards Huntington, urban entrepreneur, railroad executive, and book and art collector, played a key role in the physical configuration, economic expansion, and cultural climate of southern California His name remains prominent in the Los Angeles basin—Huntington Beach, the Huntington Hotel, and the Huntington Library—but his significance as the region's de facto regional planner is often overlooked.

Born in Oneonta, New York, Huntington was educated in public and private schools. At the age of 17, he went to work in a local hardware store. In 1871, his uncle, railway magnate Collis P. Huntington, employed the young man to manage a sawmill, and thus began their close, thirty-year business association. Huntington moved rapidly through a number of positions in his uncle's various railway enterprises and became a highly skilled railroad manager. When blocked by stockholders from following his deceased uncle as president of the Southern Pacific Railroad in 1900, Huntington used his experience and vast inheritance to create his own business empire in southern California.

Undoubtedly, Huntington's close ties to his uncle were instrumental in his business career, but they were also important in shaping his personal life. In 1873, he married Mary Alice Prentice, the sister of his uncle's adopted daughter, and the couple had four children. Divorced in 1906, he married his uncle's widow, Arabella Duval Huntington, in 1913.

Once in Los Angeles, Huntington invested large amounts of his personal fortune into three related businesses important for urban growth: street railways, real estate development, and electric-power generation and distribution. With these three companies, Huntington dominated regional development. His street railways (the Los Angeles Railway and the Pacific Electric) held a near monopoly over the basin's public transportation; by 1910, Huntington trolley systems stretched over nearly thirteen hundred miles of southern California. His real-estate holdings, largely concentrated in the northeastern portion of Los Angeles County, made him one of the area's largest landowners. And by 1913, his Pacific Light and Power Company, besides providing electricity to his streetcars, supplied 20 percent of the power needs in the city of Los Angeles.

Because Huntington operated at a time when local planning commissions had little regulatory power, he acted, in effect, as the area's metropolitan planner. By building trolley lines where and when he wanted, he determined the physical layout of the area. Then, as a large-scale subdivider, he dictated the socio-economic mix of many suburbs.

Huntington further encouraged development in southern California through his involvement in local agriculture,

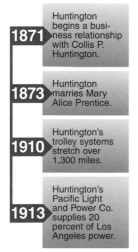

1871 Huntington begins a business relationship with Collis P. Huntington.

1873 Huntington marries Mary Alice Prentice.

1910 Huntington's trolley systems stretch over 1,300 miles.

1913 Huntington's Pacific Light and Power Co. supplies 20 percent of Los Angeles power.

The Huntington Library, Art Collections, and Botanical Gardens

Henry Edwards Huntington was one of the country's most prominent collectors of rare books and artworks. In 1919, Huntington and his wife Arabella bequeathed their library, art collections, and gardens to a non-profit educational trust, thereby creating the Hunting Library, Art Collections, and Botanical Garden, which today hosts over 500,000 visitors and scholars each year. Three art galleries and a library set amidst 207 acres of gardens in San Marino, California, showcase the Huntington holdings. The Huntington is one of the largest research libraries in the United States with about 4 million books, manuscripts, prints, photographs, and maps ranging from 3500 BCE to the present. The library boasts an impressive collection of rare books and manuscripts in the fields of British and American literature and history. Holdings include the earliest known manuscript of Chaucer's *Canterbury Tales* (ca. 1410), a Gutenberg Bible (ca. 1455), several of Shakepeare's original folios and quartos, Benjamin Franklin's handwritten autobiography, and a double-elephant folio edition of Audubon's *Birds of America*. The library also holds many rare books on science and maritime history. The Huntington Art Collections feature British and French art of the 18th and 19th centuries, including a fine collection of 18th centuries portraits. Masterpieces of the collection include the familiar Blue Boy (ca. 1770) by Thomas Gainsborough and Pinkie (1794) by Thomas Lawrence. The extensive Huntington Botanical Gardens include a 12-acre desert garden, a Japanese garden, lily ponds, camellia gardens, and jungle gardens.

industry, the hotel business, and many leading social and civic groups. To enrich and foster the region's intellectual and cultural life, he established the now famous Huntington Library, Art Collections, and Botanical Gardens in San Marino, a wealthy suburb northeast of downtown Los Angeles. ◆

Ilfeld, Charles

1847–1929 ● WHOLESALE MERCHANT

The founder of the largest wholesale merchandise business in New Mexico, Charles Ilfeld immigrated to New York from Hamburg, Germany, at the age of 18. He left for New Mexico almost immediately after landing and worked for Adolph Letcher in Taos as a clerk in a new company, A. Letcher and Company, formed to purchase grain for the surrounding military posts. When the company moved to Las Vegas, New Mexico, Ilfeld became a partner, and after his marriage to Adele Nordhaus in 1874, he bought out his partner and began to expand his wholesale operations.

In 1883, Ilfeld brought his wife's younger brother, Max Nordhaus, from Germany to serve as an apprentice, and four years later, Nordhaus and Ilfeld became partners. When the railroad came to New Mexico, Ilfeld and Nordhaus concentrated on sheep and wool, financed inventories of country stores, and extended them credit. The company assumed aspects of commercial banking—accepting deposits, paying interest, and introducing a check-writing system. Country stores established in El Monton de Alamos, Tecolate, La Junta, and Springer in the 1870s had disappointing financial returns, but by the 1890s, Ilfeld and Nordhaus controlled successful stores at Puerto de Luna, Liberty, and Tucumcari and directly invested in stores at Fort Sumner, Pastura, and Corona. In the twentieth century, Ilfeld's warehouses and country stores blanketed New Mexico.

Throughout his career, Ilfeld, a Jewish American, enjoyed tremendous respect from the Anglo community and the Spanish dons of New Mexico. He served as postmaster in Tiptonville after 1876. He was a member of the board of

> Ilfeld, a Jewish American, enjoyed tremendous respect from the Anglo community and the Spanish dons of New Mexico.

129

regents of the Normal School in Las Vegas, and when his wife died, he gave the campus a building and auditorium in her name. ◆

Jobs, Steven Paul

1955–PRESENT ● COMPUTER DEVELOPER

> *"I'm convinced that about half of what separates the successful entrepreneurs from the non-successful ones is pure perseverance."*
>
> Steve Jobs, 1995

Steven Paul Jobs was born on February 24, 1955, orphaned, and raised by adoptive parents, Paul and Clara Jobs. Steve's adopted father was a machinist at Spectra-Physics. When Steve was 5, he moved with his parents to Palo Alto, California, because his father had been transferred. It was from his father that Steve acquired his first interest in mechanical things and electronics.

Steve was 12 when he saw his first computer at Hewlett-Packard. The company had invited a group of schoolchildren to the plant for lectures and some hands-on practice. The experience left Jobs in awe of the device and he wanted one of his own. Several months later, Steve phoned directly to William Hewlett, co-founder of Hewlett Packard, to ask for some help in building a frequency counter, a device used to measure the speed of electronic impulses, for a school project. Hewlett provided Steve with some parts. He also offered him a job for the summer after his high school freshman year, putting screws in frequency counters at Hewlett-Packard.

Steve Jobs was 16 when he met his eventual business partner, Stephen Wozniak, then 21. Both had a gift for putting
technology to lighthearted uses. One idea they marketed was
a "blue box" that permitted its users to make long-distance
telephone calls free. They sold about 200 boxes and then
stopped producing them, as it bordered on the illegal. Jobs
further developed his business skills in high school, fixing
stereos and selling them to classmates.

In 1972, Jobs graduated from Homestead High School in
Cupertino, California. That fall he went to Reed College in
Portland, Oregon, but dropped out during the second semester. He stayed around campus for another year, attending
classes occasionally and reading a good deal about Eastern
religions. He left Reed College for good in early 1974. He
then returned home and got a job as a video game designer for
Atari. Jobs worked at night, and Wozniak often came by to
play with the company's video games.

The introduction of the Altair microcomputer had led to
the formation of computer clubs all over the country. The
turning point in Jobs's life came when he began dropping by
the Homebrew Computer Club, an organization of computer
enthusiasts in Silicon Valley. Wozniak, a founding member of
Homebrew, had been designing calculators at Hewlett-
Packard during this time.

In 1975, Wozniak and Jobs started building their own
microprocessor-based computer. They used an 8-bit 6502
microprocessor designed by MOS Technology. The computer
consisted of only a printed circuit board without a keyboard,
case, memory, or power supply. It could, however, be used for
developing programs, playing games, and running BASIC lan-
guage programs. The computer was called the Apple I. Jobs
and Wozniak set up a partnership, Apple Computer, Inc., to
market the product. All told, they sold about 175 Apple I
computers for $500 each, netting about half that sum in prof-
it. (The retail price of the Apple I was $666.66.)

In 1977, Jobs and Wozniak went on to develop a more
sophisticated computer, the elegant-looking Apple II. This
computer had a sleek, lightweight, beige plastic case; the keyboard and computer merged in a modular design. The $1,350
Apple II weighed 12 pounds and was easy to use. It became
known as the Volkswagen of computers. Two milestones in
Apple history are especially noteworthy. One was the

announcement in the summer of 1978 of the availability of a disk drive, which provided faster, more efficient access to the computer's memory. The second milestone was the arrival of the spreadsheet program called VisiCalc. It was at first available exclusively on Apple II computers, beginning in October 1979, and sold for only $100. By September 1980, more than 130,000 Apple II computers had been sold. By the end of 1983, 6 years after its incorporation, Apple Computer had almost 4,700 employees and $983 million in sales.

In January 1984, Apple Computer announced the Macintosh computer. This was Steve Jobs's electronic baby. He shaped it, nourished it, and pampered it into life. Working on the Macintosh project was the most exciting and absorbing thing Jobs had ever done. The Macintosh became one of the most exciting and easy-to-use computers of all time.

In September 1985, after a management disagreement with Apple president John Sculley, Jobs's resigned as chairman of Apple Computer. He established a new firm, called NeXT, Inc. His plan was to market a sophisticated "scholar's workstation" for under $10,000 to universities and colleges.

In 1988, after 3 years of secretive designing and building, Jobs unveiled the NeXT computer system. The machine, which sold for $6,500, was so sophisticated it could animate almost lifelike three-dimensional images. It was as easy to use as a personal computer, but as powerful as workstations used by scientists and engineers that cost twice as much.

But the NeXT computer system did not succeed in the market. As a result, NeXT changed its name to NeXT Software Inc. in 1993, and the company began to concentrate on software. In 1996, 11 years after Jobs's departure, Apple Computer bought NeXT Software Inc. for $400 million and hired Jobs as an advisor. Apple planned to create a new operating system by combining NeXT and Apple software. ◆

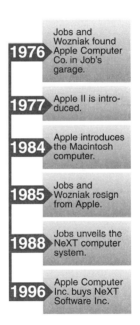

1976 Jobs and Wozniak found Apple Computer Co. in Job's garage.

1977 Apple II is introduced.

1984 Apple introduces the Macintosh computer.

1985 Jobs and Wozniak resign from Apple.

1988 Jobs unveils the NeXT computer system.

1996 Apple Computer Inc. buys NeXT Software Inc.

Johnson, John Harold

1918–PRESENT ● PUBLISHER

J ohn H. Johnson rose from a humble origin to found the country's largest African-American publishing empire and become one of the wealthiest men in the United States. Johnson was the only child of Leroy Johnson and Gertrude Jenkins Johnson and was reared in the Mississippi River town of Arkansas City. His father was killed in a sawmill accident when young Johnny (the name with which he was christened) was 8 years old. The following year, 1927, his mother married James Williams, who worked a bakery shop deliveryman.

Because the public school curriculum for blacks in Arkansas City terminated at the eighth grade and because Johnson and his mother had heard of greater opportunities in Chicago, they became part of African-American migration to that city in 1933. Johnson enrolled in DuSable High School and proved himself an able student. Perhaps the crucial event in his life occurred when he delivered an honors convocation speech heard by Harry H. Pace, president of the Supreme Liberty Life Insurance Company.

Pace, who often helped talented black youths (among them Paul Robeson), encouraged Johnson to attend college. Pace gave Johnson a part-time job at the insurance company that enabled his protégé to attend the University of Chicago. But Johnson's interest focused on the impressive operations of the black-owned insurance firm, and he eventually dropped his university studies, married Eunice Walker in 1941, and assumed full-time work at Supreme Liberty Life.

Among Johnson's duties at Supreme Liberty Life was to collect news and information about black Americans and prepare a weekly digest for Pace. Johnson thought that such a "Negro digest" could be marketed and sold. In 1942 he parlayed a $500 loan using his mother's furniture as collateral to publish the first issue of *Negro Digest*, a magazine patterned after *Reader's Digest*. Although there were format similarities between the two publications, Johnson noted in his 1989 autobiography, *Succeeding Against the Odds*, that *Reader's Digest* tended to be upbeat whereas *Negro Digest* spoke to an audience that was "angry, disillusioned and disappointed" with social equalities in the United States. Within eight months *Negro Digest* reached $50,000 a month in sales.

In 1945 Johnson launched his second publication, *Ebony*, using the format made popular by the major picture magazine *Life*. Central to his philosophy was the concept that African Americans craved a publication that would focus on black achievement and portray them in a positive manner. Six years later he created *Jet*, a pocket-sized weekly carrying news, society, entertainment, and political information pertinent to African Americans. In ensuing years Johnson added other enterprises to his lucrative empire, including new magazine ventures, book publishing, Fashion Fair cosmetics, several radio stations, and majority ownership of Supreme Liberty Life Insurance Company.

Despite the wide range and diversity of his business holdings, Johnson admitted his management style to be hands-on and direct, with every detail of operations requiring his personal approval. While tasks may be delegated, Johnson believes that his staff requires daily monitoring and oversight to ensure performance. Although he named his daughter, Linda Johnson Rice, president and chief operating officer in the late 1980s, he clearly remained in charge but asked "her opinion on decisions I plan to make."

By 1990 Johnson's personal wealth was estimated at $150 million. He has been a confidant of several U. S. presidents of both political parties and served as a goodwill ambassador to various nations throughout the world, including Eastern Europe and Africa. ◆

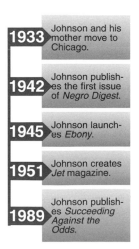

1933 Johnson and his mother move to Chicago.

1942 Johnson publishes the first issue of *Negro Digest*.

1945 Johnson launches *Ebony*.

1951 Johnson creates *Jet* magazine.

1989 Johnson publishes *Succeeding Against the Odds*.

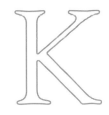

Kaiser, Henry J.

1882–1967 ● CONSTRUCTION
CONTRACTOR

> *"Problems are only opportunities in work clothes."*
>
> Henry J. Kaiser

A native of rural New York, Henry J. Kaiser left school at the age of 13 to help support his family. An energetic man who for most of his life worked eighteen to twenty hours a day, Kaiser was living in Washington State and working for a gravel and cement dealer by 1913. When a Canadian client, a road-building company, went out of business, Kaiser borrowed money to take over the company's project, and he turned a quick profit. From 1914 to 1926, he built dams in California, **levees** in Mississippi, and highways and bridges throughout the Pacific Northwest and along the West Coast. In 1926, he branched out to Cuba, where he constructed some two hundred miles of roads and highways around the island by 1930.

levee: a bank built to prevent flooding.

When the Bureau of **Reclamation** let bids for the construction of the massive Boulder Dam (now Hoover Dam) as part of the New Deal's bold foray into public works, Kaiser regarded the chance to build the dam as a key to large-scale industrial development in the West and an opportunity for

reclamation: the process of recovering unusable land.

Westerners to declare economic independence from the East. He argued that Western contractors should combine their resources to take on what at that time was the world's largest construction venture, and he reasoned that, should they do so, they would pick up lucrative contracts sure to follow. Thus the Six Companies—a consortium of mostly little known Western construction companies incorporated in 1931—won the contract and made some $10 million in profit from the $50 million paid out by the bureau. True to Kaiser's predictions, Boulder Dam launched the Six Companies (Bechtel and Kaiser and MacDonald and Kahn in San Francisco; Morrison Knudsen Corporation in Boise, Idaho; Utah Construction Company in Salt Lake City; and J. F. Shea and the Pacific Bridge Corporation of Portland, Oregon) on a path that would lead individual contractors to become multinational giants and that would mark the birth of the basic **infrastructure** of the modern American West. Working sometimes as a group, sometimes in smaller combinations, sometimes individually, but almost always with the Bureau of Reclamation, the Six Companies won contracts for building both the Bonneville and Coulee dams on the Columbia River and for numerous other projects. When they barely lost out in the bidding for California's Shasta Dam, Kaiser immediately came back with the lowest bid for cement for its construction, even though he did not own a cement plant. When he got the job, he built a mammoth cement plant at Permanente, California, and met the terms of the contract.

infrastructure: the underlying foundation of a system.

With the help of the New Deal's favored banker, Amadeo Peter Giannini, whose Bank of America had backed Kaiser from the beginning, Kaiser guided the Six Companies in Washington, D.C. He became one of the more savvy business operators in the nation's capital and spent his long workdays assiduously cultivating New Deal officials. When World War II broke out, Kaiser saw yet another chance to promote what he called "higher industrialization"—that is, the use of the Federal Government to spur Western development. Having made a fortune using the federal government to help him build the West's infrastructure, he now made a second one using the government to help him build the manufacturing industries that infrastructure made possible. At the beginning of the war, with an enormous $45 million line of credit from Giannini, Kaiser and his associates went into shipbuilding,

1914 ▶ Kaiser begins building dams and bridges along the West Coast.

1926 ▶ Kaiser begins building roads in Cuba.

1961 ▶ Kaiser sells the Hawaiian Village resort to Hilton.

1965 ▶ AFL-CIO presents Kaiser the Murray-Green Award.

first securing a contract to produce thirty ships for England, then supplying the United States. The government provided him with the capital he needed to build ships and hire workers and loaned him $150 million for a steel mill in Fontana, California. Using the new facility, the Pacific Coast's first completely integrated iron and steel plant, Kaiser developed prefabrication techniques that allowed him to turn out ships at an incredible rate in his seven new shipyards, six on the West Coast, one on the Atlantic. In less than four years, Kaiser built 1,490 ships; at his Richmond, California, shipyard, he produced a 10,500-ton Liberty ship in four days and fifteen hours; at the peak of production, his yards launched a new vessel every ten hours. By the end of the war, the federal government had sunk $5 billion into shipbuilding in California alone; employment in San Francisco's shipyards had expanded from four thousand to more than a quarter-million jobs; Kaiser's shipbuilding empire stretched from San Francisco Bay to the Columbia River; and the press was calling the rotund industrialist, cheerfully ensconced in his Oakland, California, headquarters, "Sir Launchalot."

Wartime pressures had allowed Kaiser and the government bureaucrats who worked with him to redefine the basic relationship between government and business in the American West. Government put up the capital for creating an industry; Kaiser (and other corporate leaders) provided the organization and the management—the "brains," Kaiser said—that made the new corporations successful. What had worked for him in concrete and steel, also worked in magnesium and, after the war, in aluminum. During the war, the New Deal Reconstruction Finance Corporation loaned him $20 million to finance Permanente Metals, which produced magnesium for bombs and planes, and after the war, the government sold him at bargain-basement rates its Columbia aluminum plants, which he used to launch his Kaiser Aluminum Company. He suffered perhaps his only major failure immediately after the war with an ill-advised venture into auto making. By the mid-1950s, however, he had spread his empire to Hawaii, where he constructed the Hawaiian Village resort center, which he sold to the Hilton hotel chain in 1961.

Fortune Magazine snipped that, having learned of the money to be made from federal contracts, Kaiser simply

> Kaiser pioneered comprehensive medical coverage for workers under the Permanente Foundation, later renamed the Kaiser Foundation.

"backed a truck up to the mint," and some accused Kaiser (and Giannini) of being responsible for California's economic "colonizing" of other Western states. Kaiser's workers, however, loved him. During the war, he sent labor recruiters around the country, chartered trains to bring workers to the West, and paid them even before they went to work just to make sure they were available. He promised (and delivered) high wages, housing, and medical care. He pioneered comprehensive medical coverage for workers under the Permanente Foundation, later renamed the Kaiser Foundation, by producing the country's first health maintenance organization, or HMO, which became a model for federal programs in the late twentieth century. In 1965, two years before his death, he became the first industrialist to receive organized labor's highest honor when the AFL-CIO bestowed on him its Murray-Green Award. ◆

Kellogg, Will Keith

1860–1951 ● BREAKFAST CEREAL MAGNATE

Will Keith Kellogg was born in Battle Creek, Michigan, on April 7, 1860. He was the son of John Preston and Ann Jeannette (Stanley) Kellogg. His first paternal American ancestor was Joseph Kellogg, who came to this country from England in 1654 and lived successively in Farmington, Connecticut, and Boston before settling in Hadley, Massachusetts. From Joseph and his wife, Joanna, the descent was through Nathaniel and Sarah Boltwood, Nathaniel and Sarah Preston, Gardner and Thankful Chapin, and Josiah and Hannah Smith, the grandparents of Will K. Kellogg.

Kellogg received a scanty public school education, which he supplemented with a four-month course in Parson's Business College, Kalamazoo, Michigan, in 1879, against the wishes of his parents. As a youth he worked part-time and later full-time in his father's broom factory in Battle Creek,

W. K. Kellogg with family and friends.

and he spent one year as superintendent of a new broom factory in Texas. His older brother, John H. Kellogg, a physician, in 1876 founded the Battle Creek Sanitarium, and in 1880 Kellogg became associated with him in this enterprise as business manager of the institution. For more than two decades he was involved in the sanitarium's rise to prominence. He was also business manager of the Sanitas Nut Food Company, which was established by his brother to manufacture numerous health foods developed at the sanitarium; supervised the charity activities of the sanitarium: directed the business affairs of the Modern Medicine Publishing Company, which published his brother's numerous books and other writings; and conducted numerous experiments in new health foods. As an outcome of these experiments the first successful flaked cereal was developed in 1896, the result of a search for a more digestible bread. This product, a wheat flake, found immediate acceptance as a food and at the turn of the century forty-two different brands of wheat flakes were offered for sale in the Battle Creek area alone, its manufacture not having been limited to one company.

Meanwhile, Kellogg began experimenting with the flaking of corn, and his cornflakes were first marketed by the Sanitas Nut Food Company about 1901, and by 1905 had developed into a substantial mail-order business, particularly

Kellogg's wheat flake, developed in 1896, found immediate acceptance as food.

"Eat half as much, sleep twice as much, drink three times as much, laugh four times as much, and you will live to a ripe old age."
John Harvey Kellogg

among former sanitarium patients. Recognizing the commercial possibilities of the product, in 1906 Kellogg organized the Battle Creek Toasted Corn Flake Company with assets of $35,000 and became its president. The company was capitalized at $225,000, Kellogg having received $170,000 in stock as the purchase price of his corn-flake rights. He immediately launched an intensive program of newspaper and magazine advertising and, whereas the Sanitas company was producing thirty-three cases a day by November 1905, the new concern was manufacturing 1000 cases a day by July 1906. During the next year this had been increased to nearly 4000 cases a day. Following a disastrous fire in 1907, a new plant was constructed and at that time the company, then capitalized for $1 million, began an immense expansion program.

In 1911 Kellogg purchased the interests of his brother, who preferred to be free to devote his time to the sanitarium and to the founding, with the proceeds of the sale of his stock, of the Betterment Foundation. In December 1922, the Battle Creek Toasted Corn Flake Company was succeeded by the Kellogg Company. Kellogg served as president, with the exception of 1924 and 1929-31, when he was chairman of the board, until October 1939, after which he again served as board chairman until he resigned in May 1946. During those years the original small plant, which employed twenty-five workers, had grown into an international enterprise employing 6000 workers; to the original products were added numerous others, such as Shredded Wheat, Pep, Krumbles, All-Bran, Rice Krispies, and Raisin Bran, and plants were established in Boston, Chicago, Cleveland, Omaha, and Lockport, Illinois; as well as in Manchester, England; London, Ontario, Canada; Sydney, Australia; Spring, South Africa; and Queretero, Mexico. In 1924 the Battle Creek Toasted Corn Flake Company in London, Ontario, was reorganized as the Kellogg Company of Canada Ltd. Three years later the business of the Kaffe Hag Corporation, Cleveland, was acquired, a company that developed the first caffeine-free coffee; that interest was sold in 1937. By the time that Kellogg retired in 1946, the company had annual sales of $80 million.

Kellogg pioneered in introducing many progressive labor relations policies. Early in the company's history he reduced the working day from 10 to 8 hours, and late in 1930, before President Herbert Hoover inaugurated a program for unemployment relief, the 6-hour working day was adopted at the Battle Creek plant, marking an innovation in American industry. Under this plan the plant operated 24 hours a day, with four 6-hour shifts in order to employ additional workmen, and a minimum wage of four dollars a day was set for its more than 2000 employees. Many years prior to the adoption of this plan a nursery for children of women employees was provided, and first aid care for plant injuries and a program of periodic physical examination for employees were provided through the company's health service. Believing that business should be the benefactor of society, Kellogg waited until the profits had accumulated before expending them on philanthropic causes.

In December 1930, he founded the W. K. Kellogg Child Welfare Foundation with an initial gift of $1 million for the purpose of segregating physically and mentally impaired children, remedying their shortcomings, and bringing them to the greatest possible efficiency by the most recent scientific and medical treatment. A year later the name was changed to the W. K. Kellogg Foundation and provisions were made to increase its funds eventually to $50 million. During the Second World War period the foundation expanded its work to national and international fields. Furthermore, at Lake Wintergreen, near Battle Creek, Kellogg developed a bird sanctuary that became the largest and most complete in the world. This sanctuary, covering 700 acres and an experimental farm near Gull Lake was presented by him in 1930 to the Michigan State College of Agriculture and Applied Science, although he retained a deep interest in it and continued to acquire rare birds for it. His own estate at Gull Lake was used during the early part of the Second World War as a U.S. Coast Guard reception center and later was presented to the federal government as an adjunct of the Percy Jones Hospital Center and became known as the army hospital's W. K. Kellogg Annex. Subsequently, the estate was given by the Kellogg Foundation to Michigan State University. His Florida estate at Dunedin Isles was used during the war as an amphibious-tank training station for the U.S. Marine Corps and was sold in 1946.

In 1925, Kellogg established an 800-acre horse-breeding farm in Pomona, CA, and this he presented in 1932 to the University of California along with his herd of registered

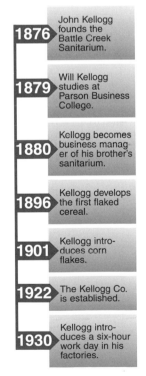

1876 John Kellogg founds the Battle Creek Sanitarium.

1879 Will Kellogg studies at Parson Business College.

1880 Kellogg becomes business manager of his brother's sanitarium.

1896 Kellogg develops the first flaked cereal.

1901 Kellogg introduces corn flakes.

1922 The Kellogg Co. is established.

1930 Kellogg introduces a six-hour work day in his factories.

husbandry: farm management.

Kellogg's products included Shredded Wheat, Pep, Krumbles, All-Bran, Rice Krispies, and Raisin Bran.

Arabian horses and an endowment of $600,000 as a foundation for teaching and research in animal **husbandry**. It became a tourist attraction and during the Second World War was transferred to the U.S. Army for use as a remount station. In 1948 the Army turned the ranch over to the Department of Agriculture. Later an act of congress transferred the ownership of the ranch to the Kellogg Foundation, and subsequently the ranch was deeded to the State of California for use in expanding educational programs of California State Polytechinic College. In Battle Creek he gave funds for the erection of the Ann J. Kellogg School, in memory of his mother, and a summer home, outside the city for underprivileged children. For a grade and high school in Middleville, MI, he contributed one-third of the expenses and the funds for all health facilities. To Battle Creek he also presented a municipal auditorium, a youth center featuring a swimming pool and gymnasium, and an airport. He constructed both the Kellogg Hotel (later Hart Hotel) and the Kellogg Inn (later The Inn), because he felt that such structures were needed by the city, but he later insisted that his name be removed from both.

For years, Kellogg shunned publicity, and he had few social contacts outside of those which came from business and the surveillance of his philanthropies. For some years he was active in the affairs of the Boy Scouts of America, and he was the recipient of the organization's Silver Beaver in 1933. Politically a Republican, he was a member of the eight-man charter commission that drafted the Battle Creek City charter, which was adopted in 1913 and was still in use at the time of his death. He was a member of the Masonic order (Knight Templar, Shriner) and the Athelstan and Rotary clubs of Battle Creek. He devoted much time to worldwide travel. He was married twice: (1) in Battle Creek, November 3, 1880, to Ella Osborn, daughter of Obadiah Davis, also of Battle Creek; they had five children: Karl Hugh; John Leonard; Will Keith; Elizabeth Ann; and Irvin Hadley. Kellogg's first wife died in 1912. And (2) in Grand Rapids, Michigan, January 1, 1918, to Carrie Staines, a physician. Will K. Kellogg died in Battle Creek, Michigan, on October 6, 1951. ◆

Knott, Walter

1889–1981 ● BERRY FARMER

Walter Knott was successful farmer and businessman who popularized the boysenberry and developed the first theme park in the United States, Knott's Berry Farm. He was born on December 11, 1889, in San Bernardino, California, the son of Elgin Columbus Knott and Margaret Virginia Dougherty. His father, a southern Methodist minister, died in 1896 after a train accident and many years of suffering from tuberculosis. The older of two brothers, Walter Knott did his best to help his mother, who worked in a laundry after her husband died. At 7 years old, Walter asked his neighbors if he could grow crops on their vacant lots and give the owners a share of his produce. He attended Pomona High School from 1905 to 1906 but did not graduate. He married Cordelia L. Hornaday, his high school sweetheart, on June 3, 1911. They had four children and later adopted two more; they would remain married until her death in April 1974.

In 1909 Knott acquired his first full-time job, harvesting cantaloupes in the Imperial Valley while fighting mosquitoes and thirst. He **homesteaded** an initial 10 acres in 1911 and by 1917 had bought 160 acres on a spur of the Mojave Desert. As a farmer in Coachella, Knott eliminated the middleman. He picked up orders from Colton, the nearest town on the rail line, and delivered directly to wholesalers and grocers. Native American women worked for him for silver, and his commission man agreed to a fixed price for his produce, evening out the peaks and valleys of supply and demand. Since money was tight, Knott found additional employment as a carpenter, roadworker, and rancher in San Luis Obispo County. Cordelia sold homemade candies to raise money to purchase a car, and together they grew giant cabbages and dwarf Arizona Hopi corn.

In 1919 Knott formed a partnership with his cousin Jim Preston. They rented twenty acres in Buena Park, where they planted berries. The Knotts had a Model T Ford and $2,500 saved from months of **austere** living, which had included eating black-eyed peas flavored with salted pig's jowls. The part-

homestead: to acquire public land as a home.

austere: harsh, simple.

ners were successful with the youngberry, but frosts and sky-rocketing land prices caused Preston to abandon the effort. Knott decided to make every effort, however, to retain his "berry patch." The Knotts could not survive farming in the Mojave so in 1922 they moved to Buena Park; the old homestead and the surrounding areas such as Calico mine later became part of Knott's theme park. Cordelia sold jams and jellies, and their children helped sell rhubarb and flowers to pay the mortgage. The family purchased ten more acres during the Great Depression. At the suggestion of a Department of Agriculture employee, Knott in 1927 contacted Rudolph Boysen concerning a hybrid plant, a blackberry, raspberry, and loganberry combination. Knott was successful with these vines, called boysenberries, which produced berries so large that twenty-five filled a standard half-pound basket.

By 1934 Cordelia Knott had started a successful fried chicken restaurant, while Walter Knott continued his berry production and began a mail order nursery for plants. Knott foresaw that freezing would be a better way of packing fruit than canning. When the local banker denied him a loan to expand his business, Knott decided to proceed alone. By 1937 Knott had a new restaurant, and he turned down the local banker's offer to finance a national chain. Knott continued to buy produce from local farmers and emphasized local motifs with a mural in his restaurant depicting Indian chiefs created by the artist Paul von Klieben. Family settings ruled the day, and the grounds were kept free of litter.

In 1940, inspired by the pioneer stories his grandmother told him of covered wagon travel to the West, Knott built Ghost Town on his farm to capture those scenes. With whistling trains, braying burros, clanging cable cars, and people in costume telling stories, Ghost Town included a Wells Fargo Express, a livery barn, Ghost Town Boot Hill Cemetery, and a blacksmith shop. An irrigation pipe to the town was hidden inside a volcano and a cactus garden, and he moved an old hotel to his property from Prescott, Arizona.

In 1951 Knott turned the old mining town of Calico in the desert between Los Angeles and Las Vegas into a tourist attraction stocked by the real railroad, the Rio Grande Southern, and staffed by former employees of the railroad. There visitors sampled the flavor of the nineteenth century, rode the San Francisco Street Railway's cable cars, and mined

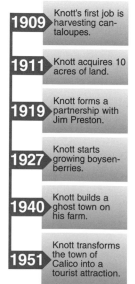

1909 Knott's first job is harvesting cantaloupes.

1911 Knott acquires 10 acres of land.

1919 Knott forms a partnership with Jim Preston.

1927 Knott starts growing boysenberries.

1940 Knott builds a ghost town on his farm.

1951 Knott transforms the town of Calico into a tourist attraction.

The Rise of Theme Parks

The origins of the theme park date back to the late 19th century beach clubs, such as those along Coney Island in Brooklyn, New York, where people drank, socialized, and watched musical productions in pavilions. Mechanical rides were added later and by the 1930s these areas had developed into amusement parks. In 1955, Walt Disney built the first amusement theme park, Disneyland, in California, where he combined fantasy with rides, food, and shows in a safe, clean, family environment. In the 1990s there were ten major types of theme park: multi-theme, such as Disneyland and Six Flags Great Adventure; water theme, such as Water Country USA in Virginia; holiday theme, such as Holiday World in Indiana; imaginary character theme, such as Sesame Place in Pennsylvania; movie theme, such as Universal Studies; musical theme, such as Dollywood in Tennessee; marine life theme, such as Sea World; historic theme, such as Frontier City in Oklahoma; and nature theme, such as Busch Gardens in Florida. The largest theme park is Walt Disney World in Florida.

for gold. When Disneyland opened nearby in 1955, Knott was **sanguine**, seeing competition as healthy. Indeed, as early as 1936 he instituted profit-sharing program for his employees. In 1963 he built a replica of Philadelphia's Independence Hall, complete with a cracked "Liberty" bell. In 1968 he built the Log Ride and, in 1971, the John Wayne Theater, which featured country-western shows and songs. The oldest theme park in the nation, Knott's Berry Farm was attracting more than four million tourists and employing more than 3,000 local workers by the 1980s. Knott's berry-preserves business was also still ongoing at the time of his death, from Parkinson's disease, in Buena Park, California. He is buried at Loma Vista Memorial Park in Fullerton, California.

Knott, a trim, feisty man with blue eyes, believed in himself, in God, and in following his dreams. His dream of farming in the desert, even though he lacked the financial resources for irrigation, was revived in a sense with his Calico Town (he never sold his old desert homestead). He was a pioneer in his love of the soil, in entrepreneurship, and in adapting to changing circumstances. His newsletter to his employees showed his marketing skills based on common sense and a love of people. Knott was known as a spokesman for constitutional rights and conservative causes, influenced by his distrust of big government. Even into his seventies, he worked from early to late, which spoke louder than his trumpeting of free enterprise against government regulations. ◆

sanguine: hopeful, cheerful.

Knott's wife sold jellies and jams, and his children sold rhubarb and flowers to help pay the mortgage.

Kroc, Raymond Albert

1902–1984 ● FOUNDER OF McDONALD'S

> *"It's a matter of having principles. It's easy to have principles when you're rich. The important thing is to have principles when you're poor."*
>
> Ray A. Kroc

Kroc was born in a suburb of Chicago, where his widowed, Bohemian grandmother had settled with her four children, including Ray's father, Louis Kroc, in the early 1890s. To help support the family, Louis Kroc quit school at age 12. Despite his scanty formal education, he made a career as a minor executive in Western Union's subsidiary, the American District Telegraph. He also bought speculative real estate at bargain prices, but he was wiped out in the Great Depression. He died in 1932 of a cerebral hemorrhage at his desk at the Pyramid Vacant Real Estate Company. Ray's mother was Rose Mary Hrach, a piano teacher. Ray was the oldest child, with a brother and a sister, and one of his mother's best piano pupils. She taught him how to perform, which he enjoyed and which provided a source of extra income throughout his early career. Otherwise Kroc was not a highly motivated student. Bored by books, his most vivid memory of his high school days was his success as a debater. He dropped out of Oak Park High School at the end of his sophomore year.

Kroc worked one summer at his uncle's drugstore soda fountain in Oak Park. There he learned "that you could influence people with a smile and enthusiasm and sell them a sundae when they'd come for a cup of coffee." In the summer of

1917, soon after the United States entered World War I, Kroc lied about his age and enlisted in the Red Cross ambulance driver training program, then served overseas. After the armistice in 1918, he returned to Oak Park High School but dropped out again after only one semester. "Algebra," he wryly observed in later years, "had not improved in my absence." He yearned to be a salesman, and although he was still a teenager, he got a job traveling from city to city representing a ribbon novelty firm. On the side, he continued to look for piano "gigs."

In the summer of 1919, Kroc left the ribbon company to take a full-time job playing piano with a dance band at a Michigan resort called the Edgewater. There he met Ethel Fleming, whose parents owned a hotel on the other side of Paw-Paw Lake. Ray and Ethel's summer romance remained warm throughout the next year, and in 1922 they married. They had one child. Ray Kroc got a daytime job selling paper cups for Lily Tulip Company and a night job playing the piano on radio station WGES in Oak Park.

By 1925 Kroc had hit his stride as a salesman, but the paper cup business was traditionally slow in wintertime, and the Florida land boom beckoned him. He took a leave of absence from Lily, piled Ethel, her sister, and his baby into a new Model T Ford, and headed for the Sunshine State, where he quickly found employment with a real estate firm in Fort Lauderdale. His specialty consisted of rounding up wintertime tourists from the Chicago area. He showed them building lots still under water that were to be raised to the surface with earth dredged from the then uncompleted inland waterway. A "closer" lurked nearby to collect $500 deposits from the convinced.

When the Florida real estate boom turned to bust after a hurricane in 1926, Kroc found a job playing piano in a plush Miami nightclub. But Ethel and their daughter stayed home alone every night, and soon Kroc realized that his young family had to return to Chicago. He sent them ahead by train and set out alone in the Model T, traveling over primitive roads in miserable weather.

In 1926 Kroc returned to the Lily Tulip paper cup company and in time became the Midwest sales manager. His strong point was innovation. He persuaded Walgreen, the Midwest's foremost drugstore chain, to introduce take-out food service

1919 Kroc takes a job playing piano for a dance band.

1926 Kroc becomes Midwest sales manager of Lily Tulip paper company.

1941 Kroc founds Prince Castle Multimixer Co.

1955 Kroc charters McDonald's System Inc.

1955 The first McDonald's franchise opens in Des Plaines, Illinois.

1965 McDonald's Corporation goes public at $22.50 per share.

1972 Kroc receives the Horatio Alger Award.

1974 Kroc buys the San Diego Padres.

In the 1950s, the idea of going out as a family to enjoy an inexpensive dinner became attractive to million of parents with cars.

at its lunch counters, which enabled a drugstore to double the number of lunches sold during the rush hour. It also doubled the number of paper cups that Walgreen bought. Another of Kroc's large Chicago customers was the Prince's Castle chain of ice cream parlors. At Kroc's urging, the owner, Earl Prince, reluctantly introduced a new milk shake formulation that, in Kroc's words, was "a colder and more viscous drink that people preferred to the thin, semi-cool conventional shake." Prince's chain was soon buying a million Lily cups a year from Kroc.

Meanwhile, Prince, who had been trained as a mechanical engineer, perfected a mixing machine that could make five milk shakes simultaneously. Kroc arranged for Lily Tulip to distribute the mixer, and Prince and Lily representatives signed a contract in 1939. When Lily Tulip's parent company in New York rejected the deal, Kroc decided to go ahead on his own. This was not easily accomplished. Securing the right to distribute the new mixer, called the Multimixer, cost him every nickel he could borrow, and he was forced to refinance the mortgage on his house in suburban Arlington Heights, Illinois. According to Kroc, the debt of almost $100,000 and the inherent risks of the new venture were too frightening for Ethel, and they began to drift apart.

Kroc was a superior salesman. His new company, started in 1941 as Prince Castle Multimixer Company and later called the Prince Castle Sales Division, prospered. But when the United States entered World War II, copper, an essential component of the mixer motors, disappeared from the civilian market. So did much of the sugar necessary to make ice cream, the basic ingredient of the drinks produced in the mixers. Kroc survived economically during the war years by finding and offering milk additives, based on corn syrup, that imitated the taste and texture of ice cream. After the war ended, the Multimixer business boomed once again, but not for long. Dairy Queen, Tastee-Freeze, and similar soft ice cream stands came into vogue, and this market had little use for milk shake mixers. Indeed, the world of take-out food changed completely in the late 1940s and early 1950s. Americans were moving to the suburbs, miles away from the drugstore soda fountains and malted milk stands. At the same time, the idea of going out as a family to enjoy an inexpensive dinner became attractive to millions of parents with cars.

Most fast-food outlets required only one or two Multimixers, but Richard ("Dick") McDonald and Maurice ("Mac") McDonald, brothers who owned a hamburger stand in San Bernardino, California, purchased eight, enough to make forty shakes simultaneously. In 1954 Kroc went to San Bernardino to find out why they needed so much capacity. He found a spotlessly clean restaurant. The kitchen gleamed with immaculate stainless steel counters and custom-designed aluminum griddles. Service was swift. In only a minute or two, a customer could receive tasty, freshly grilled hamburger (fifteen cents), crispy french fries (eight cents), and a sixteen-ounce milk shake (twenty cents) or a cup of coffee (a nickel). The stand had no pay phones, no vending machines, no carhops, and no place to "hang out." Nevertheless, customers, mostly young families, flocked to McDonald's. "I was amazed," Kroc said in later years, at "this little drive-in having people standing in line. The sales volume was incredible. . . . If they had a hundred stores like that one, I thought, I could sell them 800 Multimixers."

The McDonald brothers gave Kroc a thorough briefing, including a look at the architect's drawings of a new building surmounted by golden arches. The McDonalds' prior attempts at licensing had been disappointing, but Kroc urged them to franchise their name and unique assembly-line system. When Kroc returned to Chicago, he called Dick McDonald to ask if they were still looking for a franchise agent. "How about me?" Kroc asked.

Kroc's meeting with Dick and Mac McDonald was providential but by no means an accident. Kroc, who was 52 years old and suffered from diabetes and arthritis, needed to close a deal. He later said, "I was just carried away by the thought of McDonald's drive-ins proliferating like rabbits, with eight Multimixers in each one." Kroc was so carried away that he did not even bother to get his own lawyer. The McDonald brothers' attorney wrote the agreement that Kroc signed. It called for a franchise fee of $950 to be paid to Kroc's future company by each new franchisee. Operators were required to copy the San Bernardino store in every detail, including the sign, menu, and architecture. The smallest deviations were to be approved in writing by the McDonald brothers and sent by registered mail. Each franchise remitted 1.9 percent of its gross sales to the franchisor, of which 0.5 percent belonged to

> *"I was just carried away by the thought of McDonald's drive-ins proliferating like rabbits, with eight Multimixers in each one."*
>
> Ray Kroc

"It is ridiculous to call this an industry. This is rat eat rat, dog eat dog. I'll kill 'em, and I'm going to kill 'em before they kill me. You're talking about the American way of survival of the fittest."

Ray Kroc, 1975

Dick and Mac McDonald, who had no other franchising function. Kroc's new franchising company kept the remaining 1.4 percent, which was not enough cash flow to finance growth, as Kroc learned.

On 2 March 1955, Kroc chartered McDonald's System Inc., which was later renamed McDonald's Corporation. On 15 April 1955 he and a golfing friend opened a "model" McDonald's in Des Plaines, Illinois, near Kroc's home. Kroc checked the store at 7:00 each morning before he caught the commuter train to his Multimixer office in downtown Chicago, and he visited it again on his way home. According to Fred Turner, the future McDonald's president who began his career as a grill man in Des Plaines: "Every night you'd see [Kroc] coming down the street, walking close to the gutter, picking up every McDonald's wrapper and cup along the way. He'd come into the store with both hands full." On weekends Kroc, hosed down the parking lot, scrubbed the trash cans, and scraped chewing gum off the concrete.

In 1956 three franchised stores opened in Fresno, Los Angeles, and Reseda, California. It was easier, Kroc discovered, to close deals in California after franchisees visited the successful operation in San Bernardino. Nevertheless, during the last eight months of 1956, Kroc established eight more franchises, only one of which was in California. The most successful early McDonald's was in Waukegan, Illinois, on Lake Michigan north of Chicago. The day after the doors opened, the owner-manager ran out of cash register space for all the dollar bills that flooded in. Kroc publicized those results to attract the type of franchisee he wanted—working- or lower-middle-class family men who would devote their full time to the store.

During his years selling paper cups and milk shake mixers, Kroc studied the emerging fast-food industry closely. He found that most franchisors sought quick income rather than long-lasting, mutually profitable relationships with their dealers. The franchise sellers profited from high license fees and marked-up supplies and foodstuffs that operators were required to buy exclusively from them. Kroc's approach was different. He strove to build up his franchisees rather than exploit them. McDonald's dealers ordered directly from approved suppliers, and McDonald's Systems earned nothing from these transactions.

Kroc was almost indifferent to money. He appeared to enjoy closing a sale more than its fruits. Until 1961, he drew neither salary nor expenses from McDonald's Systems, living on his modest Multimixer sales income alone. He was especially proud of his Hamburger University, which started in the early days of the McDonald's chain in the storeroom of a restaurant and eventually moved in 1983 to a $40 million campus in Elk Grove Village, Illinois. Much more than a public relations effort, it taught new franchise owners how to cook french fries and hamburgers according to McDonald's precise specifications as well as how to keep ledgers. Kroc compared his "university" to Harvard and Stanford, and its graduates became "bachelors of hamburgerology."

By 1957 Kroc had put together a small cadre of first-rate, young operating executives. Although McDonald's appeared poised for rapid growth, from a financial point of view it seemed headed for disaster. The cash flow was inadequate to handle the system's overhead or to generate a profit. Making McDonald's profitable was the achievement of Harry J. Sonneborn, who had scouted Kroc's model store in Des Plaines and foresaw the growth potential of the chain. He resigned a well-paid executive post at TasteeFreeze in 1956 to work for Kroc at a starting salary of only $100 a week.

Sonneborn used a new leaseback system to turn McDonald's into a money machine. His staff selected sites, and restaurants were built and paid for by local real estate investors and their banks. McDonald's agreed in advance to lease the completed restaurants at a flat rent, then subleased them to new franchisees at a rent equivalent to 5 percent of sales or 140 percent of McDonald's rental cost, whichever was greater. The franchise fee, boosted by $550 in 1963, continued to be low. This system made it easier to fund new outlets and enabled Sonneborn to tell potential lenders and investors, who feared the vagaries of the restaurant business, that McDonald's was actually a real estate company.

Kroc's marriage to Ethel had become, in his own words, "a cold war." In 1957 he met Joan Smith, who played the electric organ in a nightclub in Saint Paul, Minnesota. Her husband, Rawley Smith, a railroad engineer, was about to become a McDonald's restaurant manager. In love with Joan, Kroc moved out of his Arlington Heights house and proposed that they both get divorces so they could marry each other. At first

Kroc compared his Hamburger University to Harvard and Stanford, and its graduates became "bachelors of hamburger-ology."

An investor
who paid
$2,250 for 100
McDonald's
shares in 1965
saw the value of
that investment
rise to more
than $400,000
by 1986.

Smith agreed, but under pressure from her mother and her 14-year-old daughter, she backed out. Kroc was devastated.

McDonald's continued to expand. By the end of 1957, 31 restaurants were in operation and by 1960 the number had increased to 228. However, the McDonald brothers' one-sided contract with Kroc remained a major stumbling block. Because the McDonalds never answered Kroc's letters, the "prior approval" clause of the contract was ignored out of necessity, but it hung over Kroc's head like a sword. In 1961 he asked the brothers to name a price for the exclusive right to the unfettered use of the McDonald's name and systems. They demanded $2.7 million in cash. "A million for me, a million for Mac, and $700,000 for Uncle Sam," was the way Dick McDonald put it. Raising so much money seemed impossible at the time, but Sonneborn convinced a group of institutional investors, including Princeton University, to lend Kroc the money.

In the spring of 1962 Kroc, by then divorced, moved to California because his leadership was needed on the booming West Coast, where imitators had slowed McDonald's growth to a trickle. That year he met Jane Dobbins Green, a script assistant to John Wayne. Two weeks later, they married and moved into a large house in Beverly Hills. They had no children. In 1965 Kroc purchased a ranch house in Santa Ynez, California, to use as a conference center for his senior executives.

By 1965 the total number of McDonald's restaurants was almost 700 and growing at the rate of 100 a year. To put some cash in Kroc and Sonneborn's pockets and to create a market for McDonald's stock, the corporation went public on April, 15, 1965, at $22.50 per share. Kroc collected $3 million for the shares he sold at the offering price, but within a day the market price had risen to $30 a share. It quickly soared to nearly $50, and Kroc's remaining shares suddenly had a market value of $32 million. During the next twenty years, McDonald's experienced eight stock splits and one stock dividend. An investor who paid $2,250 for 100 shares in 1965 would have seen the value of that investment rise to more than $400,000 in 1986.

The McDonald's chain made restaurant and stock market history, but Sonneborn, who had become president in 1959, quit in 1967 after a series of bitter disagreements with Kroc. Turner, Kroc's levelheaded and loyal protégé, took over as president. Kroc retained the title of chairman until 1977, when his board named him senior chairman.

In the fall of 1968, Joan Smith and her husband attended a McDonald's convention in San Diego. Somehow, Rawley Smith was sequestered while Kroc and Joan Smith spent the night playing the piano and talking. Once again they agreed to divorce their mates and marry each other. This time they did. On March 8, 1969, they married in the ranch house in Santa Ynez. They had no children.

Kroc attended McDonald's dealer conventions, and his personal charm remained a key factor in the company's growth. A longtime colleague said that Kroc was the most inspiring **extemporaneous** speaker he had ever heard. Kroc was also obsessed with neatness and cleanliness. A former McDonald's executive declared, "When Ray read out an operator with a dirty store, you could hear him six blocks away."

extemporaneous: done without preparation.

In his later years Kroc turned his energies and some of his dollars to other activities. He lectured at Dartmouth College, which gave him an honorary doctorate. He celebrated his seventieth birthday by giving more than $7 million to such Chicago institutions as Children's Memorial Hospital, the Lincoln Park Zoo, and the Harvard Congregational Church in Oak Park, which he had attended as a child. He also gave substantial quantities of McDonald's stock to senior employees. In 1972 Kroc received the Horatio Alger Award from Norman Vincent Peale, the preacher and author. Kroc was hailed for "overcoming obstacles," as the inscription said, "through Diligence, Industry and Perseverance" on his way to a success achieved.

In 1974 Kroc fulfilled his lifelong dream of owning a major league baseball team when he bought the San Diego Padres. His frustrations as a team owner began at the first home game in 1974, during which the Padres made error after error, capped by a horrendous baserunning mistake. Kroc grabbed the stadium announcer's microphone, apologized to the fans, and **berated** the team.

berate: to scold angrily.

In 1976 Kroc established the Kroc Foundation in Santa Ynez to support research in diabetes, arthritis, and multiple sclerosis and placed his younger brother, Robert L. Kroc, an **endocrine** expert, in charge. In 1977 Turner was elected

endocrine: concerning the thyroid, pituitary, and other endocrine glands.

Fast Food in America

The fast-food industry has undergone enormous changes since its humble beginning in 1921 when E.W. Ingram served five-cent hamburgers at his White Castle stand in Wichita, Kansas. Brothers Richard and Maurice McDonald opened the first hamburger drive-in in San Bernardino, California, in 1948; Ray Kroc turned their golden arches into national franchises in 1955, opening his first McDonald's in Des Plaines, Illinois. Soon, fast food outlets spread throughout the country offering doughnuts, pizza, chicken, and tacos. By the early 1990s an estimated 46 million U.S. consumers patronized the nation's 160,000 fast-food restaurants daily. Each person spent an average of $250 a year. Because of an increased workweek and less leisure time, more two-earner families, and a more hurried technological society, the fast-food industry earned $74 billion a year in the early 1990s and provided low-paying service jobs for millions. Indeed, McDonald's replaced the U.S. Army as the nation's largest employer and job trainer, and one of every fifteen workers claimed they entered the work force via a job at McDonald's. The fast-food industry has adapted to changing tastes. In order to cater to health-conscious consumers, many outlets began in the late 1980s to offer items such as lean hamburger and fresh vegetables. In 1991, Kentucky Fried Chicken changed its name to KFC to avoid the word "fried." McDonald's, Wendy's and Burger King all switched from beef tallow to vegetable oil in preparing their french fries. Fast-food outlets also joined environmental groups in efforts to recycle waste. McDonald's abandoned its polystyrene packaging in favor of paper containers and was the largest user of recycled paper in its field. But environmentalists questioned the value of the changeover because McDonald's still generated vast amounts of garbage.

chairman of the McDonald's board, and Kroc assumed the honorary title of senior chairman. In 1979, when the baseball league fined Kroc heavily for a violation of the free agent rules, he became "disgusted" with baseball and, in midseason, placed operating control of the team in the hands of his son-in-law. By 1979 more than 6,000 McDonald's restaurants girdled the globe, and Kroc's personal fortune had grown to more than $500 million. Weakened by arthritis, Kroc died of a cardiac disorder in the Scripps Memorial Hospital in San Diego.

No doubt Kroc's qualities of perseverance and industry were important, but more than anything else his success can be attributed to strong self-dependence and his talents as a salesman. Like many other great salesmen, he was imaginative and willing to take risks. His career demonstrates that it is never too late to succeed. ◆

Lathrop, Austin E. (Cap)

1865–1950 ● BUSINESSMAN

A private businessman who invested his profits in Alaska, Austin E. ("Cap") Lathrop became an advocate of private development in Alaska and was probably the territory's first millionaire.

Born in Lapeer, Michigan, and raised in a farming family, "Cap" Lathrop left home as a teenager after one year of high school. In Seattle at the time of the great fire in 1889, he began a business clearing rubble, an enterprise he developed into a **teamstering** company. He went to the Cook Inlet region of Alaska in 1896 when there was a minor gold rush there. His profitable freighting business allowed him to add general construction to his activities. He married in 1901 (his wife died in 1910, and he never remarried) and moved to the new town of Cordova in 1907 where the Guggenheim Corporation was constructing a railroad to provide access to copper deposits. He served as mayor of Cordova and became an aggressive advocate for private development. He believed that emigrants to Alaska could develop the territory more rapidly without governmental bureaucracy than with government help. In 1911, he participated in and may have led a mob of three hundred men who dumped a shipload of imported coal into the bay at Cordova in protest over the government's refusal to open coal lands for investment and development. In the aftermath of the Klondike Gold Rush, investors clashed with government Progressives who sought to manage economic development in the name of resource conservation and equality of opportunity. Lathrop put himself in the forefront of those urging a return to the unrestricted **laissez-faire** policies of the past.

teamstering: made up of members of a transportation workers union.

laissez-faire: the principle that business should not be regulated.

Lathrop's businesses continued to prosper, and in the early 1920s, he acquired coal lands along the Alaska Railroad in the Nenana region north of Anchorage. He also secured the Alaska franchise for the Olympia Brewing Company of Washington State and joined the company's board of directors.

Unlike many investors, Lathrop stayed in Alaska, rather than relocating elsewhere, and reinvested his earnings in Alaska enterprises. His businesses included movie theaters in Anchorage and Fairbanks, radio and later television stations, and eventually a newspaper, the *Fairbanks News-Miner*. In 1933, he became president of the First Bank of Cordova. During World War II, his companies provided experienced and reliable construction expertise for the unprecedented military buildup.

In the meantime, Lathrop formed a movie company, in 1923, for the filming of *The Cheechakos*, a successful full-length motion picture about the Klondike gold rush

He became involved in politics in the 1920s and served as a territorial legislator for one term and later as a representative to the Republican National Committee. After World War II, he provided leadership and support for forces opposed to Alaska statehood. He believed Alaskans should further develop industry and commerce before undertaking the additional costs and taxation associated with governmental administration. After statehood was achieved in 1958, he continued to develop his enterprises, especially his coal business. He was killed at the age of 85 in a railroad accident while working at his mining properties. ◆

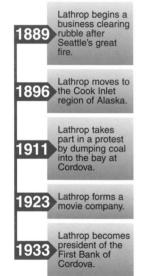

1889 Lathrop begins a business clearing rubble after Seattle's great fire.

1896 Lathrop moves to the Cook Inlet region of Alaska.

1911 Lathrop takes part in a protest by dumping coal into the bay at Cordova.

1923 Lathrop forms a movie company.

1933 Lathrop becomes president of the First Bank of Cordova.

Lay, Herman W.

1909–1982 ● FOOD INDUSTRY TYCOON

Herman Lay was born June 3, 1909, in Charlotte, North Carolina. He was the son of Jesse N. Lay and Bertha Erma Parr. Jesse Lay grew up on a farm and became a farm machinery salesman. His son later recalled how good a salesman his father was, selling "softly and with care. It was a pleasure to watch him because he did it so well." Herman s own first sales experience was when he was 10. The family had moved to Greenville, South Carolina, into a house across the street from the Greenville baseball park. Herman took advantage of the location by setting up a stand to sell soft drinks to fans. He did well and soon hired assistants to help run the stand, bought himself a bicycle, and opened his own bank account.

After graduating from public school, Lay won an athletic scholarship to Furman University in Greenville. He dropped out after two years, in 1928, and worked at a variety of jobs until 1932. By then he had managed to save enough to buy a 1928 Model A Ford, so he seized an opportunity that required a car—the local distributorship covering the Nashville, Tennessee, region for Barrett Food Products Company of Atlanta. He soon had three salesmen working for him.

Despite the impact of the Great Depression, Lay was increasingly successful through the 1930s. In 1934 he created the H. W Lay Distributing Company to handle his sales district. On 28 December 1935 he married Amelia Harper; they had three children. By 1937 he was employing fifteen salesman and the company owned nine delivery trucks and had expanded to serve all of central Tennessee and southern Kentucky. Ironically, Barrett Food Products itself was struggling, so this same year Lay acquired Barrett, its plants in Atlanta and Memphis, and its Gardner's brand name. He followed this up in 1938 with the first product carrying the Lay's name, a french-fried popcorn labeled Lay's Tennessee Valley Popcorn.

In 1939 Lay consolidated his distributing company with Barrett to form the H. W Lay Company, Inc. In 1941 the company became one of the first in the world to produce potato chips with continuous production technology when it installed in its Atlanta plant a Ferry continuous potato chip machine. Lay had also expanded his sales region throughout the Southeast. By 1944 he believed his own brand was well-enough established that he could drop the Gardner's name and market all his snack foods under the Lay's label. He strengthened his product line by introducing new products, including pretzels, and by acquiring an exclusive franchise to manufacture and distribute Fritos brand corn chips in the

"Betcha can't eat just one."
Slogan for Lay's potato chips.

Southeast. (Frito, founded in 1932, was well-established in the West.) In 1956 Lay deepened his link with the Frito company by acquiring the Capital Frito Company of Maryland, which extended his franchise into the Middle Atlantic region.

During these years Lay had earned a reputation as a super salesman, one who persuaded both employees and customers to be enthusiastic about his products. He was also an innovative manager. His firm was among the first southern businesses to create professional personnel and benefit departments, institute formal training programs, and commit itself to providing steady year-round employment.

In 1959 Elmer Doolin, founder of the Frito Company, died. Given Lay's close ties to Frito—which had concentrated on just its corn chips and thus had no products competing with Lay's extensive list—it was natural for H. W Lay to merge with Frito in 1961, creating the Frito-Lay Company, headquartered in Dallas, Texas, with Lay as president and chairman of the board. The merger also permitted Lay's Potato Chips to become the first nationally distributed chip.

By 1963, with thirty-two products now carrying the Frito-Lay name, the company had introduced a new advertising slogan for its Lay's potato chips, "Betcha can't eat just one," and hired actor-comedian Bert Lahr as official company spokesman. Frito-Lay also began developing foreign markets for its products. In 1964 Lay expanded further, acquiring Bell Products and Sevilla, both olive distributors. The company also announced introduction of a new strain of potato, the Monona, which it had developed through its research program. Frito-Lay was also now developing new strains of corn in an effort to enhance its corn chip products.

1928 Lay becomes a distributor for Barrett Food Products Co.

1934 Lay creates the H.W. Lay Distributing Co.

1937 Lay buys Barrett Food Products Co.

1961 H.W. Lay merges with Frito.

1965 Frito-Lay becomes the snack food division of PepsiCo.

1969 Lay receives the Horatio Alger Award.

Frito-Lay was already established as the nation's leading snack food company, with 10,000 store routes nationally, when Lay met Donald Kendall, president of Pepsi Cola, at a grocer's convention in the early 1960s. In 1965 they agreed to merge their companies, creating a new firm, PepsiCo, Inc., with Frito-Lay as the snack food division. Kendall served as president and chief executive officer, Lay as chairman of the board. Over the next few years Frito-Lay introduced a host of new products, including Doritos tortilla chips, Cheetos, and Ruffles. In 1971 Lay moved to the position of chairman of the executive committee; he retired from PepsiCo in 1980. After leaving he started several businesses dealing in real estate, oil and gas exploration, and frozen foods. Two years after retiring, he died of cancer in Baylor Hospital in Dallas. He was buried in Dallas.

Lay received the Horatio Alger Award in 1969. He served as a director for a wide variety of companies, including Duke Power, Wilson Sporting Goods, Third National Bank of Nashville, First National Bank of Dallas, Southwestern Life Insurance Company, and Braniff Airlines. He was a strong advocate for entrepreneurship, a topic on which he gave many public talks. The U.S. Chamber of Commerce, in recognition of his leadership in that area, named its most substantial meeting room in its Washington, D.C., headquarters for him in 1984. Lay also endowed chairs in business administration at Baylor and Southern Methodist Universities. ◆

Lisa, Manuel

1772–1820 ● MERCHANT

The first merchant-capitalist to venture north from St. Louis to the headwaters of the Missouri in search of furs and trade, Manuel Lisa made a number of significant contributions to the development of the West and the nation. Born in New Orleans to Christobal de Lisa and Maria Ignacia Rodriguez of St. Augustine, Florida, Lisa early became a merchant and trader. Aggressive and ambitious, he had, by 1798, established his permanent home in St. Louis, where his principal interest was exploiting the potential wealth of the upper Missouri country.

In 1807, with partners Pierre Menard and William Morrison, Lisa led the first trading and trapping expedition northward. Establishing Fort Raymond at the junction of the Yellowstone and Bighorn rivers, he began operations by sending out explorers, including John Colter, who found the wonders of what is now Yellowstone National Park. Leaving his crew in the mountains, Lisa returned to St. Louis in the spring

> Lisa was the first in the American era to ascend the Missouri River for purposes of trade.

of 1808. There he formed the St. Louis Missouri Fur Company, a partnership including William Clark, Pierre Chouteau, Auguste Chouteau, Jr., Sylvestre Labbadie, Benjamin Wilkinson, Reuben Lewis, and Andrew Henry in addition to himself, Menard, and Morrison. With great expectations, the company sent an expedition upriver in the spring of 1809 only to meet with frustration. Hostile relations with the Blackfoot Indians and insurmountable problems of finance, transportation, and supply intimidated the conservative partners and stifled operations; the partners refused to invest further. Lisa engineered a reorganization of the company in 1812 by turning it into a limited partnership with himself, Labbadie, and Clark as the directors, but limited finances and the impending War of 1812 put him out of business in 1814.

That year, William Clark named Manuel Lisa sub-agent for the tribes along the Missouri and charged him with maintaining peace. Performing the task quickly and well, he relieved St. Louis of its anxiety over a possible Indian attack. Lisa formed yet another Missouri Fur Company in 1819, and his partners—Joshua Pilcher, Andrew Woods, John Zenoni, Joseph Perkins, Thomas Hempstead, and Andrew Drips—represented the new and burgeoning American St. Louis. The second Missouri Fur Company failed too, for the same reasons as its predecessors, but Lisa was not there to see the ultimate end. Becoming ill upriver over the winter of 1819 to 1820, he returned to St. Louis, where he died.

In his incredibly active life, Manuel Lisa was the first in the American era to ascend the Missouri River for purposes of trading and trapping, and his men were the first to cross the Continental Divide and winter in the Oregon Country. Lisa was the first to realize the benefits of leaving trappers in the mountains and supplying them from below, thus creating the prototypical mountain man. He opened the Missouri River to safe travel, and his care and concern for the various tribes with which he did business kept that water highway open. Just slightly ahead of his times, Lisa was unable to overcome the problems of finance endemic to the early fur trade, but his activities earned him the title first "King of the Missouri."

1798 Lisa establishes his permanent home in St. Louis.

1807 Lisa leads the first expedition northward up the Missouri River from St. Louis.

1808 Lisa and others form the St. Louis Missouri Fur Co.

1809 Lisa's company sends an expedition upriver.

1814 Lisa serves as subagent for the Indians along the Missouri.

Llewellyn, James Bruce

1927–PRESENT ● BUSINESSMAN

Born in Harlem to Jamaican immigrants, J. Bruce Llewellyn attended New York City public schools. Llewellyn joined the U.S. Army at the age of 16 and served in the Army Corps of Engineers from 1944 until 1948. He graduated from the City College of New York (CCNY) with a B. S. in 1955, and received a J.D. from New York Law School in 1960.

Llewellyn ran his first business, a retail liquor store in Harlem, while still in college. From 1958 to 1960, he was a student assistant in the New York County District Attorney's Office. From 1962 until 1965, after graduating from law school, Llewellyn was a partner in the small law firm of Evans, Berger, and Llewellyn. In 1965 he became the executive director of the Upper Manhattan office of the Small Business Development Corporation (SBDC), a federally funded city agency with several offices in New York City. After a brief tenure in 1965 as regional director of the federal Small Business Administration (SBA), Llewellyn returned to the SBDC between 1965 and 1968, serving as a program of officer, director of its management training program, and eventually executive director. From 1968 to 1969, he was the deputy commissioner of the New York City Housing and Development Administration. Later government service included acting from 1977 to 1981 as the first African-American president of the Overseas Private Investment Corporation (OPIC), a federal agency which facilitates private business investment in developing countries, during the Carter administration.

In 1969 Llewellyn decided to seek greater entrepreneurial opportunities. Symbolic of his philosophy that "you have to be willing to take chances" to succeed, Llewellyn bought Fedco Food Stores, a super market chain in the Bronx, after mortgaging his house and securing loans from other sources. Despite its location in one of the poorest areas of New York City, Llewellyn built the chain into a successful business. By

1958 Llewellyn becomes assistant for the New Orleans District Attorney

1965 Llewellyn becomes a director at SBDC.

1968 Llewellyn becomes deputy commissioner of NY Housing and Dev. Assoc.

1969 Llewellyn buys Fedco Food Stores.

1977 Llewellyn becomes the OPIC's first black president

1983 Llewellyn buys part of the New York Coca-Cola Bottling Co.

1975 Fedco had sales of over $30 million, had 500 employees, and was the fourth largest black-owned firm in the country. By 1983 the chain had twenty-nine stores and sales of almost $100 million. In the same year, Llewellyn broke up the company, selling each store to independent minority grocers.

With his earnings from the sale of Fedco, Llewellyn and several partners—including basketball great Julius Erving and comedian Bill Cosby—bought a stake in the New York Coca-Cola Bottling Company in 1983. Two years later, the same group purchased the Philadelphia Coca-Cola Bottling Company, becoming the first African-American owners of a Coca-Cola bottling franchise. By 1992 the company, with Llewellyn as chairman of the board and CEO, was the third largest black-owned industrial/service business in the United States, with $266 million in sales and more than 800 employees. Llewellyn has also served as the chief executive officer of the Coca-Cola Bottling Company of Wilmington, Inc.; Garden State Cablevision, Inc.; and Queen City Broadcasting, Inc., of Buffalo, New York.

Llewellyn has endeavored to make greater economic opportunities available to minorities. His purchase of Fedco was explicitly aimed toward increased opportunities for black and Hispanic workers. He was president of One Hundred Black Men, a service organization of African-American professionals, during much of the 1970s. During the 1980s, Llewellyn criticized the Reagan administration for "going backwards" in race relations and making them more antagonistic. As an adviser to various state and national organizations, Llewellyn has campaigned for maintaining affirmative action, as long as professional standards are not sacrificed. ◆

> **Llewellyn has campaigned for maintaining affirmative action, as long as professional standards are not sacrificed.**

Malone, Annie Turnbo

1869–1957 ● COSMETICS ENTREPRENEUR

nnie Turnbo Malone was born to Robert and Isabell Turnbo in Metropolis, Illinois, and attended high school in nearby Peoria. Orphaned at a young age, she was raised by her older brothers and sisters. In her twenties she began experimenting with chemicals to develop a hair straightener for African-American women. Living in Lovejoy, Illinois, Turnbo invented and sold a hot pressing-iron as well as several lotions and creams, one for restoring lost hair. In 1902 she moved her business to 223 Market Street, in St. Louis, Missouri. She and her trained assistants began selling her "Wonderful Hair Grower" and other products door to-door. One of her agents was Madame C. J. Walker, who went on to found her own hair-care company. Turnbo copyrighted the name "Poro" for her products in 1906. On April 28, 1914, she married Aaron E. Malone, who became the chief manager and president of the Poro company.

Attaining success, Annie Malone built Poro College, a beauty school, in St. Louis in 1917. The college became a social center for the black community, housing for a time the National Negro Business League as well as other organizations. After a tornado hit the city in 1927, Poro College served as a principal relief facility for the Red Cross. Poro also trained women to be agents, teaching them the rudiments of salesmanship and beauty culture. The company enjoyed tremendous expansion in the early 1920s, employing thousands of agents. Toward the end of the decade, however, the company ran into trouble and began its decline. In 1927,

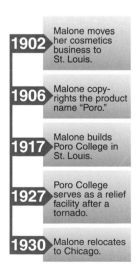

1902 Malone moves her cosmetics business to St. Louis.

1906 Malone copyrights the product name "Poro."

1917 Malone builds Poro College in St. Louis.

1927 Poro College serves as a relief facility after a tornado.

1930 Malone relocates to Chicago.

Malone and her husband had a bitter divorce and struggled for control of the company. With the support of Mary McLeod Bethune and others, Annie Malone kept control of the enterprise and settled with her husband for $200,000. In 1930, Annie Malone relocated the business and the college to Chicago. She ran into further difficulties because of her refusal to pay excise tax. Between 1943 and 1951 she was the subject of government suits. In the latter year the government seized control of the company and sold off most of Poro's property to pay taxes and fines.

Throughout her leadership of the Poro company, Malone distinguished herself as a philanthropist. In the 1920s, she gave over $25,000 to the Howard University Medical School Fund. Malone also gave substantial sums to Tuskegee University, the Citywide YMCA of St. Louis, and the St. Louis Colored Orphans' Home. The Annie Malone Crisis Center and the Annie Malone Children and Family Service Center, both in St. Louis, are named in her honor. She died in Chicago in 1957. ◆

> Malone's Poro College became a social center for the black community in St. Louis.

Marinho, Roberto

1905–PRESENT ● TELECOMMUNICATIONS TYCOON

With a net worth of $1 billion, Roberto Marinho is the third richest man in Brazil. This fortune is derived primarily from the TV Globo Network, other media, computer and telecommunications firms, as well as real estate and insurance companies (100 companies total in the group). He founded *O Globo*, one of the four main newspapers in Brazil, and Radio Globo, one of the most popular radio stations in Rio de Janeiro. In 1962, Marinho established TV Globo in joint venture with Time-Life. In 1968, after considerable controversy, that arrangement was found to violate the Brazilian Constitution and Time-Life was bought out by Marinho, who now owns 100 percent of TV Globo. By 1968, TV Globo had the first true network with

simulcast programs in Brazil and began a dominance of audience ratings that has continued until today, although competition has grown. TV Globo was favored with military government advertising and infrastucture, such as satellite and microwave links.

simulcast: broadcast over both radio and television.

The Brazilian managers Marinho hired took advantage of the growing Brazilian advertising market and built up a television production system that has been compared with the old Hollywood studios. TV Globo often produces twelve or more hours of programming a day for itself, including *telenovelas* (prime-time serials), music, news, comedy, public affairs, and talk shows. The Globo Group has expanded into records (*Som Livre*), magazines (*Globo Rural*, comic books), video and film distribution (*Globo Video*), and direct satellite broadcasting (GloboSat).

Marinho has moved into telecommunications and in formation technologies through joint ventures with NEC of Japan in areas including cellular telephony and a bid for the second generation of Brazilian telecommunications satellites. His charitable foundation, Fundação Roberto Marinho, produces television programs for education and funds historical preservation. ◆

Marriott, J(ohn) Willard (Bill)

1900–1985 ● RESTAURANT & HOTEL MOGUL

The second of eight children born to Ellen Morris and Hyrum Willard "Will" Marriott, J. Willard "Bill" Marriott grew up west of Ogden in Marriott, Utah, which was named for his grandfather John Marriott. Both grandfathers, John Marriott and William Morris, had converted to the Church of Jesus Christ of Latter-day Saints (LDS) in England and had immigrated to Utah. A farmer,

> *"Human wants are never satisfied."*
>
> J. Willard Marriott Jr.

rancher, and local leader, Marriott's father served in the bishopric of the Marriott LDS ward and in the Utah state legislature. His mother was a homemaker.

While growing up, Bill farmed row crops, herded sheep, and cattle, and attended school. Beginning at age 14, he marketed the family's sheep in San Francisco and Omaha. A good student and avid reader, he impressed his teachers at Slaterville School. Active in the LDS Church, at age 19 he began two years of service as a **proselytizing** missionary in New England and New York.

proselytizing: trying to convince others to join.

On his return, Marriott found his father's family deeply in debt. Heavy borrowing and low agricultural prices after World War I had ravaged their farming and ranching operations. In part because of his early experiences and in part because of Ralph Waldo Emerson's writings on self-reliance and hard work, Marriott sought in education and entrepreneurship a way off the farm and out of poverty. Although he had not graduated from high school, he approached his former teacher Aaron Tracy, a professor and president designate of Weber College, which had just added a junior college curriculum. Tracy agreed to enroll him. Financing his education by selling advertisements for school publications and clerking at the college bookstore, Marriott graduated with the college's first class in June 1923.

In 1927, Marriot opened a small A&W franchise in Washington D.C.

After graduation, he worked as a clothing and woolens salesman in Nevada, northern California, and the Northwest. He continued to sell during the summers while finishing his education at the University of Utah, where he graduated in 1926. Tracy induced him to return briefly to Weber College as a teacher, treasurer, and manager.

During his senior year at the University of Utah, Marriott met Alice "Allie" Sheets, an honor student. Bill and Allie were married in the Salt Lake LDS Temple on June 9, 1927; they had two children.

On May 10, 1927, Marriott and Hugh Colton opened a small A & W Root Beer franchise stand in Washington, D.C. After their marriage Allie managed a second stand (also in Washington) and kept the company's books. To capture the winter trade, they renamed the restaurants the Hot Shoppes and offered Mexican-style fast foods. In 1928 Colton returned to Utah to practice law, and Marriott bought his share of the company. During the early 1930s Marriott opened additional

J. Willard Marriott Sr.
(left) with his son J.
Willard Jr. in 1983.

Hot Shoppes in the greater Washington area and in Baltimore
and Philadelphia.

Marriott contracted **Hodgkin's disease** in 1934. Given
six months to live by his doctors, he called on two LDS leaders, who gave him a priesthood blessing. Before Christmas,
tests showed him free of the disease.

Between 1937 and 1951 Marriott enlarged his food service businesses. In 1937 his company began to furnish meals
for airline passengers. During World War II he offered
lunch-wagon services and opened cafeterias. In March 1947
the company started take-out service in Rosslyn, Virginia.
During and after the war Marriott expanded his geographic
base until by 1950 his companies operated in twelve states
and the District of Columbia. In 1953 Hot Shoppes, Inc.
(later renamed Marriott Corporation) offered stock to the
public.

Marriott also engaged in professional, church, and civic
activities. In 1948 he was president of the National
Restaurant Association. After serving as second counselor in
the presidency of the Washington, D.C., LDS stake from 1946
to 1948, he was called as stake president, a position he held
for nine and a half years. Following his term, he was an
Aaronic-priesthood adviser and Sunday-school teacher. He
served on the committee to install the Brigham Young statue
in the U.S. Capitol rotunda in 1950, and he worked actively

Hodgkin's disease:
cancer of the lymphatic
tissue.

in restoring buildings in Nauvoo, Illinois, the city from which the Mormons fled in 1846.

In 1957 the Marriott Corporation began to expand into the motor-hotel and specialty-restaurant business. Its first establishment was the Twin Bridges Motor Hotel in Arlington, Virginia. In November 1958 Marriott assigned his son Bill Jr. to launch a multimillion-dollar motor-hotel program. The Marriotts opened hotels in various cities, including Dallas, Philadelphia, and Atlanta. They also opened Fairfield Inns and the Sirloin and Saddles and Kona Kai Hawaiian restaurants. Later they started fast-food restaurants and franchises, including the Roy Rogers and Big Boy chains.

In 1964, after continuing the company's expansion program, Marriott turned over the presidency of the corporation to his son, although he remained chairman of the board. Bill Jr. borrowed heavily for a rapid expansion of the hotel business; fearing debt, Marriott was not entirely pleased with such extensive borrowing.

Bill and Allie were lifelong Republicans. She served on the Republican National Committee and as convention treasurer in 1964, 1968, and 1972. They tended to support the moderate rather than the conservative wing of the party, favoring Dwight Eisenhower, associating with Nelson Rockefeller, and supporting George Romney, a personal friend. Despite bad health during the latter part of 1968, Marriott chaired Richard Nixon's 1969 inaugural committee, a post he held again in 1973.

During the 1960s and 1970s Marriott devoted considerable time to philanthropic and public affairs. He contributed $1 million each to the University of Utah for a library and to Brigham Young University for a basketball-activities center. In 1970, in the midst of the national turmoil over U.S. involvement in Vietnam, he chaired the Independence Day celebration in Washington, D.C., a service he repeated for the Bicentennial celebration of 1976. As he remained active in business and public affairs, his health continued to deteriorate. In late 1975 and early 1976 he suffered four heart attacks. Nevertheless, he participated in the opening of new hotels and in the first of three Marriott Great America theme parks.

Marriott suffered a heart attack at his family's summer home on Lake Winnipesaukee in New Hampshire and was pronounced dead at Wolfeboro. He was buried in the

1923 Marriott graduates first in college class.

1927 Marriott and a partner open first A & W Root Beer stand.

1930 Marriott expands his Hot Shopper franchises.

1934 Marriott contracts Hodgkin's disease.

1937 Marriott's company starts providing airline food.

1950 Marriott companies operate in 12 states.

1957 Marriott begins expansion into motel/hotel business.

1969 Marriott chairs Richard Nixon's inaugural committee.

Parklawn Memorial Park in Rockville, Maryland. At the time of his death, the Marriott Corporation had operations and franchises in fifty states and twenty-seven countries, including 125 hotels and 64 flight kitchens. It owned 667 restaurants and franchised 935 more. Beyond this, it operated 2 vacation resorts, 78 airport food-service facilities, 3 cruise ships, 2,097 catering accounts, and 19 shops.

Born to a family of moderate means but local prominence, Marriott worked to pay his way through college and saved and borrowed to enter business in Washington, D.C. A man of enormous energy and exceptional business sense, he succeeded largely through attending to economy, recognizing the changing role of the automobile in the lives of people, understanding the increasing importance of family dining and fast food, researching carefully locations for his businesses, and insisting on high quality for company products and services. Significantly, we must attribute part of his success to his wife, Allie, who worked in the businesses and provided exceptional support and encouragement. ◆

Mason, Biddy

1818–1891 ● BUSINESSWOMAN

Born a slave in Georgia, Biddy Mason became the most prominent African-American woman in post-Civil War Los Angeles. Mason was the property of a Mormon planter who brought her and her three children to Salt Lake in 1848 and then to San Bernardino, California, in 1851. Five years later, she successfully petitioned for the freedom of her thirteen-member extended family. Mason subsequently settled in Los Angeles, where she became a successful midwife. She assisted in the births of hundreds of Anglo, Chicano, Native American, and African-American children between 1856 and 1891.

Using $250 she had saved, Mason purchased a parcel of land between Spring Street and Broadway, just beyond the

Mason was one of the first black female property owners in Los Angeles.

1848 Mason is brought as a slave to Salt Lake.

1851 Mason moves to Califonia.

1856 Mason begins serving as a midwife.

1866 Mason buys land in Los Angeles.

1884 Mason builds a 2-story commercial building.

city limits, in November 1866. Her purchase made her one of the first black female property owners in the Los Angeles area. Six years later, she founded the First African Methodist Episcopal Church, the oldest African-American church in Los Angeles. As downtown Los Angeles expanded, the value of her property grew. In 1884, Mason sold part of her homestead for $1,500 and constructed a two-story commercial building to house a nursery, bakeries, a restaurant, and furniture and carpet stores. The upper floor was the residence of her extended family. With the proceeds from the sale of part of the homestead, rents, and sales of other town lots, Mason generated considerable wealth. For the rest of her life, she donated regularly to charities, homeless families, and stranded settlers and became renowned for her philanthropy. ◆

Mauá, Visconde de (Irineu Evangelista de Souza)

1813–1889 ● RAILROAD MAGNATE, RANCHER, & MERCHANT

Visconde de Mauá was a Brazilian merchant, banker, industrialist, railroad magnate, rancher, and national politician who rose from obscure beginnings to become a major protagonist in imperial Brazil's banking, transportation, and industrial infrastructure. Born in Rio Grande do Sul, Mauá initiated his business entrepreneurial career in Rio de Janeiro at age 11 as a cashier in a cloth store and was later employed in a British firm, where he learned British business methods and successively held the positions of partner and sole manager by the 1830s, when the firm's founder returned to England.

Mauá invested in a variety of modernizing endeavors, most of which initially were aimed at improving Brazil's trans-

portation and industrial infrastructure. From the establishment of an iron foundry that supplied pipes for a new water
system in Rio de Janeiro, Mauá acquired concessions for a
tramway line, the first gas-lamp system built in the country,
and the first steamship company to operate on the Amazon
River. An investor in the Second Bank of Brazil, he founded
the Bank of Mauá in 1854, the same year he constructed
Brazil's first railroad line from the port of Mauá on Guanabara
Bay in Rio de Janeiro to the interior highlands, where coffee
production for the foreign market was the mainstay of the
Brazilian economy. That year he also received the title of
baron.

Mauá represented his native province of Rio Grande do
Sul in the Chamber of Deputies from 1856 to 1873, and he
received the title of viscount in 1874 after laying the first sub-
marine cable between Brazil and Europe.

Mauá's widespread banking network extended to London,
and his business ventures expanded to Argentina and Uruguay,
where he held control over Uruguayan railroads, shipyards,
gasworks, livestock farms, and meat-processing plants. His
economic liberalism was not popular among conservative economic sectors in Brazil and Uruguay, and his creditors were not
sympathetic to the losses he suffered in the Rio de la Plata
region during the War of the Triple Alliance (1864–1870). His
finances declined in the 1870s, and in 1878 he was forced into
bankruptcy. His "Exposition to the Creditors of Mauá and
Company and to the Public," written in that year, attributed
the reversal of his fortunes to his placing the well-being of the
country before personal concerns, rather than to mismanage-
ment or misdeeds. Mauá spent the remainder of his life managing a modest investment business. ◆

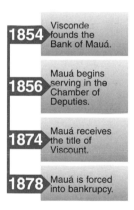

1854 Visconde founds the Bank of Mauá.

1856 Mauá begins serving in the Chamber of Deputies.

1874 Mauá receives the title of Viscount.

1878 Mauá is forced into bankrupcy.

Maytag, Frederick Louis

1857–1937 ● APPLIANCE MANUFACTURER

> *"Maytag repairman are the loneliest guys in town."*
>
> — Maytag Advertisement

Frederick Louis Maytag was born on a farm near Elgin, Illinois, on July 14, 1857. He was the son of Daniel William and Amelia (Toennebohn) Maytag, both natives of Germany. His father, a native of Lenzen, near Berlin, settle in Chicago, and thence in 1866 to Marshalltown, Iowa. Maytag passed his early years on his father's farm, spending a total of only twenty-two months in school until 1880, when he obtained employment as clerk in an implement store in Newton, Iowa. The following year he purchased a half interest in the business and purchased a lumber yard, which engaged his attention for four years.

In 1893, Maytag organized, with W. C. Bergman, A. H. Bergman, and George W. Parsons, the Parsons, Band Cutter and Self-Feeder Company, to manufacture and market a self-feeder attachment for a threshing machine, which had been invented by Parsons. The cash capital was $2400 contributed in equal shares by the four partners. On account of outside interests of other members of the firm, the active management fell to Maytag and he devoted himself with untiring energy to the development of the company and the improvement of its products. He brought the enterprise safely through two panics, overcame the disadvantages due to the seasonal nature of the demand for self-feeders by extending the line of products, and surmounted many financial, mechanical, and organizational difficulties.

Within a few years the company had become the largest manufacturer of self-feeders in the world, supplying the markets of the United States, as well as Canada, Australia, England, and South America. In 1899, a corn husker and shredder, invented by Howard Snyder, was added to its line; later a grain grader and hay press, and in 1907 a hand power washing machine. In 1909, Maytag purchased the interests of his partners, and became sole owner of the company, which by that time had a virtual **monopoly** of the feeder business supplying twenty-eight manufacturers of threshing machines.

monopoly: exclusive control.

On December 4, Maytag Company was organized under the laws of Iowa to take over the Parsons Band Cutter & Self-feeder Company and the Parsons Hawkeye Manufacturing Company, makers of self-feeders and wooden tub hand washers. Of this company, Maytag became president with T. G. Bryant as vice-president, E. H. Maytag as treasurer, and T. A. Moler as secretary. In 1911, an electric washer was produced, followed soon afterward by the development of a swinging wringer, also the invention of Howard Snyder. Gradually the manufacture of washers became the principal activity, the sales of this article in 1915 exceeding those of all other products. During that year, the company also developed a one half horse-power two-cycle gasoline engine known as the multi-motor, to furnish motive power for the washer in homes without electric current. The demand for this engine exceeded expectations, and Maytag became the world's largest maker of single-cylinder and two-cycle engines.

In 1922, the company produced a washer of a new type, know as the "Gyrafoam" washer, with which a still greater record in industrial achievement was established. This machine of the gyrator type, with a cast aluminum tub, demonstrated its superiority in speed, cleaning power, and the low rate of wear on the materials in washing. In its production, Maytag encountered and overcame a new obstacle. Several of the leading aluminum foundries or the country refused to undertake manufacturing the cast aluminum tub on the ground that it could not be made, but he built his own aluminum foundry and designed his own machinery, eventually accomplishing the result declared impossible. At the time, this foundry was one of the most completely equipped plants of its kind in the world and one of the three largest. The production of the Gyrafoam washer, which was begun in 1922, was followed by an advertising campaign that in two years found the company the fourth largest newspaper advertiser in the world. The result was a prodigious increase in the business, the volume of annual sales growing from $2,000,000 in 1921 to $53,000,000 in 1926. By the late 1990s, the Maytag Corporation was one of the largest major appliance companies in the United States and Canada, and marketed dryers, dishwashers, refrigerators, and ranges, and well as washing machines.

Maytag retired from the presidency in 1921, but continued as chairman of the board of directors for a time. He was a

> Maytag's "Gyrafoam" washer proved its superiority in speed, cleaning power, and low rate of wear on the clothes being washed.

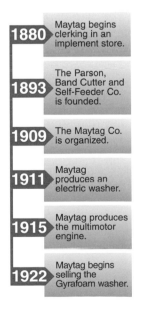

1880 Maytag begins clerking in an implement store.

1893 The Parson, Band Cutter and Self-Feeder Co. is founded.

1909 The Maytag Co. is organized.

1911 Maytag produces an electric washer.

1915 Maytag produces the multimotor engine.

1922 Maytag begins selling the Gyrafoam washer.

member of the Iowa state senate for ten years (1902–1912), becoming chairman of the committee on appropriations; was appointed the first director of the state budget (1925); and served as mayor of the city of Newton during 1923–1925. Parsons College awarded him the degree of L.L.D. in 1926 and in the same year the Home Appliance Merchants of America presented him with the world's largest and most valuable medallion, eight inches in diameter, made of pure gold and worth $25,000, in recognition of his outstanding services in originating and manufacturing electrical home appliances. Maytag was a Mason, and a member of the Knights of Pythias, Elks and odd Fellows fraternities. He was married in 1882 to Dena, daughter of William Bergman, of Newton, Iowa. They had four children: Lulu, Freda Louise, Elmer Henry, and Lewis Bergman Maytag. ◆

Fred Maytag II who headed the company after the founder died.

McCormick, Cyrus Hall

1809–1884 ● FARM EQUIPMENT MANUFACTURER

Cyrus H. McCormick's father, Robert, had been experimenting with farm machinery for years while the young man grew up. One of the father's developments was a machine for threshing grain—that is, removing the edible grain from the leaves and stems. Cyrus developed a machine to reap grain from the fields. It was essentially an oversized mowing machine that collected the "heads" of grain and saved the vast amount of human labor that had been needed previously to gather grain. The first successful McCormick reapers were developed in 1831; the machine was patented on June 21, 1834. A number of similar machines were developed and patented in the 1830s.

Cyrus McCormick's early experiments were carried on at the family farm near Lexington, Virginia. He then moved his operations to the Midwest farm area, with headquarters in Chicago, Illinois. There, he produced and sold his reaping machines, adding many improvements as time went by. The McCormick sales methods were almost as important for later American business as his reaper was for farming. He made use of "field tests" and demonstrations; he provided guarantees with his machines; he had people who used them tell of their success and endorse the product; and he introduced the idea that a manufacturer could sell merchandise and collect later

> McCormick provided guarantees with his machines and he had people who used them tell of their success and endorse the product.

for it. McCormick and his relatives became leading American businessmen, interested in railroads and mines, canals and newspapers as well as in harvesting machinery. ◆

Mellon, Andrew W.

1855–1937 ● BANKER

"If the spirit of business adventure is dulled, this country will cease to hold the foremost position in the world."
Andrew Mellon, 1923

Andrew Mellon first made a name for himself in banking in Pittsburgh, especially as the backer of high-cost, innovative industries. He financed Alcoa Aluminum in the 1890s, before most Americans knew anything about aluminum's value to industry. In the early 1900s Mellon and his family sank $15 million into Gulf Oil and backed Gulf's innovations in the petroleum business, including offshore drilling and the first corner gas stations.

By 1920 Mellon was worth close to a billion dollars, which ranked him with John D. Rockefeller and Henry Ford as one of the wealthiest men in America. After World War I, Mellon's superior grasp of economics caught the attention of national political leaders who were struggling with a stagnant economy, a rising national debt, and a crushing tax burden. Republican Warren G. Harding, winner of the 1920 presidential election, asked Mellon to be his Secretary of the Treasury and do for the American economy what he had done for aluminum and oil.

Mellon came to Washington at a crucial time in U.S. history. World War I had been a turning point in expanding the role of government in economic life. Before the war, the federal role in operating, regulating and taxing businesses was small. The federal budget was less than a billon dollars a year. The taxes needed to run the government were low and fairly easily collected; land sales and tariffs were the major sources of revenue. In the 1910s, the passing of the income tax and the outbreak of World War I thrust government regulation and taxation into much broader areas of American life.

Consequently, as Treasury Secretary, Mellon collected and studied data on the American economy. He concluded that "high rates of taxation do not necessarily mean large revenue to the Government, and that more revenue may often be obtained by lower rates." Mellon found that high tax rates caused the investment capital needed for new industry to dry up. Instead, large investors put their money into tax-free municipal **bonds**, and the federal government actually received very little tax revenue from persons with large incomes. Mellon reasoned that lower tax rates would help investors put their funds back into industry—that is, into money-making ventures that would both employ workers and produce profits.

As Treasury Secretary under Harding and Calvin Coolidge, Mellon was able to get Congress to enact his tax cuts, with the surprising result that actual tax revenues soared while tax rates dropped. In 1921, when Mellon took office, the tax rate on top incomes was 73 percent. After eight years of Mellon's tax cuts this top rate was sliced by two-thirds, to 24 percent. The tax rates of those earning less were proportionally slashed even more. For example, people earning under $4,000 per year had their rates chopped from 4 to 0.5 percent; those in the $4,000-to-$8,000 bracket had their tax burden cut from 8 to 2 percent. Tax policy, Mellon argued, "must lessen, so far as possible, the burden of taxation on those least able to bear it." Millions of citizens were removed entirely from the income-tax rolls, and when Mellon further urged the repeal of federal taxes on telegrams, telephones, and movie tickets he became one of the most popular men in

bond: a certificate promising payment with interest for money borrowed.

1890 Mellon finances Alcoa Aluminum.

1900 Mellon family sinks $15 million into Gulf Oil.

1920 Mellon is asked to be secretary of treasury.

1921 Mellon begins radical overhaul of tax policy.

1930 Mellon's taxation philosophy falls out of favor during Great Depression.

Andrew W. Mellon Foundation

The Andrew W. Mellon Foundation, a world renowned charitable trust in New York City with assets of $2.8 billion, was created in 1969 as a consolidation of two earlier trusts founded by Mellon's son, Paul Mellon, and daughter, Ailsa Mellon Bruce. The foundation's purpose is to "aid and promote such religious, charitable, scientific, literary, and educational purposes as may be in the furtherance of the public welfare or tend to promote the well-doing or well-being of mankind." Under this broad and lofty charter, the foundation currently makes selective grants to institutions in higher education; in cultural affairs and the performing arts; in population; in conservation and the environment; and in public affairs. Its board of trustees reads like a scholarly and political *Who's Who*. A quick sample of recent foundation grants includes $40 million annual support for the humanities; $12 million a year in population research, including contraceptive development and delivery of reproductive health services in developing countries and in New York City; $5 million toward research in refugee and forced migration issues; funds for basic research on natural ecosystems, and $11 million in 43 land preservation grants through the Trust for Public Land.

"A nation is not in danger of financial disaster merely because it owes itself money."

Andrew Mellon, 1933

America. Moviegoers throughout the country cheered him when he was shown on newsreels in theaters during the 1920s.

When Mellon's policies actually helped generate increases in tax revenue, even Mellon's critics were amazed. In 1921 the income tax generated $690.2 million (in constant 1929 dollars); in 1926, with tax rates slashed, the federal revenue from income taxes rose to $710.2 million This figure jumped to more than $1 billion in 1929. With taxes low and industry strong the United States had a budget surplus in each year of the 1920s.

During the 1930s, Mellon fell out of favor. Presidents Herbert Hoover and Franklin D. Roosevelt both thought that raising taxes would help fight the Great Depression. Hoover retired Mellon out of the Treasury Department into the job of ambassador to Great Britain. Mellon retired from political life in 1933. Before his death in 1937 he donated his outstanding art collection to the National Gallery of Art. ◆

Morgan, John Pierpont

1837–1913 ● FINANCIER

> *"Any man who has to ask about the annual upkeep of a yacht can't afford one."*
>
> John Piermont Morgan, attributed

John Pierpont Morgan was one of the most successful financial managers in world history. During the last twenty years of his life he was the most important financier in the United States. Morgan was born at Hartford, Connecticut, on April 17, 1837, the son of a wealthy and successful banker, Junius S. Morgan. The father had been very active in financing trade between the United States and Great Britain and "J. P." Morgan entered the family banking business in London at the age of 20. He lent money to various companies that bought and sold supplies during the Civil War and by the end of that war he was well established as a banker in New York.

He became nationally prominent in 1873 when he broke a monopoly that Jay Cooke had once held on handling government bond sales. That year, the Morgan banking firm shared with Jay Cooke the right to resell government bonds. Cooke's bank failed later in 1873 and Morgan and his associates were on hand to pick up the trade that Cooke lost. Acting as agent for the U.S. Treasury helped Morgan get many rich customers who entrusted funds to his bank for investment. He used his funds to improve American railroading operations. In the years after the Civil War, American railroads were fiercely competitive, cutting rates and trying to

Pierpont Morgan Library

The Pierpont Morgan Library in Manhattan in New York City is both a research archive for scholars and a museum holding some of the most famous manuscripts, books, and artwork in the world. It is housed in a white marble Italian Renaissance-style mansion that was built in 1906 and served as the home of J. P. Morgan Sr., the eminently successful U.S. financier. A prolific and knowledgeable collector, Morgan acquired a prodigious aggregation of medieval and Renaissance illuminated manuscripts, European paintings, Oriental porcelains, Byzantine bronzes, and a vast number of other works. Morgan's collection became the core of the Morgan Library, opened to the public by his son in 1924. Among the most interesting items are three Gutenberg Bibles, a first printing of the Declaration of Independence, Shakespeare folios, and Bach and Mozart manuscripts. Changing museum exhibits are drawn from the library's repositories. A reading room is provided for researchers. The library has been declared a National Historical Landmark.

destroy each other. Morgan controlled enough money so that he could make the roads change their practices before they could borrow what they needed to continue in operation. These investments were usually profitable for Morgan and for his banking customers, and they also gave Morgan an enormous amount of power over credit. If Morgan refused to lend money, other bankers seldom were willing to risk a loan. When a great panic swept the nation's businesses in 1893, Morgan was able to calm some of the worry by advancing funds. He also put himself in the position of becoming the most powerful single force in American banking and finance.

Morgan's power was once called on in a very unusual case. In 1895, the U.S. Treasury was in danger because its gold supplies were being drawn out and shipped to Europe. Investors were cashing in their U.S. paper money and bonds to secure government gold. President Grover Cleveland called on Morgan and his associates to protect the gold supply in the Treasury and Morgan agreed. Morgan bought a large number of government bonds himself and used his general financial power to slow down the gold outflow.

Morgan's business activities spread from railroad consolidation and international banking to the organization of very large corporations in other lines of business. One of his most daring financial deals involved the creation of the United States Steel Corporation in 1901. Morgan arranged the

1873 Morgan breaks up a monopoly on government bond sales.

1893 Morgan helps quell a financial panic.

1901 Morgan finances the creation of U.S. Steel.

1912 Morgan is investigated by a Congressional committee.

financing that enabled the steel giant to be formed by buying out the interests of Andrew Carnegie and others in smaller companies that were combined to form "big steel." He was also involved in financing companies in the farm equipment and international shipping businesses. In the early twentieth century, he lost one major business battle when he tried to win control of the Northern Pacific Railroad away from Edward H. Harriman.

Morgan's great personal power and wealth attracted a good many enemies, naturally. He was pictured as a power-grasping and ruthless man, gaining control over major elements in the country's business life and even over the Treasury of the United States itself. He was investigated by a Congressional committee in 1912 but was undamaged by the investigation. His personal prestige, in fact, improved when the committee failed to prove any serious wrong-doing. All through his career, Morgan collected great art works and rare books and manuscripts. He invested a great deal of time and money in them and his collection was one of the largest and best in the world. He presented a great part of his art collection to the Metropolitan Museum of Art in New York City, and he left his priceless collection of books and manuscripts to the public as the "Morgan Library."

His died in Rome, Italy, on March 31, 1913. ◆

> *"I am not in Wall Street for my health."*
>
> J. P. Morgan

Murdoch, Rupert

1931–PRESENT ● MEDIA MOGUL

Rupert Murdoch is an Australian-born publisher who built one of the world's largest communications empires in the late 1900s. His media business spans six continents and includes holdings in newspapers, magazines, books, television broadcasting, and film production. His most extensive holdings are in Australia, where he controls more

> *"The third world never sold a newspaper."*
>
> Rupert Murdoch, quoted in *Observer*, 1978

than half of the nation's newspaper circulation. Murdoch is known for his sensationalist tabloids and for his ability to turn financially struggling operations into profitable ones. He controls his properties through the global media holding company News Corporation Limited.

Keith Rupert Murdoch was born in Melbourne, Victoria on March 11, 1931, to Sir Keith and Dame Elisabeth (Greene) Murdoch. His father was a famous Australian war correspondent who later became a prominent chief executive of an Australian-based chain of newspapers. His mother became a Dame of the British Empire for her welfare work. Rupert grew up in Melbourne and attended Oxford University in England, where he studied economics and political science. He graduated in 1953.

In 1952 Murdoch's father died, leaving the family with the bulk of its wealth tied up in financially struggling newspapers in Adelaide and Brisbane. The family sold off the latter to meet estate taxes. In 1953, just out of college with barely a year's experience at newspapers in England, Rupert returned to Australia to take over as publisher of the family's newspapers in Adelaide, the *News and Sunday Mail*. He soon made the *News* a success, basing its journalism on sex and scandal and featuring sensationalist headlines that have since become his trademark. He went on to purchase newspapers in Brisbane, Melbourne, Perth, and Sydney, and applied a profitable formula of racy, tabloid journalism, eye-catching headlines, and heavy sports coverage to all of them.

Murdoch established Australia's first national daily newspaper, the *Australian*, in 1964. Unlike his other publications, the Australian was devoted to serious journalism and investigative reporting and it covered important local, national, and international news. He acquired his first British newspaper, a Sunday tabloid called *News of the World*, in 1969, and rankled members of the Conservative government and press by publishing weekly installments of a prostitute's memoirs, which included details of her trysts with a Russian spy and a British government official. Soon thereafter he bought a conservative London daily called the *Sun*, which he revamped into a splashy tabloid that included a daily picture of a bare-breasted woman on page 3.

Murdoch continued to expand his media empire and in 1973 he tapped into the United States market with his pur-

1952 Murdoch inherits the family's struggling newspapers.

1953 Murdoch becomes publisher of the family's Adelaide newspapers.

1953 Murdoch graduates from Oxford.

1964 Murdoch establishes Australia's first national daily newspaper.

1969 Murdoch acquires his first British newspaper, *News of the World*.

1973 Murdoch purchases the *San Antonio Express and News*.

1985 Murdoch becomes a U.S. citizen.

chase of the *San Antonio Express and News*. Shortly thereafter he launched the *National Star*, a gossipy supermarket tabloid that later became the *Star*. Throughout the 1980s and 1990s, Murdoch bought and sold a number of U.S. publications and expanded into the Pacific Rim and Asia. Some of his well-known publications have included the *Chicago Sun-Times*, the *New York Post*, *New York* magazine, *TV Guide*, London's *The Times*, and Hong Kong's *South China Morning Post*. He also invested in well-known book publishers and merged some of them in 1990 to create HarperCollins Publishers.

In 1985, Murdoch became a U.S. citizen in order to make broadcasting purchases in the United States. Under the U.S. Communications Act foreign-owned corporations could not hold U.S. broadcasting licenses. Once a citizen, Murdoch purchased 20th Century-Fox Film Corporation and several independent television stations, which he consolidated into Fox Broadcasting Company. In 1993, as part of his plan to build a global television network, he bought Star TV, a television broadcasting service that beams its satellite signals into China, India, the Middle East and the South Pacific. Banking on the popularity of sports broadcasts, Murdoch also began collecting regional sports networks and buying broadcasting rights to game coverage. By the late 1990s, he controlled broadcast rights to 69 of the 75 teams in professional baseball,

"Part of the Australian character is wanting to take on the world. It's a hard, huge continent inhabited by a few European descendants with a sense of distance from their roots. They have a great need to prove themselves."

Rupert Murdoch

Rupert Murdoch holds up a *New York Post* Oct. 5 (1978) paper after a 57-day strike.

basketball, and hockey. In 1998, he bought the Los Angeles Dodgers baseball team.

In the early 1990s, Murdoch's empire was threatened with collapse as interest rates on a number of News Corporation's loans rose and nearly $3 billion in loans became due. After months of careful restructuring and deal making with bank officials, the corporation survived. Undaunted by this narrowly averted collapse, the media baron continued the expansion of his empire, aided by a powerful lobbying effort in Washington, D.C., where federal communications agencies carefully review any of his attempts to gain control of new media properties. By the late 1990s, his net worth had topped $5 billion.

Murdoch's devotion to his empire building took its toll on his marriage with Anna Maria (Torv) Murdoch, a novelist and Murdoch's wife for more than 30 years, and the couple was separated in 1998. Murdoch has four children. ◆

Overton, Anthony

1865–1946 ● BUSINESSMAN

Although it is known that he was born in Monroe, Louisiana, in 1865, little is known of the early life of Anthony Overton. While university records are incomplete, Overton claimed that he attended Washburn College and graduated from the University of Kansas with an LL.B. in 1888. In the same year he married Clara Gregg. For several years, Overton was a judge of the Municipal Court in Topeka, Kansas. In 1898 he established the Overton Hygienic Manufacturing Company in Kansas City, Kansas. Overton moved the company to Chicago, Illinois, in 1911, where it quickly expanded, becoming popular for a "High Brown Face Powder" and other toiletry products.

Overton's business interests flourished in Chicago; in the early 1920s, he established a bank, a life insurance company, and the *Chicago Bee*, a newspaper. Eschewing luxuries himself, Overton reinvested most of his profits back into his own enterprises. The Douglass National Bank was reportedly the first national bank owned and run by African Americans in the state of Illinois.

In 1924 Overton also organized the Victory Life Insurance Company, the first black-owned insurance company to be permitted to conduct business in the state of New York, where strict regulations and legal reserve requirements made entry into the insurance market extremely difficult. As a result of the success of this company, Overton received the NAACP's Springarn Medal in 1927. Overton's empire collapsed during the Great Depression, however, when both the bank and the insurance company failed. The insurance company later reorganized under different management.

1898 Overton establishes the Overton Hygenic Manufacturing Co.

1911 Overton moves the company to Chicago.

1924 Overton reorganizes the Victory Life Insurance Co.

1927 Overton receives the NAACP's Spingarn Medal.

But the depression did not claim either the Overton Hygienic Manufacturing Company or the *Chicago Bee*, and Overton led these companies until his death. He was an active member of the board of directors of the Chicago Urban League, as well as a number of fraternal organizations. He died in Chicago in 1946. ◆

Pace, Harry Herbert

1884–1943 ● INSURANCE EXECUTIVE & MUSIC PUBLISHER

Born in Covington, Georgia, Harry H. Pace studied at Atlanta University, where he edited the school newspaper and became a student and protege of W. E. B. Du Bois. After receiving his bachelor's degree in 1903, Pace went into the printing business with Du Bois in Memphis, Tennessee. In 1905 the partners put out the short-lived magazine *The Moon Illustrated Weekly*, the first illustrated African-American journal. After the failure of the printing business in 1906, Pace taught Greek and Latin for two years at Lincoln Institute in Jefferson City, Missouri, then returned to Memphis, becoming a cashier at the city's Solvent Savings Bank.

During his time in Memphis, Pace published short stories and articles. His work eventually appeared in such publications as the *Crisis*, *Forbes Magazine*, *Colored American Magazine*, and the *New York Sun*. He also sang in church choirs and in community concerts, and began writing song lyrics. In 1908 he met composer W. C. Handy, with whom he began a collaboration. The pair's first song, "In the Cotton Fields of Dixie," was published in Memphis that year. In 1909, they formed the Pace & Handy Music Company, a sheet-music business. The company published many songs, including Handy's "Memphis Blues" (1909) and "St. Louis Blues" (1914), and Pace's own "The Girl You Never Have Met" (1909).

In 1913, Pace left Memphis and took the post of secretary-treasurer of the Standard Life Insurance Company of Atlanta.

> Pace and Handy published many songs, including Handy's Memphis Blues and St. Louis Blues.

(One of his office boys was Walter Francis White, whom he sponsored and recommended to the NAACP.) During the following years, Pace traveled the country as a life insurance and music agent, securing contracts for Handy's band and music. In 1920 Pace left Atlanta to become president of the Pace & Handy Publishing Company, by then based in New York. Composer William Grant Still was hired as chief arranger, and future band leader Fletcher Henderson was a song plugger.

Although Pace improved the financial stability of the company, he disliked Handy's business methods. In 1921 Pace resigned from the publishing company and formed the Pace Phonograph Company, the first black-owned record company. The company issued records under the Black Swan label. While it recorded many types of music, it was primarily noted for its blues records. Although Black Swan was enormously successful in its first year of business, overexpansion and white competition bankrupted the company in 1923. After Black Swan's failure, Pace left the music business and in 1930 he sold his publishing interests.

In 1925 Pace founded the Northeastern Life Insurance Company in Newark, New Jersey. After it was incorporated into the Supreme Liberty Life Insurance Company in Chicago four years later, Pace became the new company's president and built it into the largest black-owned business in the North during the 1930s. He wrote a self-help book, *Beginning Again* (1934), and served as editor of the company's monthly newspaper, *The Guardian*. (His assistant was future publisher John H. Johnson, who began his career by assembling a news digest from black periodicals for Pace.) Besides his insurance business, Pace attended the Chicago Law School, receiving his law degree in 1933, and was active in Democratic Party politics.

In the late 1930s, Pace cut back on his black community activities. In 1942, he opened a law office in downtown Chicago and bought a house in a white suburb. According to John Johnson, disgruntled employees accused Pace, who was extremely light skinned, of trying to "pass" for white, and threatened to demonstrate outside his house. The criticism hurt him deeply. He withdrew further from the black community and died the following year. ◆

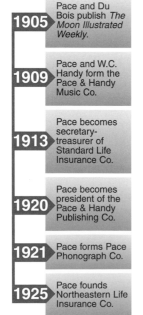

1905 Pace and Du Bois publish *The Moon Illustrated Weekly.*

1909 Pace and W.C. Handy form the Pace & Handy Music Co.

1913 Pace becomes secretary-treasurer of Standard Life Insurance Co.

1920 Pace becomes president of the Pace & Handy Publishing Co.

1921 Pace forms Pace Phonograph Co.

1925 Pace founds Northeastern Life Insurance Co.

Patiño, Simón Iturri

1860–1947 ● TIN MINER

Born in Santivañez, Cochabamba in Bolivia, Patiño spearheaded Bolivia's transition from silver to tin producer and in the process became one of the wealthiest men in the world, powerful enough to influence Bolivian politics greatly in the early twentieth century. Working first for Bolivian and German merchant houses and the Huanchaca Company, Bolivia's foremost silver-mining concern, Patiño purchased his own share of La Salvadora tin mine in 1894. After striking a rich vein in 1900, Patiño continuously modernized mining production and began purchasing other tin mines. He also began buying shares in German and, later, in partnership with U.S. venture capitalists, British tin-smelting operations in Europe. In 1924 he established Patiño Mines and Enterprises in the United States. He also bought into Malaysian tin mines. By the 1920s his Bolivian holdings were only a small fraction of his total business empire, although he continued to produce at least one-third of all Bolivian tin. With his Banco Mercantil, he was one of Bolivia's leading bankers; he also owned a majority share in the Sociedad Agícola é Ganadera de Cinti, the largest agro-industrial enterprise in Bolivia.

Given his financial clout, Patiño was a major figure in Bolivian politics. His actions led to the splintering of the Liberal Party in 1919 and so aided in the revolution that brought the Republicans to power the following year. The Catavi Massacre in 1942, in which the army killed hundreds of unarmed miners and women and children in a labor dispute with Patiño, raised nationalist fervor against the mine owner. Since Patiño had lived in Europe from the 1920s and controlled so much of the Bolivian economy, many Bolivians resented him. This resentment ultimately led to the expropriation of his mines during the 1952 revolution and the creation of Comibol, the state mining company. ◆

1894 Patiño buys a share of La Salvadora tin mine.

1900 Patiño strikes a rich vein.

1919 Patiño's actions splinter Bolivia's Liberal Party.

1924 Patiño forms Patiño Mines and Enterprises.

1942 Catavi Massacre raises ill will against Patiño.

1952 Patiño's mines are expropriated.

Patterson, Charles R.

?–1910 ● CARRIAGE MANUFACTURER

Originally from Virginia, Charles R. Patterson settled in Greenfield, Ohio, where he worked as a blacksmith before opening a buggy repair shop in 1865. His mechanical skills helped him prosper, and eventually his firm, C. R. Patterson & Sons, began manufacturing carriages and wagons. It grew to employ forty skilled mechanics and eventually produced twenty-eight buggy models, including phaetons, school wagons, funeral hearses, and surreys. One particularly popular model, a doctor's buggy, was used throughout the Southwest and Midwest.

After Patterson's death, his son Frederick Douglass Patterson (1871–1932) became general manager of the company. Frederick had been the first black student to graduate from the local high school. After receiving a bachelor of arts degree from Ohio State University in Columbus, he taught history at Louisville High School. In 1901 he married Estelline Postell of Hopkinsville, Kentucky. That same year he resigned his teaching position and returned to Ohio to work in his father's firm. Under Frederick's leadership the firm became the largest African-American-owned manufacturing company in the United States, producing 500 new vehicles and earning $75,000 annually.

In 1916 with the introduction of the Patterson-Greenfield, Frederick Patterson became the country's first and only black manufacturer of automobiles. By 1919 he had built thirty cars, but lacking the capital for production-line techniques, he was not able to compete with other manufacturers. Nevertheless, C. R. Patterson & Sons continued to be successful, building truck bodies as well as the bodies for school buses used all over Ohio, and bus bodies for the Cincinnati transit system. Frederick Patterson was a member of the Executive Committee of the National Negro Business League and the Greenfield Business League. The firm dissolved six years after his death. ◆

1865 C. Patterson opens a buggy repair shop.

1910 F. Patterson takes over his father's firm.

1916 F. Patterson begins manufacturing automobiles.

1919 F. Patterson builds his 30th car.

Peabody, George

1795–1869 ● BUSINESSMAN

G eorge Peabody began life in a poor family that could not afford to support him past the age of 11. He began work as a grocer's apprentice and rapidly learned the business of buying and selling goods. He was very successful and rose rapidly in the business world. Before he was 20, he had become manager of an important business house in the District of Columbia. The company moved to Baltimore, where George Peabody eventually became the head of the firm and an extremely rich man. He was engaged especially in importing British goods

Making money was not Peabody's main interest in life, although he made a lot of it both as a merchant and as an investor in railroads. He arranged a loan of $8 million to the State of Maryland by British bankers and refused to take a cent of commission for it. He used his own very large fortune to help the American ministers to England entertain British nobility, British political leaders, and British bankers, in their effort to represent the United States effectively. Peabody spent a great deal of time in London and acted as a channel for British bankers to invest in American business.

Peabody then undertook an unusual activity: he began giving away enormous amounts of money to causes that appeared good to him. He gave money for slum clearance and low-cost housing in London. He donated the funds for the

Peabody gave away enormous amounts of money for slum clearance and low-cost housing in London.

Peabody Institute in Baltimore (a major public library), and for scientific institutes at Yale University. Peabody money went into several branches of scientific research, including funds for his nephew, Othniel Marsh, who made the first really important American collection of fossils. One of his major gifts was the creation of the Peabody Education Fund, which was intended to support educational enterprises in the South. His name is now attached to one of the most distinguished and important schools for the training of teachers, the George Peabody College of Education at Nashville, Tennessee. His original town of South Danvers changed its name to Peabody. George Peabody's generous use of his money for the good of others made him the first important example of an American businessman who became a philanthropist. ◆

Penney, James Cash

1875–1971 ● RETAIL TYCOON

> *"Golden Rule principles are just as necessary for operating a business profitably as are trucks, typewriters, or twine."*
>
> J. C. Penney, 1902

James Cash Penney was born in Hamilton, Missouri, on September 16, 1875. He was the son of James Cash and Mary Francis (Paxton) Penney, grandson of Eli and Mildred (Burris) Penney, and great-grandson of John Penney. His father was a clergyman and a farmer. James E. Penney was educated at public schools in his native city. In 1893 he began working as a clerk in the general of John M. Hale in Hamilton. For the benefit of his health, he went to Colorado in 1897 and, after a brief period of employment in a Denver store, purchased a meat and bakery business in Longmont, Colorado. This venture proved to be unsuccessful, and he found employment as a clerk for Guy Johnson and T. M. Callahan, a mercantile partnership in Evanston, Wyoming. In 1902, his employers established a store in Kemmerer, Wyoming, and sold him a one-third interest in the store for which he invested $500 that he had saved and $1500 that he had borrowed. He served as manager of the store until 1907 when he bought the interest of his partners.

With the store in Kemmerer as his base, he began to expand his operations and established stores in Cumberland and other locations in Wyoming in 1908 and his fifth store was opened in Eureka, Utah, in 1909. He incorporated his business in 1913 under the name of J.C. Penney Company, and was president of the venture until 1917 when he chose to become chairman of the board of directors. He remained in that office until his retirement in 1958, although he was a director of the corporation until his death. The business was expanded and by the 1920s Penney stores were flourishing in forty-eight states. During the early growth of the company the stores were operated under partnership names, differing in each case in accordance with interests represented. They were often called Golden Rule stores, although that was never a corporate name, and Penney became known as the man with a thousand partners. Under that original plan the managers in each store received one-third of the profit but after 1927, they were permitted to aquire stock based upon their production earnings and financed out of such earnings. Company headquarters was maintained in Kemerer until the spring of 1908 when it moved to Salt Lake City, Utah. In 1913, it was moved to New York City. The business had annual income of $29,000 in 1902. By 1958, when Penney retired, it had annual sales of some $1.4 billion, nearly 1700 stores, and 75,000 employees.

During early years the company sold chiefly men's and women's clothing, dry goods, notions, and miscellaneous apparel. Its policy was to put one price on each article and never mark it down. The stores had no special sales, yet con-

1893 Penney begins clerking in a general store.

1902 Penney and partners establish a store in Wyoming.

1908 Penney moves his headquarters to Salt Lake City.

1909 Penney opens his fifth store.

1913 Penney incorporates the J.C. Penney Co.

1920 J. C. Penney Co. has stores in 48 states.

tinually sold goods at so low a price as to put other stores beyond competition. Later, although Penney believed in a reasonable profit, the corporation did not maintain the lowest prices, relying on its reputation to stimulate sales. It came to institute one of the most sophisticated merchandise testing centers in retailing and developed its own brands to make sure that it was offering what it considered the best quality and value. Although merchandising procedures changed with the times, it was not until the 1950s that the stores switched to more complete lines and more fashionable merchandise. It was also in the period that the company introduced credit, previously having been a strictly cash-and-carry undertaking, a policy that was greatly influenced by Penney's conservatism. After the credit plan was begun, sales rose rapidly and by the time of Penney's death were more than $4 billion annually. Penney's had become the country's fifth largest merchandising company, second in the nonfood retail industry to Sears, Roebuck, & Company.

> **Penney's policy was to put one price on each article and never mark it down.**

Penney was involved actively in religious and charitable endeavors throughout his career, and as a **nonagenarian** he kept five full-time secretaries busy with correspondence. As early as 1922, he purchased land at Green Cove Springs, Florida, and fitted up some fifty cottages for the accommodation of retired clergymen. In 1926, he purchased an additional 120,000 acres of land nearby and established Penney Farms, an experimental farming community that for a time featured an agricultural school, and built the Penney Memorial Home Community for retired clergymen, missionaries, other church workers, and their wives. The project consisted of a complex of two-story buildings, enclosing 106 apartments, as well as a separate large chapel and a library. It was completed in 1928 at a cost of $500,000 and dedicated to his parents. Penney Farms eventually became the postal address of the community. In 1946, this property was given to the Christian Herald Association of which Penney was president for a time. He founded and for many years was president of the James C. Penney Foundation, New York City. Other church-related work was that of vice president and director of the Laymen's Movement and a director Allied Youth, Inc. For many years, he spoke to religious and welfare groups in many parts of the country and was active in the work of the YMCA, Boy Scouts of America, 4-H Clubs, and kindred organizations.

nonagenarian: a person between 90 and 100 years old.

Richard W. Sears

Even in his youth, Richard W. Sears, one of American's greatest salesmen, took an interest in advertising and trade, often ordering products from catalogs and selling them to friends. While working as a station agent for the Minnesota and St. Louis Railroad, Sears started a side business trading coal and lumber. With a keen marketing eye, he observed the high retail markup on all sorts of goods, including watches. When a local jeweler received an unwanted shipment of gold-filled watches, Sears saw his opportunity, buying the watches at a greatly reduced price and selling them to agents up and down the railroad line for a slight per-unit profit. Sears netted $5000—a tidy sum for that era.

In 1886, he opened a watch business, moving in 1887 to Chicago, where he teamed up with Alvah C. Roebuck. In 1888 he launched the Sears mail-order catalog. His business relied on high volume, low profit margins, and low inventory and overhead costs. By 1895, Sears and Roebuck boasted a full-scale catalog and expanded its geographical scope to include rural areas, most of which did not have access to a wide selection of affordable goods. At this time, Sears profited not only from low prices (other firms could offer this, too) but also savvy advertising and a strong emphasis on service.

Penney married three times. He was first married in 1899 to Berta Aline with whom he had two sons, Roswell Kemper and James Cash. Berta died 1910. Penney's second wife was Mary Hortense, whom Penney married in 1919 and with whom he had a son, Kimball. Mary died in 1923. Penney married a third time in 1926 to Caroline, with whom he had two daughters, Mary Francis and Carol Marie. James C. Penney died in New York City on February 12, 1971. ◆

Perot, H(enry) Ross

1930–PRESENT ● COMPUTER
& DATA PROCESSING MOGUL

"The American Dream. Those three short, simple words encompass the hopes and aspirations of all the peoples on earth.
Ross Perot, *United We Stand*, 1992

As a child, Perot tried to make extra money selling magazines, seeds, and greeting cards.

Ross Perot was born June 27, 1930 in Texarkana, Texas, the son of Ross and Lulu May Perot. He grew up in modest circumstances in Texarkana, where he attended public schools and Texarkana Junior College. From a young age, Perot exhibited entrepreneurial inclinations. He worked at various jobs during his childhood, and often tried to make extra money selling magazines, gardens seeds, and greeting cards, among other things.

In 1949, Perot entered the United States Naval Academy in Annapolis Maryland, where he served as class president, chairman of the honor committee, and battalion commander. He graduated in 1953 and spent the next four years as a shipboard naval officer. Perot married Margot Birmingham in 1956. Upon his discharge from the navy in 1957, Perot and his wife moved to Dallas, Texas, where he began working for IBM as a salesman. He left IBM in 1962 and, with only $1,000 in his pocket, started his own data processing company, Electronic Data Systems (EDS). Under Perot's no-nonsense direction, EDS grew into a multimillion-dollar enterprise with thousands of employees. In 1984, Perot sold EDS to General Motors for $2.5 billion. He continued as the chairman of EDS for two years, then left to start a new computer services firm called Perot Systems Cooperation.

Perot became a major figure in the 1992 presidential election through his forceful personality, his apparent willingness to talk about things the major party candidates avoided, his becoming the vessel for many people's anger and frustration with the political system, and his very substantial wallet. Perot, who was born June 27, 1930, had earned his fortune largely through his computer company's success at winning contracts with the federal government for processing Medicare and Medicaid claims.

Perot had for some years been on the fringes of public policy issues. He had worked on reforming Texas's education system and its antidrug policies. But he became famous for his much-publicized efforts in 1969 to free American prisoners of war held in North Vietnam. His successful effort to free two of his company s employees who were imprisoned in Iran in 1978 was the subject of a best-selling book, *On Wings of Eagles*, and of a television miniseries. But there were some questions about Perot's version of the Iran escapade, and his persistence on the POW issue—his charges that the Reagan administration was not doing enough to help prisoners Perot believed were still being held in North Vietnam—caused failings out between him and President Reagan and also between him and then vice president George Bush.

Everything about Perot's candidacy was unconventional. He launched it on a television talk show in February 1992, saying that if volunteers placed his name on the ballot in fifty states, he would run for president. But his campaign began well before the ballot work was finished, in mid September, and Perot himself put substantial funds into the work of his "volunteers." The crew-cut, plain-talking, can-do Perot captured people's imagination and became the leader of a substantial movement. At the height of his popularity, in early June, Perot was running about even with Bill Clinton and George Bush in the polls and led in some. There was much speculation that Perot could carry enough states to keep either major party candidate from winning the election outright and that the outcome would be decided, according to the Constitution, by the House of Representatives.

But there had been signs from almost the beginning that Perot was not prepared for a presidential race. His knowledge of public affairs was fragmentary, and his temperament was wrong for the rigors of electoral politics. Also, his authoritar-

1953 Perot graduates from the Naval Academy.

1957 Perot begins working for IBM.

1962 Perot establishes Electronic Data Systems.

1969 Perot negotiates for the release of American POWs in Vietnam.

1984 Perot sells EDS to General Motors for $2.5 billion.

1992 Perot announces his plans to run for the presidency.

> *"If we decide to take this level of business creating ability nationwide, we'll all be plucking chickens for a living."*
>
> Ross Perot, 1992, about Bill Clinton's economic initiatives

ian personality was the cause of considerable unease. When Perot suddenly withdrew from the race—because he could not take the pressure—on July 16, the last day of the Democratic convention, he left many of his followers feeling abandoned. And Clinton won the bulk of Perot's supporters.

Perot's reentry into the race on October 1 was just as quirky as his withdrawal had been, but he made it clear that he did not want to be declared a quitter. His thirty-minute "infomercials"—featuring Perot sitting behind a desk and pointing to various charts about the state of the economy—broke all the rules of television, and amassed huge audiences. But Perot was not as ready as he had suggested to propose hard steps to eliminate the federal deficit. Still, he helped make the deficit an issue in the election, and he also put political reform on the agenda—especially the subjects of "revolving-door" lobbyists and lobbyists for foreign countries. In doing so, he forced Clinton to make a big play for the Perot constituency, both before and after the election so that Clinton could have a governing majority and win reelection in 1996.

Two weeks before the election, Perot began to climb in the polls again; his backing got as high as about 20 percent. But then his bizarre behavior cut into his momentum. In his appearance on the television program *60 Minutes* nine days before the election, and at a press conference the following day, he showed aspects of his personality that he had kept fairly well hidden since his reentry—signs of an overly suspicious nature and his short temper. He said that he had pulled out of the race because he had been warned that the Bush campaign would try to disrupt his daughter's wedding; he also told a not-very-credible tale about an attempt on his life in 1970 by some Black Panthers who, he said, had been sent by the North Vietnamese.

Nonetheless, his winning 19 percent of the vote representing nearly 20 million people, showed that he still had a substantial following—or that a large number of people remained unmoved by the major-party candidates. ◆

Pillsbury, Philip Winston

1903–1984 ● FOOD PROCESSING
TYCOON

P hilip Winston Pillsbury was the only son of Charles
Stinson Pillsbury and Helen Nelle Pendleton Winston.
His first paternal American ancestor, William Pillsbury,
had come to America from England seven generations earlier,
in 1640. In 1869 Pillsbury's grandfather Charles Alfred
Pillsbury, arrived in Minneapolis, Minnesota, and purchased a
share in the flour-milling business of his uncle John Sargent
Pillsbury, a prominent state politician and successful businessman. A few years later, when the uncle became governor of
Minnesota, the management of the milling business was given
to Charles Alfred. At this time various forces were about to
transform the milling industry. Charles Alfred played a major
role in taking advantage of these changes. In 1872 he, his
uncle (John Sargent), and his father organized C. A. Pillsbury
& Company, producing one of the leaders in the milling
industry. By 1889, an English syndicate purchased the
Pillsbury Mills, together with those of Senator W. D.
Washburn, combining them to form the Pillsbury-Washburn
Flour Mills Company. Under the management of Charles
Alfred, the company soon became the largest milling firm in
the world.

Charles Alfred's children, John Sargent II and Charles
Stinson, got involved in the management and operation of
the company from early ages. As the twins' relationship with
the company matured, they decided to reorganize in order to
wrest control away from the English syndicate and to return it
to American and family control. The process proved to be
lengthy. In the meantime, John Sargent Pillsbury had eight
children, and Charles Stinson Pillsbury had four—three
daughters and a son, Philip Winston. These children were to
become a new generation of Pillsbury Company leaders.

After receiving his preliminary education at Blake School
(Hopkins, Minnesota) and Hotchkiss School (Lakeville,
Connecticut), Philip Winston Pillsbury went to Yale College,

Pillsbury intro-
duced many
easy-to-prepare
food products,
such as pan-
cake, biscuit,
and cake mixes.

where he starred as a guard on the university's undefeated 1923 football team, was an All-American water polo player, and sang tenor in the glee club. Also in 1923, the family finally reacquired the milling business from the English syndicate; that summer Philip attended some of the negotiating sessions with the Pillsbury-Washburn representatives in London. His plans had been to pursue a medical career, but once the return of the properties was accomplished, his family persuaded him to cast his lot with the company. A year later, on graduation from Yale with an A.B., he became an employee of the company.

Pillsbury started work as a clerk in the "A" mill wheat department. Working at nearly every job in the mill, he stayed long enough in each job to understand and perform all the tasks required, from the receipt of the grain to shipment of the milled products. In 1928, at the age of 25, he was elected a member of the board of directors, its youngest member in history. Having mastered the art and science of milling, Philip was transferred in 1932 to the sales department and was sent to Chicago, where he ultimately became branch manager. About a year after his marriage to Eleanor Bellows on July 5, 1934, he returned to Minneapolis to assume responsibility for the company's sales in the eastern United States.

It was not too long before Philip became a senior officer of the company. In 1940 he had mustered enough experience and clout to be appointed treasurer. Six months later, pleased with Philip's integrity, experience, and insight, the Pillsbury family urged the board to appoint him president and chief executive officer.

At the time Pillsbury took over the helm, the company's sales and profits were being threatened by competition. The company was in need of innovation, reorganization, and growth. The first major decision Pillsbury made as president was to acquire a large west-coast miller, Globe Grain & Milling Company. Moreover, he launched a comprehensive plan for research and development. The main objective was to develop derivative products that could be used by households instead of food-processing factories. During World War II, the Pillsbury labs pioneered the production of formula cattle feed and enriched flour. When the war ended, the company started to introduce one "easy to prepare" food product after another, including pancakes, waffles, and biscuits, to be

1889 The Pillsbury-Washburn Flour Mills Co. is formed.

1923 Pillsbury family wrests control of company from English syndicate.

1924 Pillsbury joins the family firm as clerk.

1928 Pillsbury is elected to board of directors.

1932 Pillsbury tackles sales in Chicago.

1940 Pillsbury is appointed president and chief executive officer.

1950 Pillsbury oversees the company's expansion into a giant diversified food concern.

The Pillsbury Bakeoff

In 1949, the Pillsbury Company decided to hold a recipe contest with the goal of sharing and publicizing favorite family recipes from kitchens across America. Ordinary cooks were invited to send original recipes to Pillsbury's test kitchens, where a panel of home economists reviewed them. The cooks who submitted the best recipes were invited to New York's elegant Waldorf-Astoria Hotel for a cooking contest. Theodora Smafield of Michigan won the first Pillsbury Bakeoff with her unique No-Knead Water-Rising Twists. Since 1949, Pillsbury has sponsored bakeoffs almost every year, and many of the winning recipes have become favorites across the country. In the early years of the bakeoff, cooks were required to use Pillsbury flour in their recipes. The rules were later broadened so that contestants could use any number of Pillsbury products. Today, cooks can submit recipes in four categories: 30-minute main dishes, simple side dishes, fast and easy treats, and quick snacks and appetizers. The recipes are judged on their taste and appearance, quick and easy preparation, creativity, general appeal, and appropriate use of Pillsbury products.

followed later by cake, pie, and roll mixes. By the mid-1950s, the combination of such innovative goods, along with intensive and clever advertising (such as the annual national "Bake Off" contest), made the Pillsbury Company a leader in bringing baking convenience to the American homemaker.

In 1952 Pillsbury retired from the presidency and immediately became chairman of the board, a position he held until 1965. He continued as a director until 1974. At the time, the company's net sales were $315 million, more than seven times the level of sales at the beginning of his presidency.

He now had more time to spend with family and friends and to pursue philanthropic and civic endeavors. After the death of his wife in 1971, he married Corinne Griffith in 1977. Pillsbury died of cancer at the Abbott-Northwestern Hospital in Minneapolis, Minnesota.

Although family connections and an Ivy League education were instrumental in his rise to power, Pillsbury proved, in the course of his career, to be the right man to lead the Pillsbury Company. He oversaw the company's transformation from a milling business to a giant diversified food concern. In the process, he became a leader in introducing easy-to-prepare food products to the American household. ◆

During World War II, the Pillsbury labs pioneered the production of formula cattle feed and enriched flour.

Pullman, George Mortimer

1831–1897 ● RAILROAD CAR MANUFACTURER

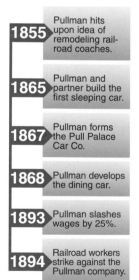

1855	Pullman hits upon idea of remodeling railroad coaches.
1865	Pullman and partner build the first sleeping car.
1867	Pullman forms the Pull Palace Car Co.
1868	Pullman develops the dining car.
1893	Pullman slashes wages by 25%.
1894	Railroad workers strike against the Pullman company.

An American industrialist, George Mortimer Pullman invented the Pullman Palace sleeping car, which made long-distance rail travel comfortable and popular. Born in Brocton, New York, Pullman apprenticed as a cabinetmaker before moving to Chicago in 1855, when he saw an opportunity to make money rebuilding and remodeling old railroad coaches. With his partner, Ben Field, he developed the idea of the sleeping car, building the first—called "the Pioneer"—in 1865. The car had a folding upper berth and seat cushions that could be extended to create a lower berth. The design rapidly found favor with the railroads, and in 1867, Pullman organized the Pullman Palace Car Company to manufacture his sleeping cars. He soon developed other types of cars, most notably the dining car in 1868. The Pullman cars made long-distance rail travel practical, comfortable, attractive, and "civilized" and gave great impetus to the ongoing construction of the transcontinental railroad. Pullman controlled the operation of the cars under contract to the railroads.

Pullman built a factory and company town, Pullman, Illinois, just south of Chicago. The town was designed along utopian lines as a clean and decent place for employees to live. Many employees, however, saw it as a kind of prison.

They were compelled to live there, pay rent to Pullman, and redeem their scrip salary at Pullman stores.

The company was the target of the great Pullman strike from May 11 to July 20, 1894. The financial panic of 1893 had prompted the company to slash wages by 25 percent without cutting company-controlled rents or company-store prices. Outraged, local members of the American Railway Union called a general strike. When Pullman refused arbitration, the union's national council, under Eugene V. Debs, mounted a nationwide boycott of Pullman cars. Sympathy strikes were triggered in twenty-seven states. In Chicago, various outbreaks of violence occurred, but the liberal governor of Illinois, John Peter Altgeld, declined to call out the militia. At last, on July 2, U.S. Attorney General Richard Olney bowed to corporate pressure and prevailed upon President Grover Cleveland to mobilize twenty-five hundred federal troops to end the strike.

The Pullman cars made long-distance rail travel comfortable, attractive, and civilized.

An old Pullman car from the Santa Fe Railroad Line. Photographed in Los Angeles, 1986.

The Pullman Strike

As a result of the financial panic of 1893, various railroad companies suffered heavy losses, which led them to curtail their operations and to reduce the wages of their employees. The Pullman Palace Car Company lowered the wages of its employees an average of 25 percent. This company, organized in 1867, carried on its chief operations at Pullman, a town which it owned just south of Chicago. When wages were reduced, no reduction was made in the rentals and fees charged employees in the company town. About 4,000 disgruntled employees joined Eugene V. Debs's American Railway Union in the spring of 1894. On May 11, 1894, about 2,500 Pullman employees quit work and forced the closing of the shops. Attempts were made to arbitrate the differences between the company and its employees, but the former took the view that there was nothing to arbitrate. Nor would the company consent to bargain with the union, although Pullman officials expressed readiness to deal with employees individually.

The local strike soon developed into a general railroad strike when members of the American Railway Union refused to handle Pullman cars. First, twenty-four Chicago-based railroads were tied up. This led to a general railroad tie-up throughout the western United States by June 28. In another two days the strike had spread to practically all parts of the country. At this juncture federal judges William A. Woods and Peter S. Grosscup issued a "blanket injunction," prohibiting all interference with trains. Strikers defied the injunction and violence broke out. President Grover Cleveland ordered federal troops into Chicago on July 4. Following their arrival, there was much mob violence and destruction of railroad property. Rioting occurred in cities as far west as Oakland, California. By July 13 some trains were running under military guard, and a few days later the strike was broken. By July 20, all federal troops were out of Chicago. During the strike, Debs was arrested and his subsequent conviction for violation of a federal injunction led to a lengthy campaign to curb the use of blanket injunctions in labor disputes. This campaign ultimately resulted in the passage of the Norris-La Guardia Anti-Injunction Act of 1932.

Paternalistic, authoritarian, and as mean-spirited as he was inventive, Pullman contributed greatly to the development and financial viability of passenger rail operations in the United States and especially over the vast distances of the west. He is buried in an elaborate mausoleum in Chicago's Graceland Cemetery; however, his most enduring physical monument, aside from the Pullman sleeping cars that still traverse America's rails, is the Victorian-Romanesque architecture of his company town, which still stands, largely unchanged, as part of what is now Chicago's South Side. ◆

Rhodes, Cecil John

1853–1902 ● SOUTH AFRICAN FINANCIER

> *"So little done, so much to do."*
> Cecil John Rhodes, last words, 1902

ecil John Rhodes was the fifth son of the vicar of Bishop's Stortford in England. Unlike his brothers, he did not attend public school because he suffered from poor health. Instead, he went to the local grammar school. His health also prevented his going into the army or becoming a **barrister** or a clergyman, all careers that he had considered.

barrister: a lawyer.

At the age of 17 he followed his brother Herbert to Natal in South Africa and went to work on a cotton farm. In 1871 Rhodes moved to the diamond mines and harsh conditions of Kimberley. Still dogged by poor health, he soon returned to England. Between 1873 and 1881 he traveled between Kimberley and Oxford, from where he finally graduated in the classics. He then wrote the first of his seven wills, leaving the fortune he did not yet possess for the founding of a secret society aimed at extending British rule "throughout the world." He dreamed of "painting the map red" and of building a railroad from the Cape to Cairo.

amalgamate: to combine into a larger whole.

syndicate: a combination of companies for a commercial purpose.

After returning to Kimberley, he began to **amalgamate** first the operations of individuals, then of **syndicates**, continually extending his control, until by 1891 he had gained a virtual monopoly of production and marketing through his De Beers Consolidated Mines company, controlling 90 percent of the world's diamond production. In 1887 Rhodes also founded Consolidated Gold Fields, one of the most powerful goldmining corporations on the Witwatersrand.

He was more interested in power than in money. He envisioned a world led by Great Britain, Germany, and the United States. He now had the wherewithal to promote his dreams of the expansion of the British Empire from its base in the Cape Colony.

Rhodes entered Cape politics and became the prime minister of Cape Colony in 1881. In 1884, after being pushed aside by General Charles Warren in Bechuanaland, he resolved that northward expansion beyond the Limpopo River would be carried out under the colonial, not the British, government, a policy of expansion and autonomy termed "colonialism." Further to this, he developed a friendship with Jan Hofmeyr, the head of the Afrikaaner Bond. They agreed on the necessity of keeping the British government out of South Africa's internal affairs and saw the future as dependent upon the cooperation of the Boers and the British, with the African tribesmen excluded from the political system. Their aim was to unite South Africa and have British imperial cooperation for trade and defense. However, they had not taken into account the determination of the Transvaal and the Orange Free State to remain independent. Led by President Paul Kruger, who held that "Africa was for the Afrikaaners," the South African Republic was equally interested in territorial expansion and commercial autonomy. Rhodes found that Kruger was one man he could never buy off.

Rhodes failed in his bid to have the Cape Colony annex Bechuanaland, the route to the northern territories of Mashonaland and Ndebeleland (which became Rhodesia), but he cleverly managed to obtain an exclusive treaty of friendship with King Lobengula, ruler of the Ndebele. He had John Moffat, a missionary, one of the few people the king trusted, sent to do this work, and Charles Rudd also obtained an exclusive concession on Rhodes's behalf over metals and minerals. Rhodes then obtained a royal charter of incorporation for his British South Africa Company that gave it the authority to make treaties, mine resources, and maintain a police force. In 1890 the company's pioneers occupied Mashonaland, and as a gesture to Britain's prime minister, who did not trust Rhodes, the latter had a newly established fort, Salisbury, named after him. The "scramble for Africa" was in full swing as Rhodes tried unsuccessfully to claim Katanga in the Congo in 1890, but the Belgians preempted him. In 1893 he sent his medical adviser and longtime personal friend, Dr. Leander Starr Jameson, to put down a serious Ndebele uprising. This led to the crushing of the Ndebele and the death of Lobengula.

Although Rhodes met with Kruger in 1890, he could not persuade him to agree to a railway and customs union. The Transvaal steadily grew in political strength after the discovery of gold in Witwatersrand. In 1895 Rhodes decided to put a stop to the Transvaal's autonomous growth, which threatened his plans for a British South African dominion. An ingenious coup was plotted in which the Uitlanders (foreigners who had come to work in the gold mines and had no political rights) were to stage a revolt intended to cause the British government to intercede and force a settlement. Rhodes managed to get colonial secretary Joseph Chamberlain's backing and had his company, Consolidated Gold Fields, foot the bill. Although the Uitlanders decided not to go through with the plan as it had no real support, Jameson impetuously led an attack in the Transvaal from Bechuanaland in 1895, and his forces were routed. Rhodes accepted responsibility for the disastrous Jameson raid and resigned his post as prime minister of Cape Colony, although he was able to keep his parliamentary seat and hold on to the British South Africa Company by blackmailing Chamberlain with threats to publish letters showing his role in the raid. The raid also served to deepen the split between the Dutch and the British colonials, as Kruger consolidated his position.

Even in the last years of his life, Rhodes was not out of the news, as a rare liaison with an adventuress, Princess Radziwill, ended in a court case in which she was charged with forging letters and bills of exchange in his name. Rhodes died before the end of the trial and was buried in the Matopo Hills in Rhodesia (now Zambia/Zimbabwe). His will included the generous scheme of scholarships at Oxford (the Rhodes schol-

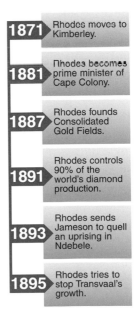

1871 Rhodes moves to Kimberley.

1881 Rhodes becomes prime minister of Cape Colony.

1887 Rhodes founds Consolidated Gold Fields.

1891 Rhodes controls 90% of the world's diamond production.

1893 Rhodes sends Jameson to quell an uprising in Ndebele.

1895 Rhodes tries to stop Transvaal's growth.

arships) for young men from the colonies, the United States, and Germany. ◆

Ripley, Edward Payson

1845–1920 ● RAILROAD EXECUTIVE

Ripley hammered the Santa Fe railroad into one of the most efficient, prosperous, and prestigious railroads in the country.

One of the more successful Western railroad executives, Edward Payson Ripley resurrected the bankrupt and nearly defunct Santa Fe Railroad. Born in Dorchester, Massachusetts, Ripley was trained as a lawyer. He entered the railroad business as the New England agent for a number of Western lines. He performed so well in this capacity that he was hired by the Burlington railroad system as an executive in the traffic department and became general traffic manager by 1888. He next moved to the Chicago, Milwaukee and St. Paul (later called the Chicago, Milwaukee, St. Paul and Pacific Railroad, or simply the Milwaukee Road) as vice president and served in that capacity until the turn of the century, when he was offered the presidency of the Atchison, Topeka and Santa Fe Railroad.

The appointment was no plum, for the Santa Fe had barely emerged from bankruptcy in the early 1890s and had been floundering ever since. Overhauling and rebuilding the line, Ripley hammered it into one of the more efficient, prosperous, and prestigious railroads in the nation. He accomplished this in part by creatively working with government regulators and supporting the Hepburn Act of 1906, which gave the government the authority to fix maximum railroad rates in cases where carriers and shippers could not agree. Ripley believed that the act would facilitate rail expansion and promote sustained profitability. When the railroads were seeking substantial rate increases to match high levels of inflation in 1910, the Hepburn Act was brought to bear. Ripley was dismayed by what he saw as the government's intransigence. He was nominated by all of the Western railroads to represent them before the Interstate Commerce Commission, which, however, failed to grant the requested rate increases. Ripley, in effect, then threw up his hands in disgust and stepped down from his role as the railroads' emissary to the government. ◆

Rockefeller, John Davison

1839–1937 ● INDUSTRIALIST

> *"I believe it is my duty to make money and still more money and to use the money I make for the good of my fellow man according to the dictates of my conscience."*
>
> John D. Rockefeller, 1905

John Davison Rockefeller was born in Richford, Tioga County, New York, where his father traded in lumber and salt. At a very early age, Rockefeller showed an aptitude for numbers, displaying an attention to detail, especially where money was concerned. At the age of seven, he had his first successful business venture—selling turkeys. The family then moved to Ohio, and at age sixteen, Rockefeller went to work in Cleveland for a produce firm. In 1859 he formed a partnership with Colonel Maurice Clark to trade produce. When Clark discovered oil, they began trading Pennsylvania oil. The idea of accruing instant wealth from oil caught their fancy. In 1863, when a new railroad line put Cleveland in a position to compete. **Refineries** sprang into existence. At

refinery: machinery for purifying petroleum.

first, Rockefeller thought refining would be merely a sideline. In 1865, after repeated arguments about expansion, he bought out his partner, Clark, for $12,500. With the purchase of the refinery, Rockefeller began to expand the business and poured his profits, plus borrowed money, into building a second refinery. He decided to open additional markets, and in 1866, put his brother William in charge of another firm in New York as the manager of the Atlantic coast trade and the export of kerosene. The growing popularity of the refining business led Rockefeller to comment: "All sorts of people went into it; the butcher, the baker, and the candlestick maker began to refine oil." His success was a result of his ability to cut costs as well as a ruthlessness in stifling competition.

In 1867 Rockefeller and his new partner, Andre, brought Henry Flagler into the business as a third partner. Flagler became a valued colleague and a close friend. In 1870 Rockefeller and a few of his people incorporated the Standard Oil Company (Ohio) and the company prospered. Rockefeller bought out his competitors by using a new method of purchase—he gave stock in his company to acquire other companies. He never owned more than 27 percent of Standard Oil stock, but even so, he became the wealthiest man in the United States with a personal fortune exceeding one billion dollars.

By the early 1880s Standard Oil had bought out or driven out of business most of its competition in Ohio. The company used its leverage to obtain reduced freight rates. It then bought pipelines and terminals, and began to buy competing refineries in other cities until Standard Oil almost had a monopoly. The company exploited every avenue to increase income and lower expenses. It not only received reduced freight rates but was also getting "drawbacks," collecting a percentage of the freight costs paid by the competition. This practice led to the enactment of anti-monopoly laws, first by the states and then by Congress. The Sherman Antitrust Act was passed by Congress in 1890, and the law was upheld in the Ohio Supreme Court in 1892.

Rockefeller was able to work around the law for a while by eliminating the Standard Oil "Trust" and renaming the company Standard Oil Company of New Jersey. The new company was the largest and most efficient producer of petroleum products. Standard Oil of New Jersey operated throughout the

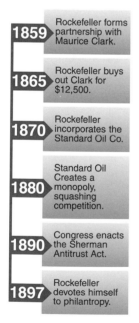

1859 Rockefeller forms partnership with Maurice Clark.

1865 Rockefeller buys out Clark for $12,500.

1870 Rockefeller incorporates the Standard Oil Co.

1880 Standard Oil Creates a monopoly, squashing competition.

1890 Congress enacts the Sherman Antitrust Act.

1897 Rockefeller devotes himself to philantropy.

world, until 1911, when the Supreme Court ruled that the company was in violation of the Sherman Antitrust Act.

Rockefeller was a generous philanthropist. As a pious Baptist he began by making relatively small contributions to the Baptist church. In 1892 he was instrumental in founding the University of Chicago. It was suggested that Rockefeller gave his spare change to the university—amounting to thirty-five million dollars. From 1897 he devoted himself exclusively to philanthropy, joined by his son, John (1894–1960). They created the Rockefeller Institute for Medical Research, later renamed Rockefeller University. In his lifetime, John D. Rockefeller contributed over half a billion dollars to charity.

In his later years, Rockefeller was well known for his habit of carrying a pocketful of shiny new dimes that he would give to the small children he met in his travels. Despite his great wealth, he was frugal with regard to personal expenses. He would wear suits until they became shiny. When he died at the age of 98, he was worth twenty-six million dollars, including a single share in Standard Oil worth $43.94. ◆

> *"I have ways of making money you know nothing of."*
> John D. Rockefeller, 1872

Rothschild Family

1744–1879 ● FINANCIERS

The name "Rothschild" was derived from the "red shield" sign over the family house in the Frankfurt-on-Main Jewish ghetto. Founder of the family was Mayer Amschel Rothschild (1744–1812). He was orphaned at the age of 12 and looked after by relatives. Intended for a rabbinical career, he left it to enter a Frankfurt banking firm, which within a few years he headed. He had a special interest in old coins and medals, producing an annual catalog that caught the attention of William IX, landowner of Hesse-Cassel, who had a great interest in numismatics. He was so impressed by Rothschild that in 1769 he appointed him sup-

Mayer
Rothschild's
sons, known as
the "Frankfurt
five," were
all financial
geniuses.

plier to the principality. When Napoleon Bonaparte began to spread his influence across Europe, William provided funds to assist his fellow rulers in face of the challenge and employed Rothschild as his agent.

Rothschild became one of the richest men in Frankfurt and deployed his five surviving sons (he had nineteen children) in different key banking capitals in Europe—Paris, London, Naples, Vienna, and Frankfurt. When William had to flee from Napoleon's armies, he entrusted his fortune to Rothschild, who first concealed it in underground hiding-places originally constructed by the Jews of Frankfurt as secret refuges in the event of danger. Rothschild was, however, able through his sons to invest the money in various countries (even in the form of loans to Napoleon) and as a result when William returned, he found his capital multiplied. He rewarded Rothschild with tax and trade concessions which allowed him to further increase his European operations.

Rothschild's sons, known as the "Frankfurt five," were all financial geniuses and through their cooperation the House of Rothschild became Europe's leading banking house. The youngest son, James Jacob Rothschild (1792–1868), established the Paris branch, Rothschild Frères. After the fall of Napoleon, he raised the money to help France pay its war **indemnity**. He continued as a leading government financier through successive regimes down to the time of Napoleon III. He also played an important role in early French railroad construction. He was an obsessive collector of objets d'art and his home was one of the great salons of Paris, presided over by his talented wife, Betty, who was also his cousin (the Rothschilds married among themselves whenever possible). There, most European artistic luminaries could be encountered—Frédéric Chopin made his French debut there, and other frequent visitors included Franz Liszt, Gioacchino Rossini, Heinrich Heine, and Honoré de Balzac (who dedicated books to both James and Betty). His son, Mayer Alphonse Rothschild (1827–1905), carried on his father's traditions in banking, art collecting, and philanthropy in both the general and Jewish communities. Like his father, he enabled the French government to pay off an indemnity after a military defeat—this time following the Franco-Prussian War (1870–1871).

The third of the brothers, Nathan Mayer Rothschild (1777–1836), was sent to England and after an initial stay in

indemnity: payment for damage or loss.

Mayer Amschel
Rothschild, founder
of the family
(1744–1812).

Manchester, moved to London. By 1815 he was the leading figure on the London stock exchange and raised money for the British campaign against Napoleon in the Peninsular War. The legend that carrier pigeon service brought him early news of the Battle of Waterloo on which he was able to profit is not authentic but both he and his brothers made early use of carrier pigeons and he was reputed better informed on developments in Europe than anyone in the British government. In 1825–1826, a period of a massive bank crash in England, he was instrumental in saving the Bank of England and bailing out the British government. Involved in many philanthropies, he set up a fund to assist victims of the Irish Potato Famine in the 1840s.

He was succeeded in the business by his son Lionel Nathan Rothschild (1808–1879). In 1847 he became the first practicing Jew elected to the British Parliament. However, because he refused to swear the Christian oath incumbent

"It requires a great deal of boldness and a great deal of caution to make a great fortune, and when you have got it, it requires ten times as much wit to keep it."
Meyer Rothschild,
ca. 1830

upon all members, he was not seated. He was reelected repeatedly but was still banned from Parliament. Finally the oath was changed, whereupon he took his place, sitting for another sixteen years in Parliament—but never once making a speech. Lionel Rothschild provided the funds for his friend Benjamin Disraeli, the prime minister, to purchase shares in the Suez Canal and hence establish British control of the waterway. ◆

Ryan, John Dennis

1864–1933 ● Mining mogul

1900 Ryan becomes president of the Daly Bank and Trust Co.

1906 Ryan buys competition, ending War of the Copper Kings.

1909 Ryan becomes president of Anaconda Co.

1912 Ryan creates the Montana Power Co.

1913 Ryan electrifies the Butte, Anaconda, and Pacific Railroad.

John Dennis Ryan's aggressive leadership of Montana's Anaconda Copper Mining Company (ACM) made him one of the nation's foremost capitalists. A native of the copper country near Houghton, Michigan, Ryan showed little interest in the industry or in college. He clerked in his uncle's store before moving to Denver, Colorado, where he became regional manager for an oil company. In that capacity, he met Montana copper magnate Marcus Daly, gained the Amalgamated (Anaconda) Copper Company's lucrative account, and won Daly's favor.

After Daly's death in 1900, Ryan moved to Butte, became president of the Daly Bank and Trust Company, and managed the Standard Oil Company's Butte properties. Amazingly, he succeeded in pacifying war ring copper kings William Andrews Clark and Frederick Augustus Heinze. By 1906, the Amalgamated had purchased the primary Butte holdings of both opponents—thus ending the War of the Copper Kings.

Ryan became president of the Amalgamated (Anaconda) Company in 1909, at the age of 44. Under his direction, the corporation consolidated its diverse holdings, expanded to Mexico and South America, and absorbed the American Brass Company, the world's largest consumer of copper. In 1912, Ryan orchestrated the creation of the Montana Power Company (MPC), which soon provided electrical power to much of Montana.

MPC electrified first the Butte, Anaconda and Pacific Railroad in 1913 and three years later the 440-mile Rocky Mountain division of the Chicago, Milwaukee, St. Paul and Pacific Railroad (Milwaukee Road). For years, Ryan served on the MPC board of directors, as well as on the board of its biggest customer, ACM.

After a short term in Washington, D.C., as a corporate volunteer during World War I, Ryan resumed his swift corporate climb and evolved from a Western promoter and executive to a national industrial lord. With the support of Anaconda executive Cornelius F. "Con" Kelley, Ryan shaped ACM into a powerful international organization, specializing in copper, silver, and brass production. A company man who launched profitable personal ventures, he invested in banks, natural gas, mining stocks, and railroads.

At the time of his death, Ryan was the head of an industrial conglomerate he had fashioned with vision, shrewd calculation, formidable negotiating skills, and determination. He was perhaps best characterized by historian Carrie Johnson as a "blend of 'modern' executive and old-fashioned financier." ◆

Ryan was a blend of modern executive and old-fashioned financier.

Simmons, Jake, Jr.

1901–1981 ● Oil tycoon

Jake Simmons's background was as unusual as his career: his great-grandfather, Cow Tom, was brought to Indian Territory as a slave to the Creek tribe in 1837; he rose to become one of the few black chiefs of a Native American tribe. Born near Muskogee, Oklahoma, Simmons was raised on the fertile ground of the former Creek nation. In 1914, his father sent him to Tuskegee Institute to study under Booker T. Washington. Simmons emulated the great educator's entrepreneurial drive and flair for oratory, soon parlaying these skills into a career as an oil broker. Operating in the racially hostile environs of Oklahoma and East Texas, he established himself as one of the few courageous enough to defend the economic rights of African-American and Native American landowners.

As he built his dynasty, Simmons gained political power and used it to further civil rights. In 1938, he and his wife, Eva Simmons, initiated one of the earliest school desegregation cases to reach the Supreme Court. As taxpayers, the couple sued the Muskogee Board of Education in federal court to bar the sale of $500,000 in bonds on the grounds that the money raised would go solely to white schools and that "no provisions have been made for the expenditure of so much as one dollar for the direct or indirect educational benefits of any Negro child, although it is proposed for Negroes to pay taxes to discharge such bonds." Appearing before a specially convened three judge federal circuit court, the Simmonses' attorney, Charles Chandler, presented compelling statistics to show that far more money was being spent on white schools

> *"How the hell can a black man stay in bed in the morning when white men rule the world?"*
>
> Jake Simmons, Jr.

and teachers than on black schools. The court gave the county a conditional go-ahead, and the Simmonses appealed their case to the Supreme Court.

The lawsuit tied up the bond issue for months, and powerful forces attempted to force Simmons to with draw the lawsuit. Economic pressure and death threats were met with defiance and news that his Muskogee home was well stocked with firearms. But the Court was unwilling to tread on the ground of segregation. Ignoring the fact that the Simmons case tore apart the legal pretense of "separate but equal," in March 1939 the Supreme Court dismissed the appeal, noting that the Simmons case was "so unsubstantial as not to need further argument."

Jake Simmons became a force to be reckoned with in the Southwest; in his words, he became "a crusader for human dignity." While serving as head of the state's NAACP during the 1960s, his opinion was said to hold sway over ten thousand voters. He used his power like a regional godfather, providing jobs and guidance for countless Oklahomans.

During the 1960s Simmons became the first African-American businessman to look for oil in postcolonial Nigeria and Ghana. As a committed nationalist, he won the goodwill of African leaders. He won important concessions for American **multinationals** like Phillips Petroleum, all the while helping African officials develop their investment codes. In 1978, Ghana awarded him its Grand Medal for his role in creating and sustaining the country's oil industry. His millionaire's fortune was built upon the percentages he received on oil deals in Africa and across the southwest United States. He often told his sons, "How the hell can a black man stay in bed in the morning when white men rule the world?" and he lived by those words until his death, in 1981, in Muskogee, Oklahoma. ◆

1914 Simmons studies with Booker T. Washington.

1938 Simmons initiates a school desegregation case.

1939 The Supreme Court dismisses Simmons' lawsuit.

1978 Ghana awards Simmons its Grand Medal

multinational: a company with branches in many countries.

Spalding, Albert Goodwill

1850–1915 ● Sportsman & Sporting Goods Manufacturer

Albert Goodwill Spalding was a sports enthusiast, a baseball promoter, and a manufacturer of sporting goods. The younger Spalding was born on a farm in Byron, Ogle County, Illinois, the son of James Lawrence and Harriet Irene (Goodwill) Wright Spalding and a descendant of Edward Spalding who became a freeman of the Massachusetts Bay Colony in 1640. The younger Spalding was educated in the public schools of Byron and Rockford, Illinois, and at the Rockford Commercial College. His first employment was as a grocer's clerk. A crippled soldier, it is said, invalided out of the Civil War, taught the boys of Rockford how to play baseball and young Spalding became an apt pupil. At the age of 17 his skill as a pitcher and batsman was such that he became an outstanding player with the Forest City team of Rockford. Largely through the prowess of Spalding and Ross Barnes, who also later became a National League player, this team attained a wide reputation. After the establishment of professional baseball, Spalding joined in 1871 the Boston team managed by Harry Wright. Spalding was pitcher and captain until 1875 and during that time the team won the championships of the National Association of Professional Base Ball Players from 1872 to 1875, inclusive.

In 1876 William A. Hulbert of Chicago, with Spalding as aid and adviser, formed the National League of Professional Base Ball Clubs, and Spalding became pitcher, captain, and manager of the Chicago team. In March of the same year he organized, with his brother James, a business firm to manufacture and sell baseball equipment and other sporting goods, under the name A. G. Spalding & Brother. Two years later his brother-in-law William T. Brown joined them and the firm name became A. G. Spalding & Brothers. In time the concern developed into the largest and most successful of its kind in the United States, with a capitalization in 1932 of

> **A crippled soldier, invalided out of the Civil War, taught Spalding how to play baseball.**

$6,000,000. Spalding maintained a connection with the Chicago Club for many years, however. Upon the death of William A. Hulbert in 1882, he became its president and continued as such until 1891, when he felt it necessary to give all his time to his sporting-goods business.

He was a big fellow physically, with a dominating personality, and a genius for organizing and directing. He was a great believer in baseball as a beneficial sport as well as an exciting public spectacle. As early as 1874 he made arrangements for a tour of England and Ireland by two baseball teams, in an endeavor to impress the good points of the game on the followers of cricket and football. Again, in 1888–89, he organized and took personal charge of a trip around the world made by his Chicago team and another group known as the All-American players. They gave exhibitions of baseball in Australia, Ceylon, Egypt, Italy, France, and the British Isles. In Egypt, a game was played on the sands near the pyramids.

In these early days of professional baseball it was necessary to stamp out rowdyism and eliminate professional gamblers who sought to corrupt teams and players for their own ends. As a player and later as a club manager, president, and league official, Spalding was a forceful leader in the fight for honest play, honest players, and a wholesome and respectable atmosphere around the ball parks. He was chosen as director of the section of sports for the United States at the Olympic Games of 1900, held in connection with the World's Fair at Paris that same year. For his work in this capacity, he later received from France the rosette of the Legion of Honor. A powerful and colorful figure, he loomed large in the field of sports for many years and, through his enthusiasm, his energy, and his keenness of mind contributed largely to the success of baseball and to the spread of many other sports. From 1878 to 1880 inclusive he edited *Spalding's Official Baseball Guide*, and in 1911 published *America's National Game*, a comprehensive history of baseball. He spent the last fifteen years of his life as a resident of Point Loma, California, and it was there that he died of heart failure, at the age of 65. His first wife, whom he married November 18, 1875, was Sarah Josephine Keith and by her he had one son; she died in 1899 and in 1900 he married Mrs. Elizabeth Churchill Mayer, who survived him. ◆

1871 — Spalding joins a Boston baseball team.

1874 — Spalding arranges British tour for two baseball teams.

1876 — A. G. Spalding & Brother is formed.

1878 — Spalding begins publishing his *Official Baseball Guide*.

1882 — Spalding becomes president of the Chicago baseball team.

1889 — Spalding arranges world tour for two baseball teams.

Spaulding, Charles Clinton

1874–1952 ● INSURANCE EXECUTIVE

Charles C. Spaulding was born in Columbus County, North Carolina. As a youth he worked on his father's farm and attended the local school until 1894, when he joined his uncle, Aaron Moore, the first black physician to practice in Durham, North Carolina. In Durham, after graduating from high school in 1898, Spaulding held a variety of jobs, before becoming the manager of a **cooperative** black grocery store. While there, he also sold life insurance policies for the North Carolina Mutual and Provident Association, founded in 1898 by seven black men, including his uncle. When the Mutual floundered in 1900 and most of the founders resigned their positions, Moore became secretary, and John Merrick, who served as president, hired Spaulding to become the general manager. The three men then constituted the board of directors. With the death of Merrick in 1919 and the reorganization of the company as the North Carolina Mutual Life Insurance Company, Spaulding became secretary-treasurer, and with the death of Moore in 1923, president, a position he held until his death in 1952. Under his leadership, the Mutual became the nation's largest black insurance company, a position it maintains today.

As the head not only of the Mutual but also of its numerous subordinate institutions—banks, a real estate company, and a **mortgage** company—Spaulding was the most powerful black in Durham and among the most powerful in the nation. His endorsement enabled black initiatives to receive financial support from prominent white foundations, such as the Duke and Rosenwald foundations and the Slater Fund. Spaulding used this power to save such black institutions as Shaw University, Virginia Theological Seminary, and the National Negro Business League from **insolvency**, and to influence the press, church sermons, school curriculums, and the allocations of public funds. With the onset of the Great Depression, both state and federal governments acknowledged Spaulding's stature, appointing him to relief committees. In 1933 the

cooperative: an organization in which members share profits and losses.

mortgage: a claim on property given as security for a loan.

insolvency: not being able to pay one's debt's.

National Urban League made him national chairman of its Emergency Advisory Council, whose purpose was to obtain black support for the National Recovery Administration (NRA) (one of the most important programs of the first phase of President Franklin D. Roosevelt's New Deal), to inform blacks about new laws regarding relief, reemployment and property, and to receive complaints of violations against blacks. Spaulding worked enthusiastically in this position, but his early hope that the NRA would bring a new era of fairness for blacks quickly soured.

As with his work for the Emergency Advisory Council, throughout Spaulding's career there was a tension between his desire to address the causes of black poverty and his need to protect his moderate image. In 1933 Spaulding introduced two local lawyers, Conrad Pearson and Cecil A. McCoy, who wanted to integrate the University of North Carolina, to NAACP secretary Walter White, but as the case, Hocutt *v.* North Carolina, gained publicity, Spaulding withdrew his support, without which it could not be won, and worked instead for reform that did not threaten segregation, such as out-of-state tuition and equal teachers' salaries. However, by the middle of the 1930s, Spaulding actively supported the return of suffrage to blacks and served as chairman of the executive committee of the Durham Committee on Negro Affairs (founded 1935), which was responsible for the registration of thousands of black voters. Because its endorsement insured candidates on average 80 percent of the black vote, the DCNA was a political force on Durham. With the onset of World War II, Spaulding became concerned almost exclusively with unifying blacks and whites in the name of patriotism. He invested much of the Mutual's assets in the war effort, buying $4,450,000 in war bonds, and traveled and gave speeches as associate administrator of the War Savings Staff. After the war, Spaulding focused on the threat he believed communism posed to business. An article he wrote for *America Magazine* proclaiming its danger was incorporated into high school text books and was reprinted in a variety of languages. ◆

1898 Seven black men found the Mutual and Provident Assoc.

1923 Spaulding becomes president of Mutual.

1933 Spaulding becomes chairman of National Urban League.

1935 Spaulding serves on the Durham Committee on Negro Affairs.

Spielberg, Steven

1947–PRESENT ● MOVIEMAKER

"The most expensive habit it the world is celluloid, not heroin, and I need a fix every few years."

Steven Spielberg, 1979

Steven Spielberg is an American film producer and director. He became one of the most successful filmmakers of the 1900s. A number of his films rank among the highest grossing movies of all time. Spielberg is known for his skill at creating riveting action scenes and his ability to capture a quality of childlike innocence on film.

Spielberg was born on December 18, 1947, in Cincinnati, Ohio. His father, Arnold Spielberg, was an electrical engineer who designed computers. His mother, Leah (Posner) Spielberg, was an accomplished concert pianist. Arnold's work took the Spielberg family to New Jersey, Arizona, and finally to California, when Steven was 16. Spielberg's family was Jewish, but the family resided in many non-Jewish neighborhoods, causing feelings of alienation in the teenage Steven.

At the age of 12, Spielberg began making his first movies, using his father's 8-millimeter camera. As a 16-year-old he produced his first feature-length film, a two-and-a-half hour science-fiction movie called *Firelight* about mysterious lights in the sky. His family hired a local theater to show the film and it grossed $500 in one night, the entire amount Spielberg had spent to make the film.

At the age of 12, Spielberg began making his first movies using his father's 8-millimeter camera.

Poor grades kept Spielberg out of the better film schools, so he enrolled at California State College in Long Beach, where he studied English and worked on films in his spare time. As an undergraduate, he bluffed his way into Universal Studios and tried to talk producers into looking at his films. His 22-minute movie *Amblin'*, about a boy and a girl who hitchhike from the Mojave Desert to the Pacific Ocean, won awards at a number of film festivals and caught the attention of Sidney Sheinberg, the head of Universal's television division. Shortly before Spielberg was to graduate from college, Sheinberg offered him a seven-year contract, which the young filmmaker eagerly accepted. He began his work at Universal by directing movie star Joan Crawford in the pilot of the suspense series *Night Gallery*. Spielberg directed other television episodes and films, including *Duel* (1971), a thriller about a traveling salesman who is pursued down rural highways by a truck with an unknown driver. *Duel* became a hit all over the world, and its success launched Spielberg's career into feature films.

His first feature film was *The Sugarland Express* (1974), a comedy-drama about a young couple who lead a police car chase in pursuit of their son, who has been placed in the hands of foster parents. A year later, at the age of 26, Spielberg achieved his first big commercial success with his second feature film, *Jaws*, a gripping thriller about a great white shark that terrorizes a seaside community. *Jaws* became the highest grossing movie of its time. Spielberg's ability to capture childlike delight and innocence became clearly evident in 1977 with his next film, *Close Encounters of the Third Kind*, a story about people who become obsessed with odd visions and eventually gather to a place where they are visited by an alien spaceship. The movie was a blockbuster hit and garnered Spielberg his first Oscar nomination for best director.

Spielberg's success continued with entertaining movies about ordinary people reacting to extraordinary events. These films included the popular "Indiana Jones" trilogy—*Raiders of the Lost Ark* (1981), *Indiana Jones and the Temple of Doom* (1984), and *Indiana Jones and the Last Crusade* (1989); *E.T.: The Extra-Terrestrial* (1982); and *Jurassic Park* (1993). He also made a number of serious films, including *The Color Purple* (1985) and *Empire of the Sun* (1987). The rich cinematogra-

1959 ▸ Spielberg makes his first movie.

1970 ▸ Spielberg lands a seven-year contract with Universal.

1974 ▸ Spielberg directs his first feature, *The Sugarland Express*.

1975 ▸ Spielberg's second feature, *Jaws*, becomes a huge success.

1977 ▸ Spielberg is nominated for an Oscar for *Close Encounters of the Third Kind*.

1994 ▸ Spielberg wins Oscars for *Schindler's List*.

1994 ▸ Spielberg and partners form Dreamworks SKG.

phy of his films coupled with memorable soundtracks and awesome special effects have become Spielberg trademarks, and his box-office success has been unrivaled. In the late 1990s *Jaws*, *E.T.*, and *Jurassic Park* ranked among the highest grossing motion pictures of all time.

Despite Spielberg's tremendous commercial success, he was criticized for years that his films lacked thematic depth. Then in 1993 Spielberg released a film that he felt was a confirmation of his Jewish roots and that critics viewed as the most important motion picture of his career. That film was *Schindler's List*, a true story based on a prize-winning book by Australia's Thomas Keneally about a group of Polish Jews who avoided extermination by the Nazis through the heroic efforts of a German industrialist. *Schindler's List* won Spielberg Academy Awards for best picture and best director in 1994. The filmmaker set up two foundations with the proceeds from the film—one devoted to the study of those who helped rescue Jews during the Holocaust and the other dedicated to keeping alive the memory of the six million Jews and others who had died in the Holocaust.

After his professional triumph of receiving an Oscar, Spielberg entered into a partnership with former Disney executive Jeffrey Katzenberg and record mogul David Geffen to form Dreamworks SKG, an entertainment company that produces films, animation, and television programs. In 1998, Spielberg released the Dreamworks film *Saving Private Ryan*. This World War II epic won raves from film critics and fans alike for its realistic depiction of war.

Spielberg has been married to actress Kate Capshaw since 1991. They have five children. ◆

Despite Spielberg's commercial success, he was criticized for years that his films lacked thematic depth.

Spreckels, Claus

1828–1908 ● SUGAR PROCESSING TYCOON

A California sugar refiner and Hawaiian planter, Claus Spreckels was born in Lamstedt, Germany. He came to the United States in 1846 and engaged in the grocery business in Charleston, South Carolina, New York City, and San Francisco, where he moved in 1856. He opened his first sugar refinery in 1863. By 1881, using technological innovations and business skill, the "sugar king" of California made his California Sugar Refinery the most modern refinery in America.

Spreckels's refineries depended on Hawaiian sugar cane. After ratification of the reciprocity treaty between the United States and Hawaii, he sailed to the islands in 1876 to establish his own sugar plantations. To obtain land leases and water rights, he allied himself with King David Kalakaua. In the decade after his arrival, Spreckels became the single largest sugar planter in Hawaii and created on Maui the Spreckelsville plantation, which he ran through his Hawaiian Commercial and Sugar Company. His plantations produced up to one-third of the entire crop, and through the factoring firm he established with William G. Irwin, Spreckels bought a substantial portion of the remaining crop.

Local planters resented Spreckels's alliance with the monarchy and eventually sought to oust him. Although he initially endorsed a plan to annex Hawaii to the United States after the Hawaiian Revolution of 1893, he soon actively opposed the plan. After annexation in 1898, the local firm of Alexander and Baldwin bought out Spreckels's company and took control of Spreckelsville plantation.

In California, Spreckels's interests also included investments in beet-sugar refineries, railroads, utilities, and trolleys. The last fifteen years of his life were marred by family warfare over the control of his companies. Nonetheless, the civic philanthropies and business interests of Spreckels and his children established the family as a dominant force in California. ◆

1846 Spreckels comes to America from Germany.

1856 Spreckels moves to San Francisco.

1863 Spreckels opens his first sugar refinery.

1876 Spreckels goes to Hawaii to establish sugar farms.

1893 Spreckels's company is bought out.

Stanford, Leland

1824–1893 ● RAILROAD DEVELOPER

"Money has little value to its possessor unless it also has value to others."
Leland Stanford, 1881

eland Stanford was one of the principal organizers of the first successful transcontinental railroads. He was president and a director of the Central Pacific Railroad, the line that constructed the rail links from the Pacific eastward to a meeting with the Union Pacific at Promontory Point, Utah. Stanford had invested money in the original surveys and was a major stockholder in the Central Pacific. He later became the president of the Southern Pacific Railroad, a railroad system that absorbed the Central Pacific and dominated rail service in California during the later years of the 19th century.

Stanford was a lawyer by training. He had moved to California in the 1850s to join two brothers in running a store. As the Civil War was about to break out, Stanford joined the Republican party and was a strong advocate of loyalty to the Union. Nominated for governor of the State, he was elected in 1861 in spite of having no previous political record. He was governor for two years and saw to it that California supported the Union government. While governor, he signed several acts that would help the Central Pacific Railroad begin its operations, including financial aid measures, which made building the railroad a matter of very little risk to the company.

Stanford believed that the railroad should be free to operate without any interference from government.

Between 1863 and 1885, he held no public office. In 1885, he was elected to the U.S. Senate. However, he and the Southern Pacific Railroad were strong influences within the State during the entire period from the creation of the railroad until Stanford's death. Stanford believed that the railroad should be free to operate without any interference from government, and that the railroad had every right to use its influence to protect itself against government action that might hinder its activities.

Leland Stanford lost his son, a boy of the same name, at the age of 15. Seeking a way to memorialize the young man, he decided to endow a school that would be a center of learning in California. The school he founded is Stanford University, one of the country's largest and most prestigious private universities. ◆

Stein, Julian Caesar (Jules)

1896–1981 ● ENTERTAINMENT TYCOON

Julian Stein's father, M. Louis Stein, owned a dry goods and shoe store in Indiana. His mother, Rosa Cohen, was an invalid whose illness kept the family in financial crisis. Both parents were Orthodox Jews. The second of five children, Julian was supporting himself at age 12 by playing the violin and saxophone, and at age 14 he had his own band and was booking other orchestras. A hard-working student, Stein skipped several grades and received his high school degree from an academy at Winona Lake, Indiana, in 1912.

At the age of 14, Stein had his own band and was booking other orchestras.

Stein attended the University of West Virginia (1912 and 1913), the University of Chicago (Ph.B., 1915), Rush Medical College (M.D., 1921), and the University of Vienna (1922). After an ophthalmology residency at Cook County Hospital in Chicago, he entered private practice in that city in 1923. Stein's 1924 manual on telescopic spectacles became a standard reference. Meanwhile, he found time to complete a correspondence course on business and serve as a first lieutenant in the U.S. Army medical reserve. While trying to focus his principal attention on his eye patients, Stein was also booking dance bands into hotels and gangster-era nightclubs in Chicago. In 1924 Stein and William R. Goodheart founded the Music Corporation of America; Stein's brother William was executive vice president of the firm until his death in 1943. In 1925 Julian Stein took "temporary" leave from his practice with another Chicago ophthalmologist and became Jules Stein, president of the growing firm. Stein would later link his medical training with his ability to deal with show business clients.

On November 16, 1928, Stein, once described by the Associated Press as a "small, slender . . . man with genial brown eyes and a chipper manner," married Doris Jones in New York; he had met her while leading a band in Kansas City. They had two daughters.

Jules and William Stein, Goodheart (who eventually left the firm shortly before World War II), and several early employees, particularly David A. "Sonny" Werblin, Lew Wasserman, and Taft Schreiber, introduced semi-monopolistic practices into the music business. This involved booking the firm's impressive roster of popular bands and requiring customers to accept a "block booking" package that included lower-grossing attractions. Client bands were required to deal exclusively through MCA. To obtain the most lucrative attractions, dance halls, theaters, night clubs, and hotels also had to book attractions exclusively through MCA. Supplementing the customary practice of booking bands for extended stays in a few big-city venues, Stein and his associates increased revenues by also routing them through a series of "one-night stands," single performances. This generated sometimes violent opposition from local musicians, but Stein consistently enjoyed the support of James Petrillo's American Federation of Musicians. The firms also supplied business management, publicity, insurance, transportation, lodging, liquor, and even confetti to clients. In effect MCA tended to become the producer as well as the booker of musical entertainment, and later of radio, film, and television programs, often attracting adverse attention from federal antitrust offi-

1910 Stein, at age 14, has his own band.

1923 Stein starts ophthalmology practice in Chicago.

1924 Stein forms the Music Corporation of America.

1925 Stein devotes himself to growing MCA firm.

1938 Stein opens film division of MCA in Hollywood.

1959 MCA expands into television, record, film and publishing ventures.

1962 U.S. Justice Department forces MCA out of talent agency business.

1981 Reagan serves as one of 76 pallbearers at Stein's funeral.

After World War II, big movie studios saw their revenues decline as audiences turned to television.

cials. Soon half of the country's top-grossing bands became clients, beginning in 1928 with the popular Guy Lombardo and Eddie Duchin. Stein, a union musician, got the permission of Petrlllo's national union to both represent and employ musicians. Petrillo became a millionaire, allegedly through MCA deals. MCA also produced a substantial number of entire programs and series for the growing mass radio audience, such as the *Lucky Strike Hit Parade*.

In 1938 Stein sent Wasserman to Hollywood to open a film division of MCA. The firm's first important film client was Bette Davis. Under Stein, Wasserman, and Schreiber's tight management, MCA came to dominate films as it had radio. Stein, who had owned a mansion in Chicago, moved to Beverly Hills, California. Under MCA's rules, film producers, in order to get the firm's top stars, would also have to hire MCA-managed directors and writers. A movie industry tradition was the seven-year contract by which a studio would engage, develop, and promote promising talent. If the actor became a big star, he or she would have to work for low pay until the contract ended. After World War II, the big studios saw their revenues declining as audiences increasingly turned to television, and they became more interested in hiring big revenue-generating stars for specific productions than long-term contract players. By negotiating single-package deals, MCA helped reduce the power of the big studios. In 1940 Petrillo and the Justice Department put pressure on the three major radio networks to cease booking talent as well as employing it. MCA bought the CBS network's representation of bands for a reported $500,000. A large factor in the firm's success was its subsequent purchase of Leland Hayward's agency with its roster of 300 stars, writers, and directors in 1945.

In 1946 Jules Stein, always the largest shareholder in the company, turned the presidency of MCA over to Wasserman. Stein remained chairman and continued planning business strategy. After World War II MCA introduced a new practice that gave major stars a percentage of a film's box office receipts and got them production deals. The landmark was James Stewart's *Winchester 73* (1950), which made Stewart rich.

With the advent of television MCA sought to create products for the new medium, as it had for radio. Ronald

Reagan, president of the Screen Actors Guild (SAG) and an MCA client, negotiated an exclusive blanket agreement with SAG in 1952 that gave MCA an exclusive, unlimited right to both represent and hire actors. Because the major studios refused to produce films for their competitor, television, MCA's Revue Productions, established in 1959, quickly became the dominant supplier of network television productions.

In 1959 the Music Corporation of America legally became MCA Inc. and began issuing stock to the general public. Stein allowed Wasserman and Schreiber to buy large blocks of MCA stock at a bargain price, giving them a substantial share in the company. He set aside another block of his stock for a profit-sharing plan for employees. Also in 1959 MCA bought Decca Records and its subsidiary Universal-International Studios. It merged Revue Productions and Universal into Universal Pictures. MCA subsequently absorbed a music publisher, a Denver savings and loan association, Spencer Gifts, book publisher G. P. Putnam's Sons, and the Yosemite Land and Curry Company. It built a new sixteen-story black steel and glass headquarters tower (1963) in Universal City, California, north of Hollywood. (The austere tower was furnished with uncomfortable antique English furniture, which Stein collected.) MCA also began to develop commercial real estate sites in the area.

In 1962 the **Antitrust** Division of the Department of Justice, joined by SAG, no longer headed by Reagan, forced the firm to opt out of its talent agency business. Reagan, called before a congressional committee, could not remember much about his role in obtaining for MCA the waiver to produce films. Six years later Stein tried to sell his extensive MCA holdings for a large profit to Westinghouse Electric, which owned radio and television stations, but the Justice Department intervened and the deal was abandoned in 1969. When Firestone Tire and Rubber offered to buy MCA, Wasserman opposed the sale because he did not want to work for a tire company. By the early 1970s MCA was known as "the factory" because of its large volume of television programs and feature films. Notable Universal films included *Airport* (1970), *The Sting* (1973), *Jaws* (1975), *The Deer Hunter* (1978), and *E. T.: The Extra-Terrestrial* (1982). Among MCA's television programs were *General Electric*

> MCA became known as "the factory" because of its large volume of television programs and feature films.

antitrust: laws to protect business from unfair practices.

Theater, with Ronald Reagan introducing the productions and taking part in and producing some of the programs, the *Ed Sullivan* and *Jack Benny Shows*, *Wagon Train*, *Wells Fargo*, *M Squad*, *Alfred Hitchcock Presents*, *Leave It to Beaver*, *McHale's Navy*, and *Marcus Welby, M.D.* The company's tour of the Universal Cities studios became a top tourist attraction.

In his later years Stein focused on promoting vision research. In 1960 he helped found Research to Prevent Blindness, Inc., which supplies research funds to promising young scientists. Through his efforts, laser therapy and **vitreous** surgery were supported in their pioneer stages. Causative factors in **cataract** formation were ascertained and chemical therapy was developed. Diabetic blindness was contained. Corneal transplants, artificial lens implants, and an array of new drugs were introduced.

The Jules Stein Eye Institute at the University of California at Los Angeles, dedicated in 1966, became the only eye center among many that Stein and his wife endowed to bear his name. It began with several million in seed money, attracted some $4 million more from show business associates, and received major public and private research funds. In fact, Stein became a principal source of funds for eye research around the country. He also helped get Congress to establish the National Eye Institute in 1968 as a separate entity within the National Institutes of Health in Bethesda, Maryland. In 1969 and 1970 Stein underwent major intestinal surgery, which required a lengthy hospitalization. He recovered and continued his active interest in business, political, and philanthropic affairs. A Republican, Stein had supported Richard M. Nixon's 1960 presidential bid. Stein and Schreiber helped raise money for Reagan's California gubernatorial campaigns in the 1960s and 1970s.

In 1973 Stein turned over the MCA chairmanship to Wasserman, but as the principal stockholder continued to help shape company policy, which included an unsuccessful attempt to market films on phonograph-like electronic discs. In the late 1970s President Jimmy Carter's Justice Department forced MCA, with other major producers, to abandon an effort to establish a cable television channel, Premier, that would have had first call on their films. (Under President Reagan's more business-friendly Justice Department, the firm

vitreous: clear jelly that fills the eyeball.

cataracts: a disease in which the eye's lens becomes cloudy.

Stein became a principal source of funds for eye research around the country.

later became a co-owner of the USA cable network.) Stein, a successful investor, was a major shareholder in Paramount Pictures. He was a member of the New York Stock Exchange and owned several New York antique stores.

When Stein died of a heart attack, President Reagan was among seventy-six honorary pallbearers from show business, medicine, and business, along with James Petrillo, Mervyn LeRoy, Hal Wallis, James Stewart, and Cary Grant. Interment was in Forest Lawn Memorial Park, Glendale, California. He left an estate worth $150 million. ◆

Steinway, Henry Englehard

1797–1871 ● PIANO MANUFACTURER

Henry Englehard Steinway, originally named Steinweg, was born in Wolfshagen, Germany. The names of his parents are not noted in the family records. In his boyhood and youth he endured many hardships. During the Napoleonic invasion of Germany several of his brothers were killed and the Steinweg house was burned, and when he was 15 his father and remaining brother were killed in an accident. In 1815 he was drafted into the army and is said to have taken part in the battle of Waterloo. Though he was without musical training and manual instruction, he had a talent for craftsmanship and an interest in the making of musical instruments. His first instrument, made after his return from the war, was a zither. In 1818 he entered the shop of an organ builder at Seesen, and became the organist of the village church; two years later he became interested in piano-making. Though his first piano is given various dates between 1825 and 1835, one account relates that it was his wedding-gift to his bride. According to family records, his marriage occurred in February 1825 and the bride was Juliane Thiemer. Seven children were eventually born to the

> *"The idea that your daughter is a schlumpf unless she plays the piano—William did more to invent that than anybody."*
> Henry Steinway, describing his grandfather William, 1988

Steinwegs: Christian Friedrich Theodore, Doretta, Charles, Henry, Wilhelmina, William, and Albert.

Steinweg's piano business prospered. In 1839 he exhibited a grand piano and two square pianos at a fair in Brunswick, Germany, where he was awarded the first prize, a gold medal, but in 1848 and 1849 the revolutions in Central Europe ruined his business, and two years later he decided to emigrate to America, where his son Charles had already gone. With his wife and daughters, and all of his sons but Theodore, he embarked from Hamburg on the *Helene Sloman* and arrived in New York, June 9, 1851.

For about two years Steinway and his sons worked in various piano factories in New York. On March 5, 1853, they joined forces again to start their own business. A year later they were awarded a medal for a square piano they exhibited at the Metropolitan Fair in Washington, D.C. In 1855 Steinweg exhibited an innovation in piano making at the American Institute, New York, a square piano with cross- or over-strung strings, and a full cast-iron frame. For five years after coming to America he concerned himself with building square pianos only, but in 1856 he manufactured a grand piano and in 1862 an upright. Meanwhile the factory quarters on Walker Street, New York, became too small for the growing business, and in 1860 a new factory was completed on Fourth (Park) Avenue at Fifty-third Street. On April 30, 1861, he and his son signed their first co-partnership agreement, and in July 1864 had their name legally changed to Steinway.

Soon after this event tragedy visited the family, for in 1865 two of the sons died. The organization was so crippled that Steinway persuaded his eldest son, Theodore, to come to America and join the business, and aid him in the technical supervision of building pianos. In 1866 he built Steinway Hall on Fourteenth Street (formally opened in 1867), a building containing retail warerooms and offices for the firm, and a concert hall that became one of the centers of New York's musical life. A few years later he died in New York, survived by his daughters and three of his sons. In his piano business, which has continuously remained in the possession of his descendants and still bears his name, he established an enterprise in which manufacturing has been regarded in the old fashion: as a craft, not as a mere commercial undertaking. ◆

1815 Steinway is drafted into the German army.

1818 Steinway visits an organ builder's shop.

1825 Steinway makes his first piano.

1839 Steinway exhibits a grand piano at Brunswick fair.

1851 Steinway arrives in New York.

1853 Steinway and sons start their own piano building business.

1866 Steinway builds Steinway Hall.

Stetson, John Batterson

1830–1906 ● HAT MANUFACTURER

Hat manufacturer John Batterson Stetson was born in Orange, New Jersey, the son of a hatter. He pursued the trade of his father until he was afflicted with tuberculosis. Hoping to regain his health in the West, he moved to Saint Joseph, Missouri, in the late 1850s and found work in a brickyard. He eventually became part owner of the enterprise before a flood washed away his investment.

Rejected for Civil War service on account of his health, Stetson joined a party of prospectors bound for the gold fields of Colorado. During the trip, he fashioned a crude, high-crowned, broad-brimmed felt hat from beaver and rabbit fur An eager teamster bought the protective headgear for five dollars.

Stetson returned to Philadelphia in 1865 and reentered the hat trade. Discouraged with local prospects, he began

Stetson's factory had turned out two million hats at the time of his death in 1906.

Cowboy Hats

While much of the typical cowboys wardrobe represented adaptations of common work clothing, a few items, including boots, spurs, and hats, were designed to meet a cowboy's special needs. Wide-brimmed, tall-crowned hats, made of straw or felt derived from beaver, rabbit, and hare fur, shielded the heads and necks of herders from scorching sun and drenching rain. The "ten gallon" air space in the hat's crown could also help keep the wearer's head cool. During cold winters in the northern plains, cowboys tied their hat brims down over their ears with a bandanna or wool scarf. Cowboys also used their hats to fan fires and signal distant comrades, and as feed and water bowls for hungry horses. Although most cowboy hats were drab light gray or black, some cowboys decorated their hats with bands made of woven horsehair or leather. The hats were also sometimes embroidered with colored thread, or decorated with small metal disks called conchas. After the Civil War, John Batterson Stetson's sturdy "boss of the plains" became the most popular hat on the Western range and synonymous with cowboy headgear.

replicating a refined version of the hat he had made in Colorado and sought a market for it in the Southwest.

Merchants eagerly embraced Stetson's new creation, christened "Boss of the Plains," and the flood of orders that followed forced him to abandon his tiny one-man shop for an expansive, modern factory erected in the suburbs of Philadelphia. In time, as many as ten thousand retailers handled Stetson's stylish yet durable creations, affectionately known in Western ranch country, as "John B.'s"

His factory was turning out two million hats at the time of his death at the age of 76. Stetson used part of his substantial fortune to endow DeLand Academy in Florida, renamed Stetson University, and served as president of its Board of Trustees. ◆

Strauss, Levi

1829–1902 ● CLOTHING MANUFACTURER

dry goods: textile products.

duck: a strong cotton or linen cloth.

Clothier Levi Strauss was born Loeb Strauss in Buttenheim, Bavaria. After his father's death, he immigrated to the United States with his mother and two sisters in 1847. He joined two brothers already in the **dry-goods** business in New York City and became a traveling salesman in Kentucky. In 1850, he founded Levi Strauss and Company and, three years later, joined his brother-in-law, David Stern, in a dry goods business in San Francisco. There, Strauss began supplying miners with stout canvas, **duck**, and denim pants produced on the East Coast and shipped west by his brothers.

In 1872, Jacob Davis, a Nevada tailor and customer of Levi Strauss and Company, announced the invention of men's work trousers with pocket seams and other weak points reinforced with copper rivets. Strauss assisted Davis in patenting the idea on May 20, 1873, and established a factory on Fremont Street to produce the improved "waist-high overalls" and later, work shirts, hunting coats, and a variety of other

The History of Blue Jeans

The first blue jeans were made in San Francisco in the late 1800s by Levi Strauss. Originally worn by men bound for the California gold rush, Strauss's indigo-blue denim work pants were adopted by lumber-jacks, miners, farmers, railroad workers, and cowboys, becoming as much a symbol of the westward trek as the covered wagon. By the early 1900s, Levi's jeans were the most popular men's work pants in the western states, where they became identified with the rugged, independent lifestyle of the men who wore them. For many years, blue jeans were only worn by outdoor laborers. Beginning in the 1930s, however, cowboy films became popular and jeans became fashionable with people who wanted to imitate their favorite movie star. In the 1940s, young Americans adopted jeans as casual wear. During the 1950s, jeans became identified with rebelliousness, and they were banned in many schools in an effort to thwart juvenile delinquency. The youth of the 1960s counterculture embraced blue jeans as a symbol of solidarity with the working class and rejection of the middle-class values of their parents. Expensive designer jeans became popular during the 1970s and 1980s, transforming what had once been simple work pants into a coveted status symbol.

garments. Meanwhile, the company continued to wholesale an assortment of other dry goods from linens to corsets.

David Stern died in 1874, and with the waning of the nineteenth century, Strauss, a lifelong bachelor, gradually retired, leaving the daily operation of his company to his four nephews, the children of his sister Fanny and David Stern. In 1890, Strauss and the Stern incorporated the company.

Praised for his fairness and integrity in business, Strauss was a charter member and treasurer of the San Francisco Board of Trade. He also served as a director of the Nevada Bank, the Liverpool, London and Globe Insurance Company, and the San Francisco Gas and Electric Company. In 1874, he became a partner in the Mission and Pacific Woolen Mills, which provided fabric to Levi Strauss and Company

A well-known philanthropist, Strauss supported many charities and endowed twenty-eight scholarships at the University of California at Berkeley in 1897. Bequests from Strauss's $6 million estate extended this benevolence, especially to orphans.

Strauss's death in San Francisco after a brief illness was widely mourned, and many local businesses closed during the funeral.

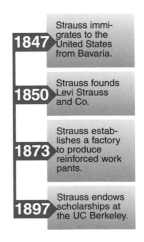

1847 Strauss immigrates to the United States from Bavaria.

1850 Strauss founds Levi Strauss and Co.

1873 Strauss establishes a factory to produce reinforced work pants.

1897 Strauss endows scholarships at the UC Berkeley.

Strauss's nephews continued to operate and expand the company, despite the devastating earthquake and fire of 1906 that destroyed its factory and headquarters. The company eventually developed into the largest manufacturer of apparel in the world with sales in the 1980s reaching more than $2.5 billion annually. ◆

Studebaker, John Mohler

1833–1917 ● Carriage manufacturer

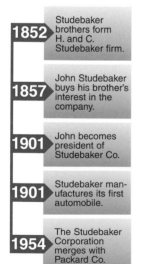

1852	Studebaker brothers form H. and C. Studebaker firm.
1857	John Studebaker buys his brother's interest in the company.
1901	John becomes president of Studebaker Co.
1901	Studebaker manufactures its first automobile.
1954	The Studebaker Corporation merges with Packard Co.

John Mohler Studebaker was a partner in the Studebaker Brothers Manufacturing Company, which, through the manufacture of more than 750,000 wagons, carts, and carriages, played a large part in America's nineteenth-century westward movement. Born in Pennsylvania, Studebaker was one of five brothers, who all eventually entered the wagon-making business. As a young man, he struck out for the gold fields of California, where his experience as a blacksmith and wagon-maker earned him more money than his gold seeking. He always had plenty of work repairing the wagons and carts of the other gold prospectors.

When he returned East in the mid-1850s, Studebaker brought with him an appreciable amount of cash that he had earned during the gold rush. In the meantime, around 1852, two of his brothers, Clement and Henry, had organized the firm of H. and C. Studebaker near South Bend, Indiana. The company was well on its way to becoming a leading manufacturer of wagons when John Studebaker bought Henry's interest in the business in 1857.

In 1868, when another brother, Peter, joined the company, the three men reorganized the business under the name Studebaker Brothers Manufacturing Company. In 1870, a fifth brother, Jacob, joined the company, which had become the world's largest manufacturer of horse-drawn wagons and

Advertisement for
Studebaker
Automobiles.
Photographed in 1902.

carts. When Clement died in 1901, John succeeded him as president of the company. He continued Clement's new focus on gasoline-powered automobiles, and the company manufactured it first automobile in 1901.

The Studebaker Corporation and the Packard Company merged operations in 1954, and the company continued to manufacture automobiles in the United States until 1963. ◆

Sutton, Percy Ellis

1920–PRESENT ● MEDIA MOGUL

Under Sutton's management, the Apollo Theater has been restored as a major Harlem cultural center and landmark.

Percy Ellis Sutton was born in San Antonio, Texas. His parents, Samuel J. Sutton and Lillian Smith, were educators and philanthropists. Percy Sutton graduated from Phillis Wheatley High School in San Antonio, and subsequently attended Prairie View Agricultural and Mechanical College, Tuskegee Institute, and Hampton Institute. When he attempted to join the Army Air Force in Texas during World War II, he was rejected (for reasons having to do with his racial background). He then successfully enlisted in New York City. As an intelligence officer with the black 99th Fighter Squadron serving in the Italian and Mediterranean theaters, Sutton earned combat stars and rose to the rank of captain.

After the war, Sutton completed his education under the G.I. Bill, graduating from Brooklyn Law School in 1950. During the Korean War, Sutton reentered the Air Force as an intelligence officer and trial judge advocate. When the war ended in 1953, Sutton opened a law partnership in Harlem with his brother, Oliver, and George Covington and worked with the NAACP on several civil rights cases throughout the 1950s. In addition to its work with the NAACP, the firm served other clients such as Malcom X and the Baptist Ministers Conference of Greater New York.

From 1961 to 1962 Sutton served as branch president of the New York City NAACP, participating in demonstrations and freedom rides in the South. During the winter of 1963–1964, Sutton and Charles Rangel cofounded the John F. Kennedy Democratic Club, later known as the Martin Luther King, Jr., Club. Sutton was elected to the New York State Assembly in 1964. In 1966, after Manhattan borough president Constance Baker Motley accepted an appointment as a federal judge, the New York City Council chose Sutton to finish Motley's term. Sutton was reelected in his own right later that year, and was subsequently reelected in 1969 and 1973. As borough president, Sutton focused on decentralizing the municipal bureaucracy, cutting city spending, and addressing the broader social causes of urban crime and poverty.

In 1970 Sutton endorsed Rangel's campaign to replace Adam Clayton Powell Jr. as congressman from Harlem. Rangel's victory marked the ascendancy of a new black political coalition in Harlem, a coalition that included not only Percy Sutton but also future New York City mayor David Dinkins. In 1971, while still Manhattan borough president, Sutton set out to purchase several black-owned media enterprises, beginning with the New York *Amsterdam News* (which he sold in 1975) and radio station WLIB-AM. In 1977 Sutton became owner and board chairman of the Inner-City Broadcasting Company, a nationwide media corporation, and through the corporation he subsequently purchased radio stations in New York, California, and Michigan. He also formed Percy Sutton International, Inc., the investments of which encouraged the agricultural, manufacturing, and trade industries in Africa, Southeast Asia, and Brazil.

In September 1977 Sutton was an unsuccessful candidate for the nomination for mayor. He retired from public office after finishing his second full term as borough president in December 1977, but he continued to advise Rangel, Dinkins, and other black politicians on electoral strategy and urban policy. In 1981 he acquired Harlem's Apollo Theater as a base for producing cable television programs. By the end of the decade Sutton's estimated net worth was $170 million. In 1990 he was succeeded as head of Inner City Broadcasting by his son, Pierre ("PePe") Montea, who raised the company's net worth to $28 million by 1992.

Sutton has been a guest lecturer at many universities and corporations and has held leadership positions in the Association for a Better New York, the National Urban League, the Congressional Black Caucus Foundation, and several other civil rights organizations. A founding member and director of Operation PUSH (People United to Save Humanity), Sutton was also a close adviser to the Rev. Jesse Jackson. He was awarded the NAACP's Springarn Medal in 1987 at the Apollo Theater, which under Sutton's management had been restored as a major Harlem cultural center and landmark. ◆

1953 Sutton opens a law firm in Harlem.

1961 Sutton begins serving as NAACP branch president.

1966 Sutton becomes Manhattan president.

1971 Sutton sets out to buy black owned media enterprises.

1977 Sutton becomes owner of Inner-City Broadcasting Co.

1981 Sutton acquires Harlem's Apollo Theatre.

1987 Sutton receives Spingarn Medal.

Trump, Donald

1946–PRESENT ● REAL ESTATE
MAGNATE

> *"The mind can overcome any obstacle. I never think of the negative."*
>
> Donald Trump

Donald Trump is a real estate developer known for his upscale properties. He has developed some of the most highly priced luxury apartment buildings in New York City and several successful casinos in Atlantic City.

Donald John Trump was born in 1946 in New York City to Mary and Fred C. Trump. His father was a real estate man, and Donald learned the business and an appreciation of buildings as a young boy. Trump's father also taught him to be competitive as a means of succeeding in the business world.

Trump attended Wharton School of Finance at the University of Pennsylvania and graduated in 1968 at the head of his class with a degree in economics. After graduation, he joined his father's real estate business, the Trump Organization, which built middle-income apartment buildings in the boroughs of New York. In 1973, the Trump Organization became embroiled in controversy when the U.S. Justice Department charged the organization with discriminatory renting practices against blacks. The company later agreed to provide housing opportunities for minority groups.

In the mid-1970s, Trump began to show the business acumen for which he has become known. Working through his father's connections in government, Trump persuaded city and state officials to build the New York convention center on the site of the bankrupt Penn Central railroad yards on the Hudson River. For this sale, he received a reported $500,000 commission from the Urban Development Corporation. With financial backing from Hyatt Corporation, a hotel management business, he then bought Penn Central's financially stricken Commodore Hotel for $10 million. He subsequently negotiated a tax abatement deal with the city that amounted to an estimated $45 million in tax savings. He then sold the hotel to the Urban Development Corporation for $1 with the understanding that he and his family and business associates would run the hotel for 99 years and the city would receive a certain percentage of the profits. The deal went through and the refurbished Grand Hyatt opened in 1980, complete with a presidential suite that rented at $2,000 a night.

In 1979, Trump began one of his best known real estate projects when he bought the site of the Bonwit Teller Department store on Fifth Avenue for $10 million with the plan of renovating the structure into luxury condominiums. He coveted the site because of its location near Tiffany's jewelry store, which he felt was good for business. Trump again attempted a tax abatement plan, but the city turned him down, saying that such tax savings were intended for modestly priced housing developments, not luxury apartments. Trump took the city to court and went all the way to the state Court of Appeals before he was granted a $50-million tax abatement. The project was the subject of further controversy after Trump promised the Metropolitan Museum of Art parts of the building's art deco facade and later demolished the structures because he considered their removal too difficult and cost prohibitive. The building finally opened in 1982 as the Trump Tower, the city's tallest and most expensive reinforced concrete structure. It became the home of celebrities and the fabulously wealthy, and its atrium featured some of the New York City's best known upscale stores.

Trump continued his real estate speculation in Manhattan through the 1980s and banks financed him left and right. His

1968 Trump graduates from the Univ. of Pennsylvania.

1973 The Justice Dept charges the Trump with discrimination.

1980 Trump's Grand Hyatt opens.

1982 New York's Trump Tower opens next to Tiffany's.

1990 Trump experiences a financial crisis.

1990 Trump divorces his wife Ivana.

1998 Trump divorces his wife Marla.

strategy was not to repay the loans by their formal terms but to refinance his properties and to buy and sell strategically.

In the late 1980s the rules on the real estate speculation game changed and Trump's wealth plummeted. The Tax Reform Act of 1986 limited depreciation on real estate, which significantly lowered his allowable tax deductions. Without the favorable deductions, investors lost interest in the inflated Manhattan real estate market, making it difficult for Trump to get money for his purchases. Trump's cash flow dried up further when the federal government tightened the lending practices of the savings and loan industry following its crisis of the 1980s and early 1990s, when more than 1,000 savings and loans failed and hundreds of others were near bankruptcy. Then creditors began to demand that Trump make insurance and interest payments that were due. Unable to pay and carrying hundreds of millions of dollars of debt, Trump faced bankruptcy.

With the help of some financial advisors, Trump survived his financial crisis, in part because his creditors were persuaded that the value of the Trump properties was closely tied to his celebrity name and that they could stand to lose millions if Trump were to go bankrupt. Trump also sold off some of his costliest and most prized assets, including the stately Plaza Hotel in New York City; the Trump Shuttle, which ran New York-Boston-Washington, D.C., routes; the *Trump Princess*, a 282-foot, $25 million yacht; and the Grand Hyatt hotel, his first big real estate venture. He then turned his attention to his gambling casinos in Atlantic City—the Trump Castle, the Trump Plaza, and the Trump Taj Mahal. By the mid-1990s, he was out of debt and a millionaire once again.

Trump has been described as smug, crude-speaking person with a fear of germs, a love of fame, and a talent for salesmanship. In 1990, he divorced Ivana Zelnickova (Winklmayr) Trump, a former fashion model and Olympic skier, with whom he had three children. He subsequently married Marla Maples, who was his mistress, then divorced her in 1998. They have one child. ◆

"A gambler is someone who plays slot machines. I prefer to own slot machines."
Donald Trump, 1990

Tupper, Earl Silas

1907–1983 ● Inventor of tupperware

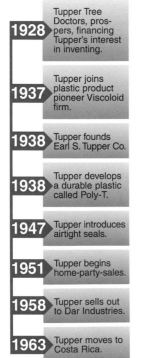

1928 Tupper Tree Doctors, prospers, financing Tupper's interest in inventing.

1937 Tupper joins plastic product pioneer Viscoloid firm.

1938 Tupper founds Earl S. Tupper Co.

1938 Tupper develops a durable plastic called Poly-T.

1947 Tupper introduces airtight seals.

1951 Tupper begins home-party-sales.

1958 Tupper sells out to Dar Industries.

1963 Tupper moves to Costa Rica.

Earl Silas Tupper was a small-town farm boy. His parents, Earnest Leslie Tupper and Lulu Clark, farmed small acreages first in New Hampshire and then in Massachusetts. Like many marginal farmers of the era, the family accepted boarders, and Tupper's mother took in laundry to supplement the family income (Tupper was one of five children). Tupper's father was an avid but only partly successful inventor who passed on this love to his son.

The family moved to the village of Shirley, Massachusetts, when Tupper was a child. His formal schooling ended with his graduation from nearby Fitchburg High School in 1925. He then worked in the family greenhouses until 1928, when, after taking a course in tree surgery, he opened his own business, Tupper Tree Doctors. The business prospered for a time, giving Tupper, who had married Marie Whitcomb Smith in 1931, the means to pursue a career as an inventor. His interest grew out of both a love of inventing and a belief that this could be his path to riches.

Events in 1936 were pivotal for Tupper. The loss of his business that year reinforced Tupper's belief that his greatest chance for success on a grand scale lay in his inventions. Consequently he began to focus on bringing some of his projects to market. In the process he met Bernard Doyle, a founder of the Viscoloid company. Viscoloid was a plastics pioneer firm located in nearby Leominster, a manufacturing center already becoming known as "plastic city." The chemical-manufacturing firm du Pont had purchased the company in 1928, and Tupper, apparently with Doyle's support, joined du Pont Viscoloid as a designer and chemist in 1937. Tupper would later recall that "my education really began" at du Pont. In his year there Tupper gained the practical chemical, design, and manufacturing experience, as well as the contacts, that enabled him to successfully strike out on his own. In 1938 he founded the Earl S. Tupper Company, which initially operated primarily as a du Pont subcontractor. The company prospered during World War II, manufacturing gas-mask parts and signal lamps. Although the company continued to do defense work for a few years after the war, Tupper's main interest had shifted to the civilian market.

Initially he devoted his prewar strategy of making goods for others. Early contracts included items such as an order for 700,000 cups from American Thermos and 300,000 cigarette cases for Camel. But he also began making his own products, such as the "Wonderlier bowl" that he sold under the Tupperware trade name. Tupper distinguished himself from competitors primarily through the superior quality of his plastic. In 1938, he had developed Poly-T, a variant of the polyethylene he had first seen at du Pont. Polyethylene had been invented in England in 1931 but attracted little interest until World War II, when researchers discovered it provided very effective insulation for the electrical wiring in radar units. Tupper's Poly-T was an unusually durable variant ideally suited to kitchen use. It was shatterproof, bendable, heat resistant, odorless, and inexpensive. This alone probably would have been enough to make Tupper a success, but in 1947 he introduced his patented airtight seal, which gave him a unique and powerful advantage over his competitors.

Tupper's seal, modeled after the lip typically found on paint cans, is the main reason Tupperware has been called "the first major [kitchen] storage breakthrough since the glass canning jar." Its partial vacuum kept foods fresh, and it was simple to use. Moreover, its Poly-T construction meant that it was also durable and inexpensive. Despite these advantages, however, sales lagged due to the lack of a suitable way to demonstrate it to the public.

Tupper found the solution to his marketing problems when Stanley Home Products, a Massachusetts firm that had developed the home-demonstration party in the 1930s, added Tupperware to its line. Some of Stanley's salespeople were enjoying great success with Tupperware, and with sales stalled in traditional retail outlets Tupper took notice. In 1948 he met with a group of Tupperware's best distributors, including a number of Stanley agents, to discuss how best to market his product. The group convinced Tupper that the product needed to be demonstrated and that the home party was its best venue. Modeled closely on the Stanley system, Tupper's marketing strategy and organization evolved between 1948 and

1951, when Tupper decided to pull Tupperware from retailer's shelves and sell it exclusively through in-home-sales parties.

Tupper chose Brownie Wise to head his new sales company, Tupper Home Parties, Inc. Much of Tupperware's phenomenal success in the 1950s can be attributed to Wise, who proved to be a skilled organizer, motivator, and spokesperson. In her first three years the sales force expanded from roughly 200 dealers to 9,000. Total sales doubled in the first full year of the new plan and tripled the following year.

Distributors convinced Tupper that his products needed to be demonstrated and that home parties were the best venue.

By the mid-1950s Tupper had achieved his boyhood dream of wealth on a grand scale, and as he had once hoped, his inventions were the root of his success. Other factors, however, had also played a part. Doyle's faith in Tupper's real but unschooled abilities had given him the chance he needed to develop his creations. Wise's ability to tap and inspire the 1950s housewives who were both Tupper's market and sales force had provided the difference between covering the market and dominating it. Overproduction of polyethylene in the early and mid-1950s had assured low prices and production that kept pace with demand.

In 1958 Tupper sold the business to Dart Industries for $16 million. He stayed on as chairman of the board of directors until 1973, when he retired and moved with his family to Costa Rica, where he became a citizen (ostensibly for tax reasons) and lived until his death, from a heart attack.

Tupper's personal and business papers are held by the Archives Center of the National Museum of American History, Smithsonian Institution. These include outlines and early drafts of Tupper's uncompleted autobiography and much of the research for a never-completed biography by Neil Osterweil. ◆

Turner, Robert Edward (Ted)

1938–PRESENT ● MEDIA MOGUL

Life is like a B-movie. You don't want to leave in the middle of it but you don't want to see it again."

Ted Turner

Ted Turner is an American broadcasting executive who built a media empire in the late 1900s. His three largest cable television stations at one time reached more than 95 percent of all cable households in the United States, and he had an estimated personal fortune of more than $3 billion. Turner is the founder of Cable News Network (CNN), the world's first 24-hour, all-news television network.

Robert Edward "Ted" Turner III was born on November 19, 1938, in Cincinnati, Ohio, to Robert Edward "Ed" Turner, a salesman, and Florence (Rooney) Turner. Ed was an alcoholic, who believed that his son would become competitive through harsh treatment, and Ted was frequently beaten for his mischievous behavior. When he was 9, the Turners moved to Savannah, Georgia, where his father had bought a billboard advertising company.

Turner attended boarding schools and military schools throughout much of his youth. In high school he displayed an interest in history and the classics and a talent for debating. When he was 17, he won the Tennessee state high school debating contest for McCallie School, a military academy for boys in Chattanooga, Tennessee.

His father sent him to Brown University in Providence Rhode Island to study business.

While at Brown, Turner pursued his interests in debating and sailing. He was the captain of the sailing team, and he won nearly all the races in which he participated. Later in life, he won many prestigious sailing trophies, including the twenty-third America's Cup, the world's most famous sailboat competition and the oldest trophy in international sports.

As a student Turner did well academically and he was known for his ability to recite Shakespeare. But his fondness for drinking and chasing women got him in trouble. He was suspended and later expelled from Brown for infractions against university rules related to his raucous behavior. After his expulsion in 1959 Turner's father sent him to work as an account executive at Turner Advertising Company in Atlanta. In 1960 he became general manager at a branch office.

In 1962, Turner's father bought the General Outdoor Advertising Company, the largest billboard company in the nation. The acquisition put the older Turner under tremendous financial pressure and in early 1963, Ed Turner began plans for selling out. Then on March 5, 1963, Ed Turner killed himself with a gun. Ted inherited the family business at the age of 24. He soon halted plans for the company sale and restored the company's profitability.

Turner began buying radio stations as a way of expanding his company, and he used his unsold billboards to advertise the stations. When he saw that TV was growing faster than any other business, he vowed to license a station. In 1970 his company went public and Turner bought Channel 17, a financially troubled, independent UHF station in Atlanta for $3 million. To program the station, originally named WTCG and later WTBS, Turner relied on old movies and sitcoms, which he promoted on the basis of their positive family values. He also captured viewers who did not watch network news by offering reruns of *Star Trek*, a popular science fiction television program, during regular network news broadcasts. WTCG also featured sports.

In 1976, Turner invested in cable television and satellite technology and became one of the first broadcasters in the world to use a communications satellite to relay programs to local cable television companies. The satellite-cable link enabled him to broadcast his programs anywhere in the country that was wired for cable access. Turner realized, however,

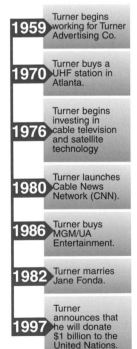

1959 Turner begins working for Turner Advertising Co.

1970 Turner buys a UHF station in Atlanta.

1976 Turner begins investing in cable television and satellite technology

1980 Turner launches Cable News Network (CNN).

1986 Turner buys MGM/UA Entertainment.

1982 Turner marries Jane Fonda.

1997 Turner announces that he will donate $1 billion to the United Nations.

that cable TV was still in its infancy and that he had to help build the cable TV audience if his own station was to succeed. He decided to offer WTCG to cable stations free of charge and to raise money through advertising revenues. He convinced the cable companies to advertise his station to help them build their customer base. The companies complied with this suggestion because WTCG was about all they could offer at no cost. His strategies paid off and by the late 1970s, WTCG was worth more than 10 times its purchase price.

In 1976, Turner purchased the Atlanta Braves baseball team and the Atlanta Hawks basketball team and telecast them on WTCG. As a new owner of the Braves, he became notorious for disregarding baseball regulations and for snubbing the authority of baseball officials. During the 1977 season, he appointed himself manager of the Braves, despite regulations against owners managing their teams. His managing career was short-lived, however. After only one game, baseball commissioner Bowie Kuhn ordered Turner to stay "in the stands, like the other owners." He was also found guilty of tampering with a player's contract after trying to buy the services of Gary Matthews, a star outfielder, who was still with the Giants, and was suspended from baseball for a year.

In 1980, Turner launched Cable News Network (CNN), an all-news network broadcast twenty-four hours a day by

Ted Turner's Donation to the United Nations

In September 18, 1997, Ted Turner astonished the audience of a United Nations Association dinner, where he had been invited to receive an award, by announcing that he planned to donate $1 billion to the United Nations. Turner later said, "I'm putting every rich person in the world on notice," expressing his hope that others would follow his example. Turner had come to his decision after seeing on a balance sheet that his personal net worth had risen from $2.2 billion in 1996 to $3.2 billion in 1997. He resolved to give his "extra billion" to the United Nations, an organization he had supported in the past. His $1 billion would rank as the largest gift ever made by an individual to a single organization. The donation was to be made in annual installments over 10 years and was based on stock that Turner owned in media conglomerate Time Warner Inc. Turner had sold WTBS to Time Warner the previous year, gaining 10 percent of the media company in the deal. United States and UN leaders praised Turner's gift, which amounted to about a year's budget for the UN. Turner intended the money to go for humanitarian programs of the UN.

"There's a lot of people who are awash in money they don't know what to do with.... It doesn't do you any good if you don't know what to do with it."

Ted Turner, 1997

satellite. Though it began as maverick cable television station, CNN developed into one of the world's most respected news programs, offering the latest-breaking news worldwide.

Turner continued to build his media empire in the 1980's and 1990's. One of his more important acquisitions came in early 1986 with the purchase of Metro-Goldwyn-Mayer/United Artists Entertainment (MGM/UA), the entertainment group that included movie studios and the MGM film library containing many Hollywood classics. Later that year, to pay off a mounting debt, he sold off a significant portion of his company and all of MGM/UA except the film library. In 1988, Turner utilized the film library in a new cable television network called TNT (Turner Network Television), which also featured TV movies and high-profile sporting events. Some of his black-and-white classics he had "colorized," a process that involved cleaning up the film prints and adding color to them. Turner's colorizing of old films stirred controversy among filmmakers and critics, who protested that adding color to black-and-white films destroyed the integrity of them.

In 1996, media giant Time Warner Inc. bought WTBS for $7.5 billion. As part of the acquisition agreement, Turner received a 10 percent stake in Time Warner and was made vice-chairman and a head of the corporation's cable-television networks.

In September 1997, Turner announced that he would donate $1 billion to the United Nations, roughly the UN's annual budget, over a period of 10 years. Turner intended the donation to benefit programs aiding refugees and children, clearing land mines and fighting disease. His gift was one of the largest ever made to an organization.

Turner is known for his gutsy business acumen, his eccentric behavior, and his staunch support of organizations promoting world peace and environmental protection. He has been married three times. In 1982, he married actress and former aerobics trainer Jane Fonda. Turner has five children. ◆

Vanderbilt, Cornelius

1794–1877 ● SHIPPING &
RAILROAD TYCOON

> *"Gentlemen: You have undertaken to
> cheat me. I won't sue you, for law is too
> slow. I'll ruin you."*
>
> Cornelius Vanderbilt,
> letter to disloyal associates, 1853

Cornelius Vanderbilt was born at Port Richmond, Staten Island, New York. (now part of New York City). He was the fourth child and second son of Cornelius and Phebe (Hand) Vander Bilt. His paternal ancestors, who came from Holland and settled on Long Island in the latter half of the seventeenth century, wrote the family name in three words, van der Bilt. The subject of the present sketch preferred to write it Van Derbilt, but during his lifetime other members of the family consolidated the name into one word. His father, a poor man with a large family, did a bit of farming on Staten Island, and some boating and lightering around New York harbor. The blue eyed, flaxen-haired, boisterous boy Cornelius had no inclination and little opportunity for education, and did not spend a day in school after he was 11. Already big in body and strong, he became at that age his father's helper. At about 13 he is said to have superintended the job of lightering a vessel, his father being engaged elsewhere. He had barely reached his sixteenth birthday when, with $100 advanced by his parents, he bought a small sailing vessel called a piragua and began a freight and passenger ferry-ferrying business between Staten Island and New York City. On December 19, 1813 when he was only 19 years old, he married Sophia Johnson, daughter of his father's sister Eleanor, and set up a home of his own near his birthplace.

The War of 1812 had opened new opportunities for him, and he was busy day and night. Among other important jobs, he had a three months' contract from the government for provisioning the forts in and around New York harbor. Before the war was over, he had several boats under his command. He built a schooner in 1814 for service to Long Island Sound, and, in the following two years, two larger schooners for the coastwise trade. These he sent out—he himself being in command of the largest—not only as cargo boats, but also as traders up the Hudson River and along the coast from New England to Charleston.

In 1818 he startled his friends by selling all his sailing vessels and going to work as a captain for Thomas Gibbons, owner of a ferry between New Brunswick, on the Raritan estuary, and New York City—an important link in the New York-Philadelphia, freight, mail, and passenger route. Gibbons was fighting for life against the steam-navigation monopoly in New York waters which had been granted to Robert Fulton by the New York legislature several years before. Vanderbilt loved a fight; he took Gibbons's one small vessel, put her in better condition, selected a hard-bitten crew and drove them to the limit of endurance, and within a year had turned a losing venture into a profitable one.

During the eleven years of his service with Gibbons, young Vanderbilt increased and broadened the business enormously. He had built seven more steamers for his employer, some for the New York-New Brunswick-Elizabeth ferries, others to ply a new line on the Delaware.

Vanderbilt had ambitions of his own; and in 1829, having accumulated a considerable nestegg, he resigned from Gibbons's employ in order to enter the steamboat business on his own. His first ventures were on the Hudson River, where other concerns were already operating; he inaugurated rate wars with a characteristic zest for conflict. Here, in a competition for the trade between New York and Peekskill, he came into collision, in 1834, with Daniel Drew. The fare between

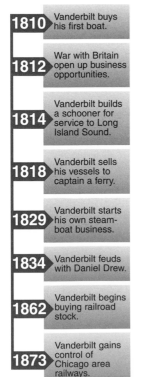

1810 Vanderbilt buys his first boat.

1812 War with Britain open up business opportunities.

1814 Vanderbilt builds a schooner for service to Long Island Sound.

1818 Vanderbilt sells his vessels to captain a ferry.

1829 Vanderbilt starts his own steamboat business.

1834 Vanderbilt feuds with Daniel Drew.

1862 Vanderbilt begins buying railroad stock.

1873 Vanderbilt gains control of Chicago area railways.

the two points was finally cut to twelve and a half cents, and then Drew sold out to Vanderbilt. The latter now entered the Albany trade, where a more powerful corporation, the Hudson River Association, was functioning. He put two boats on the Albany run and began cutting rates again. In the end his opponents paid him a goodly sum for his agreement to withdraw from competition for ten years. He next established lines on Long Island Sound and on to Providence and Boston. Later he returned to the Hudson River.

The gold rush opened new vistas to Vanderbilt, whom men were now calling "Commodore." Before the end of 1849, traffic to California was beginning to go via Panama, freight and passengers crossing the Isthmus on muleback. Vanderbilt conceived the idea of starting a line of his own via Nicaragua—through the San Juan River to Lake Nicaragua and perhaps thence by canal to the Pacific. At first he called this the American Atlantic & Pacific Ship Canal Company. A trip to England in 1850 in search of capital to finance the venture was fruitless, and he proceeded to develop the route himself. He procured from the Nicaraguan government a charter for himself in the name of the Accessory Transit Company. He then improved to some extent the channel of the San Juan River, built docks on the east and westcoasts of Nicaragua and at Virgin Bay on Lake Nicaragua, and made a fine twelve-mile **macadam** road from the latter place to his west-coast port. Meanwhile, he was beginning the construction of a fleet of eight new steamers with which he ran lines from New York, and later from New Orleans. His route was two days shorter than that via Panama; he greatly reduced the New York-San Francisco passenger fare and garnered most of the traffic.

In the middle fifties he built three vessels, one of which, the *Vanderbilt*, was the largest and finest he had yet constructed, and entered into competition for the Atlantic trade with the Cunard Line and the Collins Line, even offering to carry the mails to Havre for nothing. He found this an unprofitable venture, however, and at the beginning of the Civil War was glad to sell his Atlantic line for $3,000,000 retaining only the *Vanderbilt*, which he fitted up as a warship and turned over to the government. His connection with the expedition of Nathaniel P. Banks to New Orleans was less happy, for many of the vessels chartered by him under commission of the

> The Gold Rush opened new vistas to Vanderbilt, whom men were now calling "Commodore."

> **macadam:** made of small stones.

expunged: removed.

government proved unseaworthy. However, his name was **expunged** from the Senate resolution of censure.

Of Vanderbilt's thirteen children, one boy had died young and all of the nine daughters were living. His youngest and favorite child, George, born in 1839, was a soldier in the Civil War and died in 1866 from effects of exposure in the Corinth campaign. His second son, Cornelius Jeremiah, a gambler and ne'er-do-well, had been a great disappointment. The eldest son, William Henry, he had regarded as being of little force, and had exiled to a farm on Staten Island, though later he became aware of his ability and at last gave him opportunity to use it. This was in connection with railroad enterprises, to which Vanderbilt turned from shipping as he neared 70. He had begun buying New York & Harlem Railroad stock in 1862 when it was selling at a very low figure. He made William vice-president of the Harlem road, and thereafter his son was his first lieutenant.

He next turned his attention to the Harlem's competitor, the Hudson River Railroad, another rundown property. While buying control of the railroad, he sought authority from the

George Vanderbilt's Biltmore Estate

George Vanderbilt, grandson of Cornelius Vanderbilt and one of the heirs to his fortune, broke ground in Asheville, North Carolina, for a new family home in 1889. Construction continued until 1895, when Vanderbilt welcomed his friends and family to Biltmore to celebrate Christmas Eve. Vanderbilt combined two words when he named his estate: "bildt" from his family name and the region in Holland where the Vanderbilt family originated, and "more," which is an old English word for rolling hills, like those around Asheville. Distinguished 19th-century architect Richard Morris Hunt designed Biltmore's French Renaissance style buildings, parts of which were modeled after three famous 16th-century castles in the Loire Valley. The centerpiece of the estate is a four-story mansion with 250 rooms, including 34 master bedrooms, 43 bathrooms, 65 fireplaces, and 3 kitchens. The rooms are lavishly decorated with opulent furnishings and priceless artworks. Landscape designer Frederick Law Olmsted, who designed New York's Central Park, developed the estate's equally impressive gardens, which were originally surrounded by 125,000 acres of forest. The Biltmore estate was opened to the public in 1930 at the request of Asheville city officials, who hoped to draw tourists to the city during the Depression. Descendants of George Vanderbilt still own Biltmore, and visitors are welcome year round.

legislature to combine the two. He next sought control of the New York Central Railroad, running from Albany to Buffalo. Its directors countered by forming an alliance with Drew's Hudson River boat line and sending through freight and passengers from Albany to New York by that route. But when the river froze in early winter and the steamboats were stopped, they sought to transfer traffic to the Hudson River, road, only to discover that Vanderbilt was halting its trains on the east side of the river, a mile from Albany. Stock in the New York Central declined and Vanderbilt bought quantities of it, finally securing control in 1867. He promptly spent $2,000,000 of his own money in improving the line and buying new rolling stock. He united these two railroads by legislative act in 1869, as the New York Central & Hudson River Railroad, and in 1872 leased the Harlem Railroad to it. Out of three inefficient roads he created a single line, giving uninterrupted service.

In 1868 he sought control of the Erie Railway, a rival line to Buffalo and Chicago. He pursued the same tactics as before, buying every share of stock offered. But this time Drew, Jay Gould, and James Fisk Jr., who were in control of Erie, outmaneuvered him, throwing 50,000 shares of fraudulent stock into the market, then fleeing to New Jersey to avoid prosecution and bribing the New Jersey legislature to legalize the stock issue. Vanderbilt lost millions by this *coup*, but the plotters had to compromise with him in order to return to New York with **impunity**, and his loss was greatly reduced. Upon the insistence of his son William that extension of their rail system to Chicago was advisable, in 1873 he bought control of the Lake Shore & Michigan Southern Railway, and two years before his death the Michigan Central Railroad and the Canada Southern Railway.

In the last years of his life, his influence on national finance was stabilizing. When the panic of 1873 was at its worst, he announced that the New York Central was paying its millions of dividends as usual, and let contracts for the building of the Grand Central Terminal in New York City, with four tracks leading from it, giving employment to thousands of men. He saw to it, however, that the city paid half the cost of the **viaduct** and open-cut approaches to the station.

His fortune was estimated at more than $100,000,000, of which he left about $90,000,000 to William and about

impunity: freedom from punishment.

viaduct: a bridge over a road, railway, valley, or river.

$7,500,000 to the latter's four sons; he expressed his contempt for women by leaving less than $4,000,000 to be distributed among his own eight daughters. Vanderbilt bestowed no money philanthropically until late in life, when he gave $1,000,000 to Vanderbilt University (previously Central University) at Nashville, Tennessee, of which he is regarded as the founder. ◆

Walker,
Madam C. J.

1867–1919 ● COSMETICS
ENTREPRENEUR

Born Sarah Breedlove to ex-slaves Owen and Minerva
Breedlove on a Delta, Louisiana, cotton plantation, she
was orphaned by age 7. She lived with her sister,
Louvenia, in Vicksburg, Mississippi, until 1882, when she married Moses McWilliams, in part to escape Louvenia's cruel husband. In 1887, when her daughter, Lelia (later known as
A'Lelia Walker), was 2 years old, Moses McWilliams died. For
the next eighteen years she worked as a laundress in St. Louis.
But in 1905, with $1.50 in savings, the thirty-seven-year-old
McWilliams moved to Denver to start her own business after
developing a formula to treat her problem with baldness—an
ailment common among African-American women at the
time, brought on by poor diet, stress, illness, damaging hair-

Madame Walker gets a
manicure in her salon

> *"I am a woman who came from the cotton fields of the South. I was promoted from there to the washtub. Then I was promoted to the cook kitchen, and from there I promoted myself into the business of manufacturing hair good and preparations."*
>
> Madam Walker, in a speech, 1912

care treatments, and scalp disease. In January 1906 she married Charles Joseph Walker, a newspaper sales agent, who helped design her advertisements and mail-order operation.

While Madam Walker is often said to have invented the "hot comb," it is more likely that she adapted metal implements popularized by the French to suit black women's hair. Acutely aware of the debate about whether black women should alter the appearance of their natural hair texture, she insisted years later that her Walker System was not intended as a hair "straightener," but rather as a grooming method to heal and condition the scalp to promote hair growth and prevent baldness.

From 1906 to 1916 Madam Walker traveled throughout the United States, Central America, and the West Indies promoting her business. She settled briefly in Pittsburgh, establishing the first Lelia College of Hair Culture there in 1908, then moved the company to Indianapolis in 1910, building a factory and vastly increasing her annual sales. Her reputation as a philanthropist was solidified in 1911, when she contributed one thousand dollars to the building fund of the Indianapolis YMCA. In 1912 she and C. J. Walker divorced,

Elizabeth Arden and Helena Rubinstein

Madame Walker's successful career as an executive in the cosmetics industry was paralleled by the careers of two other cosmetics tycoons: Helena Rubinstein and Elizabeth Arden. Arden was born Florence Nightingale Graham in Woodbridge, Ontario, Canada. She moved to New York City in 1907, where she opened a beauty salon under the name of Elizabeth Arden. Arden introduced American women to eye shadow and lipstick that was tinted to compliment the color of their skin, hair, and clothes. Her business eventually grew into an international corporation. Throughout her career, Arden's primary competition came from her arch-rival, Helena Rubinstein. Rubinstein was born in Krakow, Poland, in 1870. She completed two years of medical school in Poland before immigrating to Australia in the 1880s. Rubinstein opened Australia's first beauty salon in Melbourne in 1902. She made a fortune selling face cream that was made using an old family recipe. In 1915, Rubinstein moved to New York City, where she introduced American women to waterproof mascara and face foundation. Her earlier medical training encouraged her to stress scientific preparation of her cosmetics and she provided instructions to her clients in their proper use. Together, Arden (who died in 1966) and Rubinstein (who died in 1965) helped make it acceptable and respectible for American women to wear makeup.

but she retained his name. Madam Walker joined her daughter, A'Lelia, and A'Lelia's adopted daughter, Mae (later Mae Walker Perry), in Harlem in 1916. She left the daily management of her manufacturing operation in Indianapolis to her long-time attorney and general manager, Freeman B. Ransom, factory forewoman Alice Kelly, and assistant general manager Robert L. Brokenburr.

Madam Walker's business philosophy stressed economic independence for the 20,000 former maids, farm laborers, housewives, and schoolteachers she employed as agents and factory and office workers. To further strengthen her company, she created the Madam C. J. Walker Hair Culturists Union of America and held annual conventions.

During World War I, she was among those who supported the government's black recruitment efforts and War Bond drives. But after the bloody 1917 East St. Louis riot, she joined the planning committee of the Negro Silent Protest Parade, traveling to Washington to present a petition urging President Wilson to support legislation that would make lynching a federal crime. As her wealth and visibility grew, Walker became increasingly outspoken, joining those blacks who advocated an alternative peace conference at Versailles after the war to monitor proceedings affecting the world's people of color. She intended her estate in Irvington-on-Hudson, New York—Villa Lewaro, which was designed by black architect Vertner W. Tandy—not only as a showplace but as an inspiration to other blacks.

During the spring of 1919, aware that her long battle with hypertension was taking its final toll, Madam Walker revamped her will, directing her attorney to donate five thousand dollars to the National Association for the Advancement of Color People's antilynching campaign and to contribute thousands of dollars to black educational, civic, and social institutions and organizations.

When she died at age 51, at Villa Lewaro, she was widely considered the wealthiest black woman in America and was reputed to be the first African-American woman millionaire. Her daughter, A'Lelia Walker—a central figure of the Harlem Renaissance—succeeded her as president of the Mme. C. J. Walker Manufacturing Company.

Walker's significance is rooted not only in her innovative (and sometimes controversial) hair-care system, but also in

1905 Walker moves to Denver to start her business.

1908 Walker forms the Lelia College of Hair Culture in Pittsburgh.

1910 Walker moves the company to Indianapolis.

1911 Walker contributes $1,000 to the Indianapolis YMCA.

1917 Walker advocates to make lynching a federal crime.

1992 Walker is elected to the National Business Hall of Fame.

her advocacy of black women's economic independence and her creation of business opportunities at a time when most black women worked as servants and sharecroppers. Her entrepreneurial strategies and organizational skills revolutionized what would become a multibillion-dollar ethnic hair-care and cosmetics industry by the last decade of the twentieth century. Having led an early life of hardship, she became a trailblazer of black philanthropy, using her wealth and influence to leverage social, political, and economic rights for women and blacks. In 1992 Madam Walker was elected to the National Business Hall of Fame. ◆

Walton, Sam

1918–1992 ● RETAIL MERCHANT

> *"I'm not sure I ever really figured out this celebrity business. Why in the world, for example, would I get an invitation to Elizabeth Taylor's wedding out in Hollywood?"*
>
> Sam Walton

Sam Walton was an American businessman and the founder of Wal-Mart Stores. He was one of the most successful retail merchants of his time and a revolutionary in U.S. retailing. By the time of his death in 1992, Wal-Mart was the largest retail organization in the world, with annual sales near $50 billion and family stock valued at more than $20 billion.

Samuel Moore Walton was born in Kingfisher, Oklahoma, on March 29, 1918, to Nancy Lee and Thomas Walton. His father had a number of jobs through Sam's youth, including farmer, banker, and farm-mortgage broker. The family lived in Oklahoma and Missouri, where they moved when Sam was five. Throughout his youth, Walton held odd jobs and earned much of his money delivering newspapers. He was a star athlete in high school and senior class president at the University of Missouri, where he graduated in 1940 with a degree in economics. Walton's first job out of college was as a management trainee in Des Moines, Iowa, with the J. C. Penney Company. In 1942, he was drafted into the army, where he worked as a communications officer in the Army Intelligence Corps during World War II (1939–1945).

In 1945, with the help of a family loan, Walton bought his first store, a Ben Franklin franchise in Newport, Arkansas. Seeking to expand the store's potential, Walton proposed to franchise executives a retail plan that would later serve as a blueprint for his success. He suggested that Ben Franklin target small towns, which he felt were an untapped resource. He also suggested that the stores offer discount prices on goods and that profits would come from high sales volumes. Ben Franklin executives rejected his plan, and in 1962 Walton went out on his own to open his first Wal-Mart discount store in the small city of Rogers, Arkansas.

Walton built his chain of Wal-Marts slowly. He based his retail plan on large stores that offered a wide variety of goods at cut-rate prices, and he earned his profits through high volume sales. In the early years of his business, he always located new stores in small towns and rural areas, where there was little competition. Each new Wal-Mart also was no more than a day's drive from a company warehouse, so that the store could quickly restock shelves. The typical shipping time for other retailers was two weeks. The warehouse also made large volume purchases and used Wal-Mart trucks, which reduced the cost of shipping and the price of goods.

Over the years Walton tried to visit every store at least once a year. On his visits, he always talked with employees—whom Walton called his "associates"—about how to improve sales. Walton also encouraged his employees to work hard and keep the customer satisfied, and he rewarded them through profit sharing, stock purchase plans, and incentive bonuses for keeping losses from theft and damage below corporate goals. He also held pep rallies to build company enthusiasm and would often invite groups of employees to local restaurants. Walton sometimes flew to store locations in his own twin-engine Cessna plane that he piloted himself.

In the 1980s, Walton expanded his stores from rural communities into medium-sized cities and the suburbs of large cities. Though the arrival of a Wal-Mart was generally welcomed by communities for the jobs and tax revenues it generated, it was usually feared by small businesses in town centers that were unable to compete with Wal-Mart's variety of goods and discount prices.

Walton began to diversify his stores in the 1980s, and he opened Sam's Wholesale Club (later shortened to Sam's

1940 Walton graduates from college with an economics degree.

1945 Walton buys a Ben Franklin franchise.

1962 Walton opens his first Wal-Mart discount store.

1983 Walton opens Sam's Wholesale Club.

1992 Walton is awarded the Presidential Medal of Freedom.

Club), his first warehouse club, in Oklahoma City, in 1983. The idea behind Sam's Club was to cut consumer costs by offering goods in bulk. Walton experimented with "super-store" retailing further after viewing the success of European "hypermarkets," giant stores that combined full-scale grocery stores and general merchandise stores. In 1987, he opened a pilot Hypermart USA in suburban Dallas, but found sales disappointing. Walton then scaled back the size of the hyper-market and created Wal-Mart Supercenters, which combined full-scale grocery stores and Wal-Marts.

The tremendous success of Walton's discount stores continued through the 1980s and 1990s. From 1985 to 1991, *Forbes* magazine ranked Walton the wealthiest man in the United States, a distinction that irked the successful retailer because it detracted from his down-home image. By the late 1990s, Wal-Mart Stores ranked as the nation's largest retailer, with about 2,000 Wal-Mart stores throughout the United States.

On March 18, 1992, U.S. president George Bush traveled to Wal-Mart's headquarters in Bentonville, Arkansas, to present Walton with the Presidential Medal of Freedom, the nation's highest civilian award. The award cited Walton's entrepreneurial spirit, his concern for his employees, and his commitment to his family and his community. It also praised his sponsoring of scholarships for Latin America, which reflected his desire to bring peoples together and to share with others his American ideals.

Sam Walton was known for his personal charm and warmth, his hard work ethic, and his candid, homespun style that appealed to rural customers. He lived modestly, drove around in a pickup truck, and pursued quail hunting and tennis as hobbies. Walton married Helen Alice Robson in 1943 and they had four children. He died on April 5, 1992, of cancer. ◆

From 1985 to 1991, *Forbes* magazine ranked Walton the wealthiest man in the United States.

Ward, Aaron Montgomery

1843–1913 ● MAIL ORDER MERCHANT

Aaron Montgomery Ward was born at Chatham, New Jersey, the son of Sylvester A. and Julia Laura Mary (Green) Ward. During his childhood his parents moved to Niles, Michigan, where he attended public school until he was 14. He was then apprenticed to a trade, but left his master to work in a barrel-stave factory at twenty-five cents a day and later became a day laborer in a brickyard. When he was 19 years old he went to St. Joseph, Michigan, to work in a general store for five dollars a month and his board; at the end of three years he was put in charge of the store with a salary of $100 a month. Going to Chicago about 1865, he was employed by Field, Palmer & Leiter for two years and then worked for a short time for the wholesale drygoods house of Willis, Gregg & Brown. When this firm failed, he became a traveling salesman for Walter M. Smith & Company, dry-goods wholesalers in St. Louis.

It was while he was traveling out of St. Louis that Ward obtained an intimate knowledge of rural conditions that enabled him to make a distinctive contribution to American life. A source of chronic complaint by people living in the country was the small price received for farm produce compared with the high cost of goods bought at retail. Ward conceived the idea of buying in large quantities for cash direct

> Ward was a keen judge of merchandise and he bought at prices that enabled him to sell to rural consumers at prices they could pay.

from the manufacturer and selling for cash direct to the farmer. Back in Chicago, working for C. W. Partridge, a State Street dry-goods firm, he awaited his chance to go into business for himself. He was ready to start when the Chicago fire of 1871 intervened to wipe out practically all his savings. In the spring of 1872, however, he resigned his position and invested all he had saved, $1,600, in the new business. This, with $800 contributed by George R. Thorne, his partner, constituted the total capital.

The partners began their operations in the loft of a livery stable on Kinzie Street between Rush and State streets. Their first stock was a small selection of dry goods, the first catalogue a single price sheet. Ward was a keen judge of merchandise and he bought at prices that enabled him to sell to consumers in the country at prices they could pay. From the beginning he followed the policy of satisfying the customer or allowing the return of goods. In 1873–74 purchasing agencies of the National Grange bought through him to stock their cooperative retail stores and he thus earned the good will of farmers in Illinois and Iowa. Making accessible to people in rural areas throughout the country a variety of goods that they

Mail Order Catalogues

While the origins of mail order catalogues in the United States dates to the colonial period, the expansion into the trans-Mississippi West gave these catalogues a life that continues today. Aaron Montgomery Ward established the first great national general-merchandise catalogue house. Ward organized a Chicago-based mail-order firm in 1872 with his brother-in-law, George R. Thorne. By offering its wares at low prices compared to most local merchants, Ward's mail-order business grew rapidly. In 1888, Richard Sears issued his first catalogue, primarily watches and jewelry. In 1893, he established the firm of Sears, Roebuck, and Company and began to produce more extensive general-merchandise catalogues from his headquarters in Chicago. Agricultural expansion, the completion of a continental railroad network after the Civil War, and new techniques in mass printing supported the early growth of mail-order companies. Mail-order catalogues were the "wish books" of the American West, and they offered the customer almost anything imaginable. The catalogues were an important agent in bringing the products of industrial America to every corner of the United States and, in so doing, helped break the isolation of the remote Great Plains. They reshaped the consumer market and helped established the culture of consumption for the twentieth century.

could not otherwise have enjoyed with their limited purchasing power, his enterprise succeeded from the beginning, and was forced repeatedly to move to larger quarters as sales increased. Since the business was conducted on a cash basis, it survived the panic of 1873. New lines were added after 1874 and an eight-page catalogue replaced the single price sheet. By 1876 the catalogue had 150 pages, with illustrations; by 1888, annual sales had reached one million dollars. With the building of the Ward Tower at Michigan Boulevard and Madison Street in 1900, the successful business and its founder attracted national attention. At the time of his death, annual sales amounted to some $40,000,000, customers were served in all parts of the world, and the staff of employees numbered 6,000.

Ward's public spirit was demonstrated by the protracted legal battle he carried on in the Illinois courts to maintain free from all obstruction the park between Michigan Boulevard and the lake shore, now Grant Park, and it is largely owing to his foresight and tenacity that Chicago has a lake frontage which is the heritage, not of a privileged few, but of the mass of the people, for whom Ward seems really to have cared. He retired from active management of the company in 1901, although he still retained the title of president. Since he had no sons, the management of the business passed into the hands of the five sons of his partner, Thorne. Ward spent much time at his large estate, "La Belle Knoll," at Oconomowoc, Wisconsin, where he raised fine horses. He died at Highland Park, Illinois.

On Feb. 22, 1872, in the same year in which he started his mail-order business, Ward married Elizabeth J. Cobb of Kalamazoo, whose sister had married his partner. Mrs. Ward was left the large fortune which her husband had received from the earnings of his mail-order business. During her lifetime, and through her will, she dispensed considerable sums to charitable institutions. Her principal benefactors, however, were to Northwestern University, to which institution in 1923 she gave $4,223,000 for a medical and dental school as a memorial to her husband, adding in 1926 $4,300,000 for the enlargement and maintenance of the school. She died July 26, 1926. The Wards had no children, although it was generally believed until after Mrs. Ward's will was probated that Marjorie Ward, an adopted daughter, was their own. ◆

1857 Ward goes to work in a barrel-stave factory.

1862 Ward begins working in a Michigan general store.

1865 Ward leaves his job for Chicago opportunities.

1871 Chicago fire wipes out Ward's savings.

1872 Ward starts mail-order business.

1876 Ward's catalogue swells to 150 pages.

1901 Ward retires from management to enjoy his fortune.

Waterhouse, Frank

1867–1930 ● SHIPPING MOGUL

1893 Waterhouse begins working as a stenographer.

1895 Waterhouse becomes secretary of the Pacific Navigation Company.

1898 Waterhouse establishes trading posts in Yukon.

1919 Waterhouse heads the Associated Industries of Seattle.

1921 Waterhouse heads the Seattle Chamber of Commerce.

Frank Waterhouse was born in Cheshire, England, the son of Joseph and Mary Elizabeth (Horsfield) Waterhouse. He attended private schools, but at 15 set out for America, landing in Montreal with fifty dollars in his pocket. He earned a living by hard labor during a good part of the next seven years, working in logging camps and as a hod carrier, and later serving as a constable and deputy sheriff. His wanderings took him into Minnesota and Manitoba. After three years in England, he returned to America, settling in Tacoma, Washington, where in 1893–94 he was a stenographer in the offices of the Northern Pacific Railroad. He then spent a few months selling life insurance, did a record business, and removed to Seattle as a general agent.

In January 1895 he became secretary of the Pacific Navigation Company, which operated a fleet of freight and passenger steamers on Puget Sound, and in May of the same year was appointed general manager. When the rush to the Klondike gold fields began he went to England and organized a company to furnish transportation to the northern British Columbia ports and the Yukon; in 1898 this organization established trading posts on the Yukon. He later purchased the interests of his British associates and formed an American concern, Frank Waterhouse & Company. He introduced the fresh meat business into Alaska and placed the first refrigerator boat on the Yukon.

During the Spanish-American War, he chartered a large fleet of ships for transport service, and nearly all livestock supplies from the Pacific Northwest for the army in the Philippines were shipped in his vessels. He established the first line of steamships to give regular service between Puget Sound and European ports through the Suez Canal, and the first line of freighters from the Sound to Hawaii, New Zealand, Australia, North China, and the Malay Peninsula. During the First World War, he engaged in the transportation of military supplies from Seattle to Vladivostok.

Waterhouse had many business interests other than shipping. He organized and was president of Waterhouse &

Employes, operating farms in eastern Washington, acquired iron and coal mines, the Arlington Dock Company, and other corporations; and was president of the Yellow and the Seattle taxicab companies. His civic interests were fully as numerous. He was president of the Associated Industries of Seattle, 1919–22, and of the Chamber of Commerce, 1921–22, and chairman of the Seattle chapter of the American Red Cross, 1919–26.

Waterhouse died of heart disease at his home in Seattle. In February 1893 he had married Lucy Dyer Hayden of Tacoma, daughter of John C. Hayden, and he was survived by his widow, one son, and three daughters. Another son, deceased, had been a lieutenant in the Royal (British) Flying Corps in World War I. ◆

Weinberg, Harry G.

1908–1990 ● INVESTOR & PHILANTHROPIST

Harry G. Weinberg was a businessman, investor, and philanthropist, and the founder of one of America's largest charitable foundation. He was born on August 15, 1908, in Galacia, Austria, the son of Joseph Weinberg, a tin smith and auto mechanic, and Sarah Kamserman. Harry Weinberg moved with his parents and six siblings to Baltimore, Maryland, when he was 4. He attended Samuel F. B. Morse Elementary School, until he left school in the sixth grade. After this he worked at a number of odd jobs, sold newspapers, and worked for his father's family autobody and fender repair shop.

During the Great Depression of the 1930s, Weinberg married in 1931 Jeanette Gutman, with whom he had one child, and established a business buying financially troubled homes in the city, fixing them up, for resale. He combined his real estate investments with successful investments in securities, whose price, in the depression, had fallen well below 1920s prices. He sold many of his properties at a large profit after the return of prosperity during and after World War II. He retired in 1948 with a net worth of $2 million.

Finding retirement a bore, the still youthful Weinberg began to study *Standard & Poor's* for signs of undervalued stocks. His first major move in his new career was to purchase $100,000 worth of stock in the Baltimore Brick Company. The company's real value, Weinberg discovered, lay in its ownership of vast clay pits in a central section of Baltimore. The land could be developed profitably for shopping centers. With his shares, he obtained a board membership and challenged company management to sell off these land holdings to increase the value of the company's stock. He quietly obtained support from other major stock holders and threatened wide-scale changes in the company's direction. To rid themselves of Weinberg's challenges, management bought his stock for $625,000, a huge profit on his $100,000 investment. Later, this practice would be labeled "green-mark" and would be associated with the maverick financier Carl Icahn and other financial speculators of the 1980s.

Weinberg's next major move was to use the $625,000 to secure a major holding in the Scranton (Pennsylvania) Transit Company. There he maximized the stock's value by raising fares, selling tangible assets such as garages, decreasing service, and depreciating assets where Internal Revenue Service regulations allowed. The profits from this endeavor allowed him to buy a controlling interest in the Honolulu Rapid Transit Company (HRT), and the profits from that endeavor enabled him to buy control of Dallas Transit Company and New York's Fifth Avenue Coach Lines. By 1962, his transit operations were valued at $100 million.

In the 1960s, Weinberg spent a great deal of time in Hawaii, and he finally moved to Honolulu in 1968. "Honolulu Harry," as his Baltimore associates (including his celebrity attorney Roy Cohn) called him, soon established himself as a brilliant, if often ruthless, business investor. As he had in other cities, he sought out companies with undervalued assets. In Hawaii, these were typically companies with large holdings of agriculture real estate. His targets were such prominent firms as American Factors (sugar, real estate, and

1931 Weinberg forms a business fixing and selling homes.

1948 Weinberg retires and starts investing.

1959 Weinberg founds a small charitable foundation.

1962 Weinberg's transit operations total $100 million.

1968 Weinberg moves to Hawaii.

1990 Weinberg's death enriches his charitable foundation.

shipping); Dillingham Corporation (construction and shipping); American Pacific Group (real estate, insurance, banking, laundry, and a Japanese car franchise); Maui Land and Pine (pineapples and real estate); C. Brewer and Company (agribusiness); and Alexander and Baldwin (agribusiness, shipping, and real estate).

In a series of controversial and well-publicized moves, Weinberg bought large blocks of stock in these companies, thereby driving up the stocks' price. Demanding a board membership in each company, he then pressured the land-rich companies to sell agricultural land for commercial development. Threatening to sue if his board membership was not allowed, he was typically bought out at huge profits.

In addition, Weinberg made profitable investments in shopping centers, warehouses, and ground leases (the land under dozens of hotels, apartments, office buildings, and condominiums). Given Hawaii's rapid economic growth from the 1960s to the 1980s, and the shortage of land, Weinberg's HRT company profited greatly from reassessing lease rents every ten or twenty-five years. With the rising cost of Hawaiian real estate, particularly in the last half of the 1980s, HRT realized profits exceeding 100 percent in some cases of lease reassessment.

Although Weinberg was not known for his civic mindedness by the general public, he had quietly started a small charitable foundation in Baltimore in 1959. In addition, he made periodic gifts to the Scranton Jewish Old Age Home, the University of Scranton (which awarded him an honorary doctorate in 1988), Palama Settlement in Hawaii, Baltimore's St. Agnes Hospital, Johns Hopkins Hospital, Sheppard Pratt, Ner Israel Rabbinical College, and Associated Jewish Charities.

In 1983 Weinberg surprised the public by announcing that at his death all his HRT stock (he owned 95 percent of the company) and his personal wealth would go to the Harry and Jeanette Weinberg Foundation. The primary purpose of the foundation was to assist the "poorest of the poor." Weinberg specifically chose to bypass charities that served the relatively well-to-do, such as universities, symphonies, museums, and orchestras. Instead, the foundation would provide a permanent charitable endowment in support of human services, aging services and centers, the homeless, Jewish federated giving programs, and other programs for the economically disadvantaged. Additional support was committed to programs in Israel.

Weinberg announced that at his death all his stock and personal wealth would go the Harry and Jeanette Weinberg Foundation.

Active in business up until his death from cancer in 1990, Weinberg fulfilled his promise. The Harry and Jeanette Weinberg Foundation became one of the largest in the United States, with assets valued at approximately $1 billion. By 1995, Hawaii's human services sector had become the recipient of over $40 million from the foundation, with grants made to the Young Men's Christian Association, the Young Women's Christian Association, the Hawaii Foodbank, the Association for Retarded Citizens, and Hospice Hawaii, among others. Baltimore beneficiaries have included the Salvation Army, the American Red Cross, Meals on Wheels, and the United Way of Central Maryland. ◆

Whitney, John Hay

1904–1982 ● Publisher

John Hay Whitney was a newspaper publisher, diplomat, art collector and philanthropist who presided over the *New York Herald Tribune* from 1961 to 1976. He was born on February 17, 1904, in Ellsworth, Maine. Whitney was the son of William Payne Whitney, a millionaire sportsman, and Helen (Hay) Whitney, the daughter of the distinguished author and diplomat John Hay and a well-published poet in her own right. His paternal grandfather was William C. Whitney, secretary of the navy under President Grover Cleveland. Named John Oliver Whitney at birth and christened John Hay Whitney ten months later, he was born to great wealth and earned his living by choice rather than necessity. Known as "Jock" to acquaintances, he was called "Johnny" among the family. Whitney had one sibling, a sister who was fourteen months older.

Whitney was raised in luxurious surroundings and taught by governesses until he entered school, first at Miss Chapin's and then St. Bernard's, small private schools in New York City. At 13 he entered Groton School in Groton, Massachusetts, graduating in 1922. At Yale, Whitney distinguished himself in dramatics and as a junior varsity oarsman, and graduated with a B.A. degree in 1926. He enrolled the next year at Oxford to study history and literature, and he spent considerable time in London and visiting country houses. His father presented Whitney with two thoroughbred horses for his twenty-second birthday, beginning his lifelong involvement in horse racing in both England and America.

When Payne Whitney died unexpectedly in 1927, John Whitney's inheritance exceeded $30 million. Whitney lived well and enjoyed the benefits of great wealth, but avoided extravagant display. Whitney later described himself at this period as a participant rather than a leader. His chief role was to provide capital, his supporting role was to provide good advice, but he was never asked to play the lead. Tall and handsome as well as rich, he was often regarded as shy.

Three weeks before the Great Crash on Wall Street in October 1929, Whitney took a position as a junior clerk for the investment banking firm of Lee, Higginson and Company. Having gained some practical business experience, he left the firm after a year and served actively as a director of Pan American Airways and Freeport Sulphur throughout the 1930s. He became a leading figure in what came to be called New York's café society, along with his first cousin C. V. Whitney, with whom he was sometimes confused. Most of Whitney's life passed in the glare of publicity, whether in his role as a championship polo player, a companion of Broadway and Hollywood actresses, or a movie producer. Whitney's marriage to Mary Elizabeth Altemus on September 25, 1930,

1927 Whitney inherits $30 million from his father.

1929 Whitney becomes a clerk for Lee, Higginson, and Co.

1930 Whitney become a director of Pan American Airways.

1942 Whitney enters the Army Air Force.

1946 Whitney forms the J. H. Whitney and Co. investment firm.

1957 Whitney becomes ambassador to Great Britain.

1961 Whitney becomes publisher of the *New York Herald Tribune*.

was a society event of that year. It was Whitney, as chairman of the board of Selznick International from 1936 to 1940, who purchased the screen rights to *Gone with the Wind* (1939).

Whitney had begun collecting modern art in 1929, and began his lifelong service as a trustee of the Museum of Modern Art a year later. His personal art collection was particularly strong in works of the French impressionists and postimpressionists. Beginning in 1935 Whitney also played a major role in the development of the museum's film library. In 1940 he was among the investors who supported the innovative New York City newspaper *PM*, but he sold his interest within a few months because he disagreed with the paper's increasingly liberal slant. Also in 1940, Whitney was divorced from his first wife, with whom he had had no children. On March 1, 1942, he married Betsey Cushing Roosevelt, the former wife of James Roosevelt. The couple had no children together, but Whitney adopted his second wife's two daughters from her previous marriage in 1949.

By the summer of 1940 Whitney was supporting several interventionist organizations and had attended the military training program at Plattsburg, New York. A few months later his friend Nelson A. Rockefeller named Whitney as head of the Motion Picture Division at the Office of the Co-ordinator of Inter-American Affairs. In 1942 Whitney was commissioned a captain in the Army Air Forces and assigned to staff intelligence duties in England. In August 1944, while on assignment with the Office of Strategic Services (OSS) in a newly liberated area of southern France, Colonel Whitney was captured by German troops. After eighteen days in enemy custody he managed to escape with the help of French Resistance forces. For perhaps the first time in his life, Jock Whitney had found himself in circumstances where his wealth and influence were of no value.

Whitney returned to civilian life in 1945 with a new determination to use his talent and his wealth to better purpose. He became active in venture capital investments through J. H. Whitney and Company, which he founded in 1946; that same year, he established the John Hay Whitney Foundation, which made innovative grants in education and social welfare. From 1950 onward Whitney sponsored a variety of fellowships, particularly for minority students and for high school teachers.

> **It was Whitney, as chairman of Selznick International, who purchased the screen rights to *Gone with the Wind*.**

After the war Whitney also began to show interest in politics, supporting Jacob Javits's first campaign for Congress in 1946. Whitney was an early backer of General Dwight D. Eisenhower for president, and he became finance committee chairman of Citizens for Eisenhower-Nixon in 1952. Whitney declined offers of minor government positions during Eisenhower's first term, but his success in raising campaign funds for Eisenhower was rewarded with an appointment as ambassador to Great Britain, a position once held by his grandfather, John Hay. Whitney assumed his duties in February 1957 in the aftermath of the Anglo-American disagreements over the Suez Canal crisis. He had the charm and talent for an endless round of speeches, and the wealth to entertain graciously and often, while his close relationship with the president allowed him to be more involved in policy than the typical noncareer diplomat.

When Whitney returned to New York in January 1961, it was to take up his most ambitious business project, saving the *New York Herald Tribune*. The paper had been in financial trouble for years, although it maintained its reputation for lively writing and moderate Republican editorial views. A Whitney loan rescued the *Herald Tribune* in 1958, but only in 1961 did Whitney become majority shareholder, publisher, and editor in chief. Through Whitney Communications Corporation, he controlled a group of successful magazines and small newspapers, as well as several radio and television stations, but his heart was with the *Herald Tribune*. Whitney described its closing in 1966 as "the emptiest day of my life," and he never again played an active public role in business.

Whitney was a board member and financial supporter of the Museum of Modern Art, the National Gallery of Art, and especially Yale University. He maintained an estate in Manhasset, Long Island, New York; apartments in Manhattan and London; summer residences at Fishers Island, Connecticut, and at Saratoga, a horse farm in Kentucky; a vacation estate in Greenwood, Georgia; as well as a yacht, a private airliner, and a private Pullman car. Whitney died of congestive heart failure at North Shore Hospital on Long Island in 1982. He is buried at Christ Church (Episcopal) in Manhasset. ◆

Whitney described the closing of the New York *Herald Tribune* as "the emptiest day of my life."

Winchester, Oliver Fisher

1810–1880 ● FIREARMS MANUFACTURER

Winchester's
rifles were used
considerably
during the Civil
War by entire
companies and
regiments of
state troops.

Oliver Fisher Winchester was born in Boston, Massachusetts, the son of Samuel and Hannah (Bates) Winchester. He was a descendant in the fifth generation of John Winchester, who was admitted as a freeman in Brookline in 1637. His boyhood was a difficult one, for the early death of his father threw Winchester on his own resources when he was very young, and by the time he was twenty years old he had worked on farms in various parts of New England, learned the carpenter's and joiner's trades, and clerked in stores. Between 1830 and 1837 he was employed in construction work in Baltimore, Maryland, and then opened a men's clothing store there, a feature of which was the manufacture and sale of shirts. In 1847 he sold this business to engage in the jobbing and importing business with John M. Davies in New York City. The partners also began the manufacture of shirts by a new method invented and patented by Winchester on February 1, 1848. They were so successful that about 1850 they established a new factory in New Haven, Connecticut. Winchester took entire charge and in five years accumulated an appreciable fortune.

Meanwhile, Winchester had become a heavy stockholder in the Volcanic Repeating Arms Company of New Haven and through his stock purchases became by 1856 the principal owner. In 1857 he brought about its reorganization as the New Haven Arms Company, with himself as president. The company had inherited the repeating-rifle inventions of Jennings, Tyler Henry, and Horace Smith and D. B. Wesson, as well as the services of Henry as superintendent of the factory. For the first few years Winchester manufactured repeating rifles and pistols, and gave Henry every opportunity to experiment on the improvement of both products, as well as of ammunition. The result was that in 1860 he began the production of a new repeating rifle, using a new rim-fire copper cartridge, which came to be known as the Henry rifle. Although it was primarily a sporting gun, it was privately pur-

Winya Curvignake
holding a Winchester
rifle, 1900.

chased and used considerably during the Civil War by entire companies and regiments of state troops. It was by far the best military rifle of the time but was not adopted by the federal government.

In 1866 Winchester purchased the patent of Nelson King for loading the magazine through the gate in the frame. When this invention was incorporated in the Henry rifle, a new firearm, the Winchester rifle, came into existence. Winchester then reorganized the New Haven Arms Company as the Winchester Repeating Arms Company, and established a factory at Bridgeport, Connecticut. In 1870 he erected a permanent plant in New Haven. From its first appearance the Winchester rifle was very popular, and Winchester built up an extremely successful business, augmenting it through the purchase of the patents and property of the American Repeating Rifle Company in 1869 and of the Spencer Repeating Rifle Company in 1870. In 1876 he purchased the invention of Benjamin B. Hotchkiss of the bolt-action repeating rifle, and after making necessary improvements added this to the products of his company. Finally, in 1879, he purchased the mechanism invented by John M. Browning, but the resulting Winchester single-shot rifle incorporating this invention was not produced until several years after Winchester's death.

1848 Winchester patents a method for manufacturing shirts.

1856 Winchester becomes owner of a arms manufacturing company.

1860 Winchester begins making repeating rifles.

1870 Winchester builds a plant in New Haven.

1876 Winchester buys the patent for a bolt action rifle.

Winchester served as councilman in New Haven in 1863, and the following year was presidential elector at large for Lincoln. In 1866 he was elected lieutenant governor of Connecticut on the ticket with Gov. Joseph R. Hawley. His philanthropies were many; in particular, he made generous gifts to Yale University. He married Jane Ellen Hope of Boston on Feb. 20, 1834, and at the time of his death in New Haven was survived by his widow and two children. ◆

Winfrey, Oprah Gail

1954–Present ● Media mogul

> *"I am those women. I am every one of them. And they are me. That's why we get along so well."*
>
> Oprah Winfrey, quoted in *Oprah!*
> by Robert Waldron, 1978

Born on a farm in Kosciusko, Mississippi, to Vernita Lee and Vernon Winfrey, Oprah Winfrey was reared by her grandmother for the early part of her life. At age 6, she was sent to live with her mother, who worked as a domestic, and two half brothers in Milwaukee. It was in Milwaukee that Winfrey began to display her oratorical gifts, reciting poetry at socials and teas. During her adolescence, Winfrey began to misbehave to such a degree that she was sent to live with her father in Nashville. Under the strict disciplinary regime imposed by her father, Winfrey started to flourish, distinguishing herself in debate and oratory. At 16, she won an Elks Club oratorical contest that awarded her a scholarship to Tennessee State University.

While a freshman in college, Winfrey won the Miss Black Nashville and Miss Black Tennessee pageants. As a result of this exposure, she received a job offer from a local television station and in her sophomore year became a news anchor at WTVF-TV in Nashville. After graduating in 1976, Winfrey took a job with WJZ-TV in Baltimore as a reporter and co-anchor of the evening news. In 1977 she was switched to updates on local news, which appeared during the ABC national morning show *Good Morning America*. That same year she found her niche as a talk-show host, co-hosting WJZ-TV's morning show, *Baltimore Is Talking*.

In 1984 Winfrey moved to Chicago to take over A.M. *Chicago*, a talk show losing in the ratings to Phil Donahue's popular morning program. Within a month Winfrey's ratings were equal to Donahue's. In three months she surpassed him. A year and a half later the show extended to an hour and was renamed *The Oprah Winfrey Show*. The show, which covers a wide range of topics from the lighthearted to the sensational

1976 Winfrey becomes a reporter in Baltimore.

1984 Winfrey begins hosting *A. M. Chicago*.

1986 *The Oprah Winfrey Show* is nationally syndicated.

1993 Winfrey is named America's richest entertainer.

1996 Oprah starts her book club.

The Oprah Book Club

In the fall of 1996, Oprah Winfrey introduced the Oprah Book Club. Each month Oprah chose one book and announced its title on her daily television show. She asked her viewers to read the book, then write to the show with their reactions, opinions, and insights. Four viewers were then chosen to have dinner with Winfrey and the book's author. During dinner the group discussed the book, and the discussion was later broadcast on television. Winfrey selected books that she had read and wanted to share with her viewers. Many of the books she chose were written by African American or women writers. Past selections included *Song of Solomon* and *Paradise* by Toni Morrison, *The Best Way to Play* by Bill Cosby, *The Book of Ruth* by Jane Hamilton, *I Know This Much Is True* and *She's Come Undone* by Wally Lamb, and *The Heart of a Woman* by Maya Angelou. Winfrey's influence on the public became apparent after she introduced the book club. As soon as she announced her monthly title, libraries would be inundated with requests for the book, and sales of the book increased by an average of 700,000 copies, causing a commotion in the publishing industry as Winfrey's selections created instant bestsellers. The Oprah Book Club was also instrumental in enhancing the reputations, not to mention book sales, of several relatively unknown writers.

or the tragic, was picked up for national syndication by King World Productions in 1986. By 1993 *The Oprah Winfrey Show* was seen in 99 percent of U.S. television markets and sixty-four countries. Since the show first became eligible in 1986, it has won Emmy awards for best talk show, or best talk show hostess each year except one.

In 1985 Winfrey was cast as the strong-willed Sofia in the film version of Alice Walker's *The Color Purple*, for which she received an Oscar nomination. The following year she formed her own production company, HARPO Productions, to develop projects. In 1989 Winfrey produced and acted in a television miniseries based on Gloria Naylor's novel *The Women of Brewster Place*, and in 1993 she starred in and produced the television drama *There Are No Children* Here. That same year *Forbes* magazine listed Winfrey as America's richest entertainer based on her 1992 and 1993 earnings of approximately $98 million. ◆

Woodruff, Robert Winship

1889–1985 ● SOFT DRINK TYCOON

> "It's easy to see down the valley and up the slope, but it's tough as hell to see over the next hill."
>
> Robert Woodruff

dyslexia: a disorder marked by inability to read properly.

Eldest of the four sons born to Ernest Woodruff and Emily Caroline Winship, Robert Woodruff was four years old when his family moved to Atlanta. There his father built a business empire that included banking, coal and ice, steel, and cotton ginning enterprises. In 1919 the family's prominence was further enhanced when Ernest Woodruff led a group of investors in wresting control of the growing Coca-Cola Company from Asa G. Candler.

As a boy and young adult, Robert was constantly at odds with his authoritarian father. A poor student, possibly because of undiagnosed **dyslexia**, he attended Georgia Military Academy after failing at Atlanta Boys' High School, and there he excelled in organizing events and managing organizations, while barely getting by academically. After Robert's graduation in 1908, his father sent him to Emory College (now Emory University), at the time a small two-year institution in Oxford, Georgia. He was in college only one semester before the school's president advised his father that Robert should not return for another term.

In February 1909 Woodruff began working in a bluecollar job in an Atlanta foundry. In the hope that Robert would soon marry, his father gave him a job as purchasing agent for his Atlanta Ice and Coal Company. On October 17, 1912, Robert married Nell Kendall Hodgson, who was from a wealthy Athens, Georgia, family. They had no children.

As purchasing agent, Woodruff decided to replace the company's mule-drawn wagons with trucks, buying a fleet from White Motor Company without his father's knowledge. In retaliation, the elder Woodruff reneged on a pay raise he had promised his son, and Robert quit his job, going to work as a salesman for the White Motor Company in 1913. His rise in that company was meteoric. He sold the company's trucks across the South, won a federal contract for tourist buses at Yellowstone National Park, and developed the first troop-carrying motor vehicles in World War I. He and his wife moved to Cleveland, Ohio, the corporate headquarters, and Woodruff shuttled regularly to New York City, where he established an office. He lived extravagantly and joined clubs where he could associate with the country's wealthiest and most powerful businessmen. His personality and skills attracted their confidence. By 1921 he was a vice president of White Motor Company and a protege of its president, Walter White.

The legendary Walter Teagle soon offered Woodruff the presidency of Standard Oil Company. But Woodruff returned to Atlanta in 1923 to accept the presidency of the Coca-Cola Company, which had come through serious financial difficulties and was still suffering from internal divisions caused by its hostile takeover, four years earlier, by a group of investors led by Ernest Woodruff. As president until 1939 and chairman of the board thereafter until his retirement in 1955, Robert Woodruff would lead the company in its ascent to the status of American icon, and he would continue to dominate it for another thirty years after his nominal retirement.

As president, Woodruff quickly took control of the company, marginalizing the rival Candler family and their supporters and placing executives of his own choice in positions of prominence. His father, who died in 1944, was his only per-

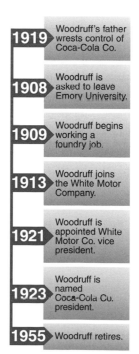

1919 Woodruff's father wrests control of Coca-Cola Co.

1908 Woodruff is asked to leave Emory University.

1909 Woodruff begins working a foundry job.

1913 Woodruff joins the White Motor Company.

1921 Woodruff is appointed White Motor Co. vice president.

1923 Woodruff is named Coca-Cola Co. president.

1955 Woodruff retires.

Coca-Cola became associated with energy, wholesomeness, and respite from the hectic pace of modern life.

trademark-infringe-ment: unlawful use of the name or picture of a competitor's product.

sistent rival for influence. Known as "the Boss," Robert Woodruff maintained a gruff demeanor and distanced himself from all but the highest tier of executives. A stocky six feet even, Woodruff's physique and dominieering personality combined to create a commanding presence in any room.

During the 1920s Coca-Cola prospered as an alternative to the alcoholic beverages forbidden by nationwide Prohibition. It benefited from saturation advertising overseen by the brilliant "idea man" Archie Lee, whose brand-image campaign associated the soft drink with energy, wholesomeness, and respite from the hectic pace of twentieth-century life. Lee covered billboards and magazine pages with the work of artists such as Norman Rockwell and Haddon Sundblom, who communicated visually the message he wanted to convey. Under Lee's guidance, Coke promoted itself as "the pause that refreshes."

Woodruff worked closely with Lee on building the image of Coca-Cola while driving competitors from the field with **trademark-infringement** lawsuits. Standardizing the product was an obsession for Woodruff. Determined that Coca-Cola would have the same taste everywhere and a reputation for purity, Woodruff sent inspectors regularly to soda fountains to test their product, and he encouraged bottlers, whose contracts with the company allowed them a great deal of independence, to improve sanitation and quality control. He converted the sales force into a corps of service personnel to work with dealers in solving their problems, and he created a statistical department, which pioneered market research.

As the seller of an inexpensive item, Coca-Cola weathered the Great Depression better than most corporations. Woodruff refused to cut salaries as other corporations did, and the company's stock actually hit a new high in 1935. Sales of Coca-Cola in bottles increased as refrigeration became available in more homes.

In World War II Woodruff masterminded a plan to make Coca-Cola available, at five cents per bottle to American troops, wherever they might be. Production of Coke in the United States remained high as the company won exemption from sugar rationing on drinks sold for consumption by military personnel, and Coca-Cola "technical officers" followed military units into combat zones, setting up and operating bottling plants and soda fountains for the thirsty troops.

The World War II experience and the ensuing Cold War helped Woodruff to realize another of his goals, worldwide marketing of Coca-Cola. Despite Woodruff's determined efforts, prewar campaigns to sell the soft drink outside the United States had been successful only in Canada, Cuba, and Germany. After the war, Coca-Cola courted elites all over the world—save in the communist countries, where Coca-Cola was officially despised as a symbol of American imperialism— and awarded bottling contracts to prominent citizens of many countries. By the early 1950s, one-fourth of Coca-Cola's sales were outside the United States; a decade later foreign sales accounted for over half of the company's revenues.

Politics, of necessity, became one of Woodruff's chief activities. To fend off government regulation and secure access to foreign markets, Woodruff employed skillful lobbyists in Washington and other capitals. Coke won many battles, including exemption from a Food and Drug Administration regulation that would have required Coke labels to reveal the addition of caffeine to the product. A Georgia Democrat, Woodruff joined the Republican business leaders who helped General Dwight D. Eisenhower win the presidency, and he took great pride in his easy access to the Eisenhower White House. He also enjoyed close relationships with Presidents Lyndon B. Johnson and Jimmy Carter.

Always preferring the background to the public eye, Woodruff made skillful use of his 30,000-acre South Georgia hunting retreat, Ichauway, to cultivate relationships with political figures. In what was then the male-only world of big business and high politics, hunting, card games, cigars, and alcohol facilitated Woodruff's access to the men who held, or aspired to hold, political power. Ichauway was one of four Woodruff residences. His Atlanta home was a white-columned mansion on elegant Tuxedo Road. He spent much of his time in New York City, where he owned a duplex apartment in Manhattan's exclusive River House, overlooking the East River. In Wyoming he vacationed at his T. E. Ranch near Cody, once the property of Buffalo Bill Cody.

In Atlanta, Coca-Cola was a major employer, a source of civic pride, and inevitably a major player in local politics. And Robert Woodruff was Atlanta's first citizen. He regularly convened the leading businessmen of the city to decide issues of public importance. Political officials generally followed

Woodruff's gift of $105 million to Emory University in 1979 was the largest private donation ever made to a university up to that time.

their lead. No issue was more important to a Southern city in the 1950s and 1960s than race, and Woodruff and his associates decided that Atlanta must accommodate itself to black aspirations for civil rights. Segregation policies were changed gradually—and Atlanta, billing itself as "'the city too busy to hate"—escaped the turmoil that engulfed Little Rock, Birmingham, and other Southern cities.

Woodruff donated immense sums of money—much of it given anonymously—to educational, artistic, and social service institutions in Atlanta. His gift of $105 million to Emory University in 1979 was the largest private donation ever made to a university up to that time. In all he gave Emory at least $225 million during his lifetime and donated an estimate estimated $100 million to other Atlanta institutions, including the Robert W. Woodruff Arts Center, a complex that was renamed for him in 1982. Raised a Methodist, Woodruff had little interest in religion as an adult.

acumen: keen insight.

In spite of Woodruff's political and business **acumen**, Coca-Cola's market lead over its chief rival, Pepsi-Cola, slipped from approximately 400 percent at the end of World War II to only 4 percent by the mid-1980s. A conservative man, Woodruff regularly rejected his subordinates' recommendations to adjust the product to changing markets. For years he refused to put Coca-Cola into larger bottles to compete with Pepsi's ten-ounce bottles, or into cans, or to develop a diet version of Coke, or to produce fruit-flavored beverages. Unwilling to allow his handpicked CEOs to make strategic decisions for the company, Woodruff kept the pace of corporate innovation slow and only reluctantly approved the **diversification** of Coca-Cola's products and packaging.

diversification: increase in the variety of products.

Only his final illness, brought on by old age, removed Woodruff for the last two weeks of his life from corporate decision-making at Coca-Cola. He died in Atlanta's Emory University Hospital and is buried in the city's Westview Cemetery.

An unquestioned genius as a manager, Woodruff often declared: "It's easy to see down the valley and up the slope, but it's tough as hell to see over the next hill." Through his understanding of changing lifestyles and consumer expectations, Woodruff made Coca-Cola a part of American culture, then won the soft drink a place in markets around the world. After the age of 70, he no longer could see so clearly over the next hill, but he refused to trust his subordinates to make decisions in the best interests of the company. As a result Coca-Cola's market supremacy was eroded.

Woodruff's contributions to the city of Atlanta are immeasurable. His donations to Emory University and other civic enterprises strengthened the cultural life of the city, and his leadership of the business community provided direction to Atlanta's emergence as a major business center. Woodruff's early recognition of the importance of eliminating racist policies moved Atlanta a step ahead of other Southern cities and helped to keep it peaceful in an era of turmoil. ◆

Woolworth, Frank Winfield

1852–1919 ● MERCHANT

"Don't be afraid to loose a little money. It advertises our stores more than anything else could."

F. W. Woolworth

Frank Winfield Woolworth, son of John Hubbell and Fanny (McBrier) Woolworth, was born on a farm at Rodman, Jefferson County, New York. In boyhood he attended country schools at Greatbend, New York, did farm work, and in his teens spent two brief terms in a business college at Watertown, the county seat. There was in his youth no augury of his future great success. In fact, although his favorite boyhood game was "playing store," although a mercantile

"I am the world's worst salesman, therefore, I must make it easy for people to buy."
F. W. Woolworth, 1888

career was the only course he craved, he seemed deplorably inept at it and was a long time in finding himself.

At 19, for the sake of experience, Woolworth took a place as clerk in a village grocery store, receiving no wages for two years. At 21 he was taken on six-months' trial at a store in Watertown, receiving no salary for the first three months, and after that $3.50 a week, which was just what he paid for board and lodging. In the course of two years his pay advanced to $6 weekly, out of which he supported himself and saved a little money. In 1875, a "ninety-nine-cent store" appeared in Watertown and did a large business. Here Woolworth got his first inkling of the notion of selling a large array of articles at one fixed price. A Watertown man decided to try the ninety-nine-cent plan in Port Huron, Michigan, and took Woolworth along as clerk at $10 a week; he was such a poor salesman that his salary was soon cut to $8.50. Discouraged, he fell ill and went back to his father's farm to recuperate.

Woolworth married Jennie Creighton of Watertown on June 11, 1876. A year later his old firm, Moore & Smith, took him back again as clerk. In 1878 he heard for the first time of a store's having a counter on which nothing but five-cent goods was sold. He induced his own employers to try the scheme, and it proved a startling success.

Woolworth now persuaded W. H. Moore to back him to the extent of three hundred dollars in a five-cent store in Utica, but the venture was a failure and was closed in three months. He came to the conclusion that the variety of goods had not been large enough and—again with Moore's help—opened a store in Lancaster, Pennslyvania (June 1879), which was a paying venture. The addition of a line of ten-cent goods was the final move that insured success. Calling his brother C. S. Woolworth, and his cousin, Seymour H. Knox, into service with him, he presently began launching other stores, as funds permitted. Those in Philadelphia, Harrisburg, and York, Pennslyvania, and Newark, New Jersey, were at first unproductive because Woolworth had not studied the locations for them with sufficient care. But others in Buffalo, Erie, Scranton, and elsewhere were successful. Two other men, F. M. Kirby and Earl P. Charlton, also became partners.

After a few years Woolworth sold his interest in the Buffalo and Erie stores to Knox, and thus began the S. H.

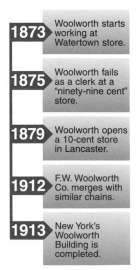

1873 Woolworth starts working at Watertown store.

1875 Woolworth fails as a clerk at a "ninety-nine cent" store.

1879 Woolworth opens a 10-cent store in Lancaster.

1912 F.W. Woolworth Co. merges with similar chains.

1913 New York's Woolworth Building is completed.

Knox & Company chain of five-and-ten-cent stores. The other partners, including C. S. Woolworth, also started chains of their own, but all remained friendly and in general avoided trespassing on each other's territory. In 1912 the four chains—Knox, Kirby, Charlton, and C. S. Woolworth—were all absorbed by the F. W. Woolworth Company, as were two stores belonging to W. H. Moore, Woolworth's early employer. More and more the Woolworth stores began having goods manufactured especially for them, sometimes taking the entire output of a factory on a year's contract. To add more articles to his line, to sell things at five and ten cents which had never sold for so little before, was Woolworth's constant aim, and a key to his success.

In fulfillment of a boyhood dream, he erected the Woolworth Building, 792 feet high, in New York City (completed in 1913), which was for some years the world's tallest building and a wonder to tourists. At his death in 1919 his company owned more than a thousand stores in the United States and Canada; its volume of business in 1918 was $107,000,000. Woolworth's own fortune was estimated at $65,000,000. He was survived by his wife and two daughters. ◆

Wozniak, Stephen G.

1950–PRESENT ● COMPUTER DEVELOPER

Stephen G. Wozniak was born in 1950. He was the son of an engineer; his father, Francis, helped design satellite guidance systems at the Lockheed Missiles & Space Company plant in Sunnyvale, California, not far from Intel and Fairchild Semiconductor. Francis taught his son the fundamentals of electronics and encouraged him to experiment on his own. Woz, as Stephen was known to his friends, became an avid electronics hobbyist. He had a talent for elec-

Steve Wozniak,
co-founder of Apple
Computer Inc., 1989.

When he was 13, Wozniak built a transistorized calculator that won first prize in a Bay Area science fair.

tronics, and he built all sorts of gadgets, including a transistor radio. By the time he was in the sixth grade, he had decided to become an electronics engineer.

Woz was bored by school. He shone in the few classes that interested him, mathematics and science, and did poorly in the rest. Electronics and computers were his greatest interests, and neither his junior high school nor his high school had much to offer him in either subject. He took to reading computer manuals and programming text books on his own, and he soon pulled ahead of his fellow students and even his teachers. When he was 13, he built a transistorized calculator that won first prize in a Bay Area science fair. He was drawn to minicomputers most of all, admiring their compactness, accessibility, and inexpensiveness. By the end of high school, Woz knew that he wanted to become a computer engineer. Woz graduated from Homestead High School in Cupertino, California.

Woz attended the University of Colorado for 1 year and later transferred to De Anza College, a junior college in Cupertino. He later left school altogether and worked for a year as a programmer for a small computer company. In 1971, he tried college again at the University of California at Berkeley. That did not last long and he dropped out and went to work as an engineer in the calculator division of Hewlett-Packard Company in Palo Alto, California.

In the summer of 1971, a friend introduced him to a quiet, intense, long-haired teenager by the name of Steven Jobs. Jobs, who was 16 years old at the time, was an electronic hobbyist as well as a student at Homestead High School, Woz's alma mater.

The introduction of the Altair microcomputer had led to the formation of computer clubs all over the country, including one in Silicon Valley known as the Homebrew Computer Club. Woz was a founding member of this club and was one of the most active members. Steve Jobs also attended meetings at the Homebrew Computer Club.

In 1975, Jobs and Woz bought a $25 microprocessor and built a computer in the living room of Jobs's parents' house in Palo Alto. Although it was not as powerful as other available computers, it was cheaper and less complicated, and it included circuits that enabled it to be connected directly to a display monitor. Woz did most of the work, but Jobs, who was trying to persuade Woz to go into business with him, chipped in with many suggestions. The computer was called the Apple I. Jobs and Woz set up a partnership, Apple Computer Inc., to market the computer.

In 1977, Jobs and Woz went on to develop a more sophisticated computer, the elegant-looking Apple II. By late 1980, more than 130,000 Apple II computers had been sold. By the end of 1983 Apple Computer had almost 4,700 employees and $983 million in sales. Today Apple Computer is a multi-billion-dollar business.

Wozniak, who was always more interested in engineering than management, took leave from Apple Computer to pursue other things, such as earning a computer science degree under an alias from the University of California in the early 1980s. In 1985, he left Apple Computer to start a company called CL9 (as in "cloud nine"). Here he designed an infrared remote control device that can operate any component of a home entertainment system, from television to VCR, regardless of the manufacturers.

CL9 eventually folded and Wozniak spent several years involved in teaching and educational projects. He briefly reunited with Apple when he became a consultant to Apple's CEO in 1996. In 1997, Wozniak joined the board of directors for Breakthrough Software, a small Internet software company based in Mountain View, California. ◆

> *"My whole life, I just did not want to be a company-runner. I just wanted to be a good engineer, wanted to write programs, design computers."*
>
> Stephen G. Wozniak, interview in *San Jose Mercury News,* 1997

1971 Wozniak meets Steve Jobs.

1975 Wozniak and Jobs build Apple I.

1977 Wozniak and Jobs develop the Apple II.

1983 Apple Computer has almost 4,700 employees.

1985 Wozniak leaves Apple to start CL9.

1996 Wozniak joins Breakthrough Software.

Wright, William

1794–1866 ● HARNESS &
SADDLE MANUFACTURER

William Wright was born near Nyack in Rockland County, New York, the son of Dr. William Wright. His father, a descendant of old Connecticut stock, came from Saybrook, Connecticut., was graduated from Yale in 1774, studied and practised medicine at New Haven, and moved across the Hudson about 1785. His death on a southern trip in 1808 made it necessary for the son to earn a living and abandon his college preparatory studies at Poughkeepsie Academy.

At fourteen Wright began his long career as a manufacturer of harness and saddlery, being apprenticed to Anson Greene Phelps, who was at that time engaged in that business in Hartford. Wright took part in the defense of Stonington in 1814 and the next year, when Phelps went to New York to make a fortune in metals, Wright, with savings of three hundred dollars, moved to Bridgeport. There he married Minerva, daughter of William Peet, who apparently financed Wright's partnership with Sheldon Smith in the saddlery business.

In 1822, the firm of Smith & Wright moved from Bridgeport to Newark, New Jersey, which was just then becoming a very active center of the leather industry; with Edwin Van Antwerp and William Faitoute later as silent partners, they developed an extensive factory. It is said to have become one of the largest establishments of its kind in the country, to have contributed much to the industrial development of Newark, and to have attained a commanding position in the southern trade. The improvement of roads and opening up of new agricultural lands stimulated the demand for harnesses and saddlery, and the European importations were poorly suited to the needs of the West and South. The West began its own saddlery but the South did little. Starting with a branch at Charleston, South Carolina, Smith & Wright soon had agents in all the principal southern cities. Wright seems to have become the dominant member of the firm and had built up a considerable fortune by the time he retired from active business in 1854.

1774 Wright graduates from Yale.

1815 Wright moves to New York to make fortune in metals.

1822 Smith & Wright move to Newark.

1840 Wright becomes mayor of Newark.

1842 Wright enters the U.S. Congress.

1853 Wright enters the U.S. Senate.

His wealth and position in the industrial world seemed to have been the chief reasons for his political prominence. From 1840 to 1843 he was the fifth mayor of Newark. In 1843 he began two terms in the national House of Representatives. He was a candidate for the New Jersey governorship in 1847 but was defeated by Daniel Haines. Never a strong partisan, he shifted about 1850 from Whig to Democrat. He was elected to the United States Senate in 1853, was defeated for reelection in 1858, but returned again to serve from 1863 until his death. He is said never to have debated in either house, and his chairmanship of the Senate committee on manufacturing alone saves him from virtual oblivion in the records. The congressional eulogists stressed his **urbanity**, integrity, toleration, and spotless life. His portrait indicates a man erect, dark, and smooth-shaven, with an expression of marked strength and determination. An Episcopalian, he was the chief benefactor of the House of Prayer at Newark. He died at his home in Newark after a painful illness, survived by his wife, a son, and a daughter. ◆

urbanity: polite and refined.

Wrigley, William, Jr.

1861–1932 ● CHEWING GUM MANUFACTURER

William Wrigley Jr. was born in Philadelphia, Pennsyvania on September 30, 1861, son of William and Mary A. (Ladley) Wrigley, grandson of Edward and Susan (Paxson) Wrigley, and great-grandson of Edmund and Jane Wrigley, natives of Knowe, near Saddleworth, England. William Wrigley's grandfather was an early woolen manufacturer in Philadelphia and his father was the founder (in 1870) and president of the Wrigley Manufacturing Co., soap manufacturers. A dislike of school and a desire to enter active business induced young Wrigley to

William Wrigley

premium: gift given as incentive to buy.

jobbers: middlemen.

begin work in his father's factory at the age of 13, and after spending several years in the shop he worked as a traveling salesman in Pennsylvania, New York and New England for nearly twenty years.

In 1891, Wrigley settled in Chicago as his father's distributor, acting as his own sales manager, salesman, bookkeeper, and packer. With the design of stimulating sales, he began offering a **premium** with each box of soap, thus inaugurating a policy which ultimately made him the largest distributor of premiums in the world. In 1892 he began handling baking powder as a side line and was so successful that in a few months the sale of soap was discontinued. Among various articles used for sales premiums was chewing gum, and when he discovered that the gum was more popular than the baking powder he decided to concentrate on its manufacture and sale. Here, again, he applied the premium method to induce **jobbers** and dealers to handle his product, offering such articles as scales, coffee grinders, show cases, toilet articles, pocket knives, cutlery, guns, fishing tackle, etc., the premiums being graded to represent the purchase of stipulated quantities. Always a firm believer in the importance of advertising, the sums which he devoted to this purpose increased year by year until the William Wrigley Jr. Co. became one of the largest advertisers in America as well as the largest manufacturer and distributor of chewing gum in the world.

In 1910 the company was incorporated in West Virginia with a capitalization of $9,000,000, which was increased to $16,500,000 in 1915 and reduced to $15,000,000 in 1922 by the retirement of the preferred management of the company (1925), it had assets of approximately $60,000,000, a gross annual business of $35,000,000 and a net income of $9,000,000. For the manufacture of its products, trade-marked "Spearmint," "Double Mint," "Juicy Fruit" and "P.K.," the company operated a fifteen-acre plant in Chicago and factories in Toronto, Canada; London, England; Frankfurt, Germany; and Sydney, Australia.

Wrigley erected an office building in Chicago with a tower 400 feet above the streets, which became one of the architectural landmarks of the city. He retired from the presidency of the company in 1925, being succeeded by his son, but continued his connection as chairman of the board of directors. He was a liberal contributor to many hospitals, charities and organizations working for the education and welfare of boys and girls of all races and sects. He was also well known in the field of sports, particularly as owner of the national league baseball club of Chicago (the "Cubs") and the Angel city baseball club of Los Angeles, California, for which he built Wrigley Field.

In 1919 he purchased Catalina Island, twenty-two miles off the coast of California south of Los Angeles, and by the construction of roads, water systems, a casino and excursion steamers, transformed it into a noted pleasure resort annually visited by thousands of tourists and vacationists. In 1926 he offered a prize of $25,000 to the first swimmer of the twenty-mile Catalina channel, and a second prize of $15,000 to the first woman to finish, if the first prize should go to a man. The contest, held in January 1927, attracted international interest from the fact that the course lay through the ocean and was considered the most difficult ever attempted by swimmers. The successful contestant was George Young, a Canadian, who was in the water fifteen hours and forty-six minutes, and according to estimates, covered more than thirty miles.

Shortly after acquiring Catalina, Wrigley constructed a baseball park on the island to serve as a spring training field for the Chicago Cubs as well as for amateur and semiprofes-

"When two men in business always agree, one of them is unnecessary."
William Wrigley Jr., 1896

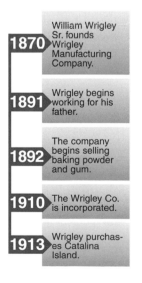

1870 William Wrigley Sr. founds Wrigley Manufacturing Company.

1891 Wrigley begins working for his father.

1892 The company begins selling baking powder and gum.

1910 The Wrigley Co. is incorporated.

1913 Wrigley purchases Catalina Island.

sional games. The island was also developed industrially and several profitable enterprises organized. Daily shipments of nearly a thousand tons of rock, sand and gravel from island quarries were brought to the mainland and used in building and paving projects throughout southern California. Deposits of a superior quality of clay led to the development of pottery and tile manufacturing. Ore deposits in commercial quantities including silver, copper and zinc were also uncovered and worked.

Wrigley acquired the Arizona Biltmore properties at Phoenix, Arizona, and was developing a winter resort there at the time of his death. In addition to the interests already mentioned, he was a director of the Erie railroad, the First National Bank, the first Trust & Savings Band and the Boulevard Bridge Bank; a trustee of the Field museum of natural history of Chicago, and a member of the executive committee of the Chicago chapter of the American Red Cross. He took an active interest in Republican politics, serving as a delegate to several national conventions. He maintained residences in Chicago, Lake Geneva, Wisconsin, Phoenix, Arizona, Pasadena, California, and on Catalina island. He was recognized as one of the leading American industrialists, the possessor of the kind of creative genius and initiative required to build a vast manufacturing enterprise. He was married September 17, 1885, to Ada E. Foote, and they had two children: Dorothy, wife of James R. Offield, and Phillip, a veteran of the World war. Wrigley died at his winter home in Phoenix, Arizona, on January 26, 1932. ◆

Yale, Linus

1821–1868 ● INVENTOR & MANUFACTURER OF LOCKS

Linus Yale was the son of Linus and Chlotilda (Hopson) Yale. He was born at Salisbury, Herkimer County, New York. He was a descendant of Thomas Yale, an uncle of Elihu Yale, who emigrated from England in 1637 and settled in New Haven. Yale inherited a mechanical temperament from his father, who was an inventor of ability, having to his credit a threshing machine, a process for pressing millstones, and a sawmill head block dog. The younger Yale was, in addition, somewhat artistic. He was well educated and for a number of years devoted himself to portrait painting.

About 1840 his father invented a bank lock, which he began to manufacture in Newport, New York, and shortly afterwards Yale undertook, independently, the same sort of business. Bank locks in those days were of very intricate construction and high in cost, and there was great rivalry among the manufacturers, all of which was a great stimulus to the industry. Yale brought out one of the first of his locks—it was the reputation of his father's locks which first caused the association of the name with the product—about 1851. This lock was made in the shop which he had established at Shelburne Falls, Massachusetts, and was called the "Yale Infallible Bank Lock." It was known as the "changeable type;" that is, the key was made up of component parts which could be separated and reassembled to change the combination. His next lock, the "Yale Magic Bank Lock," was an improved modification of his first product. It was followed by the "Yale Double Treasury Bank Lock," a masterpiece of ingenious design and skilful workmanship, the most notable of the bank locks operated by keys. About 1862, Yale began marketing his "Monitor Bank Lock," the first of the dial or combination bank locks, and the following year he brought out the "Yale Double Dial

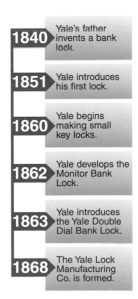

1840	Yale's father invents a bank lock.
1851	Yale introduces his first lock.
1860	Yale begins making small key locks.
1862	Yale develops the Monitor Bank Lock.
1863	Yale introduces the Yale Double Dial Bank Lock.
1868	The Yale Lock Manufacturing Co. is formed.

Bank Lock." The principles of construction used in the latter have since come into general use in the United States.

By this time Yale's reputation was well established. Between 1860 and 1865 he undertook the improvement of small key locks, devising the "Cylinder Lock," which was based on the pin-tumbler mechanism of the Egyptians. Patents covering this separate cylinder, pin-tumbler lock, using a small flat key, were issued to him on January 29, 1861, and June 27, 1865.

Since Yale's business as a consultant on bank locks left him little time and he lacked the necessary financial resources to equip his plant for the manufacture of the small locks, he went to Philadelphia in the hope of interesting others in the new venture. Through William Sellers he met John Henry Towne who brought about the establishment in October 1868 of the Yale Lock Manufacturing Company, with his son, Henry Robinson Towne, and Yale as partners. The partners immediately began the construction of a plant at Stamford, Connecticut, Yale leaving most of this activity to Towne and continuing his consulting work on bank locks. Three months later, however, while he was in New York on this business, he died suddenly of heart failure. He was married to Catherine Brooks at Shelburne Falls on September 14, 1844, and was survived by his wife and three children. ◆

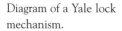

Diagram of a Yale lock mechanism.

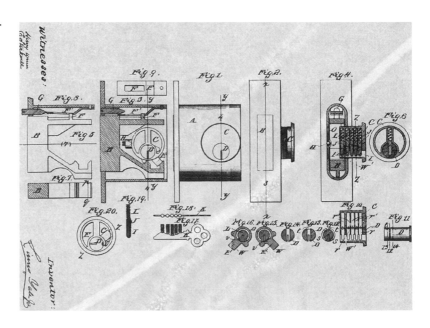

Sources

The biographies in *Macmillan Profiles: Tycoons & Entrepreneurs* were extracted from the following sources:

Dictionary of American Biography, Volumes 9 & 10, Charles Scribner's Sons, 1964.
Encyclopedia of African American Culture and History, Macmillan Reference USA, 1996.
Encyclopedia of Latin American History and Culture, Charles Scribner's Sons, 1996.
Encyclopedia of the American Presidency, Simon & Schuster, 1994.
Encyclopedia of the American West, Macmillan Reference USA, 1996.
Macmillan Encyclopedia of Computers, Macmillan Reference USA, 1992.
Record of America: A Reference History of the United States, Charles Scribner's Sons, 1996.
Scribner Encyclopedia of American Lives, Charles Scriber's Sons, 1998.
They Made History: A Biographical Dictionary, Simon & Schuster, 1993.

The following authors contributed articles to the publications listed above:

Ahmed, Siraj: Charles Clinton Spaulding
Alexander, Thomas G.: J(ohn) Willard (Bill) Marriott
Axelrod, Alan: Philip Danforth Armour, George Mortimer Pullman, Edward Payson Ripley
Bundles, A'Lelia Perry: Sarah Breedlove Walker
Carstensen, Fred: Herman W. Lay
Castle, Alfred L.: Harry G. Weinberg
Crutchfield, James A.: John Mohler Studebaker
Diaz, David: Armand Hammer
Dicke, Tom: Earl Silas Tupper
Dienstag, Eleanor Foa: Henry John II (Jack) Heinz
Dilday, Kenya: Oprah Gail Winfrey
Dillon, Richard H.: Samuel Brannan
Drew, Elizabeth: H(enry) Ross Perot
Erickson, Alana J.: James Bruce Llewellyn
Floyd, Candace: Ford Ferguson Harvey
Folsom, Burton W., Jr., and Anita P. Folsom: Andrew W. Mellon
Friedman, Walter: Annie Turnbo Malone
Friedricks, William B.: Henry Edwards Huntington
Furlong, Patrick J.: John Hay Whitney
Gill, Jonathan: Suzanne De Passe, Berry Gordy Jr.
Greenberg, Jonathan D.: Jake Simmons Jr.
Hansen, Vagn K.: Robert Winship Woodruff
Haycox, Stephen: Austin E. Lathrop
Healy, John David: James E. Casey
Hogan, Patricia: Ah Quin, Henry Culver
Jackson, W. Turrentine: John Butterfield, Charles Ilfeld
Klein, Jeffrey L.: Mifflin Wister Gibbs
Langer, Erisck D.: Simón Iturri Patiño
Luebbering, Ken: Joyce Clyde Hall

Martel, Carol M.: Jay Gould
McDonnell, Jeanne Farr: Juana Briones
McNeill, Lydia: Charles R. Patterson
Naro, Nancy Pricilla Smith: Visconde de Mauá
Oglesby, Richard E.: Manuel Lisa
Phillips, Charles: George Hearst, Henry J. Kaiser
Price, R. Byron: John Batterson Stetson, Levi Strauss
Rattenbury, Richard C.: Samuel Colt
Robinson, Gene: Harry Herbert Pace
Robinson, Greg: Robert Reed Church Sr., Earl Gilbert Graves Jr.
Schilling, Peter: Henry Allen Boyd
Seyedian, Mojtaba: Philip Winston Pillsbury
Smith, Dean: Barry Goldwater (and Family)
Spencer, Donald D.: William H. (Bill) Gates, Herman Hollerinth, Steven Paul Jobs, Stephen G. Wozniak
Stoner, John C.: Anthony Overton
Straubharr, Joseph: Roberto Marinho
Sweet, James Stouder: Julian Caesar (Jules) Stein
Taylor, Durahn: Percy Ellis Sutton
Taylor, Quintard: Biddy Mason
Vaughan, Mary Kay: Estevan de Antunano
Vos, Frank: Raymond Albert Kroc
Walter, David A.: Samuel Thomas Hauser, John Dennis Ryan
Whitehead, John S.: Claus Spreckels
Wilson, Clint C., Jr.: John Harold Johnson
Wong, Amy AnMei B.: Walter Knott
Zall, P. M.: William E. Boeing

The following articles were reprinted with permission of American Reference Publishing Company from *National Cyclopedia of American Biography*:

Name	Copyright Date	Copyright Holder	Vol/Page Number(s)
William Colgate	1906	James T. White & Company	v13:159
Herbert Henry Dow	1935	James T. White & Company	v24:12
J. Paul Getty	1946	James T. White & Company	G:121
Milton Snavely Hershey	1934	James T. White & Company	v33:23-24
Haroldson Lafayette Hunt, Jr.	1984	James T. White & Company	N-63:328-329
Will Keith Kellogg	1984	James T. White & Company	N-63:247-248
Frederick Louis Maytag	1930	James T. White & Company	v27:361
James Cash Penney	1984	James T. White & Company	N-63:269
William Wrigley, Jr.	1933	James T. White & Company	v23:64

The following articles were newly written for *Macmillan Profiles: Tycoons & Entrepreneurs*:

Name	Author
Warren Buffett	Patricia Ohlenroth
Malcolm Forbes	Patricia Ohlenroth
David Geffen	Patricia Ohlenroth
Howard Hughes	Laura Morelli
Rupert Murdoch	Patricia Ohlenroth
Steven Spielberg	Patricia Ohlenroth
Donald Trump	Patricia Ohlenroth
Ted Turner	Patricia Ohlenroth
Sam Walton	Patricia Ohlenroth

Photographs and images used in this volume were obtained from the following sources:

Stock Montage, Inc.:

Philip Danforth Armour (page 5)
John Jacob Astor (page 7)
Andrew Carnegie (page 21)
Samuel Colt (page 29)
John Deere (page 35)
Marshall Field (page 43)
James Fisk (page 45)
Henry Ford (page 49)
Henry Clay Frick (page 52)
Jakob Fugger (page 54)
Barry Goldwater (page 69)
Jay Gould (page 74)
Henry J. Heinz (page 106)

James Jerome Hill (page 113)
Henry J. Kaiser (page 137)
Cyrus Hall McCormick (page 177)
Andrew W. Mellon (page 178)
John Pierpont Morgan (page 181)
George Peabody (page 193)
George Mortimer Pullman (page 204)
Cecil John Rhodes (page 207)
John Davison Rockefeller (page 211)
Meyer Rothschild (page 215)
Leland Stanford (page 229)
Cornelius Vanderbilt (page 255)
Aaron Montgomery Ward (page 267)

Austrian Archives/Corbis: George Eastman (page 41)

Bob Krist/Corbis: Malcolm Stevenson Forbes (page 46)

Corbis-Bettmann: E. I. Du Pont (page 39), J. Paul Getty (page 67), Frederick Louis Maytag (page 176), Studebaker ad poster (page 241), Frank Winfield Woolworth (page 287), William Wrigley Jr. (page 294), Yale lock diagram (page 298)

Corbis: Henry Edwards Huntington (page 125)

Hulton-Deutsch Collection/Corbis: Sir Richard Arkwright (page 3)

Joseph Sohm;ChromoSohm Inc./Corbis: Santa Fe Pullman train (page 205)

Library of Congress/Corbis: Chinatown (page 1), Daniel Guggenheim (page 78), Edward Henry Harriman (page 93), Winya Curvignake holding Winchester rifle (page 279)

Layne Kennedy/Corbis: Motown Museum (page 72)

Lynn Goldsmith/© Corbis: William H. (Bill) Gates (page 59)

Mitchell Gerber/© Corbis: Stephen Spielberg (page 225)

Museum of Flight/Corbis: Boeing F4B-3 planes (page 11)

Neal Preston/Corbis: David Geffen (page 65)

Oscar White/Corbis: August Belmont (page 9), James Cash Penney (page 194), John Hay Whitney (page 274)

Reuters/Corbis-Bettmann: Warren Edward Buffett (page 17)

Robert Maass/Corbis: Donald Trump (page 245)

Roger Ressmeyer/© Corbis: Steven Paul Jobs (page 131), Stephen G. Wozniak (page 290)

UPI/Corbis-Bettmann: William E. Boeing (page 10), Berry Gordy Jr. (page 71), Earl Gilbert Graves Jr. (page 76), Joyce Clyde Hall (page 84), Armand Hammer (page 90), Stephen David Hassenfeld (page 96), Milton S. Hershey (page 109), Howard Hughes (page 117), Haroldson Lafayette Hunt Jr. (page 119), John Harold Johnson (page 134), Will Keith Kellogg family and friends (page 141), Raymond Albert Kroc (page 148), J(ohn) Willard (Bill) Marriott and his son (page 169), Rupert Murdock (page 185), H(enry) Ross Perot (page 198), Robert Edward (Ted) Turner (page 251), Oprah Gail Winfrey (page 280)

Underwood & Underwood/Corbis-Bettmann: Madam C. J.Walker (page 261)

Suggested Reading

AH QUIN

Griego, Andrew, Ed. "Rebuilding the California Southern Railroad: The Personal Account of A Chinese Labor Contractor, 1884." *Journal of San Diego History* (Fall 1979): 324-337.

HENRY ALLEN BOYD

Obituary. *New York Times*, May 30, 1959.

ROBERT REED CHURCH

Church, Annette, and Roberta Church. *The Robert Churches of Memphis.* 1975.

Sigafoos, Robert Allen. *From Cotton Row to Beal Street: A Business History of Memphis.* 1979.

ESTEVAN DE ANTUNAÑO

Thomson, Guy P. C. *Puebla de Los Angeles: Industry and Society in a Mexican City, 1700-1850.* 1989.

RICHARD ARKWRIGHT

Ashton, Thomas S. *The Industrial Revolution, 1760-1830.* 1948. Reprint. Greenwood, 1986.

Deane, Phyllis. *The First Industrial Revolution.* 2nd ed. 1979. Reprint, Cambridge, 1980.

Fitten, R. S., and A. P. Wadsworth. *The Strutts and the Arkwrights.* 1958.

Lane, Peter. *The Industrial Revolution.* Barnes & Noble, 1978.

Levine, David, and Keith Wrightson. *The Making of an Industrial Society: Whickham, 1560-1765.* Oxford, 1991.

Lines, Clifford J. *Companion to the Industrial Revolution.* Facts on File, 1990.

Musson, A. E., and Eric Robinson. *Science and Technology in the Industrial Revolution.* 1969. Reprint. Gordon & Breach, 1989.

PHILIP DANFORTH ARMOUR

Leech, Harper, and John C. Carroll. *Philip D. Armour and His Times.* 1938. Reprint 1979.

JOHN JACOB ASTOR

Haeger, John Denis. *John Jacob Astor: Business and Finance in the Early Republic.* Wayne State University Press, 1991.

WILLIAM W. BOEING

Boyne, Walter J. *Boeing B-52: A Documentary History.* Washington, D.C., 1981.

Norris, Guy, and Mark Wagner. *Boeing 747: Design and Development Since 1969.* Motorbooks International, 1997.

Vlach, P. R. Smith. *Boeing 747.* Specialty Press Publishers & Wholesalers, 1993.

SAMUEL BRANNAN

Bailey, Paul. *Sam Brannan and the California Mormons.* 1943.

Stellman, Louis J. *Sam Brannan, Builder of San Francisco.* 1953.

JUANA BRIONES

Bowman, J. N. "Juana Briones de Miranda." *Historical Society of Southern California Quarterly* (September 1957): 227-241.

Lothrop, Gloria Ricci. "Rancheras and the Land: Women and Property Rights in Hispanic California." *Southern California Quarterly* (Spring 1994): 59-84.

Lyman, Chester S. *Around the Horn.* 1924.

Monroy, Douglas. *Thrown Among Strangers: The Making of Mexican Culture in Frontier California.* 1990.

WARREN BUFFETT

Buffett, Mary, and David Clark. *Buffettology: The Previously Unexplained Techniques That Have Made Warren Buffett the World's Most Famous Investor.* Scribner, 1997.

Kilpatrick, Andrew. *Of Permanent Value: The Story of Warren Buffett.* Andy Kilpatrick Publishing Empire, 1998.

Greenberg, Alan C., with Warren Buffett. *Memos from the Chairman.* John Wiley & Sons, 1997.

Hagstrom, Robert G. *The Warren Buffett Way: Investment Strategies of the World's Greatest Investor.* John Wiley & Sons, 1997.

Kilpatrick, Andrew. *Warren Buffett: The Good Guy of Wall Street.* Donald I. Fine, 1995.

Lowe, Janet C. *Warren Buffett Speaks: The Wit and Wisdom from the World's Greatest Investor.* Soundelux Audio Pub., 1997.

Reynolds, Simon, with Warren Buffett. *Thoughts of Chairman Buffett: Thirty Years of Unconventional Wisdom from the Sage of Omaha.* Harperbusiness, 1998.

Train, John. *The Midas Touch: The Strategies That Have Made Warren Buffett 'America's Preeminent Investor.'* HarperCollins, 1988.

JOHN BUTTERFIELD

Conkling, Roscoe P., and Margaret B. Conkling. *The Butterfield Overland Mail, 1857-1869.* 1947.

Jackson, W. Turrentine. "A New Look at Wells Fargo, Stagecoaches, and the Pony Express." *California Historical Society Quarterly* 45 (1966): 291-324.

ANDREW CARNEGIE

Bowman, John S. *Andrew Carnegie: Steel Tycoon.* Silver Burdett, 1989.

Carnegie, Andrew. *The Gospel of Wealth.* Applewood Books. Reprint, 1998.

Jones, Theodore. *Carnegie Libraries Across America: A Public Legacy.* John Wiley & Sons, 1997.

Josephson, Matthew. *The Robber Barrons: The Great American Capitalists 1861-1901.* Harcourt Brace, 1962.

Livesay, Harold C. *Andrew Carnegie and the Rise of Big Business.* Scott, Foresman, 1987.

Simon, Charnan. *Andrew Carnegie: Builder of Libraries.* Children's Press, 1997.

Wall, Joseph F. *Andrew Carnegie.* University of Pittsburgh Press, 1989.

SAMUEL COLT

Hosley, William. *Colt: The Making of an American Legend.* University of Massachusetts Press, 1996.

Keating, Ben. *The Flamboyant Mr. Colt and His Deadly Six-Shooter.* 1978.

Sheldon, Douglas G. *Colt's Super .38: The Production History from 1929 to 1971.* Quick Vend Inc., 1997.

Sheldon, Douglas G. *Collector's Guide to Colt's 38 Automatic Pistols: The Production of the Automatic Colt Pistol,* 1987.

Webb, Walter Prescott. *The Great Plains.* 1931.

Wilson, R. L. *Colt: An American Legend.* 1985.

SUZANNE DE PASSE

"Motown Executive Brings Western to TV." *Afro-American* (February 4, 1989): 3.

Mussari, Mark. *Suzanne de Passe: Motown's Boss Lady (Wizards of Business).* Garrett Educational Corp., 1991.

DUPONT FAMILY

Mottel, William J., David E. Morrison, and Joseph F. Long. *Industrial Safety is Good Business: The Dupont Story.* John Wiley & Sons, 1997.

William, Jon M. *Corporate Images: Photography and the Du Pont Company 1865-1972.* Hagley Museum & Library, 1984.

GEORGE EASTMAN

Cumming, David. *Photography.* Steck-Vaughn, 1990.

Newhall, Beaumont. *The History of Photography, From 1839 to the Present Day,* 5th edition. Museum of Modern Art, 1982.

Rosenblum, Naomi. *A World History of Photography.* Rev. ed. Abbeville, 1989.

JAMES FISK

McAlpine, Robert W. *The Life and Times of Colonel James Fisk, Jr.* Ayer Company Publishers, 1981

Stafford, Marshall P. *The Life of James Fisk, Jr.: A Full and Accurate Narrative of All the Enterprises in Which He Was Engaged.* Ayer Company Publishers, 1981.

MALCOLM FORBES

Forbes, Malcolm with Tony Clark. *More Than I Dreamed: A Lifetime of Collecting.* Simon & Schuster, 1989.

Winans, Christopher. *Malcolm Forbes: The Man Who Had Everything.* Dufour Editions, 1991.

HENRY FORD

Batchelor, Ray. *Henry Ford, Mass Production, Modernism, and Design.* Manchester University Press, 1994.

Hardin, Wes. *Henry Ford Museum: An ABC of American Innovation.* Harry N. Abrams, 1997.

Harris, Jacqueline L. *Henry Ford.* Watts, 1984.

Kent, Zachary. *The Story of Henry Ford and the Automobile.* Children's Press, 1990.

Lacey, Robert. *Ford, The Men and the Machine.* Little, Brown, 1986.

Nevins, Allan, and Hill, F. E. *Ford.* 3 vols. Scribner, 1954-1963.

Paul, Joseph. *Henry Ford.* Ado & Daughters, 1996.

HENRY CLAY FRICK

Frick Symington Sanger, Martha. *Henry Clay Frick: A Private Life.* Abbeville Press, 1998.

Warren, Kenneth. *Triumphant Capitalism: Henry Clay Frick and the Industrial Transformation of America.* University of Pittsburgh Press, 1996.

JAKOB FUGGER

Ehrenberg, R. *Captial and Finance in the Age of the Renaissance.* 1963.

Mattheus, G. T. (editor). *News and Rumor in Renaissance Europe: The Fugger Newsletters.* 1959.

Strieder, J. *Jacob Fugger the Rich.* 1966.

BILL GATES

Boyd, Aaron. *Smart Money: The Story of Bill Gates*. Morgan Reynolds, 1995.

Dickinson, Joan D. *Bill Gates: Billionaire Computer Genius*. Enslow Publishers, Inc., 1997.

Edstrom, Jennifer, and Marlin Eller. *Barbarian Led by Bill: Microsoft from the Inside*. Henry Hold & Company, Inc., 1998

Forman, Michael. *Bill Gates: Software Billionaire*. Macmillan Children's Press, 1998.

Gates, Bill, with Nathan Myhrvold and Peter Rinearson. *The Road Ahead*. Penguin USA, 1996.

Manes, Stephen, and Paul Andrews. *Gates: How Microsoft's Mogul Reinvented an Industry-And Made Himself the Richest Man in America*. Touchstone Books, 1994.

Simon, Charnan. *Bill Gates: Helping People Use Computers*. Children's Press, 1998.

Wallace, James. *Overdrive: Bill Gates and the Race to Control Cyberspace*. John Wiley & Sons, 1997.

Wallace, James, and Jim Erickson. *Hard Drive: Bill Gates and the Making of the Microsoft Empire*. Harperbusiness, 1993.

JOHN PAUL GETTY

Getty, J. Paul. *As I See It*. Prentice Hall, 1976.

Getty, J. Paul. *How to Be Rich*. Berkeley Publishing Group, 1993.

Getty, J. Paul. *My Life and Fortunes*. Duell, Sloan & Pierce, 1963.

Hewins, Ralph. *The Richest American: J. Paul Getty*. E. P. Dutton, 1960.

Lenzer, Robert. *The Life and Loves of J. P. Getty: The Richest Man in the World*. Crown, 1986.

GIBBS, MIFFLIN WISTAR

Gibbs, Mifflin Wistar, and Tom W. Dillard. *Shadow and Light: An Autobiography with Reminiscences of the Last and Present Century*. University of Nebraska Press, reprint 1995.

GOLDWATER FAMILY

Edwards, Lee. *Goldwater: The Man Who Made a Revolution*. Regnery Publishing, Inc., 1997.

Goldberg, Robert Alan. *Barry Goldwater*. Yale University Press, 1995.

Iverson, Peter J. *Barry Goldwater: Native Arizonan*. University of Oklahoma Press, 1997.

Smith, Dean. *The Goldwaters of Arizona*. 1986.

GORDY, BERRY

Early, Gerald. *One Nation Under a Grove: Motown and American Culture*. Ecco Press, 1996.

George, Nelson. *Where Did Our Love Go?: The Rise & Fall of the Motown Sound*. St. Martin's Press, 1987.

Gordy, Berry. *To Be Loved: The Music, the Magic, the Memories of Motown*. Warner Books, 1995.

Gordy Singleton, Raynoma. *Berry, Me and Motown*. Audio Cassette Edition, Publishing Mills, 1991.

Motown Anthology. Hal Leonard Publishing Corporation, 1998

Smith, Patricia. *Life According to Motown*. Tia Chucha Press, 1991.

Waller, Don. *The Motown Story*. 1985.

Whitall, Susan. *Women of Motown: An Oral History*. Avon Books, 1998.

JAY GOULD

Grodinsky, Julius. *Jay Gould, His Business Career, 1867-1892*. Ayer Company Publishing, 1981.

Klein, Maury. *The Life and Legend of Jay Gould*. 1986.

Stuart Ogilvie, John. *Life and Death of Jay Gould and How He Made His Millions*. Ayer Company Publishing, 1981.

EARL G. GRAVES

Black Enterprise. 20th anniversary issue (August 1990).

Davis, Tim. "Graves Gets Serious." *Beverage World* 111 (October 1992): 80-84.

Graves, Earl G., Robert L. Crandall, and Wes Smith. *How to Succeed in Business Without Being White: Straight Talk on Making It in America*. Harperbusiness, 1997.

EDWARD HENRY HARRIMAN

Eckenrode, H. J. *E. H. Harriman: The Little Giant of Wall Street*. 1933.

Hughes, Jonathan. "E. H. Harriman, the Financier and the Railroads." In *The Vital Few*. 1966.

Kahn, Otto H. *Edward Henry Harriman*. 1911.

Kennan, George. *Edward Henry Harriman: A Biography*. 1922.

FORD FERGUSON HARVEY

Henderson, James David. *Meals by Fred Harvey: A Phenomenon of the American West*. 1969.

Poling-Kempes, Lesley. *The Harvey Girls: Women Who Opened the West*. 1989.

HASSENFELD, STEPHEN DAVID

Miller, G. Wayne. *Toy Wars: The Epic Struggle Between G. I. Joe, Barbie, and the Companies That Make Them*. Times Books, 1998.

Santelmo, Vincent. *The Complete Encyclopedia to G. I. Joe*. Krause Publications, 1997.

SAMUEL THOMAS HAUSER

Robbins, William G. "The Deconstruction of a Capitalist Patriarch." *Montana: The Magazine of Western History* 42:4 (Autumn 1992): 20-33.

WILLIAM RANDOLPH HEARST

Frazier, Nancy. *William Randolph Hearst*. Silver Burdett, 1989.

Hearst, William Randolph, Jr., and Jack Casserly. *The Hearsts: Father and Son*. Roberts Rinehart, 1991.

Mugridge, Ian. *The View from Xanadu: William Randolph Hearst and United States Foreign Policy*. McGill Queen University Press, 1995.

Proctor, Ben. *William Randolph Hearst: The Early Years, 1963-1910*. Oxford University Press, 1998.

Robinson, Judith. *The Hearsts: An American Dynasty*. University of Delaware Press, 1991.

Swanberg, W. A. *Citizen Hearst: A Biography of William Randolph Hearst*. Budget Book Service, 1996.

Winkler, John K. *William Randolph Hearst: A New Appraisal*. 1955.

HERMAN HOLLERITH

Lee, John A. *Computer Pioneers*. IEEE Computer Society Press, 1995.

Oakman, Robert L. *The Computer Triangle: Hardware, Software, and People*. John Wiley & Sons, 1995.

Shurkin, Joel. *Engines of the Mind: The Evolution of the Computer from Mainframes to Microprocessors*. Norton, 1996.

MILTON HERSHEY

Bailleux, Nathalie, Jeanne Bourin, and Diana Groven. *The Book of Chocolate*. Abbeville Press, 1996.

Burford, Betty, and Loren Chantland. *Chocolate by Hershey: A Story About Milton S. Hershey*. First Avenue Editions, 1994.

Charnan, Simon. *Milton Hershey: Chocolate King, Town Builder*. Children's Press, 1998.

JAMES J. HILL

Albro, Martin, and W. Thomas White. *James J. Hill and the Opening of the Northwest*. Minnesota Historical Society, 1991.

Holbrook, Stewart H. *James J. Hill*. 1955.

Pyle, Joseph Gilpin. *The Life of James J. Hill*. 2 vols. 1917.

HOWARD HUGHES

Brown, Harry Peter and Pat H. Broeske. *Howard Hughes: The Untold Story*. Signet, 1997.

Maheu, Robert, and Richard Hack. *Next to Hughes*. HarperCollins, 1992.

Phelan, James R. and Lewis Chester. *The Money: The Battle for Howard Hughes's Billions*. Random House, 1997.

Rummel, Robert W. *Howard Hughes and TWA*. Smithsonian Institution, 1991.

Thomas, Tony. *Howard Hughes in Hollywood*. Citadel Press, 1985.

H. L. HUNT

Burst, Ardis. *The Three Families of H. L. Hunt*. Grove Press, 1989.

COLLIS P. HUNTINGTON

Lewis, Oscar. *The Big Four: The Story of Huntington, Stanford, Hopkins, and Crocker and the Building of the Central Pacific*. 1938.

HENRY E. HUNTINGTON

Crump, Spencer. *Ride the Big Red Cars: How the Trolleys Helped Build Southern California.* 1962.

Friedricks, William B. *Henry E. Huntington and the Creation of Southern California.* Ohio State University Press, 1992.

Pomfret, John E. *The Henry E. Huntington Library and Art Gallery from Its Beginnings to 1969.* 1969.

Post, Robert C. *Street Railways and the Growth of Los Angeles.* 1989.

Spurgeon, Selena A. *Henry Edward Huntington: His Life and His Collection.* 1992.

Thorpe, James Ernest. *Henry Edwards Huntington: A Biography.* University of California Press, 1994.

CHARLES ILFELD

Paris, William J. *The Charles Ilfeld Company.* 1961.

Parish, William J. "The German Jew and the Commercial Revolution in Territorial New Mexico, 1850-1900." *New Mexico Quarterly* 29 (1959): 307-332.

Tobias, Henry J. *A History of the Jews in New Mexico.* 1900.

STEVE JOBS

Butcher, Lee. *Accidental Millionaire: The Rise and Fall of Steve Jobs at Apple Computer.* 1987.

Carlton, Jim. *Apple: The Inside Story of Intrigue, Egomania, and Business Blunders.* Times Books, 1997.

Garston, Christina. *Apple World: Core and Periphery in a Transnational Organizational Culture.* Coronet Books, 1994.

Kawasaki, Guy. *The Macintosh Way.* Addison-Wesley Publishing Company, 1989.

Rose, Frank. *West of Eden: The End of Innocence at Apple Computer.* 1989.

JOHN HAROLD JOHNSON

Emery, Edwin, and Michael Emery. *The Press and America.* 1978.

Falkof, Lucille. *John H. Johnson, the Man from Ebony.* Garrett Educational Corp., 1991.

Johnson, John H., and Lerone Bennett. *Succeeding Against the Odds.* Amistad Press, 1993.

Knight, Bertram. *John Harold Johnson: Magazine Magnate.* Macmillan Children's Press, 1998.

Knight, Bertram. *John Harold Johnson, the Man Who Wouldn't Take No for an Answer.* Crestwood House, 1998.

Wilson, Clint C. II. *Black Journalists in Paradox.* 1991.

HENRY J. KAISER

Adams, Stephen B. *Mr. Kaiser Goes to Washington: The Rise of a Government Entrepreneur.* University of North Carolina Press, 1997.

Foster, Mark S. *Henry J. Kaiser: Builder of the Modern American West.* University of Texas Press, 1989.

Kotkin, Joel, and Paul Grabowicz. *California, Inc.* 1982.

Lowitt, Richard. *The New Deal and the West.* 1984.

Nash, Gerald. *The American West Transformed: Impact of the Second World War.* 1985.

Heiner, Albert. *Henry J. Kaiser: Western Colossus.* Halo Books, 1991.

RAYMOND KROC

Kroc, Ray and Robert Anderson. *Grinding It Out: The Making of McDonald's.* St. Martin's Press, 1990.

Love, John F. *McDonald's: Behind the Arches.* Bantam Books, 1995.

Mascola, Marilyn, and Luciano Lazzarino. *Ray Kroc: Famous Restaurant Owner.* Rourke Book Company, Inc., 1989.

McDonald, Ronald L. *The Complete Hamburger: The History of America's Favorite Sandwich.* Birch Lane Press, 1997.

Watson, James L. *Golden Arches East: McDonald's in East Asia.* Stanford University Press, 1997.

AUSTIN E. LATHROP

Gruening, Ernest. *The State of Alaska.* 1954

Webb, Melody. *The Last Frontier.* 1984.

MANUEL LISA

Oglesby, Richard E. *Manuel Lisa and the Opening of the Missouri Fur Trade*. 1963. Reprint 1984.

LLEWELLYN, JAMES BRUCE

Berns, David L. "Ahead on the Fast Track: Entrepreneur Capitalizes on Wits, Glitz." *USA Today*, March 14, 1989, Page 1B.

Herbst, Laura. "J. Bruce Llewellyn; Helping Blacks Get Ahead." *New York Times*, June 26, 1988, Sec. 12, Page 2.

Taylor, B. Kimberly. "What Do These Millionaires Have in Common? They All Found Work with Equal Opportunity Employers Themselves." *New York Newsday*, February 1, 1994, Page 44.

BIDDY MASON

Hayden, Dolores. "Biddy Mason's Los Angeles, 1856-1891." *California History* 68 (Fall 1989): 87-99.

J. WILLARD MARRIOT

Marriott, J. Willard. *The Spirit to Serve: Marriott's Way*. Harperbusiness, 1997.

O'Brien, Robert. *Marriott*. 1977.

ANDREW W. MELLON

Finley, David E. *A Standard of Excellence: Andrew W. Mellon Founds the National Gallery of Art at Washington*. Smithsonian Institution Press, 1975.

J. P. MORGAN

Allen, Frederick L. *The Great Pierpont Morgan*. 1949. Reprint, Marboro Books, 1990.

Auchincloss, Louis. *J. P. Morgan: The Financier as Collector*. Henry N. Abrams, 1990.

Carosso, Vincent P. *The Morgans: Private International Bankers 1854-1913*. Harvard University Press, 1987.

Corey, L. *House of Morgan*. AMS Press, 1930.

Satterlee, Herbert L. *J. Piermont Morgan: An Intimate Portrait*. Ayer Company Publishing, 1975.

RUPERT MURDOCH

Block, Alex Ben. *Outfoxed: Marvin Davis, Barry Diller, Rupert Murdoch and the Inside Story of America's Fourth Television Network*. 1990.

Kiernan, Thomas. *Citizen Murdoch: The Unexpurgated Story of Rupert Murdoch—The World's Most Powerful and Controversial Media Lord*. 1986.

Leapman, Michael. *Arrogant Aussie: The Rupert Murdoch Story*. Lyle Stuart, 1985.

Shawcross, William. *Murdoch: The Making of a Media Empire*. Touchstone Books, 1997.

ANTHONY OVERTON

Obituary. *Journal of Negro History* 32, no. 3 (July 1947): 394-396.

HARRY HERBERT PACE

Johnson, John H., and Lerone Bennett, Jr. *Succeeding Against the Odds*. 1989.

Southern, Eileen. *The Music of Black Americans: A History*. 1983.

GEORGE PEABODY

Parker, Franklin. *George Peabody: A Biography*. Vanderbilt University Press, 1995.

J. C. PENNEY

Curry, Mary Elizabeth. *Creating an American Institution: The Merchandising Genius of J. C. Penney*. Garland Press, 1997.

ROSS PEROT

Barta, Carolyn, and Mike Towle. *Perot and His People: Disrupting the Balance of Political Power*. Summit Publishing Group, 1993.

Brown, Gene. H. *Ross Perot: Texas Billionaire*. Rourke Book Company, 1993.

Bredeson, Carmen. *Ross Perot: Billionaire Politician*. Enslow Publishers, 1995.

Italia, Bob. *H. Ross Perot: The Man Who Woke Up America*. Abdo & Daughters, 1993.

Levin, Doron P. *Irreconcilable Differences: Ross Perot Versus General Motors*. Signet, 1992.

Perot, Ross, and Paul Simon. *The Dollar Crisis: A Blueprint to Help Rebuild the American Dream*. Summit Publishing Group, 1996.

Perot, Ross. *Ross Perot: My Life & the Principles for Success*. Summit Publishing Group, 1996.

Perot, Ross. *Intensive Care: We Must Save Medicare and Medicaid Now*. Harper Perennial, 1995.

PHILIP WINSTON PILLSBURY

Pillsbury Company. *Pillsbury Best of the Bake-Off Cookbook; 350 Recipes from America's Favorite Cooking Contest.* Clarkson Potter, 1996.

Powell, W. *Pillsbury's Beat: A Company History from 1869.* Pillsbury Publications, 1985.

GEORGE MORTIMORE PULLMAN

Leyendecker, Liston Edgington. *Palace Car Prince: A Biography of George Mortimer Pullman.* University Press of Colorado, 1994.

CECIL RHODES

Mitchell, Lewis. *The Life and Times of the Right Honorable Cecil John Rhodes: 1853-1902.* Ayer Company Publishing, 1977.

Rotberg, Robert I. *The Founder: Cecil Rhodes and the Pursuit of Power.* Oxford University Press, 1988.

Tamarkin, M. *Cecil Rhodes and the Cape Afrikaners: The Imperial Colossus and the Colonial Parish Pump.* Frank Cass & Company, 1996.

Thomas, Anthony. *Rhodes: Race for Africa.* St. Martin's Press, 1997.

EDWARD PAYSON RIPLEY

Martin Albro. *Railroads Triumphant: The Growth, Rejection, and Rebirth of a Vital American Force.* 1992

Waters, Lawrence L. *Steel Trails to Sante Fe.* 1950.

JOHN D. ROCKEFELLER

Coffey, Ellen G. *John D. Rockefeller: Empire Builder.* Silver Burdett, 1989.

Harr, John E., and P. J. Johnson. *The Rockefeller Century.* Scribner, 1988.

Nevins, Allan. *John D. Rockefeller: The Heroic Age of American Enterprise.* 2 vols. Kraus Reprint, 1976.

ROTHSCHILD FAMILY

Gutwein, D. *The Divided Elite.* 1992

Morton, F. *The Rothschilds.* 1962.

Wilson, D. *Rothschild: A Story of Wealth and Power.* 1988.

JOHN DENNIS RYAN

Forbes, Bertie C. "John D. Ryan." In *Men Who Are Making the West*. 1923.

Johnson, Carrie. "Electrical Power, Copper, and John D. Ryan," *Montana: The Magazine of Western History* 38:4 (Autumn 1988): 24-37.

Marcosson, Isaac F. *Anaconda*. 1957.

JAKE SIMMONS JR.

Greenberg, Jonathan D. *Staking a Claim: Jake Simmons and the Making of an African-American Oil Dynasty*. 1990.

ALBERT G. SPALDING

Spalding, Albert G., and Benjamin J. Rader. *America's National Game: Historic Facts Concerning the Beginning, Evolution, Development, and Popularity of Baseball*. University of Nebraska Press, 1992.

CLAUS SPRECKLES

Adler, Jacob. *Claus Spreckels: The Sugar King in Hawaii*. 1966

Kuykendall, Ralph S. *The Hawaiian Kingdon*. Vol. 3. 1967.

STEVEN SPIELBERG

Brode, Douglas. *The Films of Steven Spielberg*. Citadel Press, 1995.

Ferber, Elizabeth. *Steven Spielberg: A Biography*. Chelsea House Publications, 1996.

Knight, Bertram T. *Master of Movie Magic*. Macmillan Children's Press, 1998.

McBride, Joseph. *Steven Spielberg: A Biography*. Simon & Schuster, 1997.

Sanello, Frank. *Spielberg: The Man, the Movies, the Mythology*. Taylor Publishing, 1996.

LELAND STANFORD

Bancroft, Hubert Howe. *History of the Life of Leland Stanford, A Character Study*. Reprint 1952.

Clark, George T. *Leland Stanford, War Governor of California, Railroad Builder, and Founder of Stanford University*. 1931.

Lewis, Oscar. *The Big Four: The Story of Huntington, Stanford, Hopkins, and Crocker, and the Building of the Central Pacific Railroad*, 1938.

Tutorow, Norman E. *Leland Stanford, Man of Many Careers*. 1971.

HENRY ENGLEHARD STEINWAY

Chapin, Miles, and Rodica Trato (illustrator). *88 Keys: The Making of a Steinway Piano*. Clarkson Potter, 1997.

Goldberg, Susan. *Steinway: From Glory to Controversy: The Family, the Business, the Piano*. Mosaic Press, 1996.

Lieberman, Richard K. *Steinway & Sons*. Yale University Press, 1995.

JOHN BATTERSON STETSON

Carlson, Laurie, and Holly Meade. *Boss of the Plains: The Hat That Won the West*. Dk Ink, 1998.

Hubbard, Elbert. *John B. Stetson*. 1912.

Lindemier, Tom, and Steve Mount. *I See by Your Outfit: Historic Cowboy Gear of the Northern Plains*. High Plains Press, 1996.

Manns, William, Elizabeth Clair Flood, and Charlotte Berney (editors). *Cowboys & the Trappings of the Old West*. Zon International Publishing Company, 1997.

Nordyke, Lewis. "Boss of the Plains: The Story Behind the Stetson." In *The Cowboy Reader*. Edited by Lon Tinkle and Allen Maxwell. 1959.

Reynolds, William, and Ritch Rand. *The Cowboy Hat Book*. Gibbs, Smith Publisher, 1995.

"Stetson: Hat of the West." *Persimmon Hill* 8 (Winter 1979): 42-51.

LEVI STRAUSS

Cray, Ed. *Levi's*. 1978.

Josephy, Alvin M., Jr. "Those Pants That Levi Gave Us." *American West* 22 (July-August 1985): 30-37.

JOHN MOHLER STUDEBAKER

Critchlow, Donald T. *Studebaker: The Life and Death of an American Corporation*. Indiana University Press, 1997.

Longstreet, Stephen. *A Century on Wheels: The Story of Studebaker: A History, 1852-1952*. Greenwood Publishing Group, 1952. Reprint 1970.

PERCY ELLIS SUTTON

Green, Charles. *The Struggle for Black Empowerment in New York City: Beyond the Politics of Pigmentation*. 1989.

Lewinson, Edwin R. *Black Politics in New York City*. 1974.

DONALD TRUMP

Baida, Peter. *Poor Richard's Legacy: American Business Values from Benjamin Franklin to Donald Trump.* 1991.

O'Donnell, John R. *Trumped!: The Inside Story of the Real Donald Trump—His Crossing Rise and Spectacular Fall.* 1991.

King, Norman. *Ivana Trump: A Very Unauthorized Biography.* 1990.

Trump, Donald, and Leershen. *The Art of Survival.* Warner Books, 1991.

Trump, Donald, and Tony Schwartz. *The Art of the Deal.*

Trump, Donald, and Kate Bonher. *The Art of the Comeback.* 1997

TED TURNER

Bibb, Proter. *Ted Turner: It Ain't as Easy as It Looks: A Biography.* Johnson Books, 1997.

Byman, Jeremy. *Ted Turner: Cable Television Tycoon* (Makers of the Media). Morgan Reynolds, 1998.

Carlson, Althea E. *Riding a White Horse: Ted Turner's Goodwill Games and Other Crusades.* Episcopal Press, 1998.

Fischer, David Marc. *Ted Turner.* Rourke Book Company, 1993.

Goldberg, Robert, and Gerald Jay Goldberg. *Citizen Turner: The Wild Rise of an American Tycoon.* Harcourt Brace, 1995.

Stefoff, Rebecca. *Ted Turner: Television's Triumphant Tiger.* Garrett Educational Corp., 1992.

CORNELIUS VANDERBILT

Auchincloss, Louis. *The Vanderbilt Era.* 1989. Reprint, Macmillan, 1990.

Patterson, Jerry E. *The Vanderbilts.* Harry N. Abrams, 1989.

Vanderbilt, Arthur T. *Fortune's Children: The Fall of the House of Vanderbilt.* Quill, 1989.

SARAH BREEDLOVE WALKER

Blashfield, Jean F. *Women Inventors: Catherine Green, Harriet Hosmer, Madame C. J. Walker, Yvonne Brill, Nancy Perkins.* Capstone Press, 1996.

Bundles, A'Lelia Perry. *Madam C. J. Walker—Entrepreneur.* 1991.

Colman, Penny. *Madame C. J. Walker: Building a Business Empire.* Millbrook Press, 1994.

Giddings, Paula. *When and Where I Enter: The Impact of Black Women on Race and Sex in America.* 1984.

Lewis, David Levering. *When Harlem Was in Vogue.* 1982.

Lommel, Cookie. *Madame C. J. Walker.* Holloway House Publishing Company, 1993.

Toby, Marlene, Carol Greene, and Steven Dobson. *Madam C. J. Walker: Pioneer Businesswoman.* Children's Press, 1995.

SAM WALTON

Ortega, Bob. *In Sam We Trust: The Untold Story of Sam Walton and How Wal-Mart Is Devouring America.* Times Books, 1998.

Vance, Sandra S., and Roy V. Scott. *Wal-Mart: A History of Sam Walton's Retail Phenomenon.* Twayne Publishing, 1994.

Walton, Sam, and John Huey. *Sam Walton: Made in America—My Story.* Bantam Books, 1993.

JOHN HAY WHITNEY

Kluger, Richard. *The Paper: The Life and Death of the New York Herald Tribune.* 1986.

OLIVER FISHER WINCHESTER

Brown, G. Allan (photographer), R. L. Wilson, and Robert D. Loomis. *Winchester: An American Legend, The Official History of Winchester Firearms and Ammunition from 1849 to the Present.* Random House, 1991.

Houze, Herbert G. *Winchester Repeating Arms Company: Its History & Development from 1865 to 1981.* Krause Publications, 1994.

Houze, Herbert G. *To the Dreams of Youth: Winchester .22 Caliber Single Shot Rifle.* Krause Publications, 1993.

Pirkle, Arthur. *Winchester Lever Action Repeating Firearms: The Models of 1866, 1873, & 1876.* North Cape Publications, 1995.

Schwing, Ned. *Winchester Slide-Action Rifles: Model 1890 & Model 1906.* Krause Publications, 1992.

OPRAH WINFREY

Decker, Jeffrey Louis. *Made in American: Self-Styled Success from Horatio Alger to Oprah Winfrey*. University of Minnesota Press, 1997.

Harrison, Barbara Grizutti. "The Important of Being Oprah." *New York Times Magazine* (June 11, 1989): 28-30.

Nicholson, Louis P. *Oprah Winfrey*. Chelsea House Publishing, 1997.

Ruth, Marianne. *Oprah Winfrey: Entertainer*. Holloway House Publishing Company, 1996.

Saidman, Anne. *Oprah Winfrey: Media Success Story*. Lerner Publications Company, 1990.

Weil, Ann. *Oprah Winfrey: Queen of Daytime TV*. Macmillan's Children Reference, 1998.

ROBERT WINSHIP WOODRUFF

Allen, Frederick. *Secret Formula: How Brilliant Marketing and Relentless Salesmanship Made Coca-Cola the Best-Known Product in the World*. Harperbusiness, 1995.

Applegate, Howard L. *Coca-Cola: A History in Photographs 1930 Through 1969*. Iconographix, 1996.

Pendergrast, Mark. *For God, Country, and Coca-Cola: The Unauthorized History of the Great American Soft Drink and the Company That Makes It*. Touchstone Books, 1998.

STEPHEN WOZNIAK

Gold, Rebecca. *Steve Wozniak: A Wizard Called Woz*. Lerner Publications Company, 1994.

Greenberg, Keith Elliot, Bruce S. Glassman, and Jim Spence. *Jobs and Wozniak: Creating the Apple Computer (Partners)*. Blackbirch Marketing, 1994.

Kendall, Martha E. *Steve Wozniak: Inventor of the Apple Computer*. Walker & Company, 1994.

affirmative action The collective term for government policies in the United States intended to promote opportunities for minorities by setting specific goals or quotas. Affirmative action favors minorities in hiring, promotion, college admissions, and government contracts to offset the effects of past discrimination against a group. The term was first used by President Lyndon B. Johnson in 1965, and the first federal policies designed to guarantee minority hiring were implemented by President Richard Nixon in 1969.

agriculture A general term for different aspects of the study and industry of managing the growth of plants and livestock for human use, also referred to as "farming." In modern times the agriculture industry has come to include a variety of different disciplines and sciences, all with the efficient production of food as their primary purpose.

antitrust Relating to legislation against trusts or combinations, specifically legislation to protect trade and commerce from unlawful monopolies or unfair business practices

apprentice A term used to refer to one who is at the beginning or starting level of learning a trade or skill under the supervision and training of a master or expert. The apprenticeship system was widely used by craft guilds during the Middle Ages, and continued to be an important and traditional way of learning a trade until the Industrial Revolution, after which it was for the most part replaced by the emergence of factories as the primary means of producing manufactured goods. An apprentice was considered a beginner in his trade, and received only room and board, along with valuable craft training, in return for the work he did. A form of apprenticeship, with terms now clearly specified in contracts and regulated by trade unions and laws, still operates in the United States today in industries that required highly trained and specialized workers.

arbitrage The procedure and practice of making purchases of securities or other financial instruments on one market and selling them on another, in order to profit from a resulting price discrepancy.

assembly line A factory arrangement, in which an item is passed along from worker to worker, each of whom performs a part of the manufac-turing process. The standardization of design and parts that was an essential factor in the Industrial Revolution of the nineteenth century made the assembly line one of the most efficient method of putting together mass-produced items, and it remains so to this day.

asset A property, such as cash, stock, or real estate, that may serve to offset or cover the liabilities of an individual or business.

barrister A British term for a professional advocate, or lawyer, permitted to plead or argue cases before the High Court of Justice. A barrister is distinguished from a solicitor, who may do so only in lower courts.

board of directors The group elected by the stockholders of a company to determine basic corporate policy and to select the top officers of a corporation. It is led by the Chairman of the Board, and may consist of a variety of individuals with different areas of expertise, financial, or personal interest in the company.

bond A financial contract sold by companies and governments to raise money. A bond pays an investor a specific rate of interest, for a specific period of time, and is essentially a loan from an investor that is to be repaid under specified terms. Many major public works, as well as company expansions, are financed by the issuing of bonds to raise capital. The sale and trading of bonds by individuals and institutions in the financial marketplace is referred to collectively as "the Bond Market."

boycott A form of protest in which a person or group refuses to buy products from or support companies with which they disagree.

broker A person who acts for another in the conducting of business transactions, such as contract negotiation, purchases, and sales in return for a fee or commission. The most common reference is to a stockbroker, who buys and sells shares on stock on behalf of individual investors.

Bureau of Reclamation Originally called the Reclamation Service, an agency of the U.S. federal government created by the Reclamation Act, signed in 1902 by President Theodore Roosevelt. Its purpose was to stimulate the settlement of 16 western states by improving the arid and sparsely populated land through irrigation. It has since grown to include such projects as flood control, preservation of fish and wildlife, the construction of dams, and providing electricity and water for millions of people.

capital Often used to refer to the large amounts of money with which a business or government public work is launched, or improvements or expansion are financed. Capital is also defined as the overall value of a company determined by its physical holdings, including such assets as land, buildings, equipment, and inventory, by which it produces income. The term "market capitalization" refers to the value of a company calculated by multiplying its dollar value per share of stock by the number of shares outstanding.

capitalism The overall term for the economic system in which individuals and companies produce and exchange goods and services through a network of prices and markets. The essential principles of what we perceive as modern capitalism were first set forth by the Scottish philosopher Adam Smith in his book *An Inquiry into the Nature and Causes of the Wealth of Nations*, published in 1776, and the term "capitalism" was introduced by Karl Marx in the mid-19th century.

catalog An itemized, descriptive list of items for sale or other public notice. Catalogs are often used by companies that specialize in retail mail order sales, or by museums or auction houses to highlight a collection or exhibit.

census A periodic government count of the population.

Chairman of the Board The presiding officer of a company's Board of Directors, elected by the Board members.

chamber of commerce A local, national, or international association of business people, established to promote business interests and attract new business to their locality. Originally made up primarily of merchants, chambers of commerce may also include bankers and manufacturers.

Chief Executive Officer The highest ranking officer in a corporation, responsible to the Board of Directors and to the stockholders for directing the management of a company. The Chief Executive Officer is appointed, or hired, by the Board of Directors.

Chief Financial Officer A high-ranking corporate officer appointed to the position by a corporation's Board of Directors.

Chief Operations Officer A high-ranking corporate officer appointed to the position by a corporation's Board of Directors.

coalition An alliance or union of two or more parties, usually temporary, established for the purpose of attaining goals favorable to those involved. The term is most often used to refer to political alliances.

common stock A capital stock other than preferred stock.

concession In business, a concession most often refers to the right of an individual or company to sell a particular item in a particular place. Concessions are usually contracts negotiated to allow a subsidiary business, such as a food stand or souvenir shop, to operate in a public place such as a ballpark or restaurant.

conglomerate A corporation created by the merger of a number of different companies with unrelated or complimentary specialties. This allows a company to reduce its dependence on a single product or market.

consultant An individual, most often a private contractor hired by a company, who offers expert advice in a particular field or is consulted before or during a particular undertaking. For example, a consultant might be hired by a corporation to provide advice when the company is considering moving into a new field, or targeting a new market segment. In such a case, a consultant might be asked to review the company's proposed course of action, and possibly offer feedback or suggestions.

contract A legal document detailing the specifics of an arrangement between two or more parties. Contracts are used for a wide variety of enterprises where there is a need to define terms and conditions beforehand. A contract is enforceable under the law and allows any of the involved parties legal recourse if the terms specified are not met.

contractor A person or company that agrees to perform a job or services for a specified price. The term is often used in reference to construction work.

corporation A business or organization created by government charter, allowing a group of people to do business under a company name. Corporations are granted certain rights and privileges, such as the issuing of stock, the right to buy and sell property, and to enter into contracts, which are conducted in the name of the corporation rather than those of the individual owners, or stockholders, limiting their personal liability. Only about one-fifth of U.S. businesses are corporations, but they account for about 90% of all business income.

controlling interest A term that refers to an individual or organization holding a sufficient quantity of stock in a company to "control" that company's policies.

data processing The conversion of raw information (data) to machine-readable form and the subsequent processing (storing, updating, combining, rearranging, printing out) by a computer.

department store Generally a large retail operation in a single building, with clearly separated areas each offering a different type of merchandise. For example, a store like Sears, which offers a wide variety of products, from menswear to lingerie to hardware and tools, in a single retail location.

depression An economic term used to refer to a phase in the business cycle of an industrial nation during which production and sales are unusually low, and business failures and unemployment are unusually high. Depressions and recessions, which are similar in effect but generally considered not as severe, result from a variety of factors, and many economists believe they are tied to other long-range economic, consumer, and industrial cycles.

economics A general term for the science and study of the production, distribution, exchange, and consumption of goods and services. It is also used to refer to a way of looking at a situation from a monetary or business point of view, and in politics "the economy" is a broad definition of the state of many different aspects of business within a country.

employee An individual who works for another individual or for a company in return for wages or other compensation.

endorsement Used mostly as an advertising or public relations tool, an endorsement is a public statement of approval or support by an individual for a specific product. For example, many sports figures endorse specific brands of athletic footwear in return for compensation from the company that produces the product.

endow To furnish a form of charity or philanthropy by which a wealthy individual or corporation provides property, money, or a source of income to an institution, or by donation causes an institution to be established, generally for the purpose of serving the common or public good. This often results in landmark public works, such as libraries or museums, that are named for their benefactors. An "endowment" refers directly to the amount or nature of the contribution.

entrepreneur A person who organizes and operates a business venture, commonly used to refer to people who seek business opportunities on their own rather than as part of an organization or corporation.

export The shipping of goods from one country for sale or consumption in another. With "import," one of a country's key economic indicators.

factory A building or group of buildings, also called a "plant," where goods are manufactured. The factory became the chief means of producing goods for mass consumption beginning with the Industrial Revolution of the late 1800s.

finance The study and management of financial resources, banking, investments, and credit. The term generally refers to the aspect of a business that deals specifically with money, or capital, apart from the other business of the company, or to a type of company called a "financial institution," such as a bank, that deals primarily with them.

financier Someone who specializes in raising and allocating public moneys; someone who deals with finance and investment on a wide scale.

flagship store The most prominent or visible store in a retail chain. The flagship store may be the chain's original location, or the store nearest its main offices, or its biggest store. Many chains have their flagship stores in the most visible shopping districts of major cities, such as New York, Los Angeles, and Paris.

foundation The founding or establishing of an institution, or an endowed institution created by a wealthy individual or company, most often with the purpose of providing charitable services or public works.

foundry A place where metal is melted or molded. A foundry may produce the metal parts that are used in a factory.

franchise In its most common usage, a "franchise" refers to a business operation, often a retail store, that has been granted the right to use a company's name or to sell its goods and services. For example, many McDonald's restaurants are franchises, owned by individuals or smaller companies, that follow rules and guidelines established by the parent corporation.

free enterprise A broad term that refers to a capitalist or other noncommunist economic system.

Freemasonry The largest and most widely established fraternal order in the world. Freemasonry began in Europe as guilds originally restricted to stonecutters. In the 17th century it began to admit men of wealth, power, or social status, and over the years the guilds became more like societies, or clubs, devoted to general principles and ideals, such as fraternity, equality, religious toleration, and peace. Much of the current structure of Freemasonry was established in England,

Ireland, and Scotland in the early 1700s, and with the patronage of members of the British nobility, the order came to be identified with social success. The Masonic belief that religion is the concern solely of the individual resulted in opposition from the Catholic Church, and Freemasonry is not permitted in some strictly Roman Catholic countries, such as Spain. The first U.S. lodges were established in Boston and Philadelphia in 1733, and American Freemasons now make up about three-fourths of worldwide membership, which exceeds 6 million.

Great Depression The worst and longest economic collapse in modern industrial society, the Great Depression in the United States began in late 1929 and lasted through the early 1940s, spreading to most of the world's other industrial countries. While the general perception is that the Great Depression was "caused" by the stock market crash in October 1929, both were actually the results of other, long-term problems in the modern economy that had been building up over a period of many years. Banks and businesses were closed, and unemployment was severe, rising from 3.2% of the American workforce in 1929 to 24.9% 1933. The nation's economy did not begin to truly recover until well after the United States had entered World War II.

Among the lasting and most profound effects of the Great Depression has been the government's role in providing aid and work to Americans affected by the economic collapse. President Herbert Hoover, a Republican, believed that providing federal relief would undermine the recipient's self-reliance, and he resisted government intervention and assistance throughout his term. In 1932, Franklin Delano Roosevelt, a Democrat, was elected president, and quickly began a series of programs collectively known as the New Deal, which have served as the basis for much of American government domestic policy ever since.

guild An organization of people with the same skills, interests, or profession. It is most often associated with the merchant guilds that were a fixture in Europe and England during the Middle Ages, where they held considerable power over trade. The power of the merchant guilds had declined considerably by the 14th century, in part due to the rise of craft guilds, which were made up of those producing specific items. The craft guilds monopolized the making and selling of those items in the cities in which they were organized, depriving the merchant guilds of their influ-

ence. The guild structure continues in the present day, especially in the areas of manufacture that require considerable human craftsmanship and skill.

Health Maintenance Organization (HMO) A private business enterprise that provides health care to groups or individuals for a set monthly premium. An alternative to traditional "fee-for-service" health insurance, in which the insured pays for service and is reimbursed, or makes a "copayment," a portion of the cost of the care, an HMO agrees to provide all necessary services, both as insurer and provider, for those covered by their plan. Membership in HMOs has grown rapidly in recent years, and by 1990 about 13.5% of the American population received their health care in this manner.

holdings A term used to describe an investor's assets, usually in terms of stocks, bonds, and cash. It may also refer to the same for a company with interests in other companies.

import To bring goods produced or manufactured in one country into another for sale or consumption. A country may import such products as it cannot produce for itself, or to increase competition or choice for consumers, or because certain items produced overseas are superior or preferred to those made domestically.

income tax A type of tax levied by a noncommunist government specifically on the income of an individual or profits of a business. In the United States, income tax usually represents a certain percentage of total earnings after eligible deductions are subtracted, and is levied on a federal level, and in many cases by states and cities as well. Originally prohibited by the Constitution, the taxing of income in this country required the enactment of the 16th Amendment to the Constitution, ratified in 1913.

industry The general term referring, in various usages, to the commercial production and sale of goods, or to a specific type of manufacture and/or trade, as in "the airline industry."

infrastructure The underlying base or structure of a business organization, or other type of system. Infrastructure also refers to the basic facilities and services of a community or society, such as laws, roads, and utilities.

initial public offering (IPO) The first-time offering of stock in a private company for purchase by outside investors. Also called "going public," an IPO is usually handled by an independent firm with some experience in promoting new offerings and determining the fair value of a company, with a set number of shares representing a certain percentage of ownership available at a set price.

inventor The person who conceives of or produces a particular thing first. The term is most often used to refer to those who create objects—for example, Thomas Edison is known as to as the "inventor" of the lightbulb, although the term inventor may also be applied to the creators of new ideas and theories.

journeyman A competent, tested worker in a skilled craft. Journeyman is the second stage in the structured learning process that begins with apprenticeship. Unlike apprentices, journeymen were considered trained workers and were paid a fixed wage for their labor. A form of this process is still used in trades that require high levels of learned skills and human craftsmanship that are best taught directly.

labor A collective term for all workers, and for the trade union movement.

laissez-faire A French term meaning literally "let things alone," a policy of government nonintervention in individual or business financial affairs. The basic principle of laissez-faire is that natural business forces such as free trade, competition, and consumer preferences can serve as effective economic regulators without the need for government interference.

lawyer An attorney or legal representative; a person authorized by another person or organization to represent them, most often in a court of law. In the United States, the training and qualification of lawyers is regulated by individual states, which generally require a certain level of general education, followed by the study of law, and sometimes a clerkship or apprenticeship under an established attorney. Lawyers must pass an examination before being certified to practice law.

liability As opposed to an asset, an obligation, responsibility, or debt of a company or individual.

licensing Licensing is the right conferred by a company to another company or individual to produce products using legally protected material. For example, the Walt Disney Company may license a toy company to produce toys featuring the characters protected by the Disney Company's copyrights, such as Mickey Mouse.

magnate A powerful or influential person, most often used to refer to those in business and industry.

manager The person in charge of running a specific organization and training others to perform their specific jobs. In business, the term may refer in a broader sense to the man-

ager of a company or organization, but is most often used to describe the person who runs a retail establishment.

management The theory and practice of managing. This term is often used in the larger sense, to refer to the principles and strategies, often specific to an individual or school of thought by which a company is run.

manufacturing The process of producing finished goods from raw materials, especially in a large-scale, industrial sense.

market research A form of study involving the use of surveys, tests, statistic studies, and other examinations of data to analyze consumer trends and try to determine the acceptance or impact a particular product or service might receive. The same tools are also used to determine what kinds of products consumers are looking for, or to help spot trends in other areas of interest that might be used to help sell a company's product. Market research is used extensively in producing and targeting advertising campaigns designed to sell products to specific market segments.

marketing The process of selling and promoting a product or service. Specific aspects include advertising, packaging, and a number of other factors that determine how a product is presented to the public. Marketing is considered one of the most important and effective tools in determining the success or failure of consumer products.

merger The joining of two or more smaller companies together to form a single business unit. A merger may be between more or less equal partners in a single field, creating a powerful or dominant organization, or between companies of any size in totally different areas, when one or both may benefit from the resources of the other. Because of strict antitrust regulations, mergers require the approval of the federal government.

mill Another term for a factory.

mine The physical excavation and operation from which ore or minerals are extracted from the earth.

mogul A term used to refer to a rich or powerful person.

monopoly An economic situation in which only a single company sells or produces an item or service, allowing it to control availability and pricing. While advantageous to a business, monopolies do not allow consumers the freedom of choice. When this involves something considered essential, it gives the company holding the monopoly an unfair advantage over the consumer. For this reason, the U.S. government has worked to curb monopolies through "antitrust" laws and regulations.

mortgage A legal contract that uses property, most often a home, as security for a loan. The process allows consumers to make purchases without having to pay the full amount outright by "guaranteeing" the loan with something of value that may be taken if the loan is not paid. The term is most often used to refer to the standard agreement by which individuals purchase their homes.

NAACP An acronym for the National Association for the Advancement of Colored People, an organization founded in 1909 to protect the rights and improve the living and working conditions of black Americans. Over the years, the NAACP has been an effective force in promoting and protecting the civil rights of African Americans, leading the efforts that resulted in the enacting of the Civil Rights Acts of 1957 and 1964, along with other important regulation aimed at overcoming discrimination and abuse in business as well as social affairs.

NASDAQ An acronym for the National Association of Security Dealers Automated Quotation system, a market for trading stocks. The NASDAQ is one of the largest stock markets in the world, with more that 5,500 companies listed, the majority of them smaller and lesser known than those found on older and more established markets such as the New York Stock Exchange. Unlike other exchanges, the NASDAQ has no central location where stock trading takes place, and its business is done for the most part over the telephone or the Internet. In recent years, thanks in part to its many listings of technology firms such as Microsoft, the NASDAQ Composite has gained acceptance as an economic indicator on much the same level as the Dow Jones Industrial Average.

New Deal The collective name given to a large-scale program of domestic government policies enacted under President Franklin D. Roosevelt, especially those intended to counteract the effects of the Great Depression between 1933 and 1938. Programs ranged from the creation of new organizations such as the Federal Deposit Insurance Corporation (FDIC) to regulate banking and provide protection for depositors, to government subsidies and public relief efforts such as the Work Projects Administration, which put unemployed people to work on public projects. A controversial and hugely influential program, the New Deal continues to have considerable effect on domestic government policy.

New York Stock Exchange (NYSE) One of the largest centralized markets for trading stocks and bonds, listing more than 2,900 companies. Trading is done by stockbrokers who buy and sell stock on behalf of investors or institutions, who work with certain members of the exchange called specialists, who focus on trading specific stocks, to negotiate a price. Located on Wall Street in New York City, the NYSE is recognized as one of the most important financial centers in the world.

numismatics The study or collection of money, most commonly used to refer to coin collecting.

panic A sudden widespread scare concerning financial affairs that results in a depression of values that is caused by extreme measures to protect property (such as securities).

parent corporation A form of corporation that includes within its activities and holdings other companies or corporations. A parent corporation allows for a single, relatively small organization to oversee a group of diverse businesses, providing overall direction and corporate philosophy.

partnership In legal terms, a formal arrangement between two or more individuals involved together in a business venture. In a partnership, as opposed to a corporation, the parties involved agree to invest their own labor and property in the company, and are personally liable for losses and partake directly of profits, in terms that must be clearly specified in the partnership agreement.

patent The legal grant, made by a government, that gives an inventor the exclusive right to benefit from his or her invention for a specified number of years. A patent may be granted for specific machines, manufactured items, industrial processes or designs, or for significant improvements on previously invented items. In the United States, patents last for twenty years, and are administered by the U.S. Patent and Trademark Office, an agency of the Department of Commerce.

philanthropy In business, a term used to describe the ongoing practice or philosophy, usually of an individual, of giving to or establishing charitable or humanistic causes or foundations. Many wealthy persons who express a desire to "give something back" to their communities or to the general public support or create such public-serving organizations as charities, scholarships, libraries, and museums, either during the course of their lifetimes, or in the form of bequests made in wills and estates.

plant Another term for a manufacturing facility, or factory.

poverty An economic condition in which people lack the income to obtain the minimal levels of such essentials as food, clothing, medical services, and housing necessary to maintain an adequate standard of living. In a strict sense, the "poverty line" is defined as those households earning a certain percentage below the average family income. In the United States, the group that currently makes up the largest portion of the population living in poverty are single mothers, who account for roughly one-third of all poor people in this country.

profit The amount of money, after all expenses are deducted, gained on an investment, business undertaking, or sale.

recession A period of decline in the economic cycle of an industrialized country, often indicated by increased unemployment and reduced investment in new business activity and production. Similar to a depression, but generally used to refer to a period where the characteristic symptoms shared by both are not as severe.

refinery Most often used to refer to a factory or plant at which a crude substance, such as oil or sugar, is purified.

retail Retailing is the business of selling goods and services directly to consumers. Most often used to describe storefront businesses, a retail operation most often offers individual products that may be purchased or ordered on the spot. There are a number of different sorts of retailers, including specialty stores, which offer a variety of products usually defined by a single category, such as shoes or women's clothing; department stores, which offer a wide variety of product lines and an extensive selection within each line; discount stores, such as Wal-Mart and Kmart, which sell an assortment of products at low prices; and chain stores, which are a group of separate locations that carry much the same merchandise and are operated under a single set of policies. Retail operations also include supermarkets, catalog and direct sales, Internet and phone solicitation, and vending machines.

robber baron A colorful and mostly derogatory term applied to certain business people who capitalize on the misfortunes of others or exploit an unfairly advantageous position to make their money. The term is derived from a group of rebellious noblemen eventually subdued by Louis VI in the 12th century. In the United States, a capitalist of the late 19th century who became wealthy through exploitation of, for example, natural resources, government influence, or low wage scales.

Rotary Club A local organization, part of the larger Rotary International, dedicated to high vocational standards, community service, and international understanding. A Rotary club is comprised of one representative of each business and profession in a community. Established in the United States in 1905, Rotary is the oldest service club organization in the world, and Rotary International includes more than a million men and women in nearly 27,000 Rotary clubs in 149 countries.

Securities and Exchange Commission (SEC) Created by the U.S. government in the Security Exchange Act of 1934, the SEC regulates stock exchanges and requires publicly traded companies to disclose information that allows potential investors to better evaluate their stock. The SEC was created in response to the stock market crash of 1929. Prior to that time, there were no strict rules governing the trading of stock, allowing for unfair practices and cheating of investors that were factors in the crash. The new regulations played a great part in restoring investors' faith in the stock market after the end of World War II.

share As in a share of stock: one unit of ownership in a company or corporation. Shares entitle their holders to a "share" in the profits of a company, which may be paid out at specified intervals in the form of dividends, as well as a portion of the proceeds if a company is sold. The number of shares in any particular company varies, and the worth of one share is determined by dividing the total value of a company by the number of shares.

shareholder One who owns shares of stock in a company or corporation. A shareholder "shares" in the profits of a company, and is allowed a voice, proportionate to the amount of stock they own, in selecting the Board of Directors, the officers of the company, and determining company policies.

Sherman Antitrust Act A government act regulating the operations of corporations, passed by the U.S. Congress in 1890. It declared illegal attempts to restrain trade, such as monopoly, and specified criminal penalties. It has been amended and supplemented by several subsequent acts. It is named for Senator John Sherman of Ohio, whose efforts were instrumental in its enactment.

smelting The process of melting or fusing metal ores to separate the basic metal constituents.

speculator One who buys and sells such financial items as stocks, commodities, or land in the hope of sudden increases in their value. Speculation, which is often based on research, individual intuition or "hunches," or experience in or knowledge of a particular industry or commodity, involves a certain degree of risk and has the potential for considerable profit or loss.

sponsor In advertising terms, a sponsor refers to a company or person who pays for radio or television time in return for the opportunity to promote its product. This may take the form of including a sponsor's name in the title of a show, or, more commonly, in the form of "commercials," small informative or entertaining productions intended to attract the interest of the viewing or listening public. Sporting events such as golf tournaments may also be sponsored, as are certain sports arenas and public institutions, such as museums.

stock Shares of ownership in a company or corporation. One share of stock is equal to the total value of the company, divided by the number of shares of stock the company has issued.

stock futures A contract similar to a stock option, in which a buyer and seller agree to sales or purchases of stocks or commodities on specific dates and at specific prices. Unlike an option, which may or may not be exercised, a futures contract must be fulfilled. The contracts themselves, once established, are then traded on the stock and commodities exchanges.

stock options Contracts that offer an investor the right to buy or sell a certain number of shares of a certain stock at fixed prices and over fixed time periods. A "call" option is the right to buy shares at a specific price within a specific time span; a "put" option is the right to sell under fixed terms. An investor may or may not exercise the "option" to buy or sell, and profit or loss on any transaction is determined by the movements of the market. Essentially, options are a speculative form of investing, in which an investor bets on the direction a stock is heading and pays for the right to make future purchases or sales based on their guess.

stock market Also called a stock exchange, an organized, regulated market for buying and selling stocks, stock options, and futures. Most have a specific location where the activity takes place, but stocks are also traded "over the counter," without a specific central trading location. Among the best known and most influential stock markets are the New York Stock Exchange, on Wall Street in New York City, the NASDAQ, the Tokyo Stock Exchange, and the London Stock Exchange.

stock split The process by which a single share of stock is "split" into two or more shares with a total value equal to the original share.

supply and demand An economic term referring to the two basic factors that determine the price of goods or services. The theory of supply and demand states that when the supply, or amount available for sale, exceeds the demand, or amount purchasers are willing to buy, sellers must lower prices to drive sales, and when the demand exceeds the supply, buyers may bid up prices as they compete to buy goods.

strike An organized work stoppage carried out by a group of employees, usually as a tactic to enforce demands or protest unfair labor conditions. Strikes are most frequently conducted by workers organized into trade unions, and are often used as a bargaining tool during contract negotiations. A strike made primarily for symbolic purposes may have a set duration, but most often strikes are continued until an agreement is reached between labor and management representatives. A strike carried out for the purpose of obtaining better relations for employees is considered an economic strike, and an employer may then seek to hire replacements for the striking workers, and is not obligated to rehire those who have been replaced. In a strike called because of alleged unfair labor practices, the employer loses the right of replacement and is obligated to rehire any workers who were discharged or replaced during the strike. One of the most feared and effective tools available to organized labor, strikes have been instrumental in changing the course of labor relations in this country.

tariff A tax levied by the government on imported or exported goods. Although primarily a source of government revenue, a tariff system may also be a part of economic policy, helping to protect domestically produced goods from less expensive imports.

trust A legal document or title to property being held by one individual or corporation for another. Also refers to the actual property being held. Trusts, or trust funds, are often held for minors.

tycoon A term used to refer to a wealthy and powerful businessperson, a magnate.

union Also called a craft or trade union, an organization or association of workers established to improve or protect their working conditions. A union represents its members in negotiations with management regarding wages, working conditions, and benefits through the process known as collective bargaining. Unions may also be politically active, with representatives in government centers who work toward the passage of laws that will benefit union members. Most unions in the United States are affiliated with the American Federation of Labor and the Congress of Industrial Organizations (the AFL-CIO).

Unions were first established in the United States and Western Europe in response to the rise of industrialization in the late 18th century. At that time, great numbers of people left rural areas to compete for a relatively few factory jobs in urban centers. This made workers increasing dependent on their employers. The first unions were formed among skilled craftsmen and artisans, and they encountered great opposition from employers and government and were considered illegal and in restraint of trade. During the 19th century, court decisions and favorable legislation removed legal barriers, but the first unions were unable to survive the economic instabilities of the first half of the 19th century. It was not until the 20th century that unionization spread to semiskilled and unskilled workers, and became the economic and industrial force that it is today.

venture capitalist An individual or institution that provides money or capital for new or unproved business ventures. Because venture capitalists face higher risk, they demand a higher return on their investment, and often insist on owning a share of the business, to better oversee how their money is spent. Venture capitalists are often specialists, who expect some of their investments to do well and some to do poorly, and their success depends on picking more successful investments than unsuccessful ones.

Wall Street Located in the lower Manhattan area of New York City, the site of many major United States stock exchanges and financial interests, including the New York Stock Exchange. The term "Wall Street" has become the generic term for the U.S. financial markets, especially the stock market.

war bonds Bonds issued by the federal government for the purpose of financing the expenses of a war.

wholesale The sale of goods in large quantities, generally from a supplier to a retailer, at a lower price than the retailer will charge the public. The difference in price, less the retailer's operational expenses, represents the profit on the sale.

Index

A

A. G. Spalding & Brothers, 221-22
A. Hammer Cooperage Company, 89
A. Letcher and Company, 129
Abolition movement, 68
Abraham, Joe, 82
Accessory Transit Company, 257
advertising, 83, 252, 284, 294-95
Aerosmith, 64
affirmative action, 164
African-American tycoons and entrepreneurs, 12-13, 26-27, 33-34, 55-58, 68-69, 71-74, 76-77, 134-35, 163-66, 171-72, 187-90, 192, 219-20, 223-24, 242-43, 261-64, 280-82
After Hours, 64
Agnelli, Giovanni, 107
Ah Quin, 1-2
Airport, 233
Alabama, 120
Alaska, 1, 23, 157-58, 270
Alcoa Aluminum, 178
Alexander, Maria A., 68
Alexander and Baldwin, 228, 273
Alfred Hitchcock Presents, 234
Allegheny Conference, 107
Allen, Paul, 59-61
Allied American Corporation, 88
Altair computer, 60-61, 132, 291
Altemus, Mary Elizabeth, 275
Altgeld, John Peter, 205
aluminum, 175-76, 178
A.M. Chicago, 281
Amalgamated (Anaconda) Copper Company, 216
Amblin', 226
American Atlantic & Pacific Ship Canal Company, 257
American Bible Union, 28
American Brass Company, 216
American District Telegraph, 148
American Express Company, 18, 20
American Factors, 272-73
American Federation of Musicians, 231-32

American Messenger Company, 24
American Pacific Group, 273
American Railway Union, 205
American Repeating Rifle Company, 279
American Smelting and Refining Company, 78
American Thermos, 249
America's Cup, 252
Amsterdam News (New York newspaper), 243
Anaconda Copper Mining Company, 101, 216-17
Andrew W. Mellon Foundation, 180
Andrews, Samuel, 212
Angelou, Maya, 281
animal husbandry, 144
Ann J. Kellogg School, 144
Annie E. Casey Foundation, 25
Annie Malone Children and Family Service Center, 166
Annie Malone Crisis Center, 166
anti-Semitism, 51
antitrust laws, 94
antiques. *See* art and antiques
Antuñano, Estevan de, 2-3
Antwerp, Edwin Van, 292
Anza, Juan Bautista de, 15
Apollo Theater, 243
Apple Computer, Inc., 61, 132-33, 291
appliances, 174-76
arbitrage, 54
architecture and buildings, 5, 44, 56, 67, 86, 102, 104, 108, 204-5, 206, 258, 263, 285, 289, 295
Arden, Elizabeth, 262
Argentina, 173
Arizona Biltmore, 296
Arizona Territory, 69-70
Arkansas, 68-69, 119-20, 134, 265-66
Arkansas City, Arkansas, 134
Arkwright, Sir Richard, 3-5
Arlington, Virginia, 170
Arlington Dock Company, 271
Arlington Heights, Illinois, 150
Armand Hammer Museum, 91-92

Armand Hammer United World College, 92
Armour, J. Ogden, 6
Armour, Philip Danforth, 5-6
Armour Institute, 6
art and antiques, 48, 52-53, 60, 65, 66-67, 89, 90, 92, 102, 104, 125, 180, 182, 183, 214, 258, 276. *See also* museums
Asheville, North Carolina, 258
assembly-line production, 51, 151
Associated Industries of Seattle, 271
Associated Jewish Charities, 273
Association, the, 63
Astor, John Jacob, 7-8
Astor Library, 7-8
Astoria, Oregon, 7
Asylum Records, 63
Atari computer, 132
Atchison, Topeka and Santa Fe Railroad, 210
Atlanta, Georgia, 282-87
Atlanta Braves, 253
Atlanta Hawks, 253
Atlanta Ice and Coal Company, 283
Atlanta University, 189
Atlantic City, New Jersey, 245, 247
Atlantic White Lend, 28
Augsburg, Bavaria, 53, 55
Australia, 183-86, 262
Australian, 184
automobiles, 49-51, 139, 192, 241
aviation, 10-11, 117-19

B

Bahamas, The, 118
Baker, Melinda Harriet, 20
Baker Hughes Incorporated, 119
baking powder, 294
Ball, George Willard, 38
Baltimore, Maryland, 193-94, 271, 273-74, 278, 281
Baltimore Brick Company, 272
Baltimore Is Talking, 281-82

Balzac, Honoré de, 214
Banco Mercantil, 191
Bank of America, 138
Bank of England, 215
Bank of Mauá, 173
bankers and banking, 9, 12, 27, 28, 99, 129, 158, 173, 178-83, 187, 191, 213-16, 246-47, 296
Banks, Nathaniel P., 257
Barnes, Ross, 221
Barrett Food Products Company, 159
baseball, 155-56, 221-22, 253, 295-96
basketball, 253
Battle Creek, Michigan, 140-44
Battle Creek Sanitarium, 141
Battle Creek Toasted Corn Flake Company, 142
B.C.I. Marketing, Inc., 77
beauty schools, 165, 262-63
Bechtel and Kaiser, 138
Bell Products, 160
Belleville, Canada, 36
Bellows, Eleanor, 202
Belmont, August, 9
Ben Franklin Stores, 265
Bentonville, Arkansas, 266
Bergman, A. H., 174
Bergman, W. C., 174
Berkshire Hathaway Inc., 17-19
Bernardsville, New Jersey, 47
Berne, New York, 19
berry farming, 145-47
Bethune, Mary McLeod, 166
Betterment Foundation, 142
beverage distributors, 164, 282-87
Beverly Hills, California, 232
Big Boy restaurants, 170
billboards, 252, 284
Billings, Dr. John, 116
bills of exchange, 54
Biltmore, 258
bird sanctuaries, 143
Black Enterprise, 77
Black Swan label, 190
Blackfoot Indians, 162
Blake, Dorothy, 36
Blake, Joseph, 36
"block booking," 231
blue jeans, 239
Boeing, William E., 10-11
Boeing Air Transport, 10
Boeing Airplane Company, 11
Bolinas, California, 15
Bolivian tycoons and entrepreneurs, 191

Bolton, England, 4
Boltwood, Nathaniel, 140
Boltwood, Sarah, 140
Bomarc missiles, 11
Bonaparte, Napoleon, 214, 215, 235
Bonneville Dam, 138
Boston, Massachusetts, 278
Boulder Dam (Hoover Dam), 137-38
Boulevard Bridge Bank, 296
box office percentage, 232
Boy Scouts of America, 77, 144
boycotts, 57, 86, 205
Boyd, Henry Allen, 12-13
Boyd, Richard Henry, 12
Boyer International Laboratories, 56
Boyer National Laboratories, 56
Boysen, Rudolph, 146
Brannan, Samuel, 13-15
Brazil, 166-67, 172-73
Brazilian tycoons and entrepreneurs, 166-67, 172-73
Breakthrough Software, 291
Breedlove, Minerva, 261
Breedlove, Owen, 261
Bridgeport, Connecticut, 279, 292
Brigham Young University, 170
Briones, Juana, 15-16
Briones, Marcos, 15
Briones, Pablo, 15
Bristow, Texas, 82
British Columbia, 68, 270
British Empire, 207-10, 216
British South Africa Company, 209
British tycoons and entrepreneurs, 3-5
Broadwater, Charles Arthus, 100
Broadway shows, 64
Brocton, New York, 204
Brokenburr, Robert L., 263
Bronx, New York, 88
Brooklyn, New York, 46, 62-63, 76
Brooklyn College, 63
Brooklyn Law School, 242
Brooks, Catherine, 298
Brown, William T., 221
Brown University, 251-52
Browne, Jackson, 63
Browning, John M., 279
Bruce, Ailsa Mellon, 180
Bryant, T. G., 175
Budenz, Louis, 122
Buena Park, California, 145-46
Buffalo, New York, 114

Buffett, Howard Homan, 17
Buffett, Lila (Stahl), 17
Buffett, Warren Edward, 17-19, 47
Buffett Partnership, 18
buildings. *See* architecture and buildings; libraries; museums
Bureau of Reclamation, 137-38
Burlington Railroad, 210
Bush, President George, 91, 199, 266
businessmen, 1-2, 12-15, 17, 23-26, 53-55, 105-8, 157-58, 163-64, 187-88, 193-94. *See also specific businesses*
businesswomen, 171-72
Butte, Anaconda and Pacific Railroad, 217
Butterfield, John, 19-20
Butterfield, Wasson and Company, 20
Byron, Illinois, 221

C

C. A. Pillsbury & Company, 201
C. Brewer and Company, 273
C. R. Patterson & Sons, 192
Cable News Network (CNN), 251, 253-54
California, 1-2, 24, 37, 67, 70, 102, 104, 131, 138, 139-40, 222. *See also* Los Angeles; San Francisco
computers in, 289-91
farming in, 145-47
fast food in, 151-56
filmmaking in, 225-29, 232-34
gold rush in, 13-15, 124, 239-40, 257
ranching in, 15-16
real estate in, 30-31, 100-101, 125-27, 295-96
California Southern Railroad, 1-2
California Star, 14
California State College, 226
California State Polytechnic College, 144
California Sugar Refinery, 228
Callahan, T. M., 195
cambiro arbitrio, 54
Camel cigarettes, 249
Canada, 7, 36, 68, 262, 270
Canada Southern Railway, 259
Candelaria, Nevada, 23
Candler, Asa G., 282

Candler family, 283
candy, 109-12
Canton, China, 1
Capital Cities/ABC Inc., 19
Capital Frito Company, 160
Capote, Truman, 107
Capshaw, Kate, 227
Carnegie, Andrew, 21-23, 52
Carnegie Company, 22
Carnegie Corporation of New
    York, 22
Carnegie Museum of Art, 108
carriages, 192, 240-41
carrier pigeons, 215
Carter, President Jimmy, 234,
    285
Case School of Applied Science,
    36, 38
Casey, Annie E., 23
Casey, Henry J., 23
Casey, James E., 23-26
Casey Family Program, 25-26
Catalina Island, 295-96
catalogues, mail order, 197, 268
Cats, 64
cattle operations, 99
CBS, 63
Central Pacific Railroad, 75, 94,
    124-25, 229
cereals, 140-44
Chamberlain, Joseph, 209
Chandler, Charles, 219-20
Chapin, Gardner, 140
Chapin, Thankful, 140
Charles V, Holy Roman emperor,
    54-55
Charleston, South Carolina, 228,
    292
Charlotte, North Carolina, 158
Charlton, Earl P., 288-89
Chatham, New Jersey, 267
Chattanooga, Tennessee, 251
Cheechakos, The, 158
chemicals, 36-40
Cher, 64
Cheshire, England, 270
chewing gum, 293-96
Chicago, Burlington, and Quincy
    Railroad, 94
Chicago, Illinois, 56, 148, 155,
    177, 221-22, 230-32, 281-82,
    294-96
  candy making in, 109
  publishing in, 134-35, 187-88
  Pullman strike in, 204-6
  retailing in, 43-44, 197, 267-69
  stockyards in, 5-6

Chicago, Milwaukee, St. Paul and
    Pacific Railroad, 217
Chicago, Milwaukee and St. Paul
    Railroad, 210
Chicago Bee, 187-88
Chicago Cubs, 295-96
Chicago Law School, 190
Chicago Sun-Times, 185
child care, 143
Children's Memorial Hospital, 155
Chinese American tycoons and
    entrepreneurs, 1-2
Chisholm Steel Shovel Works, 36
chocolate, 109-12
Chopin, Frédéric, 214
Chorley, England, 4
Chouteau, Auguste, Jr., 162
Chouteau, Pierre, 162
Christian Herald Association, 196
Church, Robert Reed, 26-27
Church, Robert Reed, Jr., 27
Church of Jesus Christ of
    Latter-Day Saints, 13-14,
    167-68
Church of St. Ann (Augsburg), 55
Churchill, Winston, 86, 107
Cincinnati, Ohio, 225, 251
Citizen Kane, 104
Citizens Savings Bank and Trust
    Company, 12
City College of New York, 163
Citywide YMCA of St. Louis, 166
civil rights, 12-13, 27, 219-20,
    224, 242-43, 263, 286-87
Civil War, 9, 21, 39-40, 45, 181,
    257, 258
Clark, Lulu, 248
Clark, Colonel Maurice, 211-12
Clark, William, 162
Clark, William Andrews, 100, 216
Class Act, 34
Cleveland, President Grover, 100,
    101, 182, 205, 275
Cleveland, Ohio, 211, 283
Clinton, President Bill, 65,
    199-200
Close Encounters of the Third Kind,
    226
clothing, 81-84, 237-38, 238-40,
    278
Coachella, California, 145
coal, 113
Cobb, Elizabeth J., 269
Coca-Cola Bottling Company of
    Wilmington, Inc., 164
Coca-Cola Company, 19, 282-87
Codex Leicester, 60

Cody, Buffalo Bill, 285
Cody, Wyoming, 285
Cohen, Rosa, 230
Cohn, Roy, 272
Coke, Thomas, Earl of Leicester,
    60
Cold War, 285
Coleman, Thelma Louise, 71
Colgate & Co., 28
Colgate, James Boorman, 28
Colgate, Robert, 27, 28
Colgate, Samuel, 28
Colgate, William, 27-28
Colgate University, 28
Collins Line, 257
colonialism, 208
Color Purple, The, 226, 282
Colorado, 195, 216-17, 237, 261
Colored American Magazine, 189
"colorization," 254
Colt, Samuel, 29-30
Colter, John, 161
Colton, Hugh, 168
Columbia University, 18, 88, 114,
    116
Columbus County, North
    Carolina, 223
Comanche Indians, 29
Comibol, 191
Commodore computers, 61
Commodores, the, 33
Common Carrier, 25
communications, 19-20. *See also*
    newspapers; radio;
    telecommunications; television
communism, 87-89, 122-23, 224,
    285
Community Chest, 107
Computer Center Corporation, 59
computers, 59-62, 114-16, 131-33,
    198-200, 289-91
Computing-Tabulating-Recording
    (C-T-R) Company, 116
Comstock, Henry T. P., 100-101
Comstock Lode, 100
Congo, 209
Connecticut, 25, 29-30, 181,
    278-79, 292, 297-98
Connelly, Marc, 86
Consolidated Gold Fields, 208,
    209
construction contractors, 137-40
continuous production technology,
    159
Convers, Albert E., 36
Cooke, Jay, 181
Coolidge, President Calvin, 179

copper, 78, 216-17
Corbis, 60
Cordova, Alaska, 157-58
Cosby, Bill, 164, 281
cosmetics, 165-66
Cosmopolitan, 104
Coulee Dam, 138
Council of National Defense, 37
Courier Newspaper Group, 56
Covington, George, 242
Covington, Georgia, 189
Cow Tom, 219
cowboy hats, 237-38
Crawford, Joan, 226
credit plan, 196
Creek Indians, 219
Creighton, Jennie, 288
Crisis, 189
Cromford, England, 4
Cruise, Tom, 64
Cuba, 103
Culver, Henry, 30-31
Culver City, California, 30-31
Culver Investment Company, 30
Cunard Line, 257
Curvignake, Winya, 279
customer satisfaction guarantee, 268

D

Daily Worker, 122
Dairy Queen, 150
Dakota Territory, 114
Dallas, Texas, 82-83, 123
Dallas Pant Manufacturing Company, 82-83
Dallas Transit Company, 272
Daly, Marcus, 100, 216-17
Daly Bank and Trust Company, 216
Daniel Guggenheim Fund, 79
Dart Industries, 250
Dartmouth College, 155
data processing, 114-16, 198-200
David Geffen Foundation, 65
Davies, John M., 278
Davies, Marion, 104
Davis, A. J., 99
Davis, Bette, 232
Davis, Jacob, 238
De Anza College, 290
De Beers Consolidated Mines, 208
de Passe, Suzanne, 33-34
de Passe Entertainment, 34

Dearborn Independent, 51
Death of a Salesman, 86
Debs, Eugene V., 205
Decca Records, 233
Deer Hunter, The, 233
Deere, John, 35
DeLand Academy, 238
Delaware, 39-40
Delaware County, New York, 27
Delta, Louisiana, 261
Democratic Party, 9, 65, 70, 100, 190, 285
Denver, Colorado, 195, 216-17, 261
Denver Pacific, 75
Derry, Pennsylvania, 109
Des Moines, Iowa, 264
Des Plaines, Illinois, 152, 153
Desilu Productions, 31
Detroit, Michigan, 10, 49-51, 71-74
Detroit Automobile Company, 50
DHS cattle operation, 99
diamonds, 208
Diana, 33
Diehl, Joan, 105
Dilday, Elizabeth Ann, 86
Dillingham Corporation, 273
Dinkins, David, 243
diplomats, 180, 277
discount stores, 288-89. *See also* retailers
Disney, Walt, 86
Disneyland, 147
Disraeli, Benjamin, 216
Dole, Robert Joseph, 49
Doolin, Elmer, 160
door-to-door sales, 56
Dorchester, Massachusetts, 210
Dougherty, Margaret Virginia, 145
Douglass, Frederick, 68
Douglass National Bank, 187-88
Dow, Grace Anna, 38
Dow, Henry, 36
Dow, Herbert Henry, 36-38
Dow, Joane (Nudd), 36
Dow, Joseph Henry, 36
Dow, Sarah Jane (Bunnell), 36
Dow Chemical Company, 36-37
Dow Process Company, 36-37
Doyle, Bernard, 248, 250
Dozier, Lamont, 73
Drake, Francis, 13
"drawbacks," 212
Dreamgirls, 64
Dreamworks SKG, 65, 227
Drew, Daniel, 75, 256-57, 259

Drips, Andrew, 162
Du Bois, W. E. B., 189
du Pont, Henry Algernon, 40
du Pont, Samuel Francis, 39-40
du Pont de Nemours, Eleuthère Irénée, 39
du Pont family, 39-40
Duchin, Eddie, 232
Dudley, Nancy, 84
Duel, 226
Dunfermline, Scotland, 21
Durham, North Carolina, 223-24
Durham Committee on Negro Affairs, 224

E

E. I. du Pont de Nemours & Co., 39, 248-49
Eagles, the, 63
Earl G. Graves Associates, 76
Earl G. Graves Publishing Company, Inc., 77
Earl S. Tupper Company, 248-49
East Texas Field, 120-21
Eastman, George, 41-42
Eastman Kodak Company, 41-42
Eastman School of Music, 42
"easy to prepare" foods, 202-3
Ebony, 57, 135
Ed Sullivan Show, The, 234
Edison Illuminating Company, 50
education, 110-12, 144
EGG Dallas Broadcasting, Inc., 77
Egtvedt, Claire, 10
Eisenhower, President Dwight D., 86, 107, 123, 170, 277, 285
El Dorado, Arkansas, 120
electric-power generation, 126
Electronic Data Systems (EDS), 198
Elektra/Asylum Records, 63
Elgin, Illinois, 174
Elgin, Texas, 81
Elk Grove Village, Illinois, 153
Ellsworth, Maine, 274
Ely & Walker, 82
"embalmed-beef" scandal, 6
Emerson, Ralph Waldo, 168
Emory University, 282-83, 286, 287
Empire of the Sun, 226
endorsements, 83
England, 3, 4-5, 27, 36, 67, 193, 215, 270, 293. *See also* British Empire

Englewood, New Jersey, 46
entertainment executives, 33-34,
    62-65, 71, 230
entrepreneurs, 68-69
Epstein, Edward Jay, 92
Equitable Life Assurance Society,
    94
Erie Canal, 20
Erie Railroad, 45, 75, 259, 296
Erving, Julius, 164
Escondido, California, 15
E.T.: The Extra-Terrestrial, 226-27,
    233
Eton, Grace, 73
Eureka, Utah, 195
Evanston, Wyoming, 195
Ewing, Jane, 107

F

F. W. Woolworth Company, 289
Fact Forum, 122
Fairbanks News-Miner, 158
Fairchild Semiconductor, 289
Fairfield Inns, 170
Faitoute, William, 292
Falmouth, Kentucky, 99
farm equipment, 35, 174-75,
    177-78
farmers, 145-47
fast food, 148-56, 170
Fayette County, Illinois, 119
Fedco Food Stores, 163-64
Federal Home Loan Mortgage
    Corporation (Freddie Mac), 19
Federal Securities Act, 57
ferries, 45, 255-57
Field, Ben, 204
Field, Marshall, 6, 43-44
Field, Palmer & Leiter, 267-69
Field Museum of Natural History,
    44, 296
Fifth Avenue Coach Lines, 272
films and filmmaking, 33-34, 64,
    73, 104, 117-19, 158, 183-86,
    225-27, 232-34, 276, 282
financial panics, 75, 182, 205, 215,
    259, 269. *See also* Great
    Depression
financiers, 53-55, 93-94, 181-83,
    193, 207-10, 213-16, 272-73.
    See also bankers and banking
firearms, 29-30, 278-80
Firestone Tire and Rubber, 233
First Bank of Cordova, 158

First National Bank, 296
First Vigilance Committee, 14
Fisk, James, 45-46, 75, 259
Fisk University, 13
Flagler, Henry, 212
Fleming, Ethel, 149-50, 153
Fletcher, Chaplain, 13
Florida, 149, 196
flour mills, 201-3
Fonda, Jane, 254
Fontana, California, 139
Food and Drug Administration,
    285
food industry, 105-8, 140-44,
    158-61, 201-3, 228
Foote, Ada E., 296
Foote, Dorothy, 296
Forbes, Adelaide (Stevenson), 46
Forbes, Bertie Charles, 46
Forbes, Bruce, 47
Forbes, Gordon, 48
Forbes, Malcolm "Steve," Jr.,
    48-49
Forbes, Malcolm Stevenson, 46-49
Forbes, Wallace, 48
"Forbes Four Hundred," 47, 48
Forbes Inc., 47-48
Forbes magazine, 46-48, 189, 266
Ford, Edsel, 51
Ford, President Gerald R., 123
Ford, Henry, 49-51, 178
Ford, Henry, II, 51, 106
Ford Foundation, 51
Ford Motor Company, 50-51, 71
Fort Lauderdale, Florida, 149
Fort Raymond, 161
Fortune Magazine, 139-40
foundations, 25, 51, 62, 65, 83, 98,
    111-12, 140, 142, 143-44, 155,
    180, 196, 273-74, 276
Fox Broadcasting Company, 185
Fragonard, Jean-Honoré, 53
franchises, 151-53, 265
Franco-Prussian War, 214
Frank Waterhouse & Company,
    270
Fred Harvey Houses, 95
Fred Harvey Indian Department,
    95
Freeport Sulphur, 275
French, Abigail, 36
French, Daniel Chester, 6
French, Joseph, 36
Frick, Henry Clay, 52-53
Frito-Lay Company, 160
Fritos, 159-60
Fugger, Jakob, I, 53

Fugger, Jakob, II, 53-55
Fugger, Johannes, 53
Fuller, Alfred C., 55
Fuller, Lestine, 56
Fuller, S. B., 55-58
Fuller Brush Company, 55
Fuller Products Company, 55-58
Fulton, Robert, 256
Fundação Roberto Marinho, 167
fur traders, 7-8, 161-62
Furman University, 159

G

G. P. Putnam's Sons, 233
Gabriel, Peter, 64
al-Gadhafi, Mu'ammar, 91
Galacia, Austria, 271
Garden State Cablevision, Inc.,
    164
Gardner, Ava, 118
Gates, William H. (Bill), 47,
    59-62
Gates Library Foundation, 62
gay rights, 65
Gaye, Marvin, 73
Geffen, Abraham, 62-63
Geffen, Betya (Volovskaya), 62-63
Geffen, David, 62-65, 227
Geffen Film Company, 64
Geffen Records, 64
Geffen-Roberts, 63
General Electric Theater, 233-34
General Foods Corporation, 19
General Motors, 198
General Outdoor Advertising
    Company, 252
George F. Getty, Inc., 66
George III, King of England, 4-5
George Peabody College of
    Education, 194
Georgia, 189, 251, 282-87
Germany, 9
Getty, George Franklin, 66
Getty, James, 66
Getty, Jean Paul, 66-67
Getty, John, 66
Getty, Margaret (Cross), 66
Getty, Martha (Wiley), 66
Getty, Nelly, 66
Getty, Sarah Catherine
    McPherson (Risher), 66
Getty Arts Center, 67
Gettystown, Ireland, 66
Ghana, 220

Giannini, Amadeo Peter, 138, 140
Gibbons, Thomas, 256
Gibbs, Mifflin Wister, 68-69
Gila City, Arizona, 70
Gilbert, Mary, 28
Gillette Co., 18-19
Globe Grain & Milling Company, 202
Globo Group, 167
gold panic, 45, 75
gold reserves, 182
gold rush
    in Alaska, 23, 157-58, 270
    in Black Hills, 100-101
    in British Columbia, 68
    in California, 13-14, 30, 100, 124, 239, 240, 257
    in Colorado, 237
    in Montana, 99
    in South Africa, 208
Goldwater, Baron, 70
Goldwater, Barry, 69-71
Goldwater, Joseph, 69-70
Goldwater, Michel, 69-70
Goldwater, Morris, 70
Gone with the Wind, 276
Good Housekeeping, 104
Goodheart, William R., 231
Gookin, R. Burt, 108
Gordy, Berry, Jr., 33, 71-74
Gordy Industries, 73-74
Gould, Jay, 45, 74-76, 259
Graceland Cemetery (Chicago), 6, 206
Graham, Benjamin, 18
Graham-Newman Corporation, 18
Grand Canyon National Park, 95
Grand Central Terminal, 259
Grant, Cary, 235
Grant, President Ulysses S., 45
Graves, Earl Gilbert, Jr., 76-77
Great Depression, 27, 56, 86, 104, 105, 121, 146, 148, 159, 180, 187, 223, 271-72, 284
Great Northern Railroad, 113-14
Green, Jane Dobbins, 154
Green Cove Springs, Florida, 196
"green-mark," 272
Green Pastures, 86
Greenfield, Ohio, 192
Greenville, South Carolina, 159
Greenwich, Connecticut, 25
greeting cards, 84-87
Gregg, Clara, 187
Griffith, Corinne, 203
Grimes County, Texas, 12
Guadalupe College, 12

Guggenheim, Daniel, 78-79
Guggenheim, Meyer, 78
Guggenheim Corporation, 157
guilds, 53
Gulf Oil, 178
gunpowder, 39
Guns N' Roses, 64
Gutman, Jeanette, 271
"Gyrafoam" washer, 175-76

H

H. and C. Studebaker, 240
H. J. Heinz Company, 105-8
H. W. Lay Company, Inc., 159
H. W. Lay Distributing Company, 159
Habsburg family, 54-55
Haggar, Joseph Marion, 81-84
Haggar Company, 83-84
Hague, The, 23
Haines, Daniel, 293
hair care, 165, 261-64
Hajjar, Khalil, 81
Hale, John M., 195
Hall, Donald, 86
Hall, George Nelson, 84
Hall, Joyce Clyde, 84-87
Hall, Rollie, 85
Hall, William, 85
Hall Brothers, Inc., 85
Hallmark Cards, 85-87
Hallmark Hall of Fame, 86
Hamburger University, 153
hamburgers, 151-56
Hamilton, Jane, 281
Hamilton, Missouri, 194
Hamilton, New York, 28
Hamilton Literary and
    Theological Seminary, 28
Hammer, Armand, 60, 87-92
Hammer, Harry, 88
Hammer, Julian, 89
Hammer, Julius, 87
Hammer, Rose (Lipschitz), 87
Hammer, Victor, 88
Hammer Galleries, 89
Hampton, New Hampshire, 36
Hampton Institute, 42, 242
Handy, W. C., 189-90
Harding, President Warren G., 178-79
Harlem, New York, 33, 163, 243
Harlem Railroad, 259
Harlem Renaissance, 263

Harlow, Jean, 118
harnesses, 292-93
Harper, Amelia, 159
HarperCollins Publishers, 185
Harper's Bazaar, 104
HARPO Productions, 282
Harriman, Edward Henry, 93-94, 183
Harry and Jeanette Weinberg
    Foundation, 273-74
Hartford, Connecticut, 29-30, 181
Hartford county, Maryland, 27
Harvard College, 101
Harvard Congregational Church, 155
Harvard University, 60
Harvey, Ford Ferguson, 95
Harvey, Fred, 95
Hasbro Children's Foundation, 98
Hasbro Company, 96-99
Hassenfeld, Henry, 96
Hassenfeld, Herman, 97
Hassenfeld, Hillel, 97
Hassenfeld, Merrill, 96
Hassenfeld, Stephen David, 96-99
Hasting, Thomas, 53
hats, 237-38
Hauser, Samuel Thomas, 99-100
Havana, Cuba, 9
Hawaii, 14, 139, 228, 272-73
Hawaiian Commercial and Sugar
    Company, 228
Hawaiian Revolution, 228
Hawley, Governor Joseph R., 280
Hay, John, 275, 277
Hayden, Lucy Dyer, 271
Hayes, President Rutherford B., 68
Hayward, Leland, 232
health foods, 141
health maintenance organizations, 140
Hearn Academy, 12
Hearst, George, 100-101
Hearst, Phoebe Apperson, 101
Hearst, William Randolph, 101-4
Hearst Castle, 102, 104
Hearst Corporation, 102
Heine, Heinrich, 214
Heinz, H. John, III, 105
Heinz, Henry John, II (Jack), 105-8
Heinz, Howard, 105
Heinz, Rust, 105
Heinz Hall, 108
Heinze, Frederick Augustus, 216
Hell's Angels, 118
Hempstead, New York, 93

Hempstead, Thomas, 162
Henderson, Fletcher, 190
Henry, Andrew, 162
Henry, Tyler, 278
Hepburn, Katharine, 118
Hepburn Act, 210
Hershey, Catherine (Sweeney), 112
Hershey, Fannie (Snavely), 109
Hershey, Henry, II, 109
Hershey, Milton S., 109-12
Hershey, Pennsylvania, 109-12
Hershey Chocolate Co., 110
Hershey Chocolate Corp., 110, 112
Hershey Industrial School, 110-11, 112
Hershey Junior College, 112
Hershey Museum, 111
Hershey Park, 111
Hewlett, William, 131
Hewlett-Packard Company, 131-32, 290
Highland Park, Illinois, 269
Hill, James Jerome, 94, 113-14
Hitler, Adolf, 92
HLH Aloe Vera Cosmetics, 121
HLH Medical Center Drugs, 121
HLH Products, 121
Hobbs, Abigail, 36
Hobbs, Samuel, 36
Hodgson, Nell Kendall, 283
Hofmeyr, Jan, 208
Holland, Brian, 73
Holland, Eddie, 73
Hollerith, Herman, 114-16
Hollingbourn, England, 27
home-demonstration parties, 249-50
Homebrew Computer Club, 132, 291
Homestake Lode, 100-101
Homestead, Pennsylvania, 52
Honeywell, 60
Honolulu, Hawaii, 272-73
Honolulu Rapid Transit Company (HRT), 272-73
Hoover, President Herbert, 142-43, 180
Hoover Dam, 137-38
Hope, Jane Ellen, 280
Hornaday, Cordelia L., 145-47
horse racing and breeding, 74, 143-44, 269, 275, 277
"hot comb," 262
Hot Shoppes, 168-69
Hot Springs, California, 14
Hotchkiss, Benjamin B., 279
hotel developers, 95, 139, 167-71

Houghton, Michigan, 216
House of Rothschild, 214
Houston, Texas, 117
Howard Heinz Endowment, 108
Howard Hughes Medical Institute, 119
Howard University, 77
Howard University Medical School Fund, 166
Hrach, Rose Mary, 148
Hudson River Association, 257
Hudson River Railroad, 258-59
Hughes, Allene, 117
Hughes, Howard, 117-19
Hughes Aircraft Company, 118, 119
Hughes Electronics Corporation, 119
Hughes Space and Communications Company, 119
Hulbert, William A., 221-22
Hungary, 54
Hunt, Caroline, 124
Hunt, Ella Rose (Myers), 119
Hunt, Haroldson Lafayette, 119, 124
Hunt, Haroldson Lafayette, Jr., 119-24
Hunt, Helen Lakelley, 124
Hunt, Lamar, 124
Hunt, Lydia, 123
Hunt, Ray Lee, 124
Hunt, Richard Morris, 258
Hunt, Ruth, 124
Hunt, Ruth June, 124
Hunt, Swanee Grace, 124
Hunt, William Herbert, 124
Hunt Oil Co., 120-21
Huntington, Arabella Duval, 126
Huntington, Collis Potter, 124-25, 126
Huntington, Henry Edwards, 125-27
Huntington Library, 127
Huron Street Hospital College, 36
Hypermart USA, 266

I

IBM. *See* International Business Machines (IBM) Corporation
Ilfeld, Charles, 129-30
Illinois, 35, 56, 119, 150, 152, 153, 165, 170, 174, 269. *See also* Chicago

Illinois Central Railroad, 93
Illinois Institute of Technology, 6
Ince, Thomas H., 31
Indian Wars, 29
Indiana, 230, 240
Indiana Jones and the Last Crusade, 226
Indiana Jones and the Temple of Doom, 226
Indianapolis YMCA, 262
Industrial Revolution, 3-5
industrialists, 21-23, 39-40, 52-53, 87-92, 211-13
"infomercials," 200
Inner-City Broadcasting Company, 243
insurance, 13, 94, 134-35, 187-90, 223-24
Intel, 289
International Business Machines (IBM) Corporation, 61, 116, 198
Interstate Commerce Commission, 25, 94, 211
inventors, 3-5, 248-50, 262, 297-98
investors, 17-19, 26-27, 271-74. *See also* financiers
Iowa, 174-76, 264
Irish Potato Famine, 215
iron, 21, 114, 173
Irwin, William G., 228
Italy, 9

J

J. B. Colgate &Co., 28
J. C. Penney Company, 195-97, 264
J. F. Shea, 138
J. H. Whitney and Company, 276
J. M. and Rose Haggar Foundation, 83
Jack Benny Show, The, 234
Jackson, Reverend Jesse, 58, 243
Jackson Five, 33-34, 73
Jacksons: An American Dream, The, 34
James C. Penney Foundation, 196
Jameson, Dr. Leander Starr, 209
Javits, Jacob, 277
Jaws, 226-27, 233
Jean Nadal Cosmetics, 56-57
Jefferson City, Missouri, 189
Jennings, 278

Jersey City, New Jersey, 28
Jet, 57, 135
Jobs, Clara, 131
Jobs, Paul, 131
Jobs, Steven Paul, 131-33, 291
John, Elton, 64
John Hay Whitney Foundation, 276
Johns Hopkins Hospital, 273
Johns Hopkins University, 97
Johnson, Earvin "Magic," 77
Johnson, Gertrude Jenkins, 134
Johnson, Guy, 195
Johnson, John Harold, 57, 134-35, 190
Johnson, Leroy, 134
Johnson, President Lyndon B., 123, 285
Johnson, Mary, 72
Johnson, Phil, 10
Johnson, Sophia, 256
Joiner, Columbus M., 120
Jones, Doris, 231
Juárez, Benito, 14
judges, 68-69
Jules Stein Eye Institute, 234
Jurassic Park, 226-27

K

Kaffe Hag Corporation, 142
Kaiser, Henry J., 137-40
Kaiser Aluminum Company, 139
Kaiser Foundation, 140
Kalakaua, King of Hawaii, 228
Kalamazoo, Michigan, 140
Kamserman, Sarah, 271
Kansas, 95
Kansas City, Missouri, 85-87, 95
Kansas Pacific, 75
Katzenberg, Jeffrey, 65, 227
Kay, Sylvia, 96
Kefauver, Estes, 122
Keith, Sarah Josephine, 222
Kelley, Cornelius F. "Con," 217
Kellogg, Ann Jeannette (Stanley), 140
Kellogg, Elizabeth Ann, 144
Kellogg, Irvin Hadley, 144
Kellogg, John H., 141
Kellogg, John Leonard, 144
Kellogg, John Preston, 140
Kellogg, Joseph, 140
Kellogg, Karl Hugh, 144
Kellogg, Will Keith, 140-44, 144

Kellogg Company, 142
Kellogg Company of Canada Ltd., 142
Kelly, Alice, 263
Kemmerer, Wyoming, 195
Kendall, Donald, 160
Keneally, Thomas, 227
Kennedy, President John F., 122, 123
Kennedy, Robert F., 76
Kentucky, 99, 238
kerosene, 212
Khan, Aly, 107
Kimberley, South Africa, 207-9
King, Nelson, 279
King Brand Overall Company, 82
Kingfisher, Oklahoma, 264
Kirby, F. M., 288-89
Klieben, Paul von, 146
Knott, Elgin Columbus, 145
Knott, Walter, 145-47
Knott's Berry Farm, 147
Knowe, England, 293
Knox, Seymour H., 288-89
Kona Kai Hawaiian restaurants, 170
Korean War, 242
Kosciusko, Mississippi, 280
Kroc, Louis, 148
Kroc, Raymond Albert, 148-56
Kroc, Robert L., 155
Kroc Foundation, 155
Kruger, Paul, 208-9
Kuhn, Bowie, 253

L

La Constancia Mexicana, 2
La Paz, Arizona, 70
Labbadie, Sylvestre, 162
labor contractors, 1-2
labor relations, 2, 6, 22, 26, 52, 87, 108, 140, 142-43, 147, 164, 204-5, 265
Lady Sings the Blues, 33, 73
Lahr, Bert, 160
Laidlaw, Roberta Remsen, 48
Lake Ontario Southern Railroad, 93
Lake Shore & Michigan Southern Railway, 259
Lake Village, Arkansas, 119-20
Lake Wintergreen, Michigan, 143
Lamb, Wally, 281
Lampoon, 101

Lamstedt, Germany, 228
Lancaster, Ohio, 47
Lancaster, Pennsylvania, 109, 288
Langford, Nathaniel P., 99
Lapeer, Michigan, 157
Las Vegas, Nevada, 118
Las Vegas, New Mexico, 129
Lathrop, Austin E. (Cap), 157-58
Lawton, Pliny, 29
lawyers, 163
Lay, Herman W., 158-61
Lay, Jesse N., 158-59
Lead, South Dakota, 100-101
leaseback system, 153
Leave It to Beaver, 234
Leavenworth, Kansas, 95
Lebanon, 81
Lee, Archie, 284
Lee, Higginson and Company, 275
legal issues, 4, 57, 62, 91-92, 94, 114, 118, 125, 166, 210-13, 219-20, 231-32, 233, 242, 243, 245-46, 269
Leiter, Levi, 44
Lelia College of Hair Culture, 262
lend-lease policy, 89, 92
Lenin, Vladimir I., 88, 92
Lennon, John, 64
Leominster, Massachusetts, 248
Leonardo da Vinci, 60
L'Ermitage Galleries, 89
LeRoy, Mervyn, 235
Letcher, Adolph, 129
Levi Strauss and Company, 238-40
Lewis, Reuben, 162
Lexington, Virginia, 177
libraries, 7-8, 22-23, 62, 127, 182-83
Libya, 91
Liles, Raynoma, 72-73
Lily Tulip Company, 149-50
Lincoln, Abraham, 6
Lincoln Institute, 189
Lincoln Memorial, 6
Lincoln Park Zoo, 155
Lisa, Christobal de, 161
Lisa, Manuel, 161-62
Liszt, Franz, 214
Little Rock, Arkansas, 68-69
Little Shop of Horrors, 64
Livingston, Crawford, 20
Livingston, Fargo and Company, 20
Llewellyn, James Bruce, 163-64
lobbyists, 125, 138, 186, 200, 285
Lobengula, King of the Ndebele, 208-9

Lockheed Missiles & Space Company, 289
locks, 297-98
Lombardo, Guy, 232
London, England, 193, 215
Lonesome Dove, 34
Long Beach, California, 37
Longmont, Colorado, 195
Lord & Taylor department store, 24
Los Altos Hills, California, 16
Los Angeles, California, 30-31, 66, 73, 90, 91, 126-27, 171-72
Los Angeles Dodgers, 186
Los Angeles Railway, 126
Lost in America, 64
Louisiana, 55-56, 81, 161, 187, 261
Louisiana Territory, 7
Lovejoy, Illinois, 165
Lucky Strike Hit Parade, 232
Lyman, Chester, 16

M

M. S. Hershey Foundation, 111-12
M Squad, 234
MacArthur, Douglas, 123
MacDonald and Kahn, 138
Madagascar, 68
Madam C. J. Walker Hair Culturists Union of America, 263
Madison University, 28
Maher, Drue, 107
Maheu, Robert, 118
Mahogany, 73
mail-order business, 197, 267-69
Maine, 274
Malcolm X, 242
Malcolmson, Alexander V., 50
Malone, Aaron E., 165-66
Malone, Annie Turnbo, 165-66
management consulting, 76
management methods, 22, 25, 43, 51, 78, 83, 87, 97, 108, 114, 121, 135, 140, 152, 160, 195, 263, 284, 286-87
Manson, Charles, 64
Mantle, Mickey, 83
manufacturing
  of aircraft, 10-11
  of appliances, 174-76
  of automobiles, 49-51, 192, 241
  of candy, 109-12

of carriages, 192, 240-41
of chemicals, 36-38, 39-40
of chewing gum, 293-96
of clothing, 81-84, 238-40, 278
of farm equipment, 35, 177-78
of firearms, 29-30, 278-80
of greeting cards, 84-87
of harnesses and saddles, 292-93
of hats, 237-38
of locks, 297-98
of pencils, 88, 97
of photography equipment, 41-42
of pianos, 235-36
of railroad cars, 204
of soap, 27-28, 55-58, 293-94
of spinning machines, 3-5
of sporting goods, 221-22
of textiles, 2-3, 53
of toys, 96-99
Maples, Marla, 247
Marcus Welby, M.D., 234
Marie Antoinette, queen of France, 53
Marinho, Roberto, 166-67
Marriott, Ellen Morris, 167-68
Marriott, Hyrum Willard "Will," 167-68
Marriott, John, 167
Marriott, J(ohn) Willard (Bill), 167-71
Marriott, J(ohn) Willard (Bill), Jr., 170
Marriott, Utah, 167
Marriott Corporation, 169-71
Marsh, Othniel, 194
Marshall Field & Company, 43-44
Marshalltown, Iowa, 174
Marston, George, 1
Martin, Glenn L., 10
Maryland, 27. *See also* Baltimore
Mason, Biddy, 171-72
mass production, 51
Massachusetts, 36, 43, 210, 248, 278, 297
Massachusetts Bay Colony, 221
Massachusetts Institute of Technology, 42, 114
Matsushita Electrical Industrial Company, 65
Matthews, Gary, 253
Mauá, Visconde de (Irineu Evangelista de Souza), 172-73
Maui Land and Pine, 273
Maximilian I, Holy Roman emperor, 54

Mayer, Mrs. Elizabeth Churchill, 222
Maytag, Amelia (Toennebohn), 174
Maytag, Daniel William, 174
Maytag, Dena (Bergman), 176
Maytag, Elmer Henry, 175, 176
Maytag, Freda Louise, 176
Maytag, Frederick Louis, 174-76
Maytag, Lewis Bergman, 176
Maytag, Lulu, 176
Maytag Company, 175-76
MCA. *See* Music Corporation of America (MCA) Inc.
McCormick, Cyrus Hall, 6, 177-78
McCormick, Robert, 177-78
McCoy, Cecil A., 224
McDonald, Maurice "Mac," 151, 154
McDonald, Richard "Dick," 151, 154
McDonald's Corporation, 19, 148-56
McHale's Navy, 234
McKinley, President William, 103
McMurtry, Larry, 34
McWilliams, Moses, 261
meatpacking, 5-6
media tycoons, 101-4, 183-86, 242-43, 277, 280-82
medicine, 88
Meharry Medical College, 13
Meier, Richard, 67
Melbourne, Australia, 184
Mellon, Andrew W., 178-80
Mellon, Paul, 180
Memphis, Tennessee, 26-27, 56, 189
Menard, Pierre, 161
Menks, Astrid, 19
merchants, 43-44, 45, 69-71, 124-25, 129-30, 161-62, 172-73, 264-67, 267-69, 287-89. *See also* retailers
Merrick, John, 223
metals, 78-79, 139. *See also* mining; *specific metals*
Metro-Goldwyn Mayer (MGM), 31
Metro-Goldwyn-Mayer/United Artists Entertainment (MGM/UA), 254
Metropolis, Illinois, 165
Metropolitan Museum of Art, 183
Mexican tycoons and entrepreneurs, 2-3, 15-16
Mexico, 14

Meyner, Robert B., 47
Michigan, 7, 10, 36-38, 49-51,
    71-74, 140-44, 157, 216, 267
Michigan Central Railroad, 259
Michigan State College of
    Agriculture and Applied
    Science, 143
Microsoft Corporation, 61-62
Midland, Michigan, 36-38
Midland Chemical Company,
    36-37
midwives, 171
Miller, Arthur, 86
Milton Bradley, 98
Milton Hershey School, 111
Milwaukee, Wisconsin, 280
Milwaukee Road, 210, 217
mining, 53-54, 99-101, 114, 191,
    207-9, 216-17, 296. *See also*
    metals
Minneapolis, Minnesota, 66,
    201-3
Minnesota, 66, 113, 201-3
Minnesota and St. Louis Railroad,
    197
Minuteman missiles, 11
Miracles, the, 72
Mirror of the Times, 68
Miss Saigon, 64
Mission and Pacific Woolen Mills,
    239
Mississippi, 26, 261, 280
Missouri, 162, 189, 194, 237. *See
    also* Kansas City; St. Louis
Missouri and Pacific Railroad, 75
Missouri Fur Company, 162
Mitchell, Joni, 63
MITS, 60-61
mixing machines, 150-51
Mme. C. J. Walker Manufacturing
    Company, 263
Modern Medicine Publishing
    Company, 141
Moffat, John, 208
Moler, T. A., 175
Moline, Illinois, 35
money laundering, 88
monopolies, 6, 62, 125, 126, 181,
    212
Monroe, Louisiana, 187
Montana, 99-101
Montana Power Company (MPC),
    216-17
Montea, Pierre "PePe," 243
Monterey, California, 101
Montreal, Canada, 270
Moon Illustrated Weekly, The, 189

Moore, Aaron, 223
Moore & Smith, 288
Moore, W. H., 288-89
Morgan, John Pierpont, 181-83
Morgan, Junius S., 181
Mormon tycoons and
    entrepreneurs, 13-15, 167-71
Morris, William, 167
Morrison, Toni, 281
Morrison, William, 161
Morrison Knudsen Corporation,
    138
MOS Technology, 132
Motley, Constance Baker, 242
Motown, 33-34, 72-74
*Motown 25: Yesterday, Today,
    Forever*, 34
Motown 30: What's Goin' On, 34
Motown Historical Museum, 72
Motown Industries, 73
Motown Returns to the Apollo, 34
Moulton, Hanna, 36
Moulton, Josiah, 36
Mt. Pleasant, Michigan, 37
mountain men, 162
muckraking, 6
Murdoch, Anna Maria (Torv), 186
Murdoch, Dame Elisabeth
    (Greene), 184
Murdoch, Sir Keith, 184
Murdoch, Rupert, 183-86
Murphy, Bettye, 90
Murphy, Victoria, 90
Museum of Modern Art, 276, 277
museums, 44, 52-53, 67, 72, 91-92,
    108, 111, 180, 182, 183, 250,
    276-77, 296. *See also*
    architecture and buildings
music business, 33-34, 62-65,
    71-74, 167, 189-90, 230-35,
    235-36, 243
Music Corporation of America
    (MCA) Inc., 64-65, 73,
    231-34
Muskogee, Oklahoma, 219-20
mustard gas, 37

N

NAACP. *See* National Association
    for the Advancement of
    Colored People (NAACP)
Napoleon III, Emperor of France,
    214
Nashville, Tennessee, 12-13, 280-81

Nashville Globe and Independent, 12
National Air Lines, 10
National Association for the
    Advancement of Colored
    People (NAACP), 13, 242,
    263
National Baptist Convention,
    12-13
National Baptist Publishing Board,
    12
National Council of Churches, 13
National Eye Institute, 234
National Gallery of Art, 180, 277
National Grange, 268
National Museum of American
    History, 250
National Negro Business League,
    13, 165, 223
National Recovery
    Administration, 224
National Restaurant Association,
    169
National Star, 185
National Sunday School Congress,
    13
National Urban League, 224
Native Americans, 219
    arts and crafts of, 95
Nauvoo, Illinois, 170
Naylor, Gloria, 282
Nebraska, 17-18, 30, 85
NEC, 167
Negro Convention, 68
Negro Digest, 135
Negro Silent Protest Parade, 263
Negro YMCA of Nashville, 13
Ner Israel Rabbinical College, 273
Nevada, 23, 100, 118
New Deal, 137-39, 224
New Deal Reconstruction Finance
    Corporation, 139
New Hampshire, 36, 248
New Haven, Connecticut, 278-79,
    292, 297-98
New Haven Arms Company,
    278-79
New Jersey, 28, 29, 46, 47, 190,
    245, 247, 267, 292-93
New Mexico, 129
New Orleans, Louisiana, 81, 161
New York (city), 18, 24-25, 87,
    89, 96, 124, 129, 228, 238,
    262, 278, 283, 285, 289. *See
    also* Bronx; Brooklyn; Harlem;
    Staten Island
banking in, 9, 181-83
candy making in, 109

development of, 7-8
museums in, 52-53
piano manufacturing in, 236
politics in, 45-46, 242-43
publishing in, 13, 102-3
real estate in, 245-47
tallow chandling in, 27-28
New York (magazine), 185
New York (state), 5, 19-20, 27-28, 75, 93, 114, 124, 126, 137, 204, 211, 287-88, 292, 297-98. *See also* New York (city)
New York, Albany and Buffalo Telegraph Company, 20
New York & Harlem Railroad, 258
New York Age, 56
New York Central & Hudson River Railroad, 259
New York Central Railroad, 116, 259
New York City Housing and Development Administration, 163
New York Coca-Cola Bottling Company, 164
New York Herald Tribune, 274, 277
New York Journal, 102-3
New York Law School, 163
New York Post, 185
New York Public Library, 8
New York Stock Exchange, 93
New York Sun, 189
New York World, 103
Newark, New Jersey, 190, 292-93
Newport, Arkansas, 265
Newport, New York, 297-98
News and Sunday Mail, 184
News Corporation Limited, 184, 186
News of the World, 184
newspapers, 12, 14, 19, 51, 56, 68, 102-3, 158, 166, 183-88, 274, 276-77. *See also specific papers*
Newton, Iowa, 174-76
NeXT, Inc., 133
NeXT Software Inc., 133
Nicaragua, 257
Nigeria, 220
Night Gallery, 226
Niles, Michigan, 267
Nirvana, 64
nitrous oxide (laughing gas), 29
Nixon, President Richard M., 91, 123, 170, 234
Nordhaus, Adele, 129
Nordhaus, Max, 129
Norfolk, Nebraska, 85

North Carolina, 37, 158, 223-24, 258
North Carolina Mutual and Provident Association, 223
North Carolina Mutual Life Insurance Company, 223-24
Northeastern Life Insurance Company, 190
Northern Pacific Railroad, 114, 183, 270
Northern Securities Company, 94, 114
Northwestern University, 269
Norton, Margaret, 73
Nottingham, England, 4
numismatics, 213
Nyack, New York, 292
Nyro, Laura, 63

O

O Globo, 166
Oak Park, Illinois, 155
Oakland, California, 24
Oberlin College, 68
Oberman, D. H., 82
Occidental Petroleum, 90-92
Oconomowoc, Wisconsin, 269
Odekirk, Glen, 118
Offield, James R., 296
Ohio, 7, 47, 192, 211-13, 225, 251, 283
Ohio State University, 192
oil, 66-67, 90-92, 119-24, 178, 211-13, 219-20
Oklahoma, 66, 219-20, 264, 266
Oklahoma City, Oklahoma, 266
Olmsted, Frederick Law, 258
Olney, Richard, 205
Olympia Brewing Company, 158
Olympic Games, 222
Omaha, Nebraska, 17-19
Onassis, Aristotle, 107
One Cent Savings Bank and Trust Company, 12
One Hundred Black Men, 164
"one-night stands," 231
"one price policy," 83
Oneonta, New York, 124, 126
Operation Push, 58
Oprah Book Club, 281
Oprah Winfrey Show, The, 281-82
Ore-Ida, 108
Oregon, 7
O'Reilly, Anthony J. F., 108

Organization of Petroleum Exporting Countries (OPEC), 91
Ormsby, England, 36
Osborn, Ella, 144
Osterweil, Neil, 250
"overalls," 238
Overland Mail Company, 20
Overseas Private Investment Corporation (OPIC), 163
Overton, Anthony, 187-88
Overton Hygienic Manufacturing Company, 187-88
Oxford University, 66, 184, 275

P

Pace & Handy Music Company, 189
Pace & Handy Publishing Company, 190
Pace, Harry Herbert, 134-35, 189-90
Pace Phonograph Company, 190
Pacific Aero Products Company, 10
Pacific Bridge Corporation, 138
Pacific Electric, 126
Pacific Light and Power Company, 126
Pacific Navigation Company, 270-71
Packard Company, 241
packet boats, 20
Page, Hannah, 36
Page, Mary, 36
Page, Samuel, 36
Palama Settlement, 273
Palmer, Arnold, 83
Palo Alto, California, 16, 131, 290-91
Pan American Airways, 275
Panola Pipe Line Co., 121
Parade Gasoline Co., 121
Parents-Teachers Association, 101
Parish Monroe, Louisiana, 55
Parr, Bertha Erma, 158
Parsons, George W., 174
Parsons Band Cutter and Self-Feeder Company, 174-75
Parson's Business College, 140
Parsons College, 176
Parsons Hawkeye Manufacturing Company, 175
Partridge, C. W., 268

Patent Arms Manufacturing Company, 29
Patent Fire Arms Manufacturing Company, 30
Paterson, New Jersey, 29
Patiño, Simón Iturri, 191
Patterson, Charles R., 192
Patterson, Frederick Douglass, 192
Paul, Louis, 4
Peabody, George, 193-94
Peabody Education Fund, 194
Peabody Institute, 194
Peale, Norman Vincent, 155
Pearson, Conrad, 224
Pearson, John, 29
Peet, William, 292
pencils, 88, 97
Penney, Berta Aline, 197
Penney, Carol Marie, 197
Penney, Caroline, 197
Penney, Eli, 194
Penney, James Cash, 194-97, 197
Penney, John, 194
Penney, Kimball, 197
Penney, Mary Francis (Paxton), 194, 197
Penney, Mary Hortense, 197
Penney, Mildred (Burris), 194
Penney, Roswell Kemper, 197
Penney Farms, 196
Penney Memorial Home Community, 196
Pennsylvania, 52, 109-12, 240, 288. *See also* Philadelphia; Pittsburgh
Pennsylvania Railroad, 21
Penrod Drilling Co., 121
pension funds, 23
Peoria, Illinois, 165
Pepsi-Cola, 286
PepsiCo, Inc., 160
Percy Jones Hospital Center, 143
Percy Sutton International, Inc., 243
Perkins, Joseph, 162
Permanente, California, 138
Permanente Foundation, 140
Permanente Metals, 139
Perot, H(enry) Ross, 198-200
Perot, Lulu May, 198
Perot, Margot (Birmingham), 198
Perot, Ross, 198
Perot Systems Cooperation, 198
Perry, Mae Walker, 263
Petrillo, James, 231-32, 235
Petroleum Corporation of America, 66

pharmaceuticals, 37
Phelps, Anson Greene, 292
Philadelphia, Pennsylvania, 25, 68, 109, 237-38, 293, 298
Philadelphia Coca-Cola Bottling Company, 164
philanthropy, 6, 7-8, 12-13, 22-23, 25-26, 27, 28, 38, 42, 44, 51, 52, 55, 62, 65, 79, 83-84, 87, 92, 98, 107, 108, 110-12, 127, 129-30, 143-44, 155, 161, 166, 167, 170, 172, 180, 193-94, 196, 203, 209-10, 213, 214, 215, 223-24, 227, 228, 230, 234, 238, 253, 254, 260, 262, 264, 266, 269, 271-74, 276, 280, 286, 293, 295. *See also* foundations
Philip II, King of Spain, 55
Phillips Petroleum, 220
Philomathean Institute, 68
Phoenix, Arizona, 70
photography equipment, 41-42
pianos, 235-36
Pierpont Morgan Library, 182, 183
Pilcher, Joshua, 162
Pillsbury, Charles Alfred, 201
Pillsbury, Charles Stinson, 201
Pillsbury, Henry Adams, 203
Pillsbury, John Sargent, 201
Pillsbury, Philip Winston, 201-3
Pillsbury, Philip Winston, Jr., 203
Pillsbury, William, 201
Pillsbury-Washburn Flour Mills Company, 201-3
Pitt, William, 27
Pittsburgh, Pennsylvania, 52, 105, 178-80, 262
Pittsburgh Courier, 56
Pittsburgh Symphony, 108
Pittsfield, Massachusetts, 43
Placid Oil Co., 121
plastics, 248-50
PM (New York newspaper), 276
Point Loma, California, 222
politics
American, 9, 20, 27, 40, 45, 47, 49, 51, 65, 68, 70-71, 76-77, 87, 100, 101, 103, 105, 121-23, 144, 147, 164, 176, 178-80, 190, 199-200, 201, 220, 229-30, 234, 242-43, 280, 285-86, 293, 296
Bolivian, 191
Brazilian, 173
British, 27, 215-16

Latin American, 122
South African, 208-9
Pollit, Edward, 3-4
polyethylene, 249-50
Pomona, California, 145
pony express, 20
Poro College, 165-66
Poro Company, 165-66
Port Richmond, Staten Island, 255-56
Postell, Estelline, 192
potato chips, 159-60
Powell, Adam Clayton, Jr., 243
Prairie View Agricultural and Mechanical College, 242
Pratt and Whitney Company, 10, 115-16
prefabrication techniques, 139
Prentice, Mary Alice, 126
Prescott, Arizona, 70
Preston, England, 3
Preston, Jim, 145-46
Preston, Nathaniel, 140
Preston, Sarah, 140
Prince, Earl, 150
Prince Castle Multimixer Company, 150-51
Prince's Castle, 150
Princeton University, 46
profit-sharing systems, 25, 147
promotional schemes, 31
Prophet, The, 13
publishers and publishing, 12-13, 14, 46-49, 56, 76-77, 100-104, 134-35, 166-67, 183-86, 189-90, 274-77, 281. *See also* newspapers
Puebla, Mexico, 2-3
Pulitzer, Joseph, 103
Pullman, George Mortimer, 6, 204-6
Pullman, Illinois, 204-5
Pullman Palace Car Company, 6, 204-5
Pure Food and Drug Act, 6
Pyramid Vacant Real Estate Company, 148

Q

quality control, 284
Queen Charlotte Island Coal Company, 68
Queen City Broadcasting, Inc., 164

R

radio, 122, 158, 166, 232, 252
Radio Globo, 166
Radio Shack, 61
Radziwill, Princess, 209
Raiders of the Lost Ark, 226
railroads, 45, 74-76, 93-94,
  99-100, 113-14, 124-27,
  172-73, 181-83, 204-6, 210-11,
  229-30, 255-60
ranchers, 15-16, 172-73
Rangel, Charles, 242-43
Ransom, Freeman B., 263
Reagan, President Ronald, 92,
  232-35
real estate developers, 30-31, 95,
  126, 139, 295-96
real estate tycoons, 7-8, 14, 16, 26,
  48, 148, 149, 153, 171-72, 228,
  245-47, 271-73
Reed College, 132
refrigerated railroad cars, 5-6
Regal Theatre (Chicago), 56
Republic of Texas, 29
Republican Party, 20, 27, 68, 71,
  101, 108, 144, 170, 229, 296
Research to Prevent Blindness,
  Inc., 234
restaurant developers, 95, 148-56,
  167-71
"restraint of trade," 94
retailers, 194-97, 264-67, 278,
  287-89
Revue Productions, 233
Rhodes, Cecil John, 207-10
Rhodes, Herbert, 207-9
Rhodes scholarships, 209-10
Rhodesia, 208-9
Rice, Linda Johnson, 135
Richford, New York, 211
Richmond, California, 139
Rio de Janeiro, Brazil, 172-73
Rio Grande do Sul, Brazil,
  172-73
Ripley, Edward Payson, 210-11
Risky Business, 64
RKO studios, 31
"robber baron," 75
Robbins, Illinois, 56
Robert W. Woodruff Arts Center,
  286
Roberts, Edward, 60-61
Roberts, Elliot, 63
Robeson, Paul, 134
Robinson, Smokey, 72
Robson, Helen Alice, 266

Rockefeller, John Davison, 178,
  211-13
Rockefeller, John Davison, Jr., 213
Rockefeller, Nelson A., 170, 276
Rockefeller, William, 212
Rockefeller Institute for Medical
  Research, 213
Rockefeller University, 213
Rockford Commercial College,
  221
Rockwell, Norman, 44, 284
Rodman, New York, 287
Rodriguez, Maria Ignacia, 161
Roebuck, Alvah C., 197
Rogers, Arkansas, 265
Rogers, Will, 51
Romney, George, 170
Ronstadt, Linda, 63
Roosevelt, Betsey Cushing, 276
Roosevelt, James, 276
Roosevelt, President Franklin D.,
  89, 92, 180, 224
Root, Elisha, 30
Ross, Diana, 73
Rossini, Gioacchino, 214
Rosslyn, Virginia, 169
Rothschild, Betty, 214
Rothschild, James Jacob, 214
Rothschild, Lionel Nathan,
  215-16
Rothschild, Mayer Alphonse, 214
Rothschild, Mayer Amschel,
  213-14, 215
Rothschild, Nathan Mayer, 214-15
Rothschild family, 9, 213-16
Roxbury, New York, 75
Roy Rogers restaurants, 170
Rubinstein, Helena, 262
Rudd, Charles, 208
Rush Medical College, 230
Rust, Elizabeth "Betty" Granger,
  105
Rutland and Washington Railroad,
  75
Ryan, Claude, 24
Ryan, John Dennis, 216-17

S

S. H. Knox & Company, 289
Sacramento, California, 14, 124
saddles, 292-93
sailing, 252
St. Agnes Hospital, 273
St. Joseph, Michigan, 267

St. Joseph, Missouri, 237
St. Jude's Research Hospital, 83-84
St. Louis, Missouri, 81-82, 162,
  165, 261, 267-68
St. Louis Colored Orphans' Home,
  166
St. Louis Missouri Fur Company,
  162
St. Mary's College, 83
St. Paul, Minnesota, 113
sales premiums, 294
salesmen, 43-44, 56, 85, 149-50,
  158-60, 168, 177-78, 238, 267,
  283, 294
Salisbury, New York, 297
Salisbury, Rhodesia, 209
Salt Lake City, Utah, 195
Sam's Clubs, 265-66
San Antonio, Texas, 12, 242
San Antonio Express and News, 185
San Bernardino, California, 151,
  171
San Diego, California, 1-2
San Diego Padres, 155
San Francisco, California, 1,
  13-16, 68, 101, 139, 228,
  238-40
San Francisco Board of Trade, 239
San Francisco Examiner, 102
San Luis Obispo, California, 101
San Marino, California, 127
San Simeon, California, 102, 104
Sanitas Nut Food Company,
  141-42
Santa Barbara, California, 1
Santa Fe Railroad, 210
Santa Monica, California, 67
Santa Ynez, California, 154, 155
Sargent, John, II, 201
Savannah, Georgia, 251
Saybrook, Connecticut, 292
Schindler's List, 227
Schreiber, Taft, 231-33, 234
Scott, Thomas, 21
Scranton Jewish Old Age Home,
  273
Scranton (Pennsylvania) Transit
  Company, 272
Screen Actors Guild (SAG), 233
Sculley, John, 133
sculpture, 6
Sears, Richard W., 197, 268
Sears, Roebuck, & Company, 196,
  197, 268
Seattle, Washington, 23-26,
  59-62, 114, 157, 270-71
Seattle Taxicab Company, 271

Second Bank of Brazil, 173
Security and Exchange
Commission, 91
See's Candy Shops, 19
Sellers, William, 298
Selznick International, 276
Sevilla, 160
Sharp-Hughes Tool Company,
117-18
Shasta Dam, 138
Shaw University, 223
Sheets, Alice "Allie," 168, 170,
171
Sheinberg, Sidney, 226
Shelburne Falls, Massachusetts,
297
Sheppard Pratt, 273
Sherman Antitrust Act, 212-13
shipbuilding, 138-39
shipping, 24-26, 113-14, 255-60,
270-71
Shirley, Massachusetts, 248
Sidor, John, 82
Simmons, Eva, 219
Simmons, Jake, Jr., 219-20
Sirloin and Saddles, 170
Six Companies, 138
Skouras, Spyros, 82
Skouras brothers, 81-82
sleeping cars, 204-6
Slidel & Co., 27
Smackover, Arkansas, 120
Small Business Administration,
163
Small Business Development
Corporation (SBDC), 163
Smith, Hannah, 140
Smith, Horace, 278
Smith, Joan, 153-54, 155
Smith, Joseph, Jr., 13
Smith, Josiah, 140
Smith, Lillian, 242
Smith, Marie Whitcomb, 248
Smith, Rawley, 153, 155
Smith, Sheldon, 292
Smith & Wright, 292-93
Snyder, Howard, 175
soap, 27-28, 55-58, 293-94
Socialist Labor Party, 87
Sociedad Agífcola é Ganadera de
Cinti, 191
Society of California Pioneers, 14
Soderstrom, Charles, 24
soft drinks, 164, 282-87
Solvent Savings Bank and Trust
Company, 27, 189
Sonneborn, Harry J., 153-55

Sonora, California, 70
South Africa, 207-10
South African tycoons and
entrepreneurs, 207-10
South Bend, Indiana, 240
South Carolina, 159, 228, 292
South Center Department Store
(Chicago), 56
South China Morning Post, 185
South Dakota, 100-101
Southern Methodist University, 83
Southern Pacific Railroad, 94,
125, 126, 229-30
Soviet Union, 88, 92
Spalding, Albert Goodwill, 221-22
Spalding, Edward, 221
Spalding, Harriet Irene (Goodwill)
Wright, 221
Spalding, James, 221
Spalding, James Lawrence, 221
Spanish-American War, 103, 270
Spanish Armada, 55
Spartan Aircraft Company, 66
Spaulding, Charles Clinton,
223-24
speculators, 45-46, 74-76
Spencer Gifts, 233
Spencer Repeating Rifle
Company, 279
Spielberg, Arnold, 225
Spielberg, Leah (Posner), 225
Spielberg, Steven, 65, 225-27
spinning machines, 3-5
sporting goods, 221-22
sports broadcasting, 185-86
sports management, 74, 155, 186,
253
sportsmen, 221-22
Spreckels, Claus, 228
Springwells Township, Michigan,
49
stagecoaches, 19-20
Staines, Carrie, 144
Stalin, Joseph, 89
Stamford, Connecticut, 298
Standard Life Insurance Company,
189-90
Standard Oil Company, 212, 216,
283
Standard Oil of New Jersey,
212-13
Stanford, Leland, 125, 229-30
Stanford University, 230
Stanley Home Products, 249
Star (tabloid), 185
Star-Kist, 108
Star Trek, 252

Star TV, 185
Staten Island, New York, 255-56,
258
statistics, 115-16
Staubach, Roger, 83
steam turbine, 36
steamboats, 45, 113, 173, 256-57
steel, 21-23, 52, 182-83
Stein, Julian Caesar (Jules),
230-35
Stein, M. Louis, 230
Stein, William, 231
Steinway, Albert, 236
Steinway, Charles, 236
Steinway, Christian Friedrich
Theodore, 236
Steinway, Doretta, 236
Steinway, Henry, 236
Steinway, Henry Englehard, 235-36
Steinway, Wilhelmina, 236
Steinway, William, 236
Stern, David, 238-39
Stern, Fanny, 239
Stetson, John Batterson, 237-38
Stetson University, 238
Stewart, James, 232, 235
Still, William, 68
Still, William Grant, 190
Sting, The, 233
Stinson, Charles, 201
stock, 212
Stockbridge, New York, 5
Stokes, Edward, 45
straight-line production, 83
Strauss, Levi, 238-40
strikes, 205
Stuart, Granville, 99
Stuart, James, 99
Studebaker, Clement, 240-41
Studebaker, Henry, 240-41
Studebaker, Jacob, 240
Studebaker, John Mohler,
240-41
Studebaker, Peter, 240
Studebaker Brothers
Manufacturing Company,
240-41
Suez Canal, 216
sugar processing, 228
Sugarland Express, The, 226
Sun (London newspaper), 184
Sundblom, Haddon, 284
Sunnyvale, California, 289
supermarkets, 163-64
"superstores," 266
Supreme Court of the United
States, 94, 114, 123

Supreme Liberty Life Insurance
Company, 13, 134-35, 190
Surrey, England, 67
Sutter's Fort, 14
Sutton, Oliver, 242
Sutton, Percy Ellis, 242-43
Sutton, Samuel J., 242
Swell Hogan, 117

T

tabloid journalism, 184-86
Tabulating Machine Company,
116
Tacoma, Washington, 270
take-out food, 149-50, 169
talent agents, 63
talk-show hosts, 281-82
tallow chandling, 27-28
Tamla Records, 72
Tandy, Vertner W., 263
Taos, New Mexico, 129
Tapia, Isidora, 15
Tastee-Freeze, 150, 153
tax policies, 178-80
Tax Reform Act, 247
taxicabs, 271
Taylor, Elizabeth, 48
Teagle, Walter, 283
telecommunications, 77, 166-67
telegraphic communication, 20
television, 33-34, 73, 86, 122, 158,
164, 183-86, 226, 232-34, 243,
251-54, 280-82
Temptations, the, 73
Tenable Oil Co., 121
Tennessee, 12-13, 26-27, 56, 189,
251, 280-81
Tennessee Agricultural and
Normal School, 12
Tennessee State University, 12
Terrell, Mary Church, 27
Texarkana, Texas, 198
Texas, 12, 29-30, 81-83, 117, 120,
123, 198, 242
Texas and Pacific Railroad, 75
Texas Rangers, 29
textiles, 2-3, 53
theme parks, 111, 145-47, 170
There Are No Children Here,
282
Thiemer, Juliane, 235
Thompson, James, 58
Thompson, Susan, 19
Thorne, George R., 268

threshing machines, 174-75,
177-78
Tidewater Associated Oil
Company, 66
Time-Life, 166
Time Warner Inc., 253
Times, The (London newspaper),
185
tin, 191
toiletry products, 187-88
Tolman, Frances Barrett, 90
Torreón, Mexico, 81
tourism, 95
Towne, Henry Robinson, 298
Towne, John Henry, 298
toys, 96-99
Tracy, Aaron, 168
Trans World Airlines, 118
TransAfrica, 77
transit systems, 126, 257, 272-73
transportation, 19-20, 272. *See also*
automobiles; aviation;
carriages; railroads; shipping;
transit systems
Trinity College (Cambridge), 105
Trotsky, Leon, 88
Truman, Harry, 86
Trump, Donald, 245-47
Trump, Fred C., 245
Trump, Ivana Zelnickova
(Winklmayr), 247
Trump, Mary, 245
Trump Organization, 245-46
Trust & Savings Bank, 296
Trust for Public Land, 180
TRW, 59-60
Tulsa, Oklahoma, 66
Tupper, Earl Silas, 248-50
Tupper, Earnest Leslie, 248
Tupper Home Parties, Inc., 250
Tupper Tree Doctors, 248
Tupperware, 248-50
Turnbo, Isabell, 165
Turnbo, Robert, 165
Turner, Florence (Rooney), 251
Turner, Fred, 152, 155-56
Turner, Robert Edward "Ed,"
251-52
Turner, Robert Edward "Ted,"
251-54
Turner Advertising Company, 252
Turner Network Television
(TNT), 254
Tuscaloosa, Alabama, 120
Tuskegee Institute, 42, 166, 219,
242
TV Globo Network, 166-67

TV Guide, 185
20th Century-Fox Film
Corporation, 82, 185
Two Arabian Knights, 118
two-way radio communications, 10
Tyrol, 53-54

U

Underground Railroad, 68
Union Army, 9
Union Pacific Railroad, 75, 93-94,
229
United Aircraft, 11
United Aircraft and Transport,
10-11
United Airlines, 11
United Distillers of America, 90
United Nations, 253, 254
United Parcel Service, 23-26
United States Constitution
amendments to, 121-23
United States-Mexican War, 29
United States Naval Academy,
198
United States Steel Corporation,
23, 52, 182-83
United War Fund, 107
United Way, 107
Universal City, California, 233-34
Universal-International Studios,
233
Universal Pictures, 233-34
Universal Studios, 226
University of California
(Berkeley), 66, 239, 290-91
University of California at Los
Angeles (UCLA), 63, 64
University of Chicago, 134, 213,
230
University of Colorado, 290
University of Dallas, 83
University of Kansas, 187
University of Michigan, 38
University of Missouri, 264
University of Nebraska, 17-18
University of North Carolina, 224
University of Notre Dame, 83
University of Pennsylvania, 17,
245
University of Rochester, 42
University of Scranton, 273
University of Texas, 63
University of Utah, 168, 170
University of West Virginia, 230

Uruguay, 173
U.S. Census Bureau, 114-16
USA cable network, 235
Utah, 138, 167-68, 170, 195
Utah Construction Company, 138
Utica, New York, 19-20, 288
utilities, 126, 216-17

V

Vadina, Olga, 88-89
Valparise College, 119
"value" investing, 18-19
Vander Bilt, Cornelius, 255
Vander Bilt, Phebe (Hand), 255
Vanderbilt, Cornelius, 75, 255-60
Vanderbilt, Cornelius Jeremiah, 258
Vanderbilt, George, 258
Vanderbilt, William, 259
Vanderbilt, William Henry, 258
Vanderbilt University, 260
Venice, Italy, 53
Veracruz, Mexico, 2
Vermont, 35
Vicksburg, Mississippi, 261
Victory Life Insurance Company, 187
vigilante movements, 14
Virginia, 169, 170, 177
Virginia Theological Seminary, 223
Viscoloid, 248
Vogel, Harry, 82
Volcanic Repeating Arms Company, 278

W

W. K. Kellogg Child Welfare Foundation, 143
W. K. Kellogg Foundation, 143-44
Wagon Train, 234
Wal-Mart Stores, 264-67
Waldorf-Astoria Hotel, 8
Waldorf Towers, 25
Walgreen Drugs, 149-50
Walker, A'Lelia, 261, 263
Walker, Alice, 282
Walker, Charles Joseph, 262
Walker, Dan, 58
Walker, Eunice, 135
Walker, Madam C. J., 165, 261-64

Walker, Samuel H., 29-30
Wallace, George, 123
Wallis, Hal, 235
Walt Disney Company, 19
Walter M. Smith & Company, 267
Walton, Nancy Lee, 264
Walton, Sam, 264-67
Walton, Thomas, 264
War of 1812, 7, 162, 256
War of the Triple Alliance, 173
Ward, Aaron Montgomery, 267-69
Ward, Julia Laura Mary (Green), 267
Ward, Marjorie, 269
Ward, Sylvester A., 267
warehousing, 114
Warner Communications, 63-64
Warren, Earl, 123
Warren, General Charles, 208
Wasaff, Rose Mary, 82
Washburn, W. D., 201
Washburn College, 187
washing machines, 175-76
Washington, 137, 270. *See also* Seattle
Washington, Booker T., 69, 219
Washington, D.C., 17, 115, 168-71, 193, 217
Washington, Harold, 58
Washington Post, 19
Wasserman, Lew, 231-33, 234
Waterhouse & Employees, 270-71
Waterhouse, Frank, 270-71
Waterhouse, Joseph, 270
Waterhouse, Mary Elizabeth (Horsfield), 270
Watertown, Massachusetts, 36
Watertown, New York, 287-88
Waukegan, Illinois, 152
Webb, Walter Prescott, 30
Weber College, 168
Weinberg, Harry G., 271-74
Weinberg, Joseph, 271
Welles, Orson, 104
Wells, Henry, 20
Wells, Mary, 73
Wells and Company, 20
Wells Fargo, 234
Werblin, David A. "Sonny," 231
Wesson, D. B., 278
Western Electric Company, 115
Westinghouse Electric & Manufacturing Company, 38, 49, 233
Wharton School of Finance, 245
White, Walter, 283
White, Walter Francis, 190, 224

White Citizens Councils, 56-57
White Motor Company, 283
Whitney, C. V., 275
Whitney, Helen (Hay), 274-75
Whitney, John Hay, 274-77
Whitney, William C., 275
Whitney, William Payne, 274
Whitney Communications Corporation, 277
wholesale, 129-30
wigmakers, 3-4
"wildcat" oilwells, 120
Wilkinson, Benjamin, 162
William IX, landowner of Hesse-Cassel, 213-14
William Morris Agency, 63
William Wrigley Jr. Co., 294-95
Williams, James, 134
Williams, Josephine, 70
Willis, Gregg & Brown, 267-69
Wilmington, North Carolina, 37
Wilson, Jackie, 71-72
Wilson, Millicent, 104
Wilson, President Woodrow, 263
Winchester, Hannah (Bates), 278
Winchester, John, 278
Winchester, Oliver Fisher, 278-80
Winchester, Samuel, 278
Winchester 73, 232
Winchester Repeating Arms Company, 279
Winchester rifle, 279
Winfrey, Oprah Gail, 280-82
Winfrey, Vernita Lee, 280
Winfrey, Vernon, 280
Winship, Emily Caroline, 282-84
Winston, Helen Nelle Pendleton, 201
Winton, Alexander, 50
Wisconsin, 269, 280
Wise, Brownie, 250
Wiz, The, 73
Wolfshagen, Germany, 235
Women of Brewster Place, The, 282
women tycoons and entrepreneurs, 15-16, 33-34, 145-47, 165-66, 171-72, 261-64, 280-82
Wonder, Stevie, 72, 73
Woodbridge, Canada, 262
Woodruff, Ernest, 282-84
Woodruff, Robert Winship, 282-87
Woods, Andrew, 162
Woolworth, C. S., 288-89
Woolworth, Fanny (McBrier), 287
Woolworth, Frank Winfield, 287-89
Woolworth, John Hubbell, 287

Woolworth Building, 289
World War I, 10, 51, 179, 217, 263, 283
World War II, 11, 47, 89, 106-7, 120, 121, 138-39, 143, 150, 158, 169, 202, 224, 242, 249, 264, 272, 276, 284-85
Wozniak, Francis, 289
Wozniak, Stephen G., 132, 289-91
Wright, Harry, 221
Wright, Minerva (Peet), 292
Wright, William, 292-93
Wright, Dr. William, 292
Wrigley, Edmund, 293
Wrigley, Edward, 293
Wrigley, Jane, 293
Wrigley, Mary A. (Ladley), 293
Wrigley, Phillip, 296

Wrigley, Susan (Paxson), 293
Wrigley, William, 293
Wrigley, William, Jr., 293-96
Wrigley Manufacturing Co., 293
Wyoming, 195, 285

Y

Yale, Chlotilda (Hopson), 297
Yale, Elihu, 297
Yale, Linus, 297-98
Yale, Thomas, 297
Yale Lock Manufacturing Company, 298
Yale University, 10, 64, 105, 194, 201-2, 275, 277, 280, 292

Yellow Cabs, 271
"yellow" journalism, 102
Yellowstone National Park, 161, 283
Yellowstone Prospecting Expedition, 99
Yosemite Land and Curry Company, 233
Young, Brigham, 13, 14
Young, George, 295
Yukon, 270

Z

Zenoni, John, 162
Zevely, Angela Carey, 89